PRIMA OFFICIAL GAME GUIDE

CONTENTS

How To Use This Guide

Welcome to the official strategy guide for *The Legend of Zelda: Skyward Sword*, the game that celebrates the 25th anniversary of Nintendo's seminal *Legend of Zelda* series. This guide hopes to make your trip through Link's latest adventure as smooth and frustration-free as possible by covering all of the game's challenges and secrets. Here's a brief rundown of what's available in the guide and where you'll find key bits of information.

Chapter 1: Getting Started

Since *Skyward Sword* introduces the Wii MotionPlus to the *Legend of Zelda* series, *Skyward Sword* can play very differently than previous *Legend of Zelda* titles. This section helps introduce the tips and techniques players will need to master in order to survive the game's challenges. For veteran *Legend of Zelda* players, here you'll find a breakdown of the major ways in which *Skyward Sword* is unlike its predecessors.

HOW TO USE THIS GUIDE | GETTING STARTED | WALKTHROUGH | SECRETS & SIDE QUESTS | ITEMS, EQUIPMENT, & CRAFTING | MAPS

Playing the Game

The Legend of Zelda: Skyward Sword is built around the Wii MotionPlus and, as a result, plays a bit differently than earlier games in the *Legend of Zelda* series. Tricks and techniques that worked in older games won't work in *Skyward Sword*. You also have access to new options unlike anything possible in prior *Legend of Zelda* games.

Link's Sword

The most profound change Wii MotionPlus brings to *Legend of Zelda* in *Skyward Sword* is real-time combat based on one-to-one motion input. Link has nine basic sword strikes at his disposal, each triggered by how you move your Wii Remote. An additional four special sword strikes call upon you to use the Wii Remote and Nunchuk in tandem, and there's also the new Skyward Strike.

Because of this, Link doesn't learn any special sword skills throughout the game (like, say, the hidden skills in *Twilight Princess*). Instead, Link can access all of his possible sword maneuvers from the very moment he acquires the Goddess Sword. Your skill with the Wii Remote alone determines how effectively Link can use his blade in this game.

Link's Sword Strikes

Vertical Slashes

Moving the Wii Remote straight up and down lets Link perform a vertical slash. A rising vertical slash (down to up) is crucial in certain boss battles, while a descending vertical slash (up to down) is very useful in fighting enemies like Keese and Chuchus. It's easy to do vertical slashes very rapidly by shaking the Wii Remote up and down quickly, which is handy in boss battles where you have a limited amount of time to damage a boss's weak point. While exploring the world, you sometimes need to use descending vertical slashes to chop down stakes.

Diagonal Slashes

Link can swing his sword both ways along both diagonals, for a total of four diagonal strike possibilities. As with the two horizontal slashes, which diagonal slash you use in combat is extremely important in situations where you fight enemies that can block. It is usually most crucial in boss battles, where a boss or sub-boss may be guarding against all possible attacks except the correct rising or descending diagonal slash. If you're trying to do a horizontal slash but you aren't holding your Wii Remote level, you may get a diagonal slash instead. This can be a sign that you need to adjust your grip.

Horizontal Slashes

Moving the Wii Remote left to right (or right to left) performs a horizontal slash. Which way you execute the slash is key in situations where you're fighting an enemy that can block your attacks. Often, in these situations, the enemy will be vulnerable to attack if you swing from their unprotected direction, while you may take damage if you swing from the wrong side.

Thrust

If you hold the Wii Remote level and thrust it forward, Link thrusts his sword forward like a fencer. This sword strike is indispensable for defeating enemies that have small weak points, like Skulltulas and Beamos. You also use it frequently while solving puzzles, since it lets you use your sword to interact with mechanisms like generators. If you attempt to do a thrust and you aren't holding your Wii Remote level, you may end up doing a vertical slash instead. This can also be a sign that you need to adjust your grip on the Wii Remote.

TIP

Are you having difficulty doing thrusts or horizontal slashes consistently? You may be playing the game while sitting in a posture that inclines you to hold the Wii Remote incorrectly. In *Skyward Sword*, the game reads combat motion input relative to a Wii MotionPlus controller held in a perfectly horizontal position. If you're doing something like resting your elbows on the arms of a chair while you play, then you may be tilting the tip of the Wii Remote up or down too much for sword strikes to register correctly. It can sometimes be useful to play through battles that call for very precise motion input while standing up, which helps ensure that you hold the Wii Remote without tilting it too much.

10 primagames.com PRIMA Official Game Guide 11

Chapter 2: Walkthrough

All area maps, boss strategies, and puzzle solutions you'll need to complete the game and see the ending are located in this section. Note that this section will not cover how to acquire any items or other secrets that aren't required (or highly recommended) for simply finishing the game. Players who want to use the game's maps without following walkthrough advice can use the map section at the end of this book.

Chapter 3: Secrets & Side Quests

The *Legend of Zelda: Skyward Sword* is designed so that players can take a break from the main story and go questing for optional items and secrets whenever they wish. This section breaks down how to finish all side quests and beat all minigames.

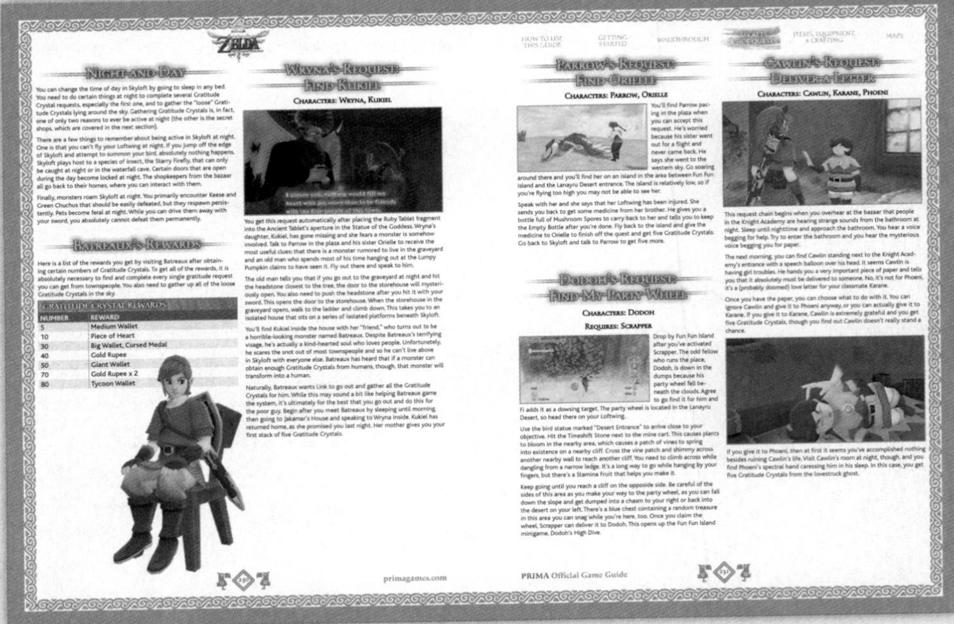

HOW TO USE THIS GUIDE · GETTING STARTED · WALKTHROUGH · SECRETS & SIDE QUESTS · ITEMS, EQUIPMENT, & CRAFTING · MAPS

Night and Day

You can change the time of day in Skyloft by going to sleep in any bed. You need to do certain things at night to complete several Gratitude Crystal requests, especially the first one, and to gather the "loose" Gratitude Crystals lying around the sky. Gathering Gratitude Crystals is, in fact, one of only two reasons to ever be active at night (the other is the secret shops, which are covered in the next section).

There are a few things to remember about being active in Skyloft at night. One is that you can't fly your Loftwing at night. If you jump off the edge of Skyloft and attempt to summon your bird, absolutely nothing happens. Skyloft plays host to a species of insect, the Starry Firefly, that can only be caught at night or in the waterfall cave. Certain doors that are open during the day become locked at night. The shopkeepers from the bazaar all go back to their homes, where you can interact with them.

Finally, monsters roam Skyloft at night. You primarily encounter Keese and Green Chuchus that should be easily defeated, but they respawn persistently. Pets become feral at night. While you can drive them away with your sword, you absolutely cannot defeat them permanently.

Batreaux's Rewards

Here is a list of the rewards you get by visiting Batreaux after obtaining certain numbers of Gratitude Crystals. To get all of the rewards, it is absolutely necessary to find and complete every single gratitude request you can get from townspeople. You also need to gather up all of the loose Gratitude Crystals in the sky.

GRATITUDE CRYSTAL REWARDS

NUMBER	REWARD
5	Medium Wallet
10	Piece of Heart
30	Big Wallet, Cursed Medal
40	Gold Rupee
50	Giant Wallet
70	Gold Rupee x 2
80	Tycoon Wallet

Wryna's Request: Find Kukiel

Characters: Wryna, Kukiel

You get this request automatically after placing the Ruby Tablet fragment into the Ancient Tablet's aperture in the Statue of the Goddess. Wryna's daughter, Kukiel, has gone missing and she fears a monster is somehow involved. Talk to Parrow in the plaza and his sister Orielle to receive the most useful clues: that there is a monster rumored to live in the graveyard and an old man who spends most of his time hanging out at the Lumpy Pumpkin claims to have seen it. Fly out there and speak to him.

The old man tells you that if you go out to the graveyard at night and hit the headstone closest to the tree, the door to the storehouse will mysteriously open. You also need to push the headstone after you hit it with your sword. This opens the door to the storehouse. When the storehouse in the graveyard opens, walk to the ladder and climb down. This takes you to an isolated house that sits on a series of isolated platforms beneath Skyloft.

You'll find Kukiel inside the house with her "friend," who turns out to be a horrible-looking monster named Batreaux. Despite Batreaux's terrifying visage, he's actually a kind-hearted soul who loves people. Unfortunately, he scares the snot out of most townspeople and so he can't live above in Skyloft with everyone else. Batreaux has heard that if a monster can obtain enough Gratitude Crystals from humans, though, that monster will transform into a human.

Naturally, Batreaux wants Link to go out and gather all the Gratitude Crystals for him. While this may sound a bit like helping Batreaux game the system, it's ultimately for the best that you go out and do this for the poor guy. Begin after you meet Batreaux by sleeping until morning, then going to Jakamar's House and speaking to Wryna inside. Kukiel has returned home, as she promised you last night. Her mother gives you your first stack of five Gratitude Crystals.

Parrow's Request: Find Orielle

Characters: Parrow, Orielle

You'll find Parrow pacing in the plaza when you can accept this request. He's worried because his sister went out for a flight and never came back. He says she went to the western sky. Go soaring around there and you'll find her on an island in the area between Fun Fun Island and the Lanayru Desert entrance. The island is relatively low, so if you're flying too high you may not be able to see her.

Speak with her and she says that her Loftwing has been injured. She sends you back to get some medicine from her brother. He gives you a bottle full of Mushroom Spores to carry back to her and tells you to keep the Empty Bottle after you're done. Fly back to the island and give the medicine to Orielle to finish off the quest and get five Gratitude Crystals. Go back to Skyloft and talk to Parrow to get five more.

Dodoh's Request: Find My Party Wheel

Characters: Dodoh

Requires: Scrapper

Drop by Fun Fun Island after you've activated Scrapper. The odd fellow who runs the place, Dodoh, is down in the dumps because his party wheel fell beneath the clouds. Agree to go find it for him and Fi adds it as a dowsing target. The party wheel is located in the Lanayru Desert, so head there on your Loftwing.

Use the bird statue marked "Desert Entrance" to arrive close to your objective. Hit the Timeshift Stone next to the mine cart. This causes plants to bloom in the nearby area, which causes a patch of vines to spring into existence on a nearby cliff. Cross the vine patch and shimmy across another nearby wall to reach another cliff. You need to climb across while dangling from a narrow ledge. It's a long way to go while hanging by your fingers, but there's a Stamina Fruit that helps you make it.

Keep going until you reach a cliff on the opposide side. Be careful of the sides of this area as you make your way to the party wheel, as you can fall down the slope and get dumped into a chasm to your right or back into the desert on your left. There's a blue chest containing a random treasure in this area you can snag while you're here, too. Once you claim the wheel, Scrapper can deliver it to Dodoh. This opens up the Fun Fun Island minigame, Dodoh's High Dive.

Cawlin's Request: Deliver a Letter

Characters: Cawlin, Karane, Phoeni

This request chain begins when you overhear at the bazaar that people in the Knight Academy are hearing strange sounds from the bathroom at night. Sleep until nighttime and approach the bathroom. You hear a voice begging for help. Try to enter the bathroom and you hear the mysterious voice begging you for paper.

The next morning, you can find Cawlin standing next to the Knight Academy's entrance with a speech balloon over his head. It seems Cawlin is having girl troubles. He hands you a very important piece of paper and tells you that it absolutely must be delivered to someone. No, it's not for Phoeni, it's a (probably doomed) love letter for your classmate Karane.

Once you have the paper, you can choose what to do with it. You can ignore Cawlin and give it to Phoeni anyway, or you can actually give it to Karane. If you give it to Karane, Cawlin is extremely grateful and you get five Gratitude Crystals, though you find out Cawlin doesn't really stand a chance.

If you give it to Phoeni, then at first it seems you've accomplished nothing besides ruining Cawlin's life. Visit Cawlin's room at night, though, and you find Phoeni's spectral hand caressing him in his sleep. In this case, you get five Gratitude Crystals from the lovestruck ghost.

primagames.com · PRIMA Official Game Guide

Chapter 4: Items, Equipment, & Crafting

Whether you're one of those players who can't bear to finish a game without forging all the best equipment possible or just someone who wants to adventure with the best shield possible at all times, this section will detail everything you need to know about crafting items. Here you'll find item lists with costs, guides to obtaining crafting materials, recipes necessary for forging all of the game's optional equipment, and a special section about catching bugs and enhancing potions.

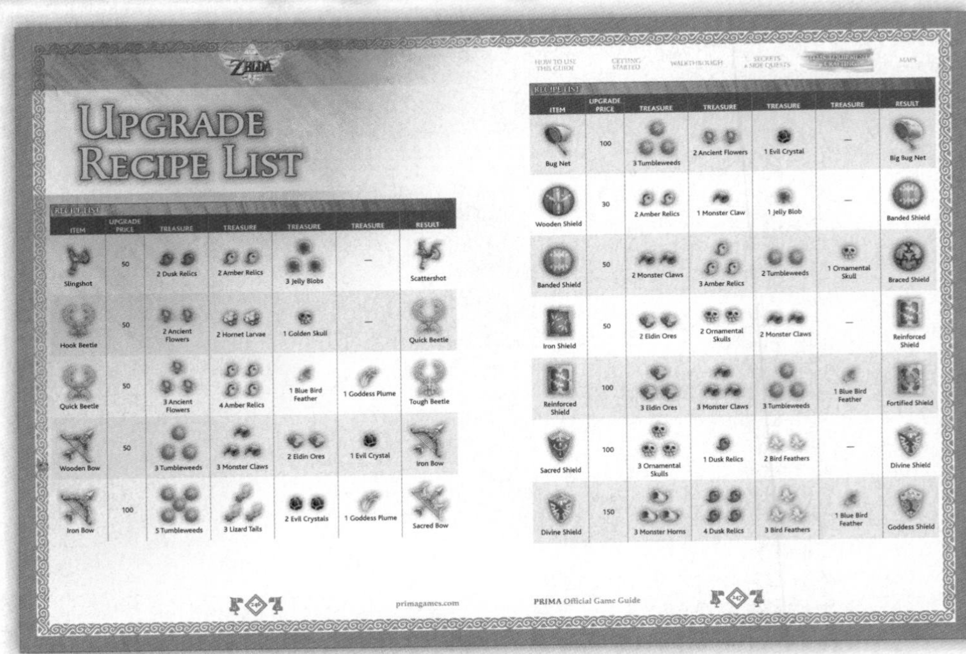

HOW TO USE THIS GUIDE · GETTING STARTED · WALKTHROUGH · SECRETS & SIDE QUESTS · ITEMS, EQUIPMENT, & CRAFTING · MAPS

Upgrade Recipe List

RECIPE LIST

ITEM	UPGRADE PRICE	TREASURE	TREASURE	TREASURE	TREASURE	RESULT
Slingshot	50	2 Dusk Relics	2 Amber Relics	3 Jelly Blobs	—	Scattershot
Hook Beetle	50	2 Ancient Flowers	2 Hornet Larvae	1 Golden Skull	—	Quick Beetle
Quick Beetle	50	3 Ancient Flowers	4 Amber Relics	1 Blue Bird Feather	1 Goddess Plume	Tough Beetle
Wooden Bow	50	3 Tumbleweeds	3 Monster Claws	2 Eldin Ores	1 Evil Crystal	Iron Bow
Iron Bow	100	5 Tumbleweeds	3 Lizard Tails	2 Evil Crystals	1 Goddess Plume	Sacred Bow

RECIPE LIST

ITEM	UPGRADE PRICE	TREASURE	TREASURE	TREASURE	TREASURE	RESULT
Bug Net	100	3 Tumbleweeds	2 Ancient Flowers	1 Evil Crystal	—	Big Bug Net
Wooden Shield	30	2 Amber Relics	1 Monster Claw	1 Jelly Blob	—	Banded Shield
Banded Shield	50	2 Monster Claws	3 Amber Relics	2 Tumbleweeds	1 Ornamental Skull	Braced Shield
Iron Shield	50	2 Eldin Ores	2 Ornamental Skulls	2 Monster Claws	—	Reinforced Shield
Reinforced Shield	100	3 Eldin Ores	3 Monster Claws	3 Tumbleweeds	1 Blue Bird Feather	Fortified Shield
Sacred Shield	100	3 Ornamental Skulls	1 Dusk Relics	2 Bird Feathers	—	Divine Shield
Divine Shield	150	3 Monster Horns	4 Dusk Relics	3 Bird Feathers	1 Blue Bird Feather	Goddess Shield

primagames.com · PRIMA Official Game Guide

Chapter 5: Maps

For quick reference, this section offers a selection of the most useful *Skyward Sword* area maps. Use this when exploring on your own to make sure you don't get lost or miss anything too interesting.

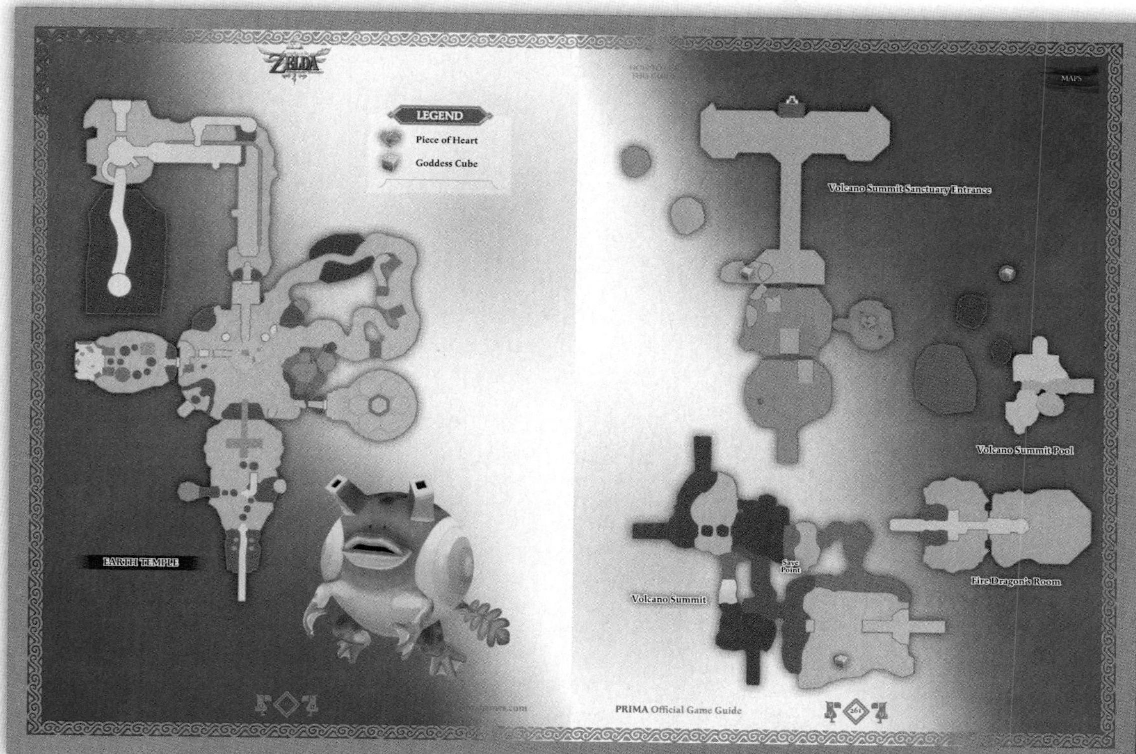

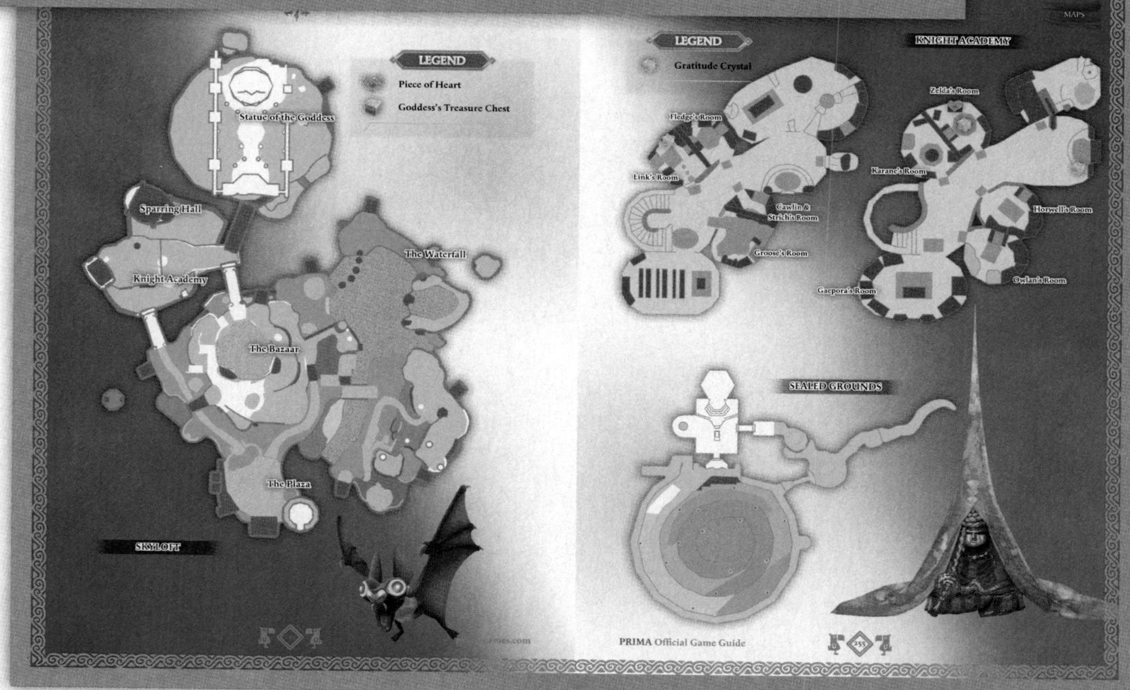

GETTING STARTED

Playing the Game

The Legend of Zelda: Skyward Sword is built around the Wii MotionPlus and, as a result, plays a bit differently than earlier games in the *Legend of Zelda* series. Tricks and techniques that worked in older games won't work in *Skyward Sword*. You also have access to new options unlike anything possible in prior *Legend of Zelda* games.

Link's Sword

The most profound change Wii MotionPlus brings to *Legend of Zelda* in *Skyward Sword* is real-time combat based on one-to-one motion input. Link has nine basic sword strikes at his disposal, each triggered by how you move your Wii Remote. An additional four special sword strikes call upon you to use the Wii Remote and Nunchuk in tandem, and there's also the new Skyward Strike.

Because of this, Link doesn't learn any special sword skills throughout the game (like, say, the hidden skills in *Twilight Princess*). Instead, Link can access all of his possible sword maneuvers from the very moment he acquires the Goddess Sword. Your skill with the Wii Remote alone determines how effectively Link can use his blade in this game.

Link's Sword Strikes

Vertical Slashes

Moving the Wii Remote straight up and down lets Link perform a vertical slash. A rising vertical slash (down to up) is crucial in certain boss battles, while a descending vertical slash (up to down) is very useful in fighting enemies like Keese and Chuchus. It's easy to do vertical slashes very rapidly by shaking the Wii Remote up and down quickly, which is handy in boss battles where you have a limited amount of time to damage a boss's weak point. While exploring the world, you sometimes need to use descending vertical slashes to chop down stakes.

Horizontal Slashes

Moving the Wii Remote left to right (or right to left) performs a horizontal slash. Which way you execute the slash is key in situations where you're fighting an enemy that can block your attacks. Often, in these situations, the enemy will be vulnerable to attack if you swing from their unprotected direction, while you may take damage if you swing from the wrong side.

Diagonal Slashes

Link can swing his sword both ways along both diagonals, for a total of four diagonal strike possibilities. As with the two horizontal slashes, which diagonal slash you use in combat is extremely important in situations where you fight enemies that can block. It is usually most crucial in boss battles, where a boss or sub-boss may be guarding against all possible attacks except the correct rising or descending diagonal slash. If you're trying to do a horizontal slash but you aren't holding your Wii Remote level, you may get a diagonal slash instead. This can be a sign that you need to adjust your grip.

Thrust

If you hold the Wii Remote level and thrust it forward, Link thrusts his sword forward like a fencer. This sword strike is indispensable for defeating enemies that have small weak points, like Skulltulas and Beamos. You also use it frequently while solving puzzles, since it lets you use your sword to interact with mechanisms like generators. If you attempt to do a thrust and you aren't holding your Wii Remote level, you may end up doing a vertical slash instead. This can also be a sign that you need to adjust your grip on the Wii Remote.

> **TIP**
>
> Are you having difficulty doing thrusts or horizontal slashes consistently? You may be playing the game while sitting in a posture that inclines you to hold the Wii Remote incorrectly. In *Skyward Sword*, the game reads combat motion input relative to a Wii MotionPlus controller held in a perfectly horizontal position. If you're doing something like resting your elbows on the arms of a chair while you play, then you may be tilting the tip of the Wii Remote up or down too much for sword strikes to register correctly. It can sometimes be useful to play through battles that call for very precise motion input while standing up, which helps ensure that you hold the Wii Remote without tilting it too much.

Link's Special Sword Strikes

Fatal Blow

This is the *Skyward Sword* version of Link's famous jumping sword attack from *The Legend of Zelda II*. While targeting an enemy that lies prone on the ground, move both the Wii Remote and Nunchuk sharply downward.

Jump Attack

Move the Wii Remote while Link is dashing, and he executes his signature jump attack attack from *Ocarina of Time* (and other 3D *Legend of Zelda* games). This move can be very useful because it knocks enemies over, setting them up for Fatal Blows.

Horizontal Spin

If you shake the Wii Remote and Nunchuk horizontally, Link performs a horizontal spinning slash that's twice as powerful as an ordinary sword strike. This move drains Link's stamina quickly, so you can't rely on it in most battles. Instead, it's best saved for situations where many enemies are crowding around you or when you're facing a particularly slow-moving enemy, like a Moblin. It's extremely useful for chopping down grass when you're scouring an area for hearts or Rupees.

Vertical Spin

While the Skyward Strike doesn't call for you to use the Nunchuk, it's worth discussing here. Link can charge energy by holding his sword above his head, then use any of his basic sword strikes to launch a sword beam. This lets Link attack enemies from a safe distance or across gaps. Some enemies take extra damage from sword beams, too.

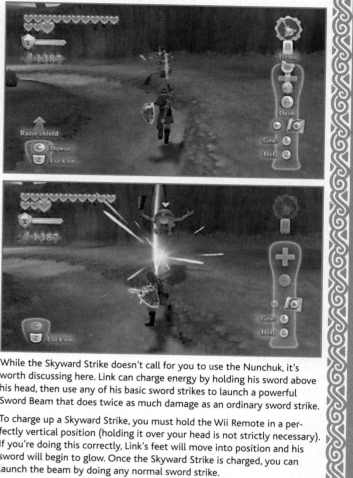

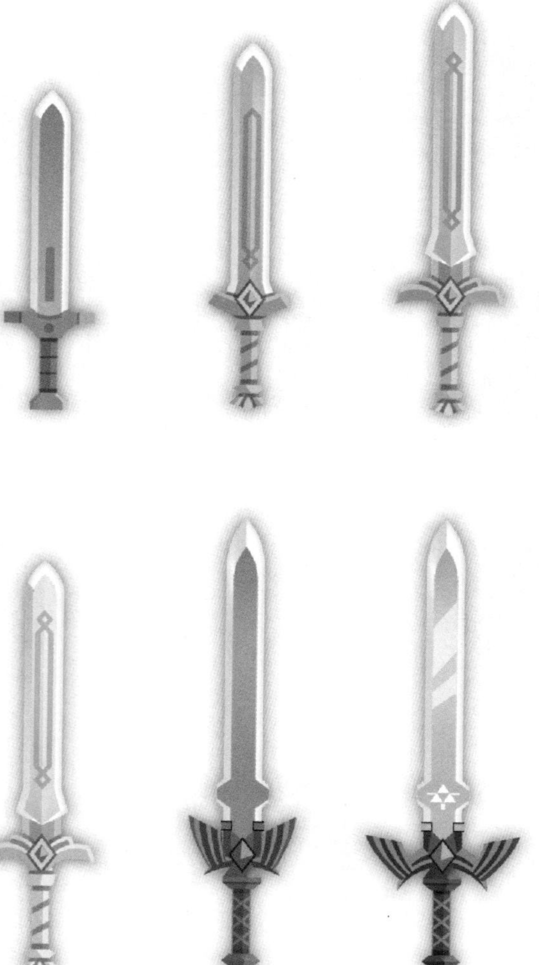

Skyward Strike

While the Skyward Strike doesn't call for you to use the Nunchuk, it's worth discussing here. Link can charge energy by holding his sword above his head, then use any of his basic sword strikes to launch a powerful Sword Beam that does twice as much damage as an ordinary sword strike.

To charge up a Skyward Strike, you must hold the Wii Remote in a perfectly vertical position (holding it over your head is not strictly necessary). If you're doing this correctly, Link's feet will move into position and his sword will begin to glow. Once the Skyward Strike is charged, you can launch the beam by doing any normal sword strike.

Because the Skyward Strike takes so long to charge, it's rarely useful in heated combat. It's typically more to your advantage to hit an enemy rapidly with regular sword strikes instead. That said, a Skyward Strike can sometimes be useful against enemies from a safe distance, such as across a gap.

TIP

Your sword can hold the charge for a Skyward Strike for a few seconds, so you can reposition Link before releasing your sword beam. The energy dissipates after a few seconds, so you can't do stuff like keep a sword beam constantly charged.

Link's Shield

Link's relationship with his shield is a bit different now, too. In previous games, the shield could deflect certain attacks but would offer little to no protection against others. In *Skyward Sword*, Link can use his shield to deflect almost any attack, but at a cost. Now your shield has its own health meter, and if your shield takes too much attack damage, it will break. Once your shield is broken, it's gone for good and must be replaced with a new one.

This means it's important to consider when it's better to absorb a blow with your shield or try to just dodge or interrupt an enemy's attack. Also, different types of shields have different properties. Wooden shields absorb electrical attacks well but can break instantly if damaged by fire. Iron shields handle fire well but are useless for defending against electrical attacks.

You now control Link's shield with the Nunchuk. Shaking it causes Link to raise his shield into a defensive posture, but this forces Link to lower his sword. If you opt to have Link attack, then his shield is automatically lowered. You must choose carefully when to defend and when to use your blade in *Skyward Sword*. You must also remember to equip your shield, as otherwise it's possible for Link to carry a shield around without using it.

You can use Link's shield to reflect attacks back at enemies or to interrupt them completely. You do this through a technique called shield bashing. If you shake the Nunchuk while Link is in a defensive posture, he swings his shield arm forward. If you time this properly with the enemy's attack, Link's shield bash can bounce projectiles or interrupt an enemy's attack.

For some enemies, the timing required to properly shield-bash their attacks is so tight that it's easier to try and overwhelm them with fast offense. Other enemies and certain bosses are extremely difficult to defeat until you learn how to properly shield bash their attacks. Learning how to interrupt a particular enemy's attack patterns with a well-timed shield-bash can be a painful and frustrating process early in the game, since only a few mistakes can result in a broken shield.

It's still an absolutely essential skill for succeeding in *Skyward Sword*. When you successfully shield-bash an enemy attack, your shield takes no damage and Link also takes no damage. A skillful player can use the shield to sail through many otherwise-dangerous fights without taking a bit of damage. In addition, many enemies will be staggered when their attacks are shield-bashed, which gives you an opening to attack them unopposed.

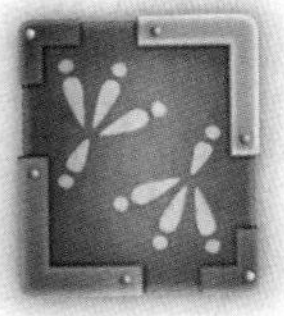

Using Tools

Through the course of his adventure, Link discovers eight special items he can use to help him explore previously inaccessible areas and defeat enemies more easily: the Slingshot, Bug Net, Beetle, Bombs, Gust Bellows, Whip, Clawshots, and Bow. Collectively, this guide refers to these items as tools, since they often help you solve problems and overcome in-game obstacles. You equip one of these items by holding down Ⓑ to bring up the tools menu, highlighting your selection with the Wii Remote's pointer, and then releasing Ⓑ.

Once a tool is equipped, you tap Ⓑ to begin using it. The game does not pause while you're switching between tools. Enemies can still attack you while you're in the tools menu. In practical terms, this means that you need to be really careful when you attempt to use tools or switch between tools during any sort of fight. Switching from a tool to your sword or shield is easy, though. If you shake the Wii Remote or the Nunchuk while Link is using a tool, he immediately puts it away and raises his sword or shield (as appropriate).

While prior *Legend of Zelda* games tended to feature enemies that were much more easily defeated by using certain tools rather than the sword, most enemies you can close to melee range within *Skyward Sword* are best battled with your sword and shield alone. There are enemies that can be defeated using tools, but usually it's best to attack these enemies from a safe distance with whatever you're using. Link moves more slowly when using most tools and will have a hard time dodging attacks.

While some prior *Legend of Zelda* games made it possible and advisable to completely defeat bosses using particular tools like the bow or bombs, in *Skyward Sword* you typically use these items only to create opportunities to damage the boss with your sword. You should only ever need to use one tool against any particular boss, usually the one you acquire in that boss's dungeon.

The Adventure Pouch

Skyward Sword introduces a separate real-time menu that you use to manage disposable and optional items that Link can use in combat. Press and hold ⊖ to bring up the Adventure Pouch menu, then select the item you'd like to use by highlighting it with the Wii Remote pointer. Some items you equip this way you then need to use other buttons to activate, like the Nunchuk for Link's shield or Ⓐ to drink a potion. Some items carried in the Adventure Pouch can have passive effects, like ammo bags, medals, or Fairies in bottles.

You begin with four slots in your Adventure Pouch and can acquire up to four more through the course of the game. Three of these slots you purchase from Beedle's Airshop, while the fourth is found in one of the goddess's treasure chests. If you find a new item and don't have space for it in your Adventure Pouch, it'll go immediately into storage at the Item Check (which is discussed more in the "Walkthrough" chapter). You can acquire far more items than you can carry even with an eight-slot Adventure Pouch, so you'll have to make decisions about what you do and don't want to carry pretty early in the game.

Since the Adventure Pouch is also a real-time menu, using potions to restore health in tense battles (like boss fights) is a little more complicated in *Skyward Sword* than it was in previous *Legend of Zelda* games. To restore health in a boss battle, you'll have to successfully retreat from the boss, find a safe spot on the battlefield, and manage to drink down the potion before the boss connects an attack. Though even basic Heart Potions restore more life, it can be useful to carry Fairies in your bottles instead just because a Fairy will revive you automatically upon death.

TIP

Skyward Sword features a Revitalizing Potion that can repair a damaged shield automatically, though it's just as difficult to use successfully during a tense battle as a Heart Potion. If you're afraid that your shield will break before a battle ends, it can be easier to just unequip it quickly through your Adventure Pouch menu then repair it later.

The Stamina Gauge

While the stamina gauge isn't part of the game's Wii MotionPlus controls, it's still a new element that you'll need to carefully manage throughout the course of your adventure. The simplest way to explain the stamina gauge is that it measures how long Link can exert himself before he gets exhausted. Any activity the game considers unusually strenuous will deplete Link's stamina. This includes dashing (running while holding down Ⓐ), spin-slash moves, dangling from ledges, carrying heavy objects, and climbing along vine-covered walls.

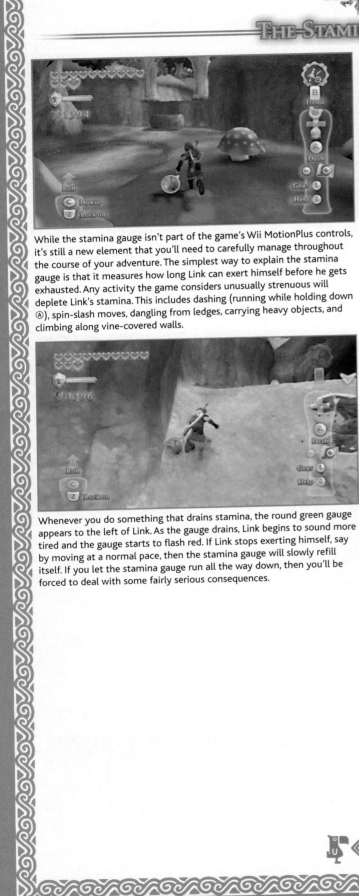

Whenever you do something that drains stamina, the round green gauge appears to the left of Link. As the gauge drains, Link begins to sound more tired and the gauge starts to flash red. If Link stops exerting himself, say by moving at a normal pace, then the stamina gauge will slowly refill itself. If you let the stamina gauge run all the way down, then you'll be forced to deal with some fairly serious consequences.

When Link's stamina runs out, he becomes exhausted. Once exhausted, Link can no longer move at a pace faster than a slow walk. If he is dangling from a ledge or wall, he will immediately fall from it. He can't dash or use any of his tools, his sword, or his shield until his stamina gauge has fully refilled. An exhausted Link is a sitting duck that bosses and strong enemies can easily kill, regardless of how many hearts Link has. Becoming exhausted while dealing with certain environmental hazards, like sinksand or conveyor belts, can instantly kill Link.

The simplest way to make sure Link doesn't become exhausted is to keep an eye on his stamina gauge. Some areas where Link must dash or climb will be dotted with Stamina Fruit, a resource that will completely restore Link's stamina if he touches it. These items replenish automatically and can be the only thing to make a dangerous area passable. You can buy a potion called the Stamina Potion that makes your stamina reduce more slowly or, if you enhance it, makes your stamina stay constant for three minutes no matter what you're doing. Using this potion is subject to all the limitations of using any other item from your Adventure Pouch.

It's important not to do things that drain Link's stamina gauge needlessly. Don't fight enemies with spin-slashes if you can defeat them just as easily with standard sword techniques, which won't drain your stamina. Don't dash unless it's necessary to escape an environmental hazard, clear a jump, or retreat from a strong enemy. Definitely don't dash or use stamina-draining attacks needlessly when fighting bosses. When it comes to managing Link's stamina, *Skyward Sword* is a game that calls for a cautious approach.

Saving Your Game

In most *Legend of Zelda* games, you can choose to save your progress at any time. This is not the case in *Skyward Sword*, where you can only save your progress at bird statues scattered throughout Skyloft (your hub city) and the surface world below. The bird statues are rather similar to the Owl Statues found in *Majora's Mask*, but the saves you make at bird statues won't be erased after you load them. Bird statues in *Skyward Sword* basically work like the save points you'd encounter in a typical console RPG.

Bird statues in the overworld are connected to Skyloft in a way that is without precedent in the *Legend of Zelda* series. When you visit a bird statue located on the surface world, you'll have the option to return automatically to Skyloft if you wish. If you visit a bird statue in a dungeon, you can't return directly to Skyloft but you can return directly to the beginning of the dungeon. Most dungeons have bird statues by the entrance, so effectively this lets you quickly leave a dungeon at any time and return to Skyloft.

The ability to return to a safe hub area full of shops at any time has a major impact on the flow of the game. In most *Legend of Zelda* games, you want to prepare carefully before you enter a dungeon. If you get overwhelmed or run out of items, backtracking can be just as dangerous as moving forward. In *Skyward Sword*, most dungeons are designed with shortcuts that you can trigger as you explore the location. So it's easy to leave a dungeon, resupply at Skyloft, and then quickly make your way back to the point in the dungeon where you were originally.

While you'll want to be fully supplied before fighting a dungeon's boss or sub-boss, you don't need to be as careful when exploring *Skyward Sword*'s dungeons as you needed to be in prior games. Whenever a dungeon is too much for you, it'll be easy to get out. If you get killed in *Skyward Sword*, you have the option to quit and simply reload your last save. You can also choose to continue, but if you do so then any items you consumed before you died will still be gone. So if you drank a bunch of potions or broke your shield, those resources are gone.

Crafting Items

In most *Legend of Zelda* games, obtaining an enhanced item like a better bow involved having to find or earn it somehow during the course of the game. In *Skyward Sword*, Link can create improved equipment himself. While fighting enemies and exploring, Link will run across 16 different types of material that he can collect. If he takes these materials to the game's Scrap Shop and has enough Rupees on hand, he'll be able to take a weak item like the basic Wooden Bow and forge it into the enhanced Iron Bow (or, given time, the Sacred Bow).

Being able to enhance items changes the flow of the game somewhat. Creating the best shield possible is always a priority, since stronger shields can absorb more damage before they break. Instead of being able to acquire certain equipment at set times, you may find you can make it very early in the game if you get some lucky drops. By the same token, you may have to set extra time aside during gameplay for gathering materials and improving items. While many of the materials you'll use regularly can drop when you defeat enemies, there are also many types that can only be found in certain locations or obtained by using a certain tool in a certain way.

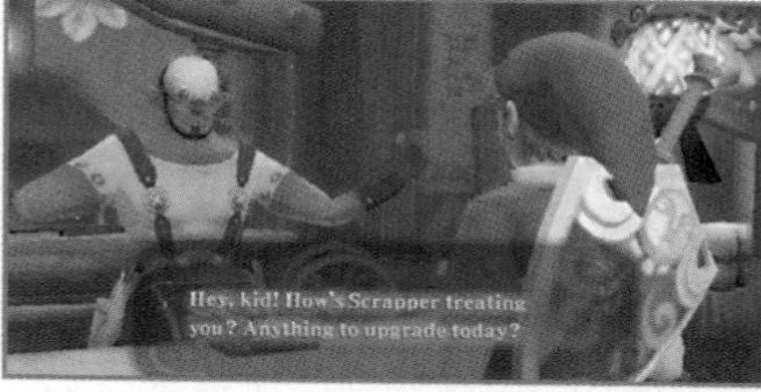

One particular vintage *Legend of Zelda* activity, hunting for bugs, is purely part of item crafting in this game. You can infuse bugs you've caught into certain potions, allowing Link to make far more powerful potions than the ones for sale at the game's Potion Shop. As a trade-off, catching bugs is now more difficult, to balance out the powerful potions you can create with them. As you play through the game, keep an eye on where you can find certain materials and how much of certain important types you've acquired. It's always worth taking a trip back to Skyloft to improve equipment if you've gathered up the right materials for it.

Note that the vast majority of the item crafting you can do in *Legend of Zelda* is both completely optional and not at all necessary if you just want to beat the game and see its ending. The walkthrough recommends crafting a handful of items that can make the game dramatically easier for you early on, but it's very possible to make virtually every major item in the game well before you reach the game's last few dungeons. Likewise, item crafting has led to a change in the role of the Hylian Shield in this game, where it's both far more powerful than ever before and far less necessary to completing the game.

For more information about item crafting and item data, consult the "Items, Equipment, and Crafting" chapter. For information about the Hylian Shield, consult the "Secrets and Side Quests" chapter.

Equipment and Items

Equipment

Link's not going to save the world with his bare hands. To battle enemies and brave dungeons, Link needs to acquire and upgrade equipment that enhances his abilities. Some of his equipment can be found in chests, some is acquired as part of the storyline, and some of it must be made by upgrading equipment with treasures.

Link's Swords

Practice Sword

Link's first sword is an ordinary, mortal blade, taken on loan from the Sparring Hall. It's fine for dueling Keese and Chuchus, but to explore the surface world Link needs something stronger.

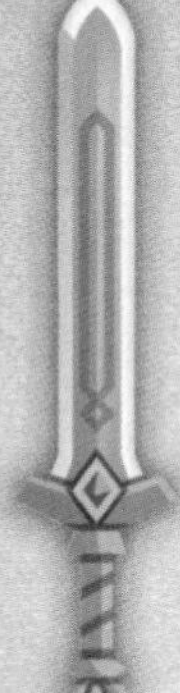

Goddess Sword

The Goddess Sword is a divine blade passed down from ancient times. It can detect objects through dowsing and fire powerful sword beams made of sacred energy. This sword is the bane of evil, but its power is limited. You acquire this from a mysterious chamber in Skyloft.

Goddess Longsword

The second form of the Goddess Sword grows longer and doubles its power after absorbing Farore's Flame in the Ancient Cistern. Using this sword, Link can adventure into more dangerous areas and defeat enemies more easily.

Goddess White Sword

The third form of the Goddess Sword. Its perfect white blade is the result of the sword's increasing purity, as its imperfections were burned away by Nayru's Flame in the Sandship. This sword has enhanced dowsing abilities, making it easier for Link to seek out treasure.

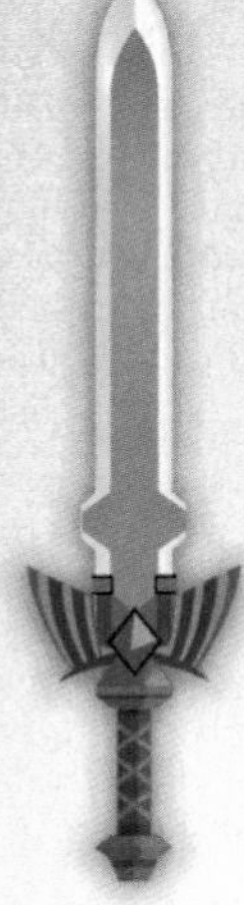

Master Sword

The near-perfect form of the Goddess Sword is created when it absorbs the holy power of Din's Flame. This blade possesses three times the power of the original Goddess Sword and is the bane of all evil, but it is not yet complete.

True Master Sword

The ultimate proof against evil is the complete form of the Goddess Sword, purified by Link's virtue and blessed by the Goddess Hylia's own hand. With the True Master Sword, Link has the power to seek out the land's greatest power, the legendary Triforce.

Link's Shields

Wooden Shields

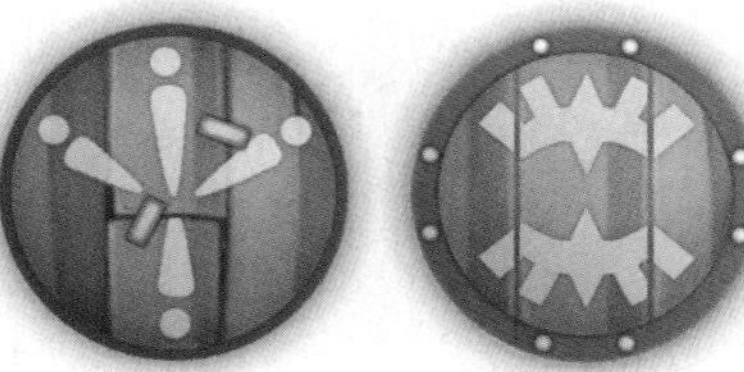

Link begins the game wielding the flimsy Wooden Shield. It can't absorb much damage and is highly flammable, but is proof against electric attacks. You can get your first Wooden Shield from Instructor Horwell at the Knight Academy, but if it breaks you must buy another one from Rupin at the Gear Shop. You can use treasures to enhance the Wooden Shield into the sturdier Banded Shield and the Braced Shield.

Iron Shields

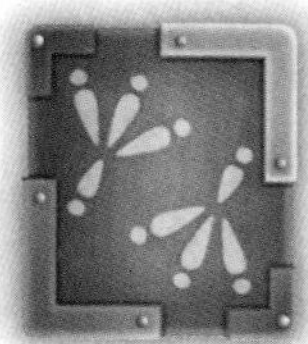

You can buy the Iron Shield from Rupin's Gear Shop once you begin adventuring in Eldin Volcano. The Iron Shield is highly resistant to flame attacks, making it ideal to use in Eldin Volcano's fiery environment. It conducts electricity, though, which makes it useless in Lanayru Desert. You can use treasures to enhance the Iron Shield into the sturdier Reinforced Shield and Fortified Shield.

Sacred Shields

You can buy the Sacred Shield from Rupin's Gear Shop once you begin questing for the three Sacred Flames. This shield is very expensive, but for good reason. It is proof against fire, electricity, and evil curses. Even better, its durability can regenerate over time on its own. You can use treasures to enhance the Sacred Shield into the sturdier Divine Shield and Goddess Shield.

Hylian Shield

A legendary treasure of the goddess, the Hylian Shield is said to be guarded by the Thunder Dragon, Lanayru. An adventurer who proved his worthiness might convince the dragon to part with it. The Hylian Shield is divine in origin and is said to be so perfectly strong that it cannot break, no matter how much damage it absorbs. The Hylian Shield is also far larger than any other shield in the game, making it more effective when it comes to protecting Link from attacks.

Ranged Weapons

Slingshot

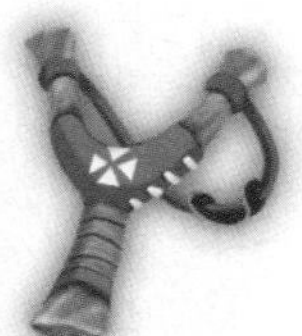

The Slingshot you obtain from the Kikwi elder in Faron Woods lets you fire Deku Seeds at enemies that are just out of Link's reach. Fire from the Slingshot can only dizzy large enemies, but sometimes this buys you valuable time. Smaller enemies like Walltulas can actually be defeated with shots from the Slingshot. You can use treasures to enhance the Slingshot into the Scattershot, which breaks Deku Seeds into nine pieces to pepper your enemies with shrapnel.

Seed Satchels

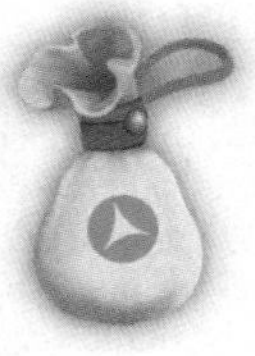

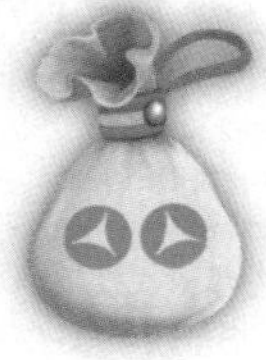

You can carry a Seed Satchel in your Adventure Pouch to hold extra ammo for your Slingshot. The Small Seed Satchel you find in a goddess's treasure chest or purchase from Rupin lets you carry 10 extra Deku Seeds. You can use treasures to enhance the Small Seed Satchel into the Medium Seed Satchel, which lets you carry 20 extra Deku Seeds, and the Large Seed Satchel, which lets you carry 30 extra Deku Seeds. You can also buy and enhance multiple Seed Satchels if you like.

Bow

You find your first bow, the Wooden Bow, in the Sandship in the Lanayru Sand Sea. You can fire the bow to damage and defeat distant enemies, or enemies like Spumes that usually lurk in areas where your sword can't reach them.

Quivers

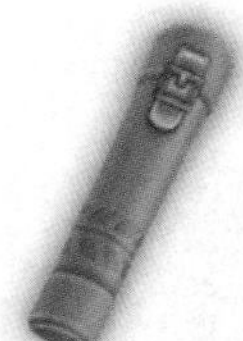

You can carry a quiver in your Adventure Pouch to hold extra arrows for your bow. The Small Quiver you find in a goddess's treasure chest or purchase from Rupin holds 5 extra arrows. You can use treasures to enhance the Small Quiver into the Medium Quiver, which holds 10 extra arrows, and the Large Quiver, which holds 15 extra arrows. You can also buy and enhance multiple quivers if you like.

Bombs

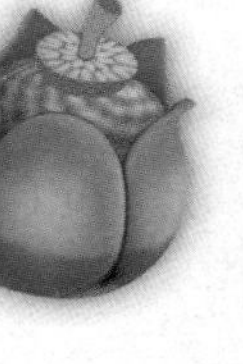

Once you obtain the Bomb Bag, Link can store and carry Bomb Flowers or buy bombs directly from Rupin. You can occasionally use bombs to defeat enemies like Spumes or to stagger enemies like Stalfos, but you primarily use bombs to solve puzzles and blast open hidden chambers.

Bomb Bags

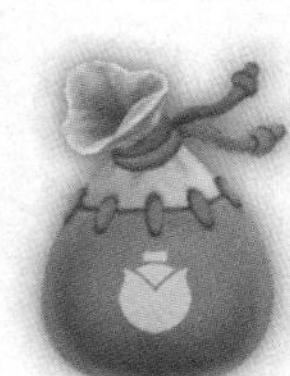

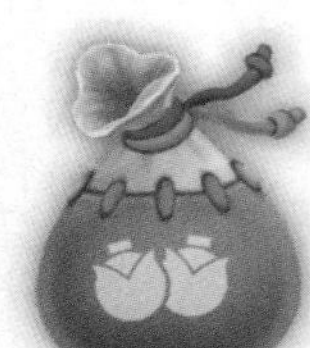

Carry a Bomb Bag in your Adventure Pouch and you can carry extra bombs. The Small Bomb Bag you find in a goddess's treasure chest or buy from Rupin lets you carry 5 extra bombs. You can use treasures to enhance the Small Bomb Bag into the Medium Bomb Bag, which holds 10 extra bombs, and the Large Bomb Bag, which holds 15 extra bombs. You can also buy and enhance multiple Bomb Bags if you like.

Tools and Special Items

Beetle

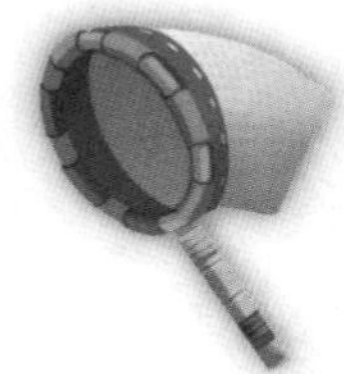

Link acquires the Beetle in the Skyview Temple. This incredibly useful tool is an ancient flying drone that can cut through ropes and, eventually, carry bombs to blast distant targets. You can use it to strike switches, attack small enemies, or just examine what the terrain ahead of you looks like. A worker robot in the Lanayru Desert upgrades your Beetle to the Hook Beetle automatically. After that, you can use treasures to upgrade the Hook Beetle to the Quick Beetle and the Tough Beetle.

Gust Bellows

Link acquires the Gust Bellows deep within the Lanayru Mining Facility. This device draws in air using a vacuum mounted at its rear, then blows it out at high speed. You can use the Gust Bellows to blow away loose sand and dirt, which is a surprisingly important task. You can also use the Gust Bellows against certain lightweight enemies, like Arachas and Froaks. In fact, blowing a Froak into a wall or something else solid makes it explode.

Clawshots

Link acquires the Clawshots by completing the Lanayru Desert's Silent Realm challenge. Each Clawshot is a glove Link can wear over his hand and use to automatically fire a powerful grappling hook. Once you have the Clawshots in your possession, you can reach all kinds of hidden areas by grappling up to wall-mounted targets and patches of vines.

Whip

Link acquires the whip in the Ancient Cistern. The whip is a curious tool made of ancient technology. The tip of the whip uses a mysterious energy to latch on to hooks and even some collectible items, like hearts and Rupees. Some enemies can be snared by the whip, allowing Link to steal items from them or stun them.

Bug Net

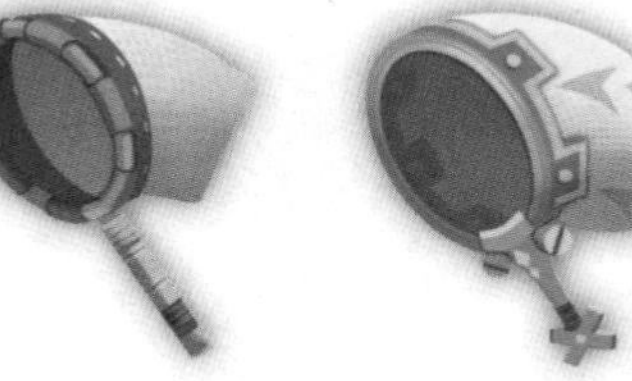

You can purchase the Bug Net from Beedle's Airshop any time after Link acquires the Slingshot. With the Bug Net, Link can catch bugs and all sorts of other things like Fairies, small birds, and Tumbleweeds. You can use treasures to upgrade the Bug Net to the Big Bug Net, which has a wider mouth that can catch targets more easily.

Goddess's Harp

Link acquires the Goddess's Harp in the Temple of Time. The harp serves no purpose in combat, but you can play it to reveal secrets like goddess walls and Gossip Stones that sometimes hide in places where Blessed Butterflies gather. You can also use it to play a musical minigame. There are five special songs the harp can play, each learned as part of your quest through the game.

Digging Mitts

A friendly Mogma gives Link the Digging Mitts in Eldin Volcano. Using the Digging Mitts, Link can dig in patches of dirt for Eldin Ores, hearts, Rupees, Fairies, and steam geysers that let you reach new places.

Mogma Mitts

A grateful Mogma gives Link the Mogma Mitts in the Fire Sanctuary. Using the Mogma Mitts, Link can dig in patches of dirt to uncover the entrances to underground burrows. Crawling around in burrows helps you reach new areas of a dungeon and solve puzzles. Sometimes, you can even find treasures hidden underground or by passing through burrows.

Water Dragon's Scale

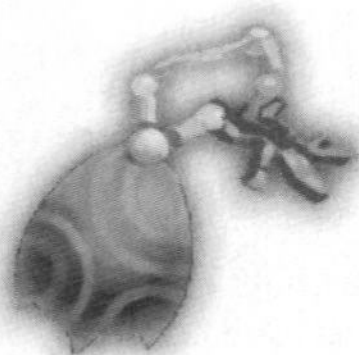

Link acquires the Water Dragon's Scale by completing the Silent Realm challenge in Faron Woods. The Water Dragon's Scale allows Link to swim freely through deep water and execute spin attacks to smash down underwater obstacles and defeat underwater enemies. You do need to collect air bubbles to keep from drowning underwater, but this is usually pretty easy.

Fireshield Earrings

Link acquires the Fireshield Earrings by completing the Silent Realm challenge in Eldin Volcano. With the Fireshield Earrings, Link becomes immune to the ravages of fire. He can walk through superheated areas that were previously deadly and can no longer be set on fire by falling in magma or being attacked by enemies.

Sailcloth

The Sailcloth is a gift from Zelda early in the game. You can use the Sailcloth to break your fall and land safely after making long dives from very high places.

Wallets

All wallets except the Small Wallet and the Extra Wallets you acquire by giving Batreaux Gratitude Crystals in Skyloft. Link can only carry as much money as his wallet will hold, so once your wallet is maxed out you can't collect any more Rupees. Well, you can, but the Rupees basically just disappear. This is pretty annoying if you find a huge number of Rupees in a chest or win some from a minigame.

Small Wallet

You begin the game with the Small Wallet. It holds a mere 300 Rupees, but what do you expect? Link was just a student when he got it. He didn't know he'd be going on a big expensive adventure back then.

Medium Wallet

With the Medium Wallet, Link can carry up to 500 Rupees. That's better, but still too little to afford a lot of the game's best items.

Big Wallet

With the Big Wallet, Link can carry up to 1,000 Rupees. That's more than enough money to afford most items in the game, though there are still a few things that'll be pretty tough to buy.

Giant Wallet

With the Giant Wallet, Link can carry up to 5,000 Rupees. That's more money than even an adventurer is ever going to need, but it's nice to not have to waste any Rupees.

Tycoon Wallet

With the Tycoon Wallet, Link can carry up to an unbelievable 9,000 Rupees. How would you even get that much money at once? Believe it or not, it's perfectly possible to fill up the Tycoon Wallet.

Extra Wallets

You can purchase Extra Wallets from Beedle's Airshop. Each wallet costs 100 Rupees and lets you add an additional 300 Rupees to your wallet's current capacity. You can purchase three Extra Wallets from Beedle, letting you add 900 Rupees to your wallet's capacity. With a Tycoon Wallet and three Extra Wallets, it's possible to carry 9,900 Rupees at once!

Adventure Pouch Items

In addition to ammo bags and shields, you can carry other items in your Adventure Pouch. Some of these items have passive effects, like the medals, while others like potions you can use at will by selecting them. You also sometimes use items from your Adventure Pouch automatically while solving puzzles or advancing the game's storyline.

Empty Bottles

You can obtain up to five Empty Bottles in *Skyward Sword*. The main purpose of Empty Bottles is holding potions, but you can also use Empty Bottles to carry Fairies, water, sacred water, various medicines, and pumpkin soup. If you carry pumpkin soup around in an Empty Bottle for more than five minutes, it becomes unappetizing cold pumpkin soup.

Glittering Spores

When you hit the mushrooms that grow in Faron Woods, they release clouds of spores. When you collect these spores in an Empty Bottle, they become Glittering Spores. You can pour Glittering Spores on collectible items like hearts and Rupees to transform them in strange ways.

Medals

Heart Medal

While you're carrying a Heart Medal, enemies drop hearts more frequently. You also find hearts more frequently when cutting down grass, digging in holes, and breaking pots. It's useful to carry when you're having a hard time fighting the enemies that patrol a certain area. It's also good for places like Eldin Volcano, where you can take a lot of damage from missing jumps and falling into lava. You obtain the Heart Medal from a goddess's treasure chest.

Rupee Medal

While you're carrying a Rupee Medal, enemies drop Rupees more frequently. You also find Rupees more frequently when cutting down grass, digging in holes, and breaking pots. It's useful to carry when you're trying to earn money for expensive but necessary items like Adventure Pouch Slots or the Sacred Shield. You obtain the Rupee Medal from a goddess's treasure chest.

Treasure Medal

While you're carrying a Treasure Medal, enemies drop treasures more frequently. It's good to carry around when you're grinding for treasures so you can upgrade an essential piece of equipment. You obtain the Treasure Medal from a goddess's treasure chest.

Potion Medal

While you're carrying a Potion Medal, potions with three-minute durations like the Stamina Potion, Air Potion, and Guardian Potion last longer. Combining a Guardian Potion with a Potion Medal can make even the toughest battles into cakewalks.

Life Medal

While you're carrying a Life Medal, Link's health meter is extended by one heart. Obtaining and carrying the game's two Life Medals is the only way to get Link's health meter all the way up to 20 hearts. Otherwise, Link's health maxes out at 18 hearts. You find one Life Medal in a goddess's treasure chest and can buy the other one from Beedle's Airshop.

Cursed Medal

The Cursed Medal confers the benefits of the Treasure Medal and the Rupee Medal all at once, but while carrying it you cannot open your Adventure Pouch at all. This means you can't use any potions, shields, or other items you might be carrying. This medal can be extremely useful when gathering treasures, since extra Rupees are always nice to have when you're paying for equipment upgrades. You can only obtain it from Batreaux.

Bug Medal

While you're carrying the Bug Medal, your in-game map automatically displays the locations of any nearby bug spawns. Note that bugs aren't always present at bug spawns and that the Bug Medal doesn't tell you which types of bugs spawn in a given area. You can purchase this medal from Beedle's Airshop after you purchase the Bug Net.

Potions

You purchase all potions from Bertie's Potion Shop. Some don't become available until later in the game. All of them can be enhanced by Bertie, if you pay a small fee and bring him the right bugs.

Heart Potions

A basic Heart Potion restores eight hearts of life when you drink it. With the right bugs, Bertie can enhance the Heart Potion into a Heart Potion+ or the Heart Potion++. A Heart Potion+ restores Link's life to maximum while a Heart Potion++ can restore Link's life to maximum twice before it's completely consumed.

Air Potions

A basic Air Potion makes Link consume air half as quickly for the next three minutes. With the right bugs, Bertie can enhance an Air Potion into an Air Potion+. After drinking an Air Potion+, Link can stay underwater without needing to breathe at all for three minutes.

Stamina Potions

A basic Stamina Potion makes Link's stamina go down half as quickly for the next three minutes. With the right bugs, Bertie can enhance a Stamina Potion into a Stamina Potion+. After drinking a Stamina Potion+, Link can do whatever he wants for three minutes without his stamina reducing whatsoever.

Guardian Potions

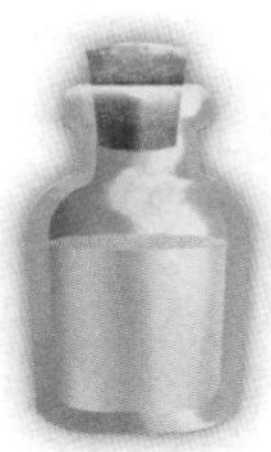 

A basic Guardian Potion protects Link for three minutes, making him take half damage from all attacks. With the right bugs, Bertie can enhance a Guardian Potion into a Guardian Potion+. After drinking a Guardian Potion+, Link will not take damage from any attacks for the next three minutes.

Revitalizing Potions

 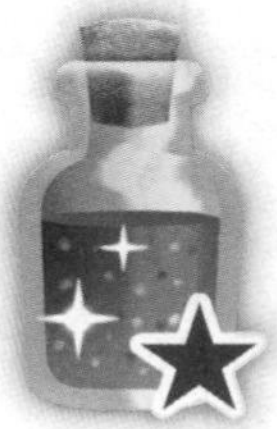 

A basic Revitalizing Potion restores four hearts of Link's health and completely restores his shield's durability. With the right bugs, Bertie can enhance a Revitalizing Potion into a Revitalizing Potion+ or a Revitalizing Potion++. A Revitalizing Potion+ completely restores the durability of Link's shield and restores eight hearts of life. A Revitalizing Potion++ does the same thing but can be used twice before it is consumed.

Bertie's Potion Shop

At Bertie's Potion Shop in the Skyloft Bazaar, you can fill up any Empty Bottles in your possession with useful potions. At the beginning of the game, you can purchase Heart Potions, Revitalizing Potions, and Guardian Potions. While the Heart Potion and Revitalizing Potion are affordable, Guardian Potions are extremely pricy at 200 Rupees. Later in the game, the Potion Shop adds Stamina Potions and Air Potions to its selection. Bertie's Potion Shop is the only place in the game where you can acquire potions.

You usually buy potions from Bertie's wife. If you visit Bertie himself, you can have him enhance potions into their + and ++ forms by paying him a fee and bringing him the right bugs. Catching bugs can be difficult and time-consuming, so think carefully about whether you really need a given potion enhancement before you decide to go get it. Some potion enhancements you won't be able to buy until you've explored far enough into the game that you can find a wide variety of bugs. For instance, you can't make a Heart Potion+ until you've been to Eldin Volcano and can't make a Heart Potion++ until you've been to Lanayru Desert.

You don't need enhanced potions to finish the main game, so this guide rarely recommends Bertie's enhancing services. If you're having a really hard time beating a particular boss, though, then you may want to consider taking a little time to prepare some enhanced potions before attempting the fight again. Consult the "Equipment, Items, and Crafting" chapter for more details.

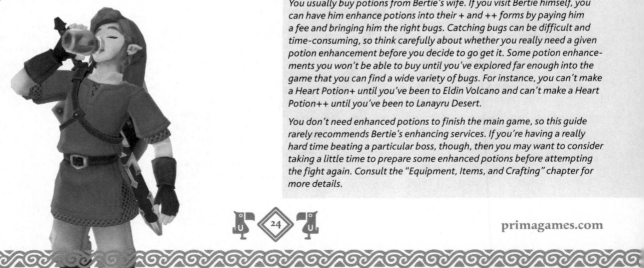

Collectible Items

Rupees

There are five types of Rupees in *Skyward Sword*. Common Green and Blue Rupees you can get by defeating enemies, cutting down grass, or digging in holes. Red Rupees can be found by defeating certain enemies, opening small chests, digging in holes, and carefully searching for hidden areas. Silver Rupees are sometimes hidden in certain dungeons and are otherwise only found in blue chests and goddess's treasure chests. Gold Rupees are only found in goddess's treasure chests. Each color of Rupee signifies a different value.

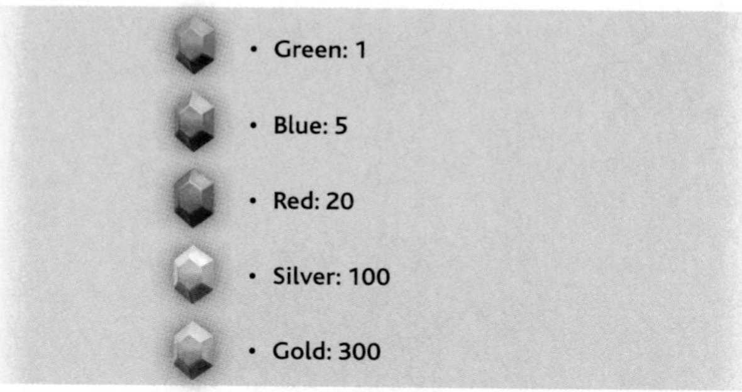

• Green: 1
• Blue: 5
• Red: 20
• Silver: 100
• Gold: 300

The Rupoor

The dreaded Rupoor is a malignant form of antimoney that somehow makes you lose 10 Rupees instantly. There are only a few points in the game where you can acquire a Rupoor, but you still want to avoid them whenever possible. Rupoors appear in the Thrill Digger minigame and can be shot down from the black crystals that line the Thrill Digger room's walls. You find them sometimes in underground burrows you can move through with the Mogma Mitts. You can also create a Rupoor sometimes by pouring Glittering Spores on a Rupee.

Hearts and Pieces of Heart

Hearts

You can find hearts growing in the wild. You can also find them by defeating enemies, cutting down tall grass, or digging in holes. Grabbing a heart restores one heart's worth of life to Link's health meter.

Pieces of Heart

There are 24 Pieces of Heart in *Skyward Sword*. Many of them you find in goddess's treasure chests, while others you have to get by playing minigames or finding hidden areas. Every time you collect four Pieces of Heart, you add an extra heart to Link's health meter.

PIECES OF HEART

PIECE OF HEART	LOCATION	HOW TO GET IT
1	Faron Woods	p. 64
2	Beedle's Airshop	p. 67
3	Goddess Chest #2	p. 72
4	Lumpy Pumpkin	p. 73
5	Skyview Temple	p. 80
6	Eldin Volcano	p. 90
7	Goddess Chest #11	p. 117
8	Goddess Wall	p. 128
9	Faron Woods	p. 133
10	Goddess Chest #6	p. 139
11	Goddess Chest #14	p. 139
12	Lanayru Desert	p. 156
13	Goddess Chest #21	p. 167
14	Sandship	p. 172
15	Goddess Chest #22	p. 182
16	Fire Sanctuary	p. 189
17	Volcano Summit	p. 204
18	Zelda's Room	p. 229
19	Batreaux	p. 230
20	Lumpy Pumpkin	p. 234
21	Rickety Coaster	p. 237
22	Pumpkin Pull	p. 237
23	Fun Fun Island	p. 237
24	Thunder Dragon's Lightning Round	p. 238

Treasures

There are 16 types of treasures you can obtain in *Skyward Sword*: Hornet Larvae, Bird Feathers, Tumbleweeds, Lizard Tails, Eldin Ores, Ancient Flowers, Amber Relics, Dusk Relics, Jelly Blobs, Monster Claws, Monster Horns, Ornamental Skulls, Evil Crystals, Blue Bird Feathers, Golden Skulls, and Goddess Plumes. You gather treasures so you can take them to Gondo's Scrap Shop and use them to upgrade your equipment. Each type of treasure is found in a particular way, either dropped by enemies or hidden throughout the world. For more information about gathering treasures and what you can do with them, consult the "Items, Equipment, and Crafting" chapter.

Bugs

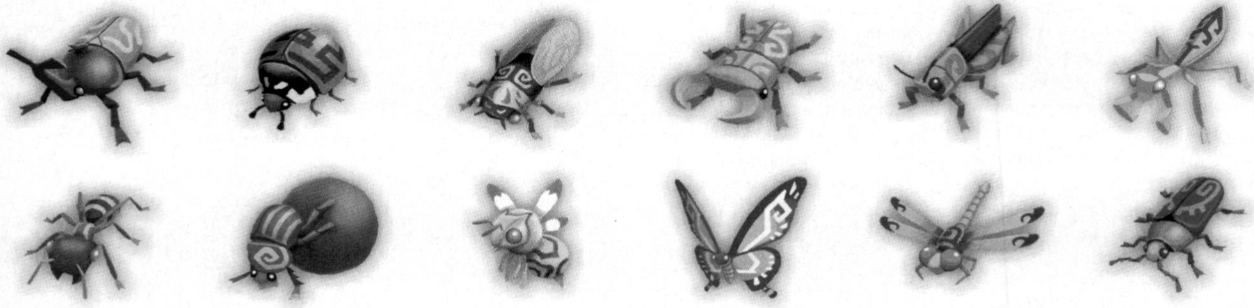

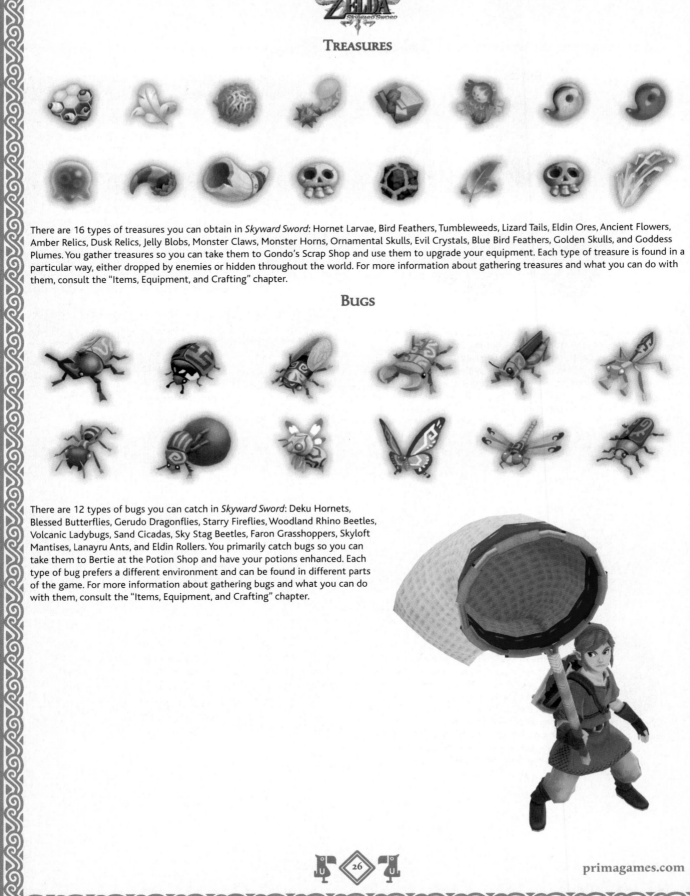

There are 12 types of bugs you can catch in *Skyward Sword*: Deku Hornets, Blessed Butterflies, Gerudo Dragonflies, Starry Fireflies, Woodland Rhino Beetles, Volcanic Ladybugs, Sand Cicadas, Sky Stag Beetles, Faron Grasshoppers, Skyloft Mantises, Lanayru Ants, and Eldin Rollers. You primarily catch bugs so you can take them to Bertie at the Potion Shop and have your potions enhanced. Each type of bug prefers a different environment and can be found in different parts of the game. For more information about gathering bugs and what you can do with them, consult the "Items, Equipment, and Crafting" chapter.

Quest Items

Stone of Trials

This mysterious stone is the reward for completing the Silent Realm challenge in Skyloft. It's said that if you find the right place in Skyloft to put it, you open the way to the Triforce.

Pieces of the Key

Bokoblins broke the key to the Earth Temple into five pieces and scattered them through Eldin Volcano. You must find them all before you can explore the Earth Temple.

Beedle's Insect Cage

Inside this cage is an extremely rare insect Beedle keeps as a pet. Beedle loves his pet very much and has spared no expense when it comes to its fancy cage.

Cawlin's Letter

Cawlin's Letter, full of florid and heartfelt (if amateurish) poetry. It's written on very nice paper.

Rattle

A baby's beloved rattle. Just imagine how angry that baby would be if it got lost.

Life Tree Seedling

A seedling that, in a thousand years, could grow into a Life Tree. Of course, you'd have to plant it in just the right soil.

Life Tree Fruit

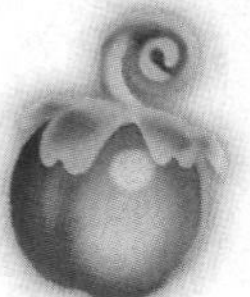

After a thousand years, the Life Tree bears a single giant fruit. This fruit is said to cure any illness, no matter how grave.

Gratitude Crystals

A few loose Gratitude Crystals appear in Skyloft and certain parts of the sky at night. There are 15 of these in all. (The remaining Gratitude Crystals you must earn by completing Gratitude Crystal requests; see the "Secrets and Side Quests" chapter for details.)

Songs

Ballad of the Goddess

A simple song, taught to you by the old priestess at the Sealed Temple. Play this in Skyloft to reveal a path that leads into the thunderhead.

Farore's Courage

A sacred song given to you at the Isle of Songs. Play it in the correct area of Faron Woods to gain entrance to the Silent Realm.

Nayru's Wisdom

A sacred song given to you at the Isle of Songs. Play it in the correct area of Lanayru Desert to gain entrance to the Silent Realm.

Din's Power

A sacred song given to you at the Isle of Songs. Play it in the correct area of Eldin Volcano to gain entrance to the Silent Realm.

Song of the Hero

A song so sacred that it was broken into four parts by the goddess. Each piece is guarded by one of the surface world's three great dragons and the sky spirit, Levias. Once it's assembled, play it in the correct area of Skyloft to gain entrance to the Silent Realm.

Puzzle Keys

Golden Carving

A strange carving that's actually the key to a door. Use it in Skyview Temple to open the puzzle door that leads to Skyview Spring.

Dragon Sculpture

A strange golden carving that resembles a dragon. Use it in the Earth Temple to open the puzzle door that leads to the final boss's room.

Ancient Circuit

A strange golden carving designed to be part of some unfathomable machine. Use it in Lanayru Mining Facility to open the puzzle door that leads to the Temple of Time.

Blessed Idol

A carving that resembles the statue that sits in the center of the Ancient Cistern. Use it to open the puzzle door that awaits inside the statue itself.

Mysterious Crystals

At first glance, it's not easy to tell what this carving was meant to resemble. Use it to open the puzzle door that awaits inside the Fire Sanctuary.

Squid Carving

An intricate carving that resembles a squid. Use it to open the puzzle that awaits inside the Sandship.

Chests

There are many chests strewn throughout Skyloft and the lands below it, each beckoning adventurers with the promise of riches. Each type of chest holds different loot inside, and some must be opened in certain ways.

Blue Chests

You can find blue chests anywhere in Skyloft or the lands below it, including both inside and outside of dungeons. A blue chest can hold special items for a dungeon, like a Small Key or Dungeon Map, as well as random treasures or even Pieces of Heart.

Jeweled Chests

Jeweled chests only appear in dungeons and always hold the key to that dungeon's puzzle door. They usually occur somewhere near the puzzle door, but not always.

Goddess's Treasure Chests

Goddess's treasure chests are strewn throughout the sky. You can't open them until you activate the corresponding Goddess Cube on the surface world. Goddess's treasure chests can hold some of the rarest treasures in the game, including unique medals, Gold Rupees, and Pieces of Heart.

ITEM CHECKLIST

ITEM	LOCATION
Banded Shield	Gondo's Scrap Shop
Beetle	Skyview Temple
Gust Bellows	Lanayru Mining Facility
Big Bug Net	Gondo's Scrap Shop
Big Wallet	Batreaux
Bombs	Earth Temple
Braced Shield	Gondo's Scrap Shop
Bug Medal	Beedle's Airshop
Bug Net	Beedle's Airshop
Clawshots	Nayru's Silent Realm
Cursed Medal	Batreaux
Digging Mitts	Eldin Volcano
Divine Shield	Gondo's Scrap Shop
Empty Bottle #1	Bertie's Potion Shop
Empty Bottle #2	Sealed Grounds
Empty Bottle #3	Goddess's Treasure Chest
Empty Bottle #4	Fire Sanctuary
Empty Bottle #5	Parrow
Extra Wallet	Beedle's Airshop
Extra Wallet	Beedle's Airshop
Extra Wallet	Beedle's Airshop
Fireshield Earrings	Din's Silent Realm
Fortified Shield	Gondo's Scrap Shop
Giant Wallet	Batreaux
Goddess's Harp	Temple of Time
Goddess Longsword	Ancient Cistern
Goddess Shield	Gondo's Scrap Shop
Goddess Sword	Skyloft
Goddess White Sword	Sandship
Heart Medal	Goddess's Treasure Chest
Hook Beetle	Lanayru Desert
Hylian Shield	Thunder Dragon's Lightning Round
Iron Bow	Gondo's Scrap Shop
Iron Shield	Rupin's Gear Shop
Large Bomb Bag	Gondo's Scrap Shop

ITEM	LOCATION
Large Quiver	Gondo's Scrap Shop
Large Seed Satchel	Gondo's Scrap Shop
Life Medal	Goddess's Treasure Chest
Life Medal	Beedle's Airshop
Master Sword	Fire Sanctuary
Medium Bomb Bag	Gondo's Scrap Shop
Medium Quiver	Gondo's Scrap Shop
Medium Seed Satchel	Gondo's Scrap Shop
Medium Wallet	Batreaux
Mogma Mitts	Fire Sanctuary
Practice Sword	Sparring Hall
Quick Beetle	Gondo's Scrap Shop
Reinforced Shield	Gondo's Scrap Shop
Rupee Medal	Goddess's Treasure Chest
Sacred Bow	Gondo's Scrap Shop
Sacred Shield	Rupin's Gear Shop
Sailcloth	Skyloft
Scattershot	Gondo's Scrap Shop
Slingshot	Faron Woods
Small Bomb Bag	Goddess's Treasure Chest, Rupin's Gear Shop
Small Quiver	Goddess's Treasure Chest, Rupin's Gear Shop
Small Seed Satchel	Goddess's Treasure Chest, Rupin's Gear Shop
Small Wallet	Batreaux
Tough Beetle	Gondo's Scrap Shop
Treasure Medal	Goddess's Treasure Chest
True Master Sword	Temple of Hylia
Tycoon Wallet	Batreaux
Potion Medal	Goddess's Treasure Chest
Water Dragon's Scale	Farore's Silent Realm
Whip	Ancient Cistern
Wooden Bow	Sandship
Wooden Shield	Knight Academy

Cast of Characters

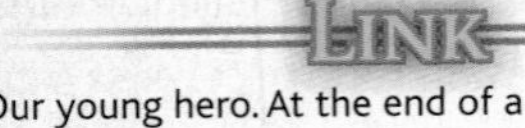

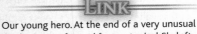

Link

Our young hero. At the end of a very unusual day he is transformed from a typical Skyloft schoolboy into a great adventurer. Link wields the Goddess Sword and is tasked with exploring the long-lost surface world.

Zelda

Link's best friend, who's known him since his childhood. Zelda usually watches out for Link, but she's gone missing after being caught in a sudden, mysterious windstorm.

Headmaster Gaepora

Zelda's father, who administers the Knight Academy where Link was studying. He knows much about the history of Skyloft and fears that Zelda's disappearance is the beginning of something great and terrible.

Groose

Link's rival, who is deeply jealous of Link's close relationship with Zelda. Although he has a bullying personality, his affection for Zelda is genuine and he can be a loyal friend when he wishes.

Fi

A mysterious woman who says she's the spirit of Link's new Goddess Sword. A faithful servant of the goddess, Fi pledges to aid Link in his journey through the surface world.

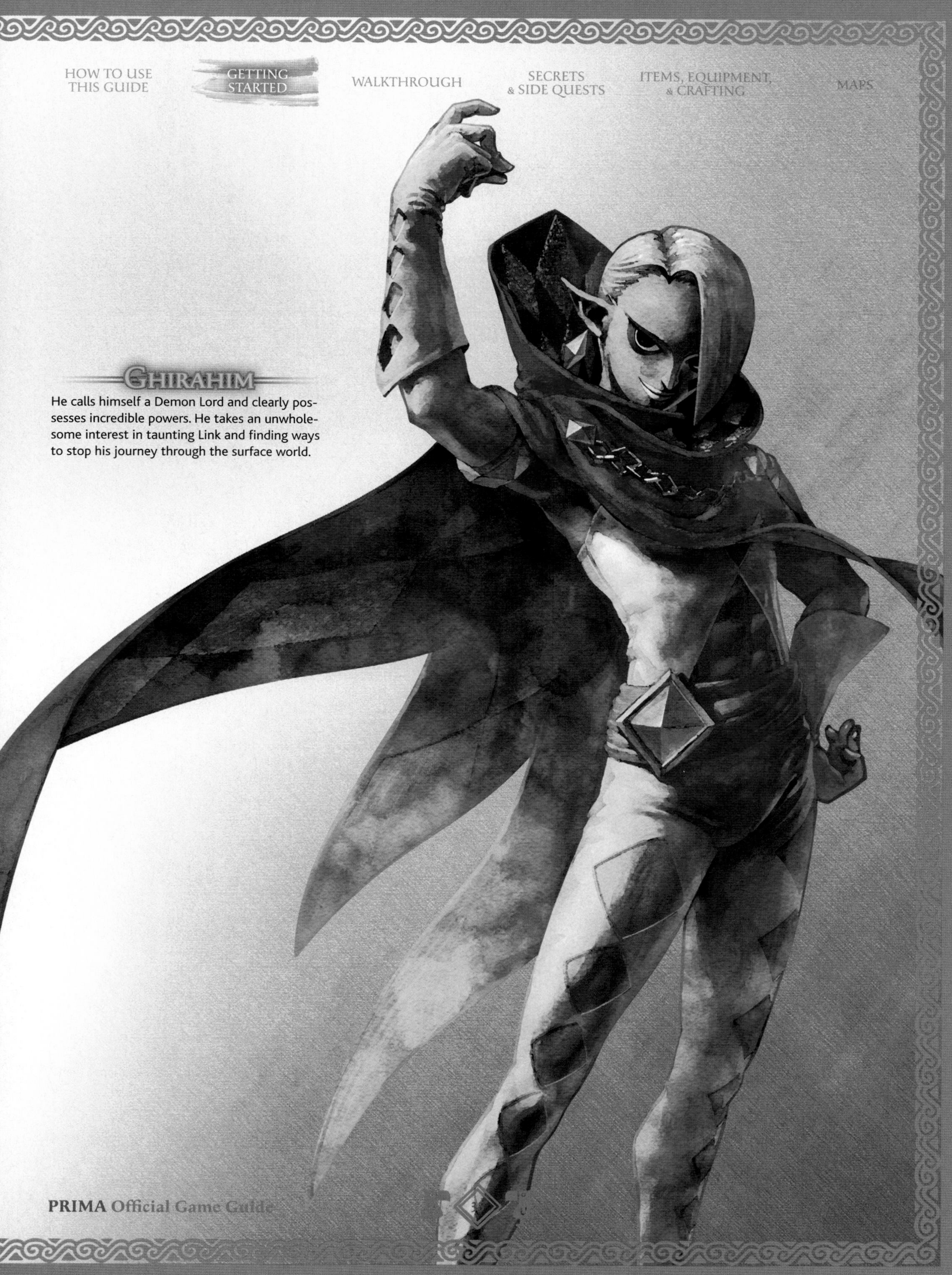

Ghirahim

He calls himself a Demon Lord and clearly possesses incredible powers. He takes an unwholesome interest in taunting Link and finding ways to stop his journey through the surface world.

The Sky

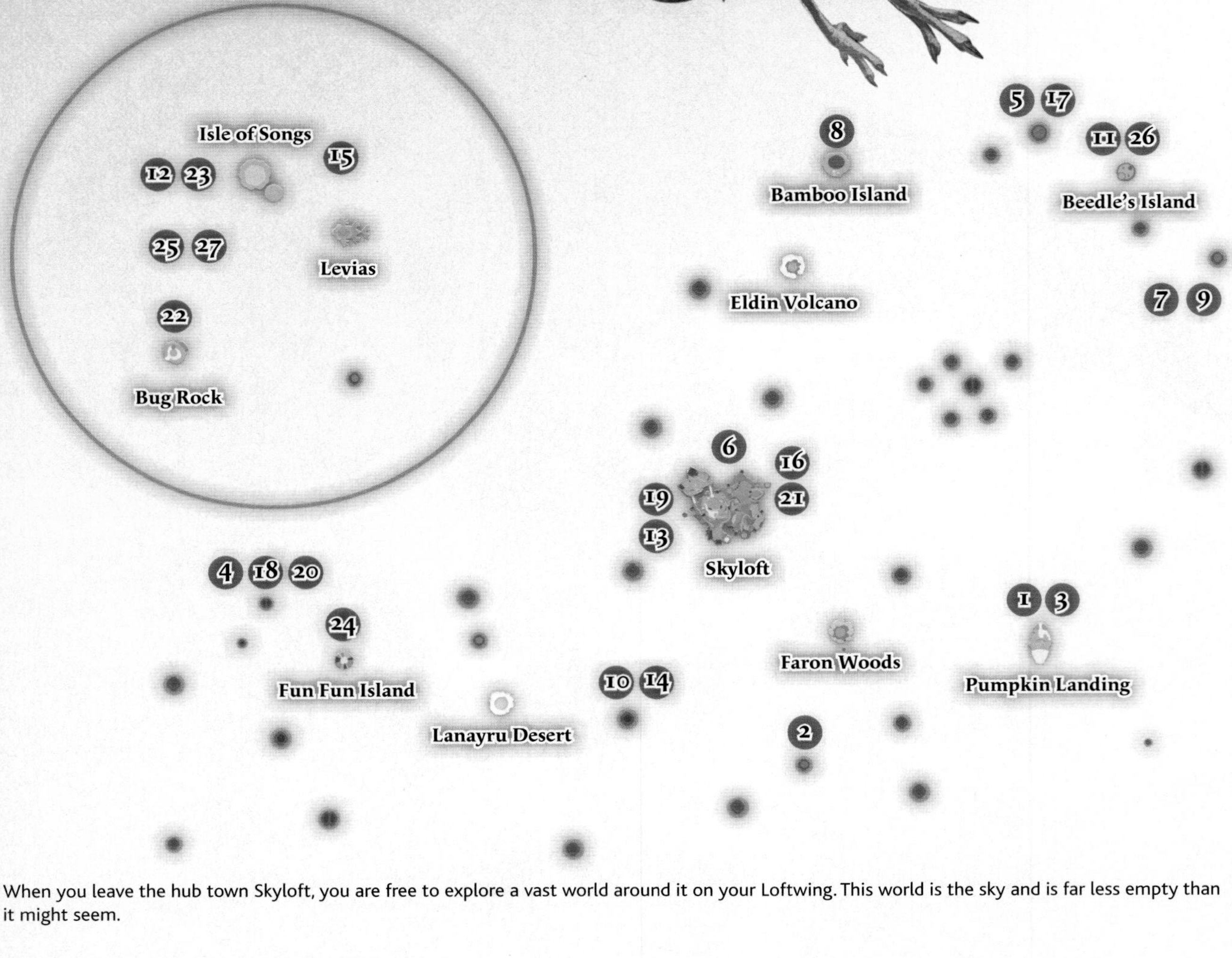

Isle of Songs
12 23
15
25 27
Levias
22
Bug Rock
8
Bamboo Island
5 17
11 26
Beedle's Island
Eldin Volcano
7 9
6
16
19
21
13
Skyloft
4 18 20
24
Fun Fun Island
Lanayru Desert
10 14
Faron Woods
1 3
Pumpkin Landing
2

When you leave the hub town Skyloft, you are free to explore a vast world around it on your Loftwing. This world is the sky and is far less empty than it might seem.

Goddess's Treasure Chests

The sky is stuffed with goddess's treasure chests that sit on small empty islands, on top of buildings, and deep within small hidden areas. You ordinarily cannot open them. You can only open a goddess's treasure chest after you've activated the Goddess Cube that corresponds to it on the surface world. Instructions for finding the Goddess Cubes are in the walkthrough.

Each Goddess Cube is numbered. The goddess's treasure chest on the map that's labeled with the same number corresponds to that cube. Some chests are a little tricky to get into once you've found them. Instructions for obtaining these goddess's treasure chests can be found in the walkthrough.

Goddess's Treasure Chest Checklist

	GODDESS CUBE #	HOW TO GET IT	CHEST CONTENTS	HOW TO GET IT
☐	1	p. 71	Adventure Pouch Slot	p. 72
☐	2	p. 72	Piece of Heart	p. 72
☐	3	p. 85	Gold Rupee	p. 85
☐	4	p. 89	Small Seed Satchel	p. 96
☐	5	p. 89	Silver Rupee	p. 96
☐	6	p. 95	Piece of Heart	p. 139
☐	7	p. 96	Treasure Medal	p. 96
☐	8	p. 94	Gold Rupee	p. 96
☐	9	p. 91	Silver Rupee	p. 109
☐	10	p. 107	Heart Medal	p. 109
☐	11	p. 114	Piece of Heart	p. 117
☐	12	p. 115	Gold Rupee	p. 117
☐	13	p. 139	Silver Rupee	p. 139
☐	14	p. 139	Piece of Heart	p. 139
☐	15	p. 139	Rupee Medal	p. 139
☐	16	p. 142	Gold Rupee	p. 157
☐	17	p. 156	Heart Medal	p. 157
☐	18	p. 156	Life Medal	p. 157
☐	19	p. 160	Gold Rupee	p. 167
☐	20	p. 161	Potion Medal	p. 167
☐	21	p. 167	Piece of Heart	p. 167
☐	22	p. 180	Piece of Heart	p. 182
☐	23	p. 180	Small Bomb Bag	p. 182
☐	24	p. 199	Gold Rupee	p. 199
☐	25	p. 179	Empty Bottle	p. 199
☐	26	p. 199	Rupee Medal	p. 199
☐	27	p. 208	Small Quiver	p. 208

Traveling the Sky

Usually when you travel the sky, you're interested in going directly from Skyloft to whatever part of the surface you want to explore. Take a moment to glance around you, though, and you can find some interesting things.

Flying Rupees

Birds called Guays fly through the sky, dangling Rupees from their claws. There's one that carries a Green Rupee, one that carries a Red Rupee, and one that carries a Silver Rupee. When you spot one of the birds, you can try to get the Rupee in its claws. You can do this by flying right under the Guay, snatching the Rupee from its claws, or you can attack it with a Dash or Spiral Charge by pressing Ⓐ. Once the Guay is destroyed, you snag the Rupee it was carrying.

Octoroks

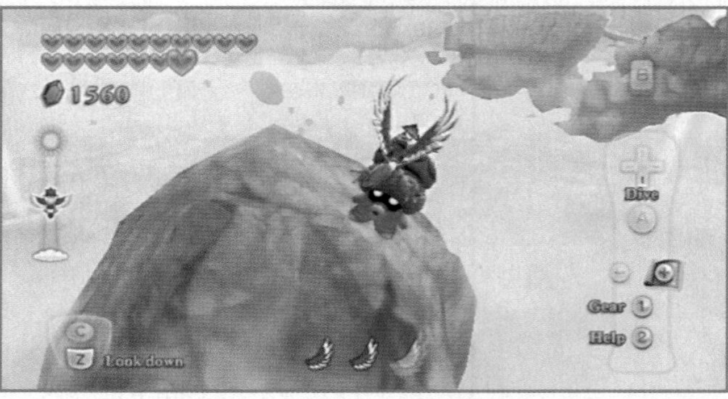

Annoyingly, some of the stones that float in the sky are infested with Octoroks. The rocks they spit can stagger your bird or damage Link, if they hit him. It is usually easiest to avoid them, but sometimes your course in the sky takes you right past an Octorok's home rock. In this case, you want to attack and eliminate the Octorok. Just slam into it with your Loftwing's Dash or Spiral Charge to defeat it.

Shortcut Stones

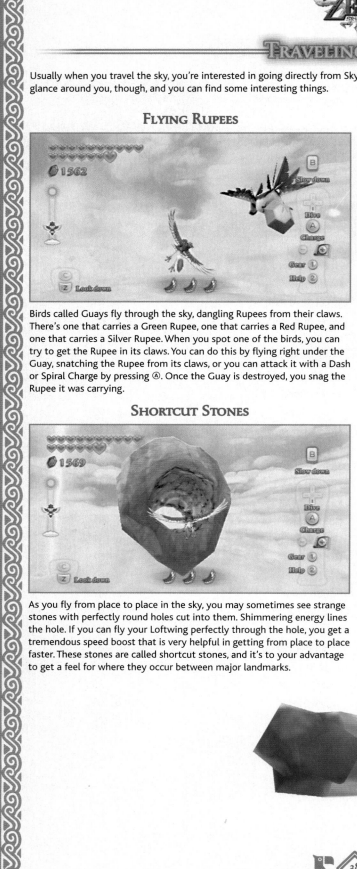

As you fly from place to place in the sky, you may sometimes see strange stones with perfectly round holes cut into them. Shimmering energy lines the hole. If you can fly your Loftwing perfectly through the hole, you get a tremendous speed boost that is very helpful in getting from place to place faster. These stones are called shortcut stones, and it's to your advantage to get a feel for where they occur between major landmarks.

Sky Attractions

You can fly to certain islands in the sky to play minigames and visit certain characters. Some minigames must be unlocked before you can play them. For more details about how to beat these minigames and what you can win from them, consult the "Secrets and Side Quests" chapter.

Lumpy Pumpkin

Kina and her father run this rustic pub that specializes in pumpkin soup and unusual chandeliers. Eventually, you can play a harp minigame here.

Peater's Clean Cut

On a round island far to the north of Skyloft dwells a man called Peater. Once the heartthrob of Skyloft, now Peater is a nervous, overweight father. Peater was famous for his skill with a sword and challenges visitors to try their luck at chopping a bamboo pole while it's in midair.

Pumpkin Pull

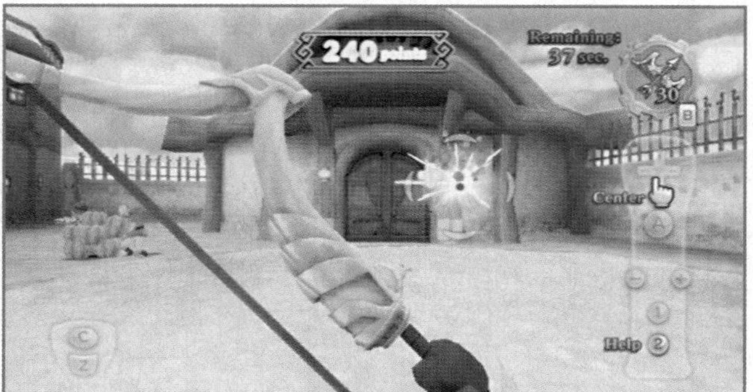

Once your friend Fledge builds up his biceps, he offers you a chance to test your archery skills in a pumpkin-shooting minigame. Fledge tosses pumpkins and you get points for shooting them down, with big bonuses if you can keep from missing. Get over 600 points in the minigame and Fledge hands over a Piece of Heart.

Dodoh's High Dive

Dodoh's High Dive is a place about "fun" run by a strange little man who thinks nothing should delight you more than being shot out of a cannon. If you can land at the right spots on the island's giant roulette wheel, you can win Rupees and one prize that's even bigger.

Strich's Bug Heaven

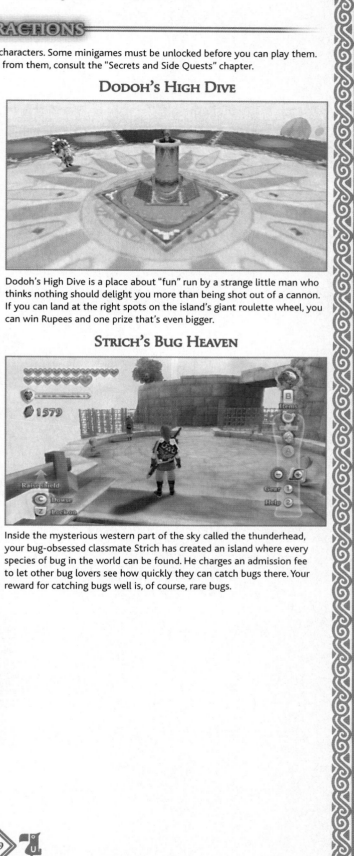

Inside the mysterious western part of the sky called the thunderhead, your bug-obsessed classmate Strich has created an island where every species of bug in the world can be found. He charges an admission fee to let other bug lovers see how quickly they can catch bugs there. Your reward for catching bugs well is, of course, rare bugs.

WALKTHROUGH

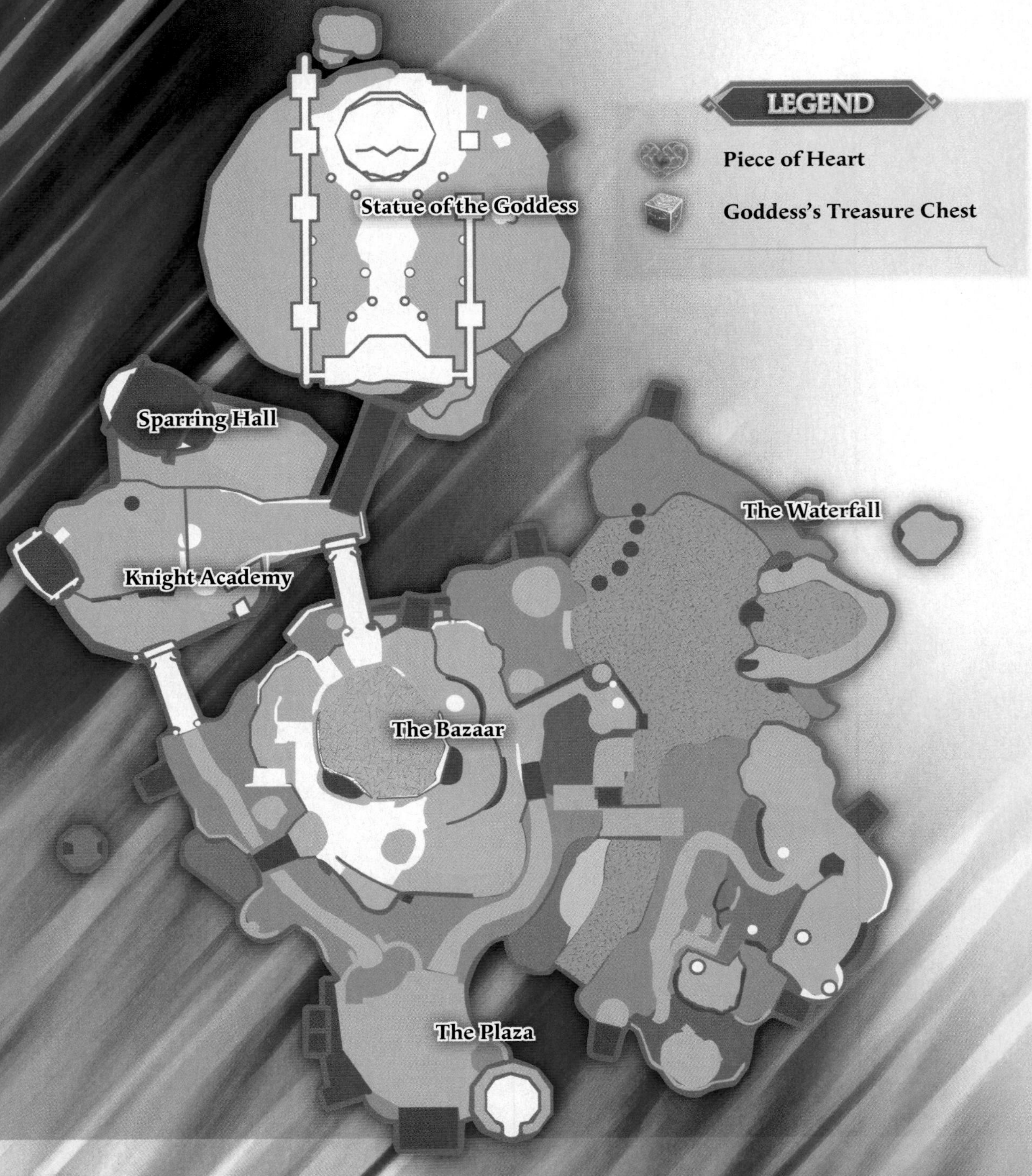

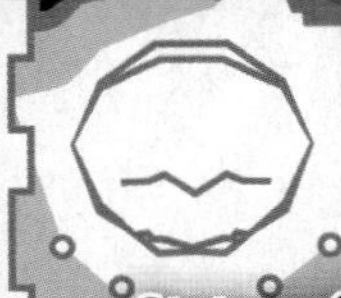

LEGEND

Piece of Heart

Goddess's Treasure Chest

Statue of the Goddess

Sparring Hall

Knight Academy

The Waterfall

The Bazaar

The Plaza

Skyloft

The Day of the Wing Ceremony

Good morning! You're Link, a freshman at the Knight Academy in Skyloft. Every citizen of Skyloft bonds to a giant bird called a Loftwing at a very young age. Having a Loftwing to ride makes getting around a lot easier, since there's not much solid ground up here.

Your partner is a Crimson Loftwing that everyone says is special, but you don't think you're any different from most other guys your age on Skyloft. Well, okay, you're not much of a morning person. Your friend Zelda is very much a morning person, though, and you promised to meet her before the big Wing Ceremony today. You'd better get going.

While you shouldn't leave Zelda waiting, you've got enough time to take a look around the Knight Academy and talk to your classmates. Most of the doors in the Academy are locked right now, so you'll have to exit through the large double doors on the first floor.

On the way out, stop to give your friend Fledge a hand with moving some heavy barrels into the kitchen. This activity acts as a little tutorial for managing the limits of your stamina gauge. Also, Fledge'll give you 20 Rupees for the help, which is pretty big money at this point in the game.

Outside the Knight Academy you find your first bird statue. Since the gate is closed, the only way to leave the area is to pass under the stone arch. When you do, you meet Instructor Horwell, who sends you through a tutorial that teaches you how to target items, climb up on objects, and leap over small gaps.

You're also tasked with rescuing the Headmaster's pet, Mia, from the Academy's rooftop, which serves as a climbing tutorial. Just dangle from the ledge next to the Academy's second-floor entrance and slowly make your way over to the left. From there, you just need to climb up the vines to an upper level and then push the box up against the wall.

LEGEND

Gratitude Crystal

Knight Academy

Fledge's Room
Link's Room
Cawlin & Strich's Room
Groose's Room
Zelda's Room
Karane's Room
Horwell's Room
Owlan's Room
Gaepora's Room

Free Money

Check your cupboard before you leave your room to find a Blue Rupee worth five Rupees. In the future, this walkthrough will only note the location of certain Red, Silver, and Gold Rupees. You can find Green Rupees (worth one Rupee) and Blue Rupees tucked away in virtually every pot and blade of grass in the land, so a little patience can yield a lot of cash.

There's a catch to this, though. Right now, you're carrying the Small Wallet, which can only hold 300 Rupees. Once you've maxed it out, any other Rupees you discover are essentially wasted. Eventually, you can obtain bigger wallets that hold more money by making purchases from shops and completing side quests. You can consult the "Items, Equipment, and Crafting" chapter for more details. The walkthrough will also give you tips for obtaining a couple of basic wallet upgrades that make finishing the game a lot easier. Later on in the game, you can work toward having a bigger wallet whenever you like.

NOTE

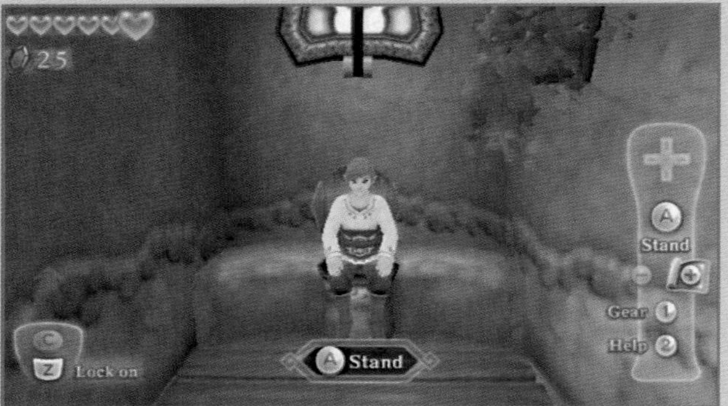

Just to the right of the first-floor exit from the Knight Academy is a restroom, complete with toilet. It is highly recommended that you have Link sit on the toilet, then stand up and leave the room. This causes something to happen that is not useful, but pretty funny.

Out in the Courtyard

Carry Mia back to Instructor Horwell to conclude the tutorial. Note that while you can toss Mia up on the two stacked boxes and the right side of the broken archway, you can't throw her across the gap. You need to actually hold her and jump across the gap to get her back to Instructor Horwell.

The Case of the Missing Loftwing

Cross the bridge that connects to the upper level of the Knight Academy and then head up the wooden stairs to reach the lofty Statue of the Goddess. This triggers a long story sequence that you can just sit back and enjoy. When it's over, go looking for your Loftwing, which has disappeared.

Say What You Feel

Sometimes during cutscenes in Skyward Sword, *you'll be allowed to pick Link's response to a question or statement made by another character. Saying different things will prompt different reactions, some of them quite funny. These choices will never affect the outcome of the story (or side quests).*

Begin your investigation by returning to the Knight Academy. Just outside the second floor entrance, speak with Instructor Horwell and the class-mate who's standing outside the door. The second floor entrance to the Academy is unlocked now, so you can go inside from there. Speak with Pipit and Fledge, who'll both have some useful information for you. When you're done, exit from the Academy's first floor entrance and go into the courtyard. The gate that connects the Academy's courtyard to the rest of Skyloft is unlocked now, so you can start exploring.

If you head directly toward the plaza, you'll pass by a kid who's trying to shake a bug out of a tree. This is a good opportunity to practice dashing and rolling into objects. You can use this to knock objects down from high places like walls and, well, trees.

Bug Catching

In Skyward Sword, *you use bugs primarily to enhance the potions you'll eventually be able to buy from the bazaar. There are 12 types of bugs in the game, which you typically catch using the Bug Net, which you'll also acquire later. The walkthrough won't discuss bug-catching very much, since you don't need any enhanced potions to complete the game. If you're interested in exploring the game's bug-catching aspect in more detail, turn to the "Items, Equipment, and Crafting" chapter for more information.*

Entering the plaza triggers a cutscene that makes it pretty clear who's responsible for your Loftwing's "disappearance." Now that it's clear that foul play was involved in this fowl play, you should report your findings to Headmaster Gaepora at the Knight Academy. His room is unlocked now, so just enter it to find him. After this meeting, exit the Knight Academy.

Pipit calls you over to the Sparring Hall area on the far left of the Academy's courtyard. Here you discover the solution to the mystery of your missing Loftwing and have its location marked on your map. Next, enter the Sparring Hall to pick up some equipment for your rescue mission. Once inside, talk to the Commander and then enter the storage room on his right to pick up the Practice Sword.

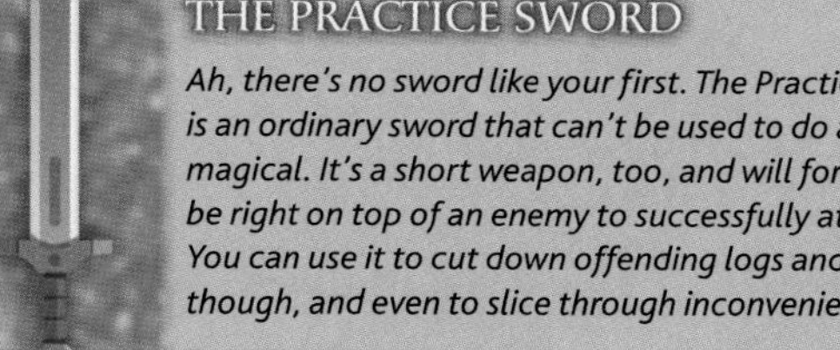

The Practice Sword

Ah, there's no sword like your first. The Practice Sword is an ordinary sword that can't be used to do anything magical. It's a short weapon, too, and will force you to be right on top of an enemy to successfully attack it. You can use it to cut down offending logs and monsters, though, and even to slice through inconvenient ropes.

Now that you've got the Practice Sword, you can begin the swordplay tutorial and practice your skills against the Sparring Hall's targets. Avoid the log-on-a-rope target, as that one's intended for shield practice. Once you can strike all of the practice targets accurately and do the spin strikes correctly, you're ready to move on toward the location Pipit marked on your map.

Head toward the waterfall at the north edge of Skyloft's main island. Cross the lagoon by leaping across the stone platforms that jut out of the water. Take a right and head up toward the cave mouth blocked off by pointed stakes. Hack the stakes apart with your sword to open up the cave, which serves as something of a tutorial dungeon.

The Waterfall Cave

This area introduces you to the basics of exploring dungeons. The waterfall cave itself is a twisting but basically direct path that you can just follow to its exit. It's patrolled by enemies that are relatively weak, but they can still hurt you. You need to adjust to combat quickly.

The Waterfall

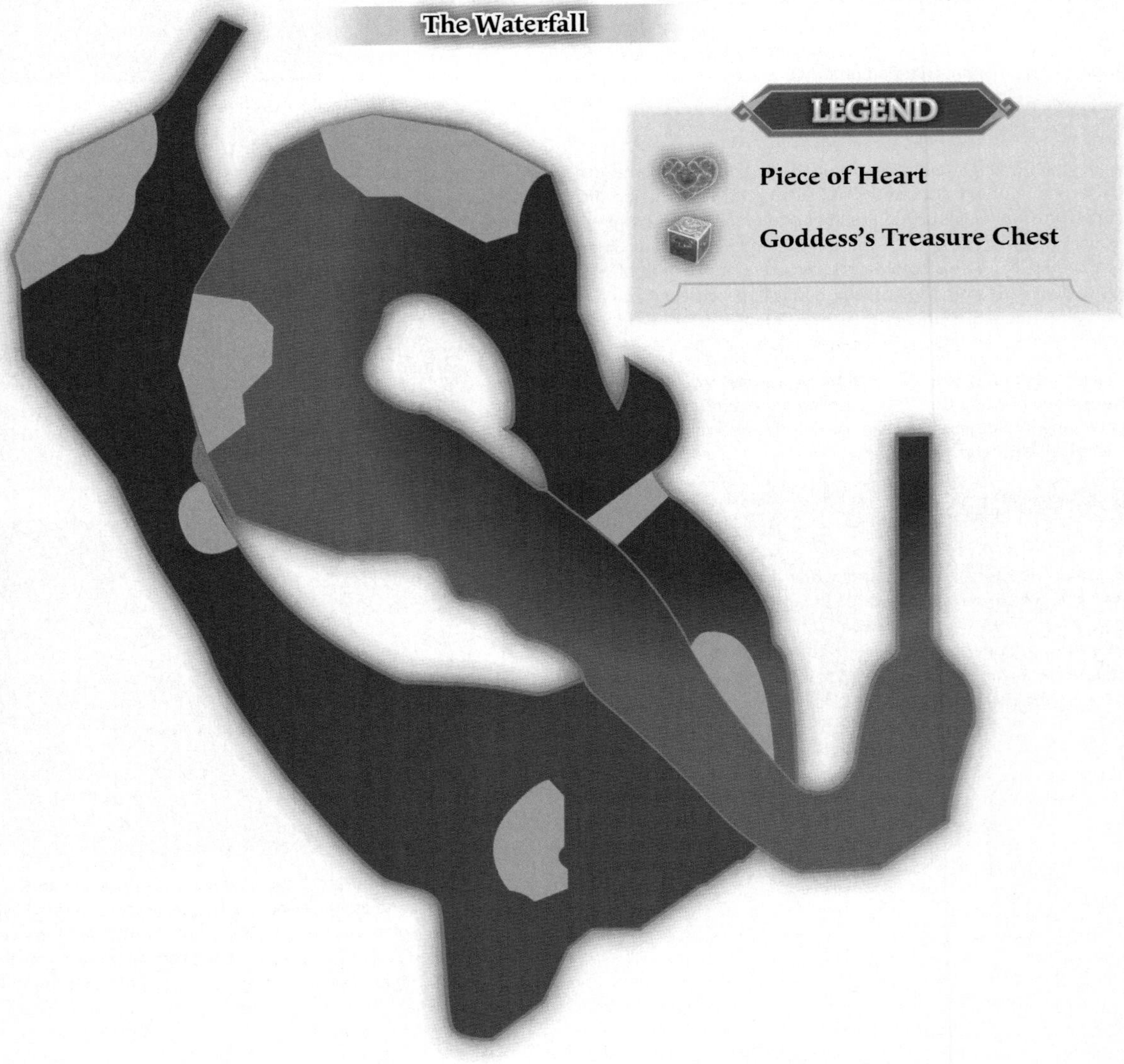

LEGEND

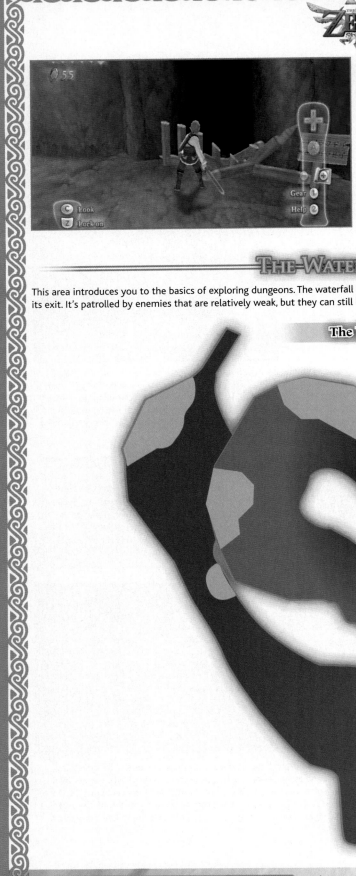

- Piece of Heart
- Goddess's Treasure Chest

ENEMY: KEESE

These bat-like creatures are a persistent annoyance throughout the game. They often swarm around you in groups, so one can attack you while you're dealing with another. You know a Keese is about to attack when its eyes change color. After that, it'll swoop down toward you and do a bit of damage (about half a heart) if it connects.

You can defeat a swarm of Keese quickly by holding down Ⓩ and executing rapid descending vertical slashes. Holding down Ⓩ lets Link automatically turn to face the next Keese that's within his attack range. Link can often interrupt a Keese's diving attacks with a vertical slash.

ENEMY: CHUCHU

These blob-like enemies ooze up out of the ground, sometimes in packs, and try to absorb Link directly into their jiggly bodies. The Chuchus in this cave are small and can be defeated with any sword slash attack (thrusting at them is useless). Later in the game, you'll encounter larger Chuchus that you can only defeat by slashing them apart into smaller blobs.

If Link is caught by a Chuchu, you can break free by rapidly shaking the Wii Remote and Nunchuk. If you can't break free quickly enough, you'll take damage. Packs of these Green Chuchus are best fought using roughly the same technique you use against Keese, holding down Ⓩ and slashing at them rapidly.

Now that you have a sword, you can cut down blades of grass to find Rupees and life-replenishing hearts. While the grassy patches in dungeons yield a bit more money than the ones you find in overworld locations like Skyloft, you don't really need to mow every dungeon lawn you come across. It can be wiser to let grassy areas stand until you badly need to find hearts, then start cutting them down.

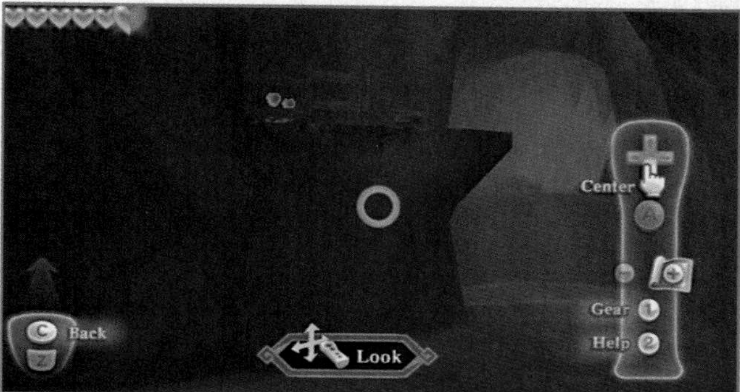

As you wind through the end of the dungeon, you eventually come to a small chest and a couple of heart flowers resting on a platform that's too high for you to reach easily.

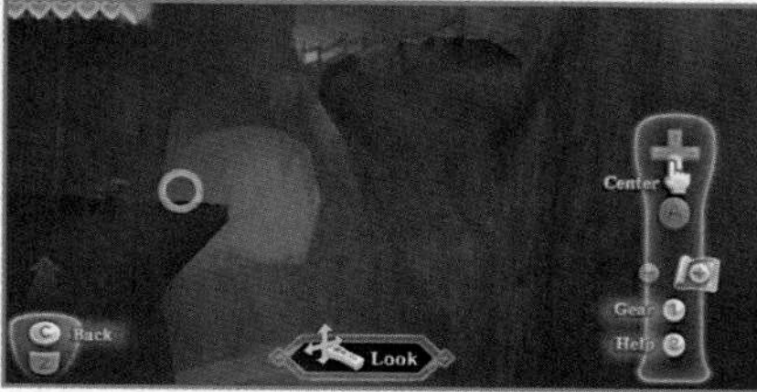

Hit Ⓒ and use the Look command to examine your surroundings carefully from a first-person perspective. This lets you see things that you couldn't spot by relying on the game's automatic camera. If you use Look and then glance to the right of the chest, you'll see an even higher platform that overlooks it. If you backtrack to that platform, you can use it to jump down to the chest.

As you fight the enemies in the waterfall cave, you may have a chance to begin gathering treasures. Keese drop Monster Claws while Chuchus drop Jelly Blobs, both of which you'll definitely want to start hoarding for future use. You can flip to the "Items, Equipment, and Crafting" chapter to get a more comprehensive list of where to find various treasures and what you can do with them. The walkthrough will only cover how to make items that are highly recommended for clearing the game. If you gather treasures diligently, though, you can make all kinds of stuff.

Be sure to keep your eyes open for vines you can climb as you traverse the cave, as you can find some hidden Red Rupees that way. Just off to the right of the waterfall cave's exit, you can spot a pair of Red Rupees spinning in a small tunnel. Link can reach them by crawling into the tunnel. Simply approach the area and Link automatically begins crawling. While you're crawling, Link moves slowly and you see the world from a first-person perspective. You can't fight enemies while crawling through tunnels, but most enemies are much too large to fit into these tiny areas anyway.

No doubt about it. That's your
Loftwing, Link!

Once you're outside, follow the grassy path. You meet up with Zelda along the way. She follows you until you reach the area where your Loftwing is held captive. The boards secured across the cave's entrance are too sturdy for your puny Practice Sword to cleave through. Instead, cut the ropes that are holding the boards in place. Two horizontal cuts and two diagonal cuts should get the job done.

With your Loftwing freed, you can think about participating in the Wing Ceremony now. Zelda takes you through a brief flying tutorial that covers the basics of charging, slowing, and diving. Then the Wing Ceremony begins automatically. In gameplay terms, the Wing Ceremony is a bird racing minigame that has two parts. The first part requires you to build up just enough speed to catch the golden Loftwing and attempt to claim the Bird Statuette it's carrying. The second part requires you to do this while Groose and his goons throw eggs at you.

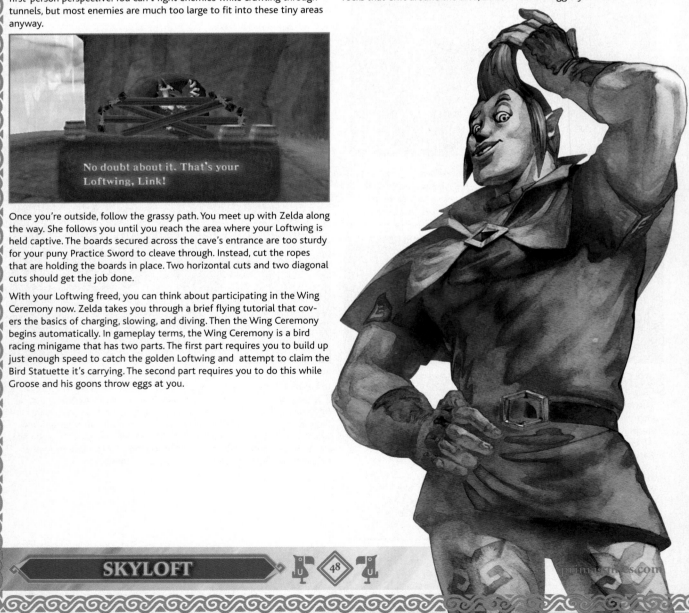

Getting the statuette the first time is a simple matter of using dives to build up a high top speed, then charging up toward the golden Loftwing. You don't need to get right on top of it, just close enough that the Catch command becomes available. As long as you don't lose track of the golden Loftwing's location, you should make steady progress. Be careful not to let your Loftwing hit one of the other competitors or any of the floating rocks that drift around the area, since this will stagger your bird.

Winning in the second part isn't as tricky as it may seem at first. Don't put a lot of effort into dodging the eggs Groose's goons throw at you. If you get hit, you won't actually lose a lot of speed. The best approach is to ignore the eggs completely and just focus on building up a high top speed, as you did in the first part. Approaching the golden Loftwing uses the same techniques that got you through the first part of the Wing Ceremony.

Next, you play a minigame that's essentially a tutorial for controlling Link's ability to dive during extremely long falls. You're asked to repeat a targeted dive from the top of the Statue of the Goddess down into the center of a stone circle over and over until you get it right. Mastering dive control is an essential skill both for finishing the game and for finding all of the game's secrets, so be patient and try to get the hang of it.

The trick to controlling Link in a dive is to remember that he only falls straight down when you hold the Wii Remote perfectly horizontal. Otherwise, he immediately drifts in whatever direction you tilt the Wii Remote, no matter how slightly it's tilted. You have to tilt the Wii Remote down to make him move forward and upwards to make him move backward. If you hit Ⓑ to activate the Sailcloth while Link's shadow is over the circle's center, you'll be able to complete the tutorial.

After the Storm

After the ceremony's conclusion, things go terribly wrong and Zelda goes missing. Link awakens in his room, disoriented. A voice is calling to him and you need to follow it. After Link steps out into the Knight Academy's hallways, follow the mysterious woman who appears before you. Catching her is impossible, but following her leads you toward your next goal.

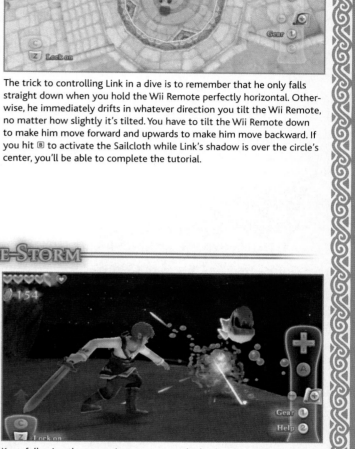

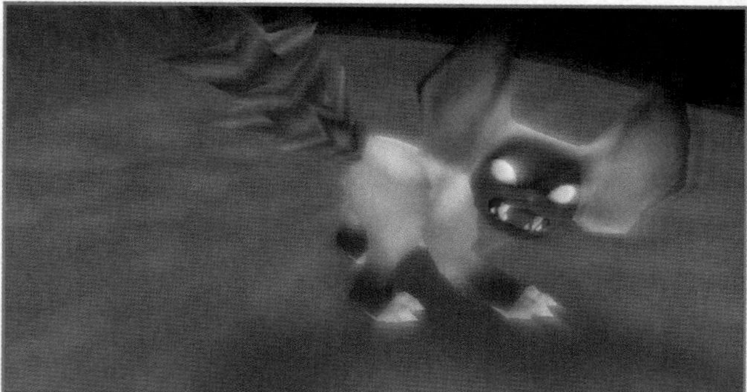

This is your first chance to travel through Skyloft during the night instead of daytime. While Skyloft is safe when the sun is shining, at night monsters roam around and tame animals become feral. Defend yourself with your sword and remember that you can't actually kill anyone's pet, just make it run away from you.

Night and Day

A little later in the game you gain the ability to switch between night and day in Skyloft and certain other areas in the sky by going to sleep. You can't change the time of day in any of the game's three surface areas, since you aren't allowed to venture forth from Skyloft at night. Generally, you only need to be active during the night in Skyloft to progress certain side quests. More details are available in the "Secrets and Side Quests" chapter.

Keep following the mysterious woman as she leads you on a fairly direct path that winds around the outside of the Statue of the Goddess. When you reach the ledge you're supposed to use to get around to the next platform, drop down to find a small chest that contains a Red Rupee and a much larger specimen of Chuchu than you've ever fought before. Don't hesitate to jump across the wide gaps you'll eventually have to cross if you want to keep following the mystery woman. The chase ends after you climb up the vines that put you just behind the Statue of the Goddess.

Enter the door that opens in the base of the Statue of the Goddess. In the ensuing cutscene, you discover that the mysterious woman is a winsome android named Fi who dwells within the Goddess Sword, a mystic weapon destined for Link's hand. Fi gives Link the first chunk of the Ancient Tablet, the Emerald Tablet, which opens the way down to the dangerous surface world below.

THE GODDESS SWORD

Now you're ready for some real adventuring. The Goddess Sword expands Link's abilities tremendously. Now you can use Skyward Strikes to attack enemies with sword beams, dowse using Ⓒ, and summon Fi to speak with you by tapping down on the +Control Pad. Almost everything you'd ask Fi about is covered in this guide anyway, of course, but she can still do some useful things like assess Link's equipment and tell you how long you've been playing.

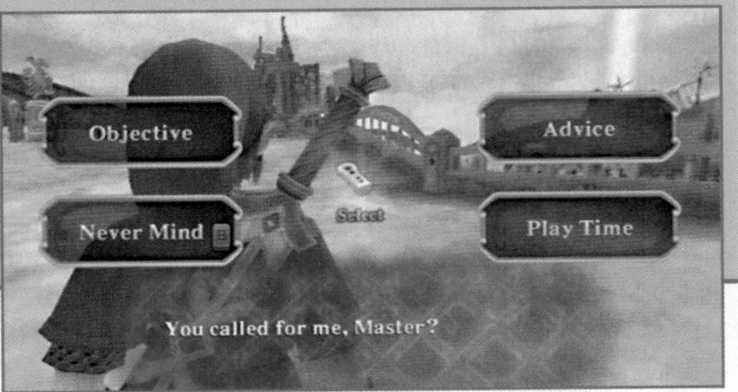

Some Final Preparations

You got a Wooden Shield!
This light wooden shield breaks easily and can burn, so be careful how you use it.

Now that Link has his mission and his knight cadet's uniform, he can prepare to begin his adventure in earnest. Your friend Fledge gives you the Adventure Pouch before you leave the Knight Academy, so now you can carry extra items. The bazaar in Skyloft is open, too, so you've got a place to buy items and enhance your gear. Your first task, though, is to pay a visit to the Sparring Hall to learn one last lesson about combat. On the way, be sure to speak with Instructor Horwell in the Knight Academy courtyard to get the Wooden Shield.

Now you can mess around with the hanging log in the Sparring Hall. Hit it with your sword to set it in motion and then use it to practice shield bashing. Don't move on until you can consistently shield-bash the log. Mastering the shield bash will prove itself useful through out the game.

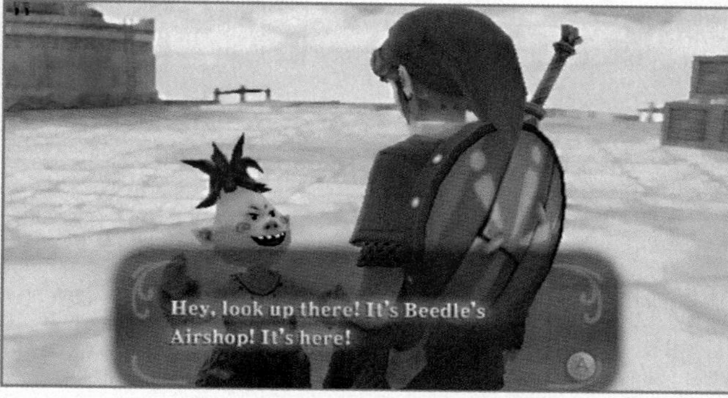

Hey, look up there! It's Beedle's Airshop! It's here!

If you visit the plaza before you leave Skyloft, your bug-loving pal will tell you that Beedle's Airshop has arrived. The airshop flies a slow circuit around Skyloft and is the only place where you can obtain the Bug Net and many other rare, valuable items. To visit the airshop, you need to find a way to ring the bell beneath it. It may be tempting to throw pots at it for a while, but the airshop will always be just a little too high to be hit that way. You can only ring the bell by using a tool you'll find in the game's next area. So ignore the airshop for now, but plan to come back to it later. Right now, you need to hit the bazaar.

For some reason, I like you, though, so I'll give you a spare Empty Bottle I've been keeping here in the stall!
Oh, it's nothing. It's my little gift.

You shouldn't need to purchase a shield at the bazaar, but you'll definitely want to get some potions. Stop by Bertie's Potion Shop and speak to its owner. She'll give you your first Empty Bottle so you can, in turn, spend money on her potions. Pick up a Revitalizing Potion, since you don't really have enough hearts yet to make a Heart Potion worth it. Also, it's fairly likely that your shield is going to get damaged sometime soon.

Once you've stocked up on supplies, fly your Loftwing toward the green pillar of light. You're ready to become the first man from Skyloft to visit the surface.

A Quick Guide to the Bazaar

The bazaar takes every sort of shop you'd want to visit in a game like this and puts them all in a single convenient hub location. There are five major stalls in the bazaar, and at different points in the game you'll need to visit them all. There are a couple that you'll probably end up visiting really frequently.

Sparrot the Fortune-Teller

For 10 Rupees, the fortune-teller will give you some hints about whatever you're currently doing in the game, even if it's just advice about what kind of equipment it'd be best to carry. You can also ask him about where to obtain certain types of treasures. This advice can be really useful—except you already own this strategy guide, which will give you much more detailed advice. So you'll probably only visit the fortune-teller when the game's storyline or finishing up a side quest demands it.

Bertie's Potion Shop

At the Potion Shop, you can fill up any Empty Bottles in your possession with useful potions. The Potion Shop sells five types of potions, but only three are available right now—and only two are affordable. Fortunately, these happen to be the only two that really make finishing the game easier: red Heart Potion (20 Rupees) and dark violet Revitalizing Potion (30 Rupees). Heart Potion restores up to eight hearts while Revitalizing Potion repairs your shield and restores up to four hearts. The shimmering violet Guardian Potion can also be useful during boss battles, since it reduces the damage you take from enemies for three minutes. Right now it's so expensive (200 Rupees a bottle) that it's not really worth it.

If you visit the Potion Shop owner's husband, you can enhance potions to make their effects more powerful. For instance, an enhanced Heart Potion will restore all of your health, no matter how many hearts you have. Enhancing potions costs some Rupees and requires you to gather ingredients to add to the potion, usually bugs you need to go out and catch. You don't need enhanced potions to finish the game, so the walkthrough isn't going to recommend his services. Some of the high-end potions can be very useful toward the end of the game, though. Consult the "Items, Equipment, and Crafting" chapter for more details.

Rupin's Gear Shop

As you might guess from this description, the Gear Shop sells odds and ends that help Link on his journey. Right now, it won't be very useful to you since you don't have any tools that use ammo yet, but you'll definitely be back here if you manage to break your shield. As you progress through the game and acquire tools, the Gear Shop's inventory will begin to expand. Eventually, you'll be able to purchase different types of shields as well as ammo bags that let you carry extra ammo.

Peatrice's Item Check

You know why the Item Check girl always looks so bored? Because you're going to spend the first part of the game ignoring her. Item Check lets you manage your item storage, which is basically where you have to put all the extra items that won't fit in your Adventure Pouch. Eventually, you'll have way more items you could carry than you could ever fit into your Adventure Pouch, so you'll have to carefully choose which ones to take. For now, though, it's pretty easy to carry everything with you.

Gondo's Scrap Shop

You can do two enormously useful things at the Scrap Shop: upgrade your items and repair your shield. What's nice about repairing your shield is that it only costs 10 Rupees, no matter how damaged it is. Fixing a shield is always going to be much cheaper than having to replace one that busted.

To upgrade items, you need to spend some Rupees and have the right treasures on hand (like those Jelly Blobs and Monster Claws you might've picked up earlier). It's quite difficult to get through the game without upgrading at least some of your items, particularly your shields, so expect to spend a lot of time here. For lists of what the Scrap Shop can upgrade and recipe lists, check the "Items, Equipment, and Crafting" chapter.

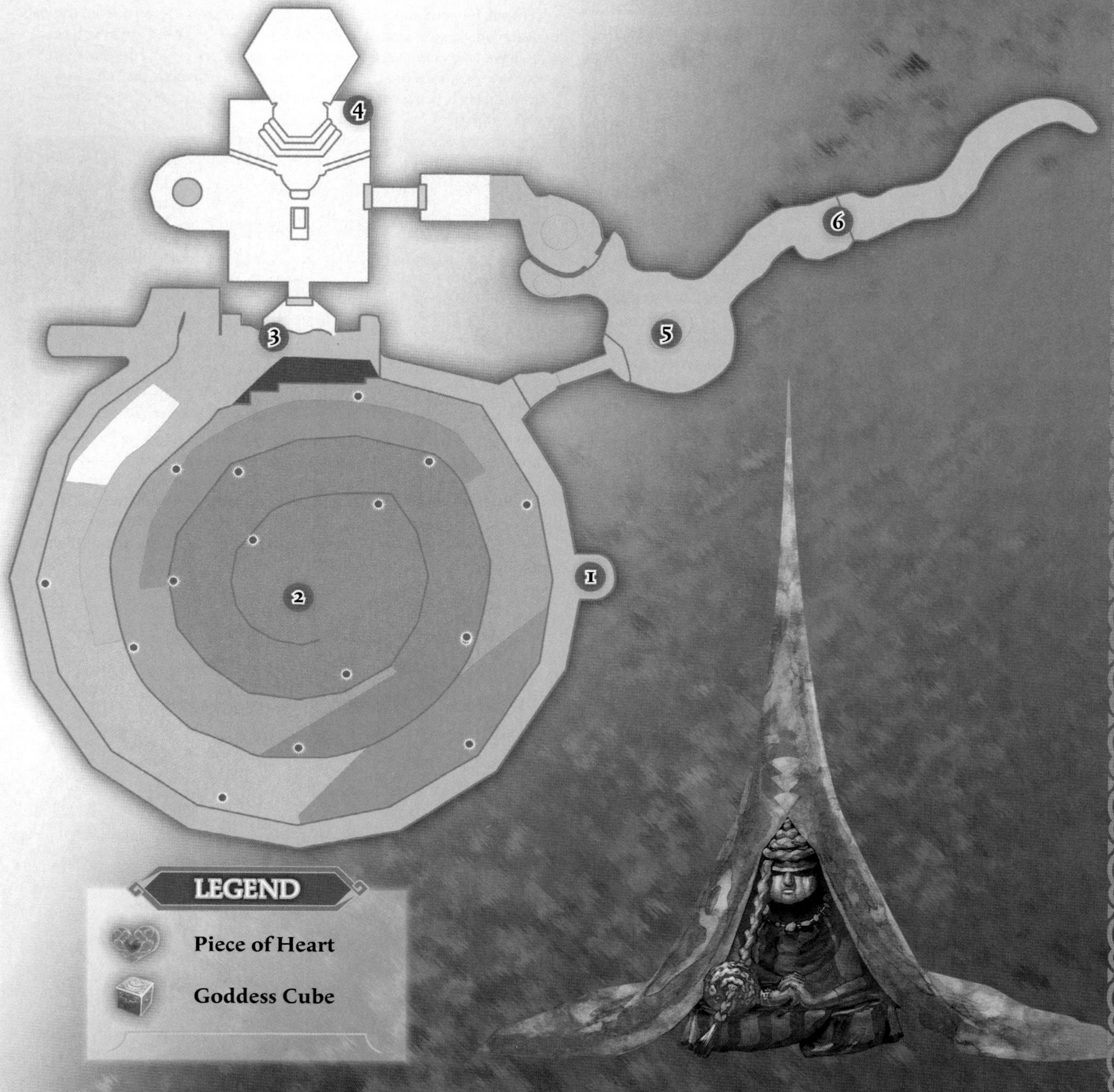

1
2
3
4
5
6

LEGEND

Piece of Heart

Goddess Cube

Sealed Grounds

ENEMY: DEKU BABA

Deku Babas aren't quite as obnoxious in Skyward Sword *as they could be in earlier* Legend of Zelda *games, but they're still pretty dangerous. Deku Babas rise up on their long stalks as you approach, letting their mouths hang open. If you linger too long in their striking area, they'll rapidly lunge forward and headbutt you. This attack is difficult, but not impossible, to shield-bash.*

You can only damage a Deku Baba when its mouth is open, by using strikes that correspond to the orientation of its mouth opening. So you need to hit Deku Babas whose mouths open horizontally with horizontal slashes and ones whose mouths open vertically with vertical slashes.

The one advantage you have when fighting Deku Babas is mobility. You're pretty nimble while your enemy is rooted in place. The most efficient way to defeat one can be to simply run up to it and hit it with the appropriate type of sword strike immediately after it awakens. You can also stand just far enough away that the Deku Baba can't hit you and use Skyward Strikes to kill it, though sometimes a Deku Baba will defend against this at the last second by closing its mouth.

1. Welcome to the Jungle

Immediately upon landing in the Sealed Grounds, you'll be menaced by new monsters. Fortunately, this is when Fi mentions her ability to relay enemy data to you. Most of what Fi tells you is just for flavor, but often she can tell you a lot of useful things about an enemy's weak points. Of course, so can this strategy guide.

2. The Pit

Just walk forward until you trigger the next cutscene. Head toward the door covered in glowing orange sigils and examine it. You can't get in yet, but you'll want to come back here after the next story event. For now, make your way down toward the bottom of the deep, spiraling pit. You can walk down slowly if you want to examine the area, or just jump down the sides if you're impatient.

When you reach the stake conspicuously leaking evil power at the bottom, let the cutscene play. Then lock on to the stake with Z and hit it with a Skyward Strike. The holes that dot the ground in the spiral pit begin gushing with steam and hot air. This is a good thing! Walk toward one of the hot air geysers and you'll automatically use the Sailcloth to ride it up to the pit's next level. Now you can get back up to the top of the pit quickly.

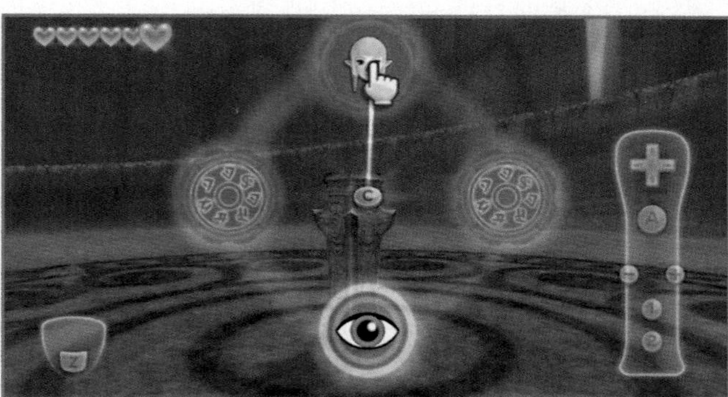

You also unlock Fi's ability to dowse for objects. It works as an enhancement of the Look command, so you trigger it with Ⓒ. By swinging your sword slowly around in the manner of a dowsing rod, you can find out in roughly what direction the object you're dowsing for is located. Eventually you'll be able to dowse for a lot of different things, but right now you'll use it to dowse for the location of story-related objects. If you just want to use the regular Look command, hold down Ⓒ, highlight the eye icon at the bottom of the dowsing menu, and then release Ⓒ.

3. Into the Temple

If you dowse for Zelda's presence, your sword will point you toward the sealed door at the top of the pit. Ride the geysers up in that direction. When you approach the sealed door now, you trigger a cutscene that causes it to automatically unseal itself. Now you can enter the Sealed Temple, the upper area of the Sealed Grounds map.

Save your game at the bird statue, then head up the steps to trigger a cutscene. After the cutscene ends, you'll have the route into Faron Woods clearly marked on your map. You'll also unlock the ability to place beacons on the in-game map. Just move the cursor over the area where you'd like to place a beacon and tap Ⓒ to place it. You can also tap Ⓒ over any beacon you've placed to remove it.

Beacons you've placed on the map screen appear as tall blue pillars of light when you're moving about the game world. You shouldn't need to use beacons frequently in the immediately upcoming areas of the game, but you'll find them really useful a bit later on.

4. Take This

Anyway, don't head out for Faron Woods just yet! Make sure you pick up the treasure chest mentioned in the cutscene. It's just to the right of the old priestess, alongside some pots. The chest contains another bottle full of Revitalizing Potion. The free potion is nice, but the real boon here is getting a second bottle! That means you'll be able to carry two potions around with you. Keep the bottles in your Adventure Pouch at all times.

5. The Gang

As you head toward the area marked on your map, you'll stumble across a hapless creature being menaced by five nasty-looking humanoids. Obviously, this situation calls for heroic intervention. If you're a *Legend of Zelda* fan, you'll recognize this as a friendly Goron being menaced by bad guys who turn out to be *Skyward Sword*'s take on the Bokoblins.

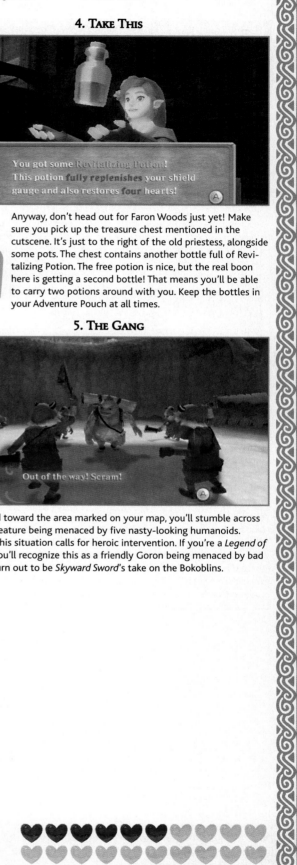

ENEMY: RED BOKOBLIN

Red Bokoblins roam many regions of the surface world and will attack Link on sight. You're just as likely to encounter them in packs like this as you are patrolling territory alone. Bokoblins will rush directly at Link, screaming to alert others nearby, and attempt to slash at him with their rusty, cleaver-like swords. Although Bokoblins seem to be slow creatures, they can use their thick blades to block your sword strikes quite nimbly.

You can stagger Bokoblins by shield-bashing them when they attempt to hack at you with their swords. The timing for this is very forgiving, so you shouldn't have difficulty accomplishing it when fighting only one or two Bokoblins. When dealing with large groups like this, focus on offense rather than defense to help thin the enemy's numbers out.

If the Bokoblins crowd around you, use a horizontal spin slash to help clear the area. Try to maneuver so that you can see all the enemies you're trying to fight. Hold down Z to make sure you stay locked on to an enemy. Rush forward and begin attacking. If the Bokoblin blocks you, then switch up your attack so you're targeting an area that the Bokoblin isn't blocking. For instance, if he holds his sword above his head to block vertical slashes, then use a rising diagonal strike to damage him. If he's holding his sword up to block swings coming from the right, then begin swinging from the left.

It takes three normal sword strikes to defeat a Bokoblin. Fortunately, breaking through their guard staggers them automatically. So once you land the first blow, you should be able to land two more immediately after. If you're holding down Z and haven't let any enemies get behind you, you should automatically turn to face your next foe and begin doing the whole thing over again. You won't be able to auto-target enemies who get behind you, so if the combat music is still playing and you can't lock on to an enemy, it means you need to turn around fast.

It turns out this particular friendly Goron is an amateur archaeologist fascinated with myths and legends about Skyloft and the ancient human civilization that predated it. Some of these stories are, uh, slightly less than accurate, but your new Goron pal is good at finding the grains of truth hidden in old folktales. You'll meet him throughout the game, giving you hints about how to find many mysterious and useful things hidden throughout the world.

NOTE

From this point onward, you can return to Skyloft automatically from any outdoors bird statue. These statues glow orange instead of blue. You can also land at any outdoors bird statue you've used when diving down into a region. Basically this means you should feel free to backtrack to Skyloft whenever you wish.

6. Into the Woods

For now, save your game at the bird statue and continue. Climb up the vines and enter the cave to access a narrow area with a massive log at the end. Walk toward the log and you'll find that Link can opt to push it. By pushing the log down the narrow cliff, you've created a shortcut you can use to enter the area behind the Sealed Temple more quickly. This isn't a tremendously useful shortcut in and of itself, but remember how you created it. You'll need to create lots more like this in the game's next area.

Now head toward the red X marked on your in-game map. Push the log you find so that it's right up against the cliff that's just a bit too tall for you to climb. Once you're up on the cliff, just keep running forward to enter Faron Woods.

FARON WOODS

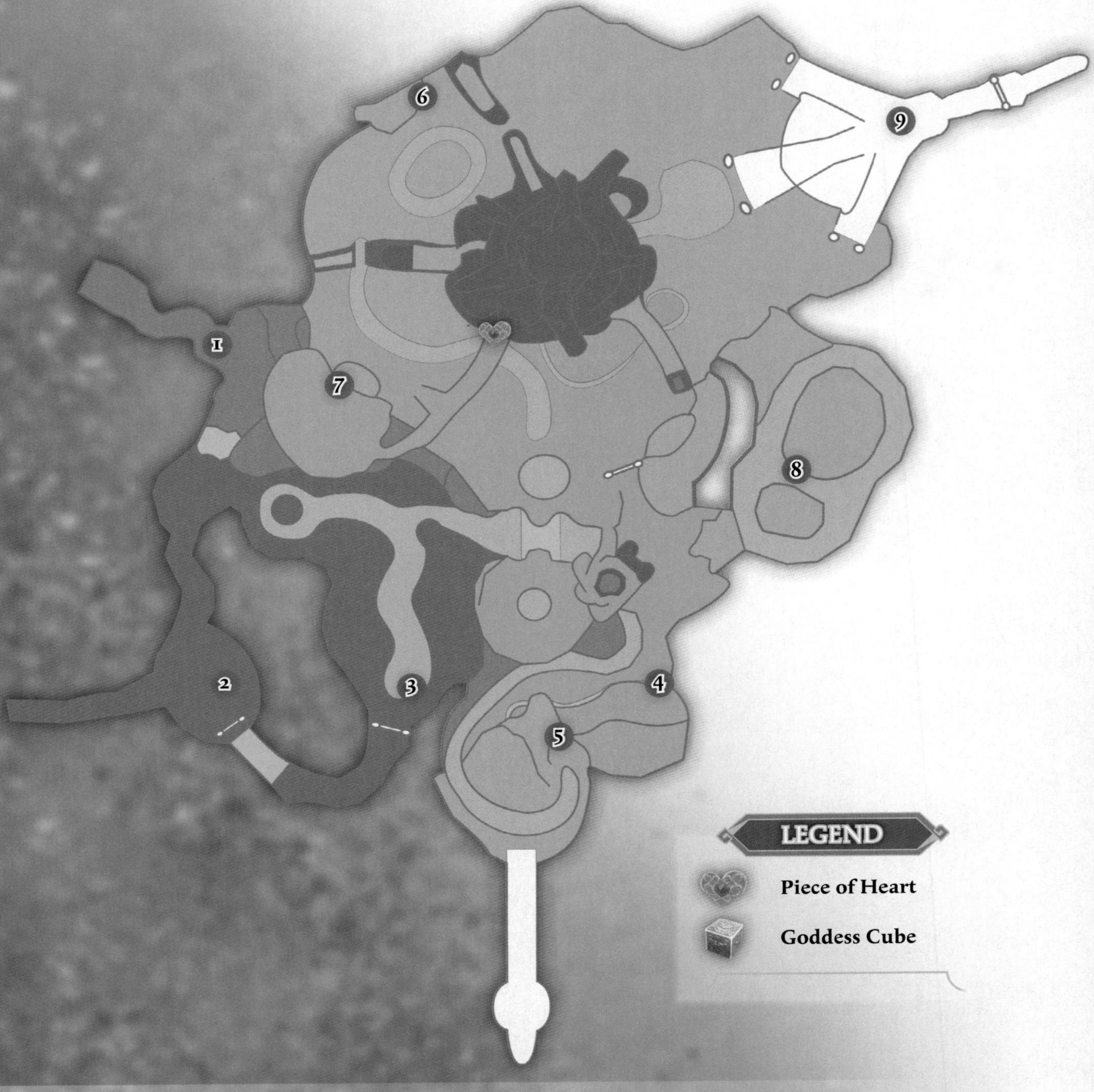

LEGEND

Piece of Heart

Goddess Cube

FARON WOODS

115
Gear 1
Help 2
Lock on

1. Swinging

Forests in video games have a tendency to be twisty, disorienting mazes. While Faron Woods is less blatantly maze-like than most video-game forests, it's still a huge area teeming with dangerous enemies where it's extremely easy to get lost. Learning how to navigate Faron Woods correctly is one of the first major challenges you face in the game.

For now, dowse for Zelda and head in that direction. Take a running leap at the rope dangling over the pit to grab onto it. Once you're hanging, swing the Wii Remote forward and back to make Link swing over to the ledge. Press Ⓐ to leap off the rope when it looks like you'll clear the pit. You'll be doing a lot of rope-swinging to get through this trip to Faron Woods.

2. Fighting

Continue down the path once you're on the other side of the rope pit. Use your sword to hack down the saplings blocking your way. Once you're past the saplings, you'll find a pair of Bokoblins menacing a...plant? Maybe? Well, those guys can't be up to any good, so go introduce them to the business end of your Goddess Sword.

Go talk to the "plant" after you've taken care of the bad guys. It reveals itself as a small plant-bird creature called a Kikwi that's so timid, it's absolutely terrified of you. For some reason, it turns up as a false positive when you dowse for Zelda. Maybe it's met her sometime recently? You'll have to go chase it down to find out.

3. Chasing

The only way to get up the slope ahead of you is to dash. This takes you to a large open area full of mushrooms. Follow the dirt path down to a circular area at the end, either dodging or fighting the Deku Baba ahead of you. Just beyond the circular area is a shortcut log you should take a moment to push over. After you push it you'll find an Amber Relic, a treasure that can be very useful to you at this part of the game.

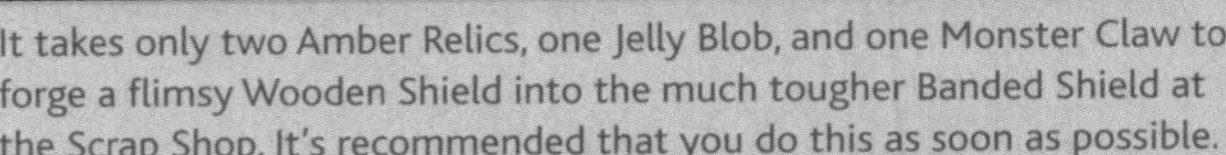

It takes only two Amber Relics, one Jelly Blob, and one Monster Claw to forge a flimsy Wooden Shield into the much tougher Banded Shield at the Scrap Shop. It's recommended that you do this as soon as possible.

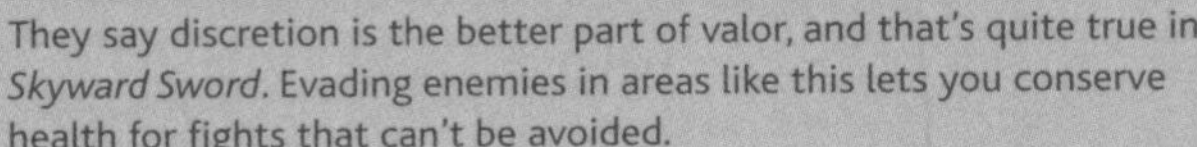

They say discretion is the better part of valor, and that's quite true in *Skyward Sword*. Evading enemies in areas like this lets you conserve health for fights that can't be avoided.

Now, backtrack down a dirt path that branches off to the right. The Kikwi is hiding behind a mushroom just to the right (from this direction) of the branching dirt path. The Kikwi runs around the large mushroom, always trying to stay on the opposite side from you. Even if you dash until your stamina gauge runs out, you won't quite be able to keep up with the speedy Kikwi.

Glittering Spores and You

When you hit the mushrooms to spook the Kikwis, you may notice fine clouds of spores waft into the air. Try catching some of these spores in an Empty Bottle. This transforms the spores into Glttering Spores, an item that's fun to play with and occassionally very useful. You can pour Glittering Spores on hearts and Rupees to transform them.

If you use Glittering Spores on a Rupee, you transform the Rupee into another denomination (or the dreaded Rupoor). This effect is unpredictable, so you're gambling whenever you choose to do this. If you pour Glittering Spores on hearts, then the heart becomes a Fairy. This aspect of Glittering Spores is extremely useful at this point in the game.

You can't chase down the Kikwi, but there's another trick you can use to force it out of hiding. Strike the mushroom the Kikwi is hiding behind with your sword. This panics the little creature so much that it bolts toward another hiding place. Dowse and you'll find it's hiding behind a different mushroom. You can force it out of hiding with another sword strike.

After the Kikwi runs away, dowse again. This time the Kikwi is hiding behind the tree in the circular dirt area you visited earlier. This time you can approach and speak to him. Now you find out that the creature's name is Machi, while Machi finds out he's not your idea of food. A cutscene ensues and you get your next task, dowsing for Zelda in hopes that she's with the Kikwi elder.

4. The Waterfall

Dowsing directs you to leave this area by dashing up a slope. A Deku Baba stands guard on it, but it's pretty easy to just pass it by. You can find another Amber Relic as you move down the path at the top of the slope, as well as some Bokoblins and other enemies waiting in the waterfall area.

ENEMY: OCTOROK

Octoroks have bedeviled Link since the beginning of the Legend of Zelda *series, but they might be at their most maddening during this part of* Skyward Sword. *Octoroks masquerade as bushes, rising briefly from the ground to spit rocks at you. You cannot damage them with your sword. If you try to do something like pick up the bush the Octorok hides under, you'll just hurt yourself.*

You can only kill an Octorok by using the rocks it spits at you. You can shield-bash the rocks or attempt to swat them at the Octorok with your sword. This sends the rocks flying back at the Octoroks, killing them in a single blow. Shield bashing is a little safer, since if your timing is off your shield absorbs the damage.

TIP

Having a Banded Shield instead of the Wooden Shield can help if you're struggling to shield-bash the Octoroks' rocks consistently. A Banded Shield can take twice as much damage as a Wooden Shield before breaking.

5. The Second Swing

Make your way past the waterfall lagoon and up a sloping area. You need to cut down some saplings to proceed. There are more Octoroks at the top, as well as a wall bearing a curious sigil. For now, you're looking for a rope attached to a tree branch that's tied to a fern. It's being guarded by a Deku Baba.

Once that enemy is defeated, cut the fern that's holding the rope taut. Now you can swing across the gap. Run and jump at the rope and Link will grab on automatically. Be careful to have the camera centered behind Link correctly, or you may accidentally run and jump past the rope. Once you execute the swing correctly, you'll be able to meet the Kikwi elder, Bucha. He thinks that maybe he met Zelda, but maybe he's so worried about the three Kikwis missing from his tribe that he can't recall any details.

Link needs to dowse for the three missing Kikwis now. They're scattered around the Faron Woods area and should be easily found by utilizing the dowsing ability. You can find these Kikwi in any order you wish. The order presented in the guide is merely a suggested order.

6. The First Kikwi

Swing back out of the elder's area the way you entered. Head to the beginning of the dirt path that winds around the great tree. Dowse your way down the dirt path. At the end there should be a tunnel in a tree root, partially hidden behind some blades of grass. Defeat the Octorok that stands guard nearby, then crawl through. You'll emerge into an area where three Bokoblins patrol a circular dirt path around a tree. Take care of the enemies, then head toward the platforms off to the tree's left. Run up a giant tree root nearby and then grab onto some vines so you can begin climbing up toward them. Leap across from the first set of vines toward the other to your left. The first Kikwi, Erla, hides in the center of the tall grass.

Like the others, this Kikwi thinks Link might be a predator and won't willingly come out of hiding. If you start cutting down the tall grass, the Kikwi will attempt to crawl (very slowly) away from you. Just run around cutting down grass until a thought balloon appears over the Kikwi's head. This indicates that interacting with it now will advance the plot.

TIP

Keep an eye out for these thought balloons. They also appear when interacting with a character will trigger or advance a side quest's chain of events.

7. The Second Kikwi

To find the next Kikwi, circle around the Great Tree at the center of the Faron Woods map. You're looking for an area where one of its roots slopes into the ground, creating a way for you to explore some high plateaus that you can't otherwise reach. An Octorok stands guard near the correct root.

Head to your left once you've ascended the tree root guarded by the Octorok and proceed towards the trunk of the Great Tree. On the far side of the tightrope is a Piece of Heart. By collecting four, you can add another heart onto Link's health meter. The walkthrough covers how to obtain all of the Pieces of Heart you can get by finding chests or otherwise exploring the world. All other Pieces of Heart must be obtained by going on side quests or playing minigames and are covered in the "Secrets and Side Quests" chapter.

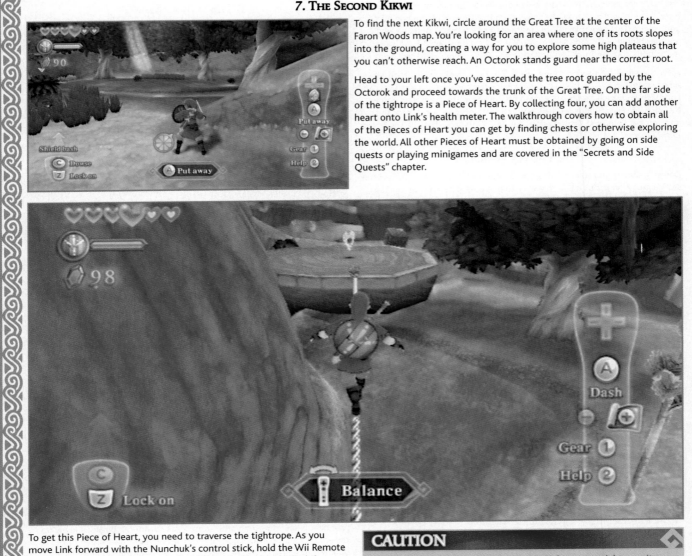

To get this Piece of Heart, you need to traverse the tightrope. As you move Link forward with the Nunchuk's control stick, hold the Wii Remote perfectly upright. When Link begins to tilt too much toward the left or right, tilt it a few times in the opposite direction to straighten him up. Don't tilt the Wii Remote more than about 45 degrees to either side, as the controls aren't calibrated to pick up that kind of motion. Instead, if Link is badly tilting to the left, tilting your Wii Remote quickly to the right a couple of times will help straighten him up. If Link tilts too far in either direction, he'll fall off the rope. Link always catches himself with his hands, so you'll be able to push him back up with the control stick and resume your tightrope walk if this happens.

CAUTION

If you're having a very hard time getting Link across a tightrope, it can indicate that your Wii MotionPlus has lost calibration. Try opening the map with ⊕ and holding down on the Wii Remote's +Control Pad to restore calibration.

Once you've gathered the Piece of Heart, head down the root path until you reach a Deku Baba. Defeat it, then continue on until you reach a wide plateau guarded by an Octorok. Defeat it, then head past the patch of tall grass to find a hole in the ground. Drop down into it. Follow the path that leads away toward your left. This takes you into an area hidden behind a crumbling brick wall, where the second Kikwi hides. This one is disguising itself as a bush. Try picking it up.

8. The Third Kikwi

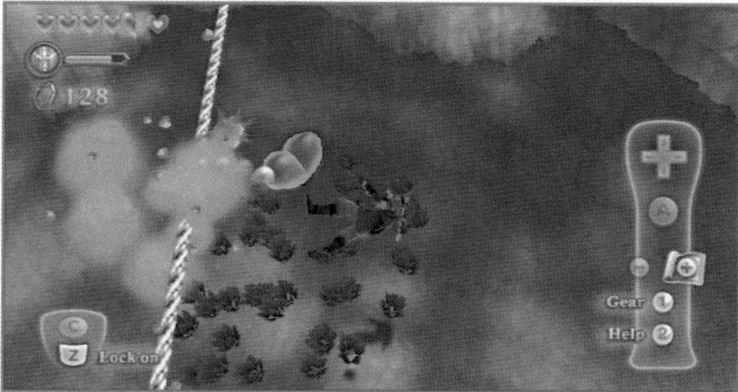

Once you've marked Oolo's location down, you can set out to find the third Kikwi. Head back to the elder's location and then enter a small tunnel located behind him. This opens up into a small area inside part of the Great Tree. Climb up the vines in the back of the "room," then cross the rope bridge you find waiting for you at the top.

This bridge has a pair of prickly burrs stuck to it. If they attach to Link, they'll turn red and eventually explode. This only inflicts a quarter-heart's worth of damage, but it also knocks Link off the rope bridge. Shake the Wii Remote a little when prompted to jostle the burrs enough that they fall off the rope (or fall off Link, if they've attached to him). Jostling can make Link fall, but if so he'll catch himself with his hands. This isn't the case if an exploding burr knocks him off. On the other side of the rope bridge, drop into a wide, pit-like area.

Enemy: Red Bokoblin Leader

The Bokoblin leader distinguishes himself from lesser Bokoblins with his stylish head bandana and the Monster Horn he carries. A Bokoblin leader can blow the Monster Horn to summon his followers to attack Link en masse. Otherwise, a Bokoblin leader is no different from any other Bokoblin. He uses the same attack patterns and can be defeated using the same tactics.

The Red Bokoblin leader will summon four other Bokoblins and rush you in a group. Handle this fight the same way you handled the Bokoblin free-for-all in the Sealed Grounds. Once you've defeated all the Bokoblins, the last Kikwi will come out of hiding. Unfortunately, he's stuck up a tree so you need to help the little guy down. Dash and roll into the tree to knock down both the Kikwi and a vine rope. After this, the Kikwi introduces himself as Lopsa.

Now that you've rescued all the missing Kikwis, use the vine rope to swing your way out of this area. You can use the control stick to move Link up and down the rope, so long as it's not moving. To make the rope swing, jerk your Wii Remote sharply downward the way you would to make your Loftwing flap its wings. This makes Link kick forward, which swings the rope into motion. You can make the rope swing farther and faster by having Link kick again while the rope is in motion. Just jump off the rope while it's swinging forward to get back into the rest of Faron Woods.

You got the Slingshot! Use this projectile-shooting weapon to fling Deku Seeds at your foes! The hard seeds will stun your enemies.

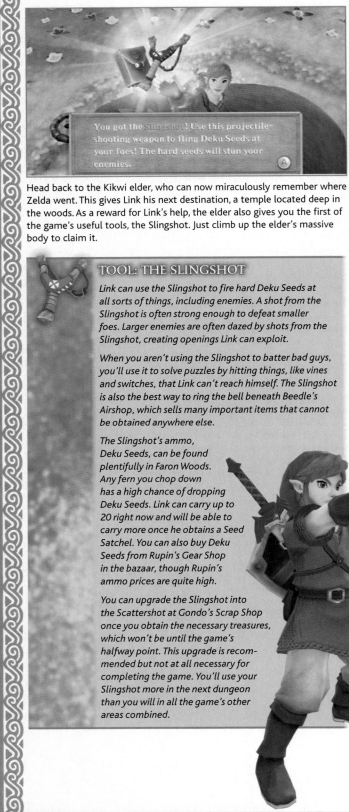

Head back to the Kikwi elder, who can now miraculously remember where Zelda went. This gives Link his next destination, a temple located deep in the woods. As a reward for Link's help, the elder also gives you the first of the game's useful tools, the Slingshot. Just climb up the elder's massive body to claim it.

TOOL: THE SLINGSHOT

Link can use the Slingshot to fire hard Deku Seeds at all sorts of things, including enemies. A shot from the Slingshot is often strong enough to defeat smaller foes. Larger enemies are often dazed by shots from the Slingshot, creating openings Link can exploit.

When you aren't using the Slingshot to batter bad guys, you'll use it to solve puzzles by hitting things, like vines and switches, that Link can't reach himself. The Slingshot is also the best way to ring the bell beneath Beedle's Airshop, which sells many important items that cannot be obtained anywhere else.

The Slingshot's ammo, Deku Seeds, can be found plentifully in Faron Woods. Any fern you chop down has a high chance of dropping Deku Seeds. Link can carry up to 20 right now and will be able to carry more once he obtains a Seed Satchel. You can also buy Deku Seeds from Rupin's Gear Shop in the bazaar, though Rupin's ammo prices are quite high.

You can upgrade the Slingshot into the Scattershot at Gondo's Scrap Shop once you obtain the necessary treasures, which won't be until the game's halfway point. This upgrade is recommended but not at all necessary for completing the game. You'll use your Slingshot more in the next dungeon than you will in all the game's other areas combined.

9. The Viewing Platform

Use your new Slingshot as the elder instructs, to knock a vine down from a tree. Swing across the vine to create a shortcut that leads into the area immediately at the base of the Great Tree. Make your way toward the temple-like structure the elder showed you earlier. This isn't the next dungeon, but it opens up the area that leads to it. As you draw near your destination, you encounter an annoying new enemy.

ENEMY: GUAY

Guays are crow-like birds that take perverse pleasure in dropping noxious...stuff on the heads of hapless adventurers who happen to be passing through. This doesn't do a lot of damage, but it's really gross and annoying to run around with a clump of bird stuff attached to your head or shoulder.

Most of the time, you can just dash past Guays before they attack you. At this point in the game, they're difficult to defeat unless they swoop low enough to be hit with your sword. You can fire at them with the Slingshot but Guays are quick and difficult to hit. If you do land a shot, it'll kill the Guay instantly.

Guays always drop Red Rupees after they're defeated. You might be tempted to try hunting them awhile to earn Rupees quickly, but this is not recommended. Guays are very time-consuming to kill until you acquire the Wooden Bow, which happens much later on in the game. By then, you'll have discovered better ways to amass a lot of Rupees quickly.

Save your game at the bird statue that awaits at the top of the viewing platform. At this point, it is highly recommended that you backtrack to Skyloft to acquire something that's very useful in the next area.

Head toward the area where the airshop circles. Now you should have little difficulty ringing the bell by shooting a Deku Seed at it with your Slingshot. Once you've rung the bell, the shop stops and drops a rope. Grab onto it and you're automatically raised into the airshop. Be sure you have enough Rupees to buy something, as Beedle doesn't care much for window shoppers.

Beedle's Airshop

On this particular trip, you want to pick up a Bug Net, but expect to return to Beedle's Airshop frequently throughout the game. He sells a lot of unique high-end items that are otherwise unobtainable, including three of the eight possible Adventure Pouch slots and one of the game's two Life Medals. You basically want to visit this shop whenever you've amassed enough Rupees to buy one of the available items.

AIRSHOP WARES

ITEM NAME	PRICE
Bug Net	50
Extra Wallet (1st)	100
Extra Wallet (2nd)	100
Extra Wallet (3rd)	100
Adventure Pouch Slot (1st)	300
Adventure Pouch Slot (2nd)	600
Adventure Pouch Slot (3rd)	1,200
Life Medal	800
Piece of Heart	1,600
Bug Medal	1,000

It's worth noting that you can buy up to three Extra Wallets before Beedle stops stocking them, allowing Link to carry a maximum of 9,900 Rupees once he obtains the game's largest wallet, the Tycoon Wallet. Stocking up on Extra Wallets also makes the game quite easy to complete with only the Small or Medium Wallet, too.

Beedle sells four items at a time, with some spawning only after you've bought others. You can't purchase the Bug Medal, for instance, until you've bought the Bug Net. Beedle doesn't offer his Piece of Heart for sale until you've bought every other item he sells, so it'll probably be fairly late in the game before you can get it.

TOOL: THE BUG NET

You may be wondering why this tool is essential, given that this very walkthrough has told you that bug-catching is completely optional. Well, for one, it's nice to have a Bug Net on hand when you encounter life-restoring Fairies. A Fairy caught in a Bug Net can be stored in any Empty Bottle you have on hand and saved for use in a desperate situation.

There are also some things you can do with a Bug Net that are completely indispensable for upgrading your gear. Three treasures necessary for crafting improved shields, tools, and other items simply can't be obtained short of using your Bug Net to catch certain small objects and creatures found in certain areas of the game. This is discussed more in the "Items, Equipment, and Crafting" chapter and the appropriate areas of the walkthrough.

There's a third use of the Bug Net that's really specific to a hazard you encounter in the next area of the game, too. Understanding that you can do this is an essential part of figuring out how bug-catching works if you're interested in that aspect of the game, too. Read on for details.

As a final note, you can improve the Bug Net's usefulness tremendously by upgrading it into the Big Bug Net. You won't be able to obtain the treasures necessary for this until about halfway through the game, but it's highly recommended for any player who's serious about bug-catching or forging maxed-out gear.

Head back to the bird statue at the viewing platform so you can resume exploring right where you left off. Turn around and you'll find a cliff that's just a little bit too high for you to jump up, but which dowsing indicates is the way Zelda went. There's a coiled vine just above it that you can shoot down with your Slingshot. Use this to swing up to the top of the cliff and pass through the stone doorway to the game's next area.

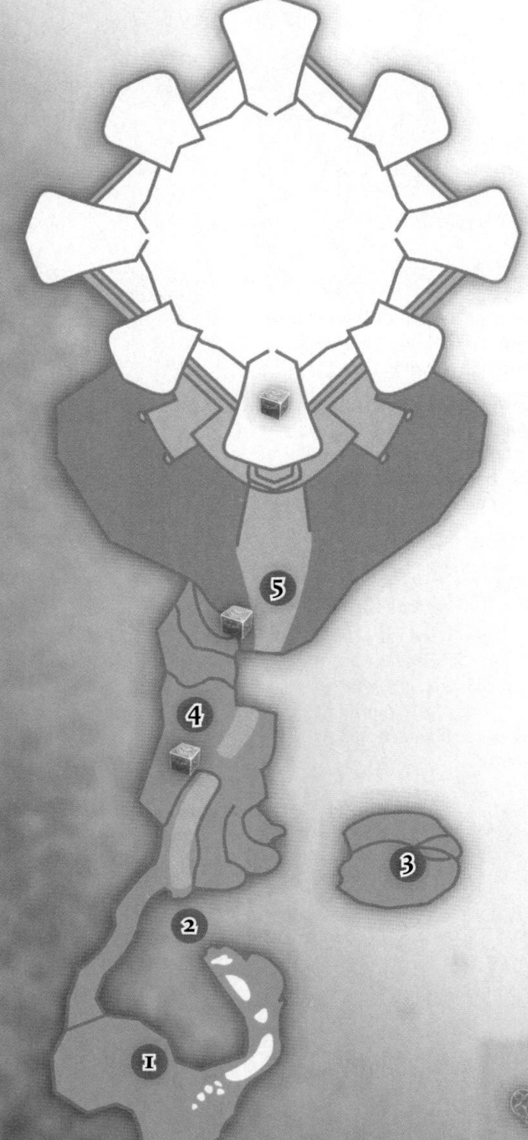

LEGEND

 Piece of Heart

 Goddess Cube

The Deep Woods

1. Deku Hornets

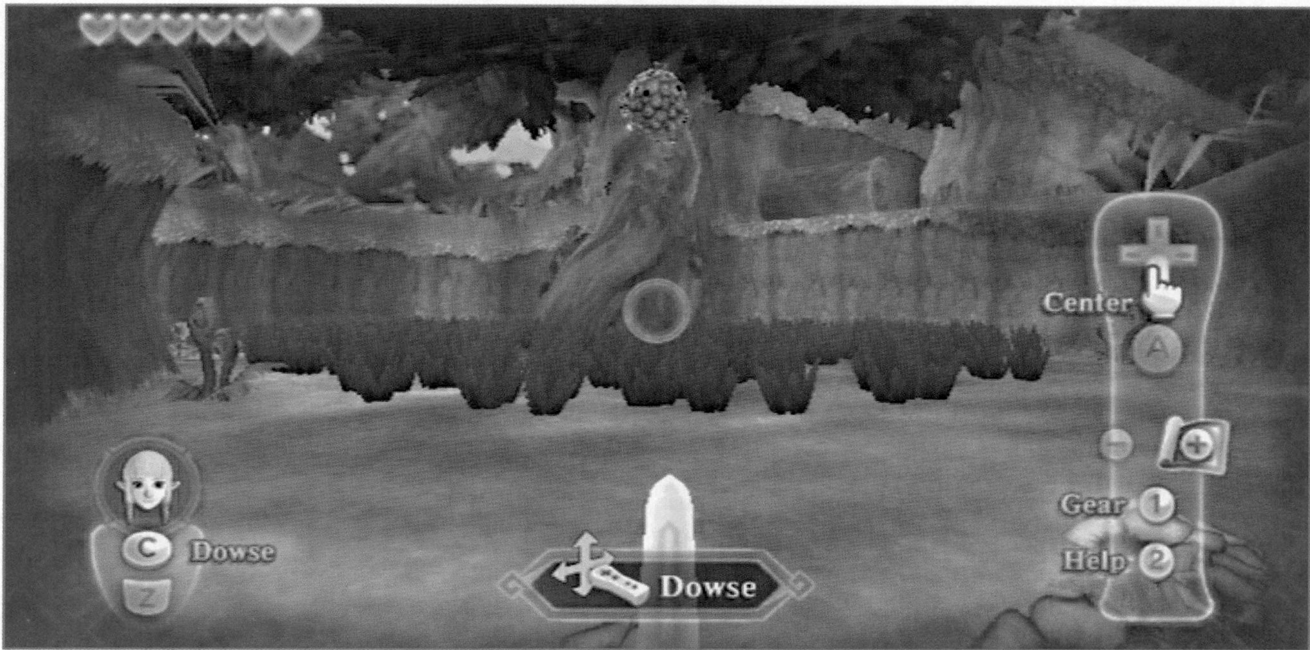

This is a treacherous area that you must pass through to find the entrance to that temple you were told about earlier. You're immediately attacked by a Bokoblin leader and a pair of his followers, which is just the beginning of your problems. Up ahead, if you happen to dowse before you move forward, you'll see a Deku Hornet nest hanging from a tree.

If you approach the nest, a swarm of nine (or so) Deku Hornets will fly out and harass you. This particular nest you can just avoid, but there are other nests that won't be dealt with so easily. While a Deku Hornet's sting only does a quarter-heart's worth of damage, there are around nine of them and you'll quickly discover that attacking them with your sword is futile. You need to deal with Deku Hornet problems another way.

Our recommended method is to shoot down a Deku Hornet nest as soon as you spot it, then get out your Bug Net. Once the Bug Net is out, just wave it around. You don't need to try to catch the Deku Hornets, though it's quite likely you'll end up catching a few without trying. Just by waving around your Bug Net, you'll make the Deku Hornets want to retreat.

NOTE

A basic rule of bug catching in *Skyward Sword* is that swinging your net too violently while bugs are in the area will make them retreat from you. This rule usually serves to make catching bugs more difficult, since it means that to be successful you ideally creep slowly toward a bug and then catch it with a single sudden swing of your Bug Net. In this case, though, you can exploit it to work in your favor.

2. More Deku Hornets

Head forward, down a path that winds through the roots of a giant tree, battling some Bokoblins along the way. At the end of the path, you come to a rope bridge with a Deku Hornet nest dangling over it. Shoot down the nest and then use your Bug Net to drive off or capture the Deku Hornet swarm before you try to cross. If you try to cross without taking care of the hornets' nest first, the Deku Hornets will sting you until you fall.

3. Up and Over

Once on the other side, continue down the path and battle the Bokoblin and Octorok you encounter just before you reach a deep pit. You must find a way to go around. Before you do that, though, head back toward the rope bridge to discover a path you can use to create a shortcut back to the area's entrance. This will be very useful whenever you need to backtrack into this area later.

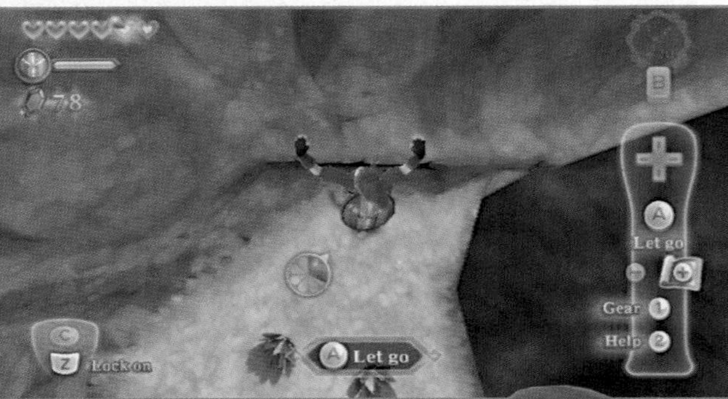

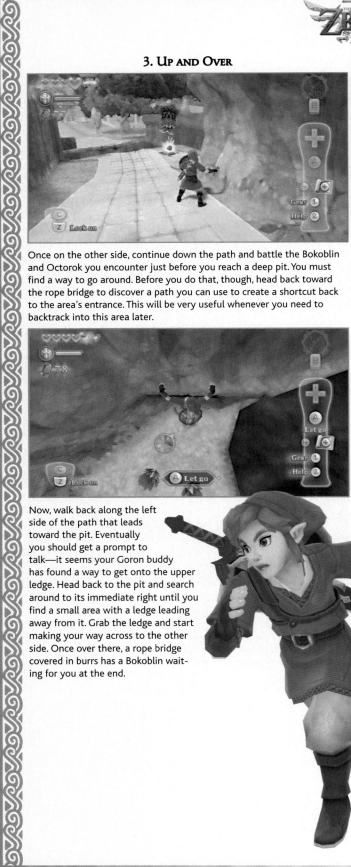

Now, walk back along the left side of the path that leads toward the pit. Eventually you should get a prompt to talk—it seems your Goron buddy has found a way to get onto the upper ledge. Head back to the pit and search around to its immediate right until you find a small area with a ledge leading away from it. Grab the ledge and start making your way across to the other side. Once over there, a rope bridge covered in burrs has a Bokoblin waiting for you at the end.

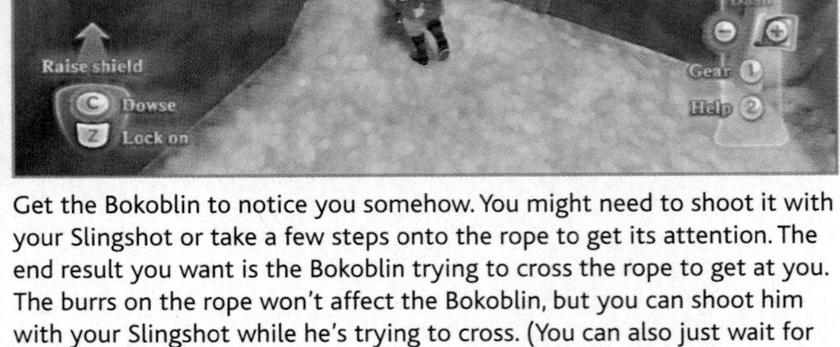

Get the Bokoblin to notice you somehow. You might need to shoot it with your Slingshot or take a few steps onto the rope to get its attention. The end result you want is the Bokoblin trying to cross the rope to get at you. The burrs on the rope won't affect the Bokoblin, but you can shoot him with your Slingshot while he's trying to cross. (You can also just wait for him to cross and defeat him normally, but the Slingshot thing is much funnier.)

Now you can cross the rope—just make sure to jostle the burrs off. After that, follow the path and be sure to save your game at the bird statue. Use the rope to swing across the pit at the end of the dirt path. Waiting for you on the other side of the pit is a new enemy.

Enemy: Quadro Baba

The Quadro Baba is a golden yellow Deku Baba. It has twice as much health as a Deku Baba, so you need to spin-slash it twice or hit it with your current sword four times before it goes down. The Quadro Baba takes its name from its ability to change the orientation of its mouth at will. That is, the Quadro Baba can choose whether to have its mouth open horizontally or vertically. It tends to switch from one to the other after each of its attacks or if you attack it unsuccessfully. Otherwise, the Quadro Baba uses the same basic attack pattern as a Deku Baba. You can handle it with roughly the same tactics. Since the Quadro Baba takes twice as long to kill, though, it's much easier to make a mistake and get damaged while trying to attack it.

4. The Cube

Once you're past the Quadro Baba, make your way over to your Goron pal, who's pondering a giant metal cube inexplicably sitting in the middle of the forest. This cube is called a Goddess Cube, and you activate it by hitting it with a Skyward Strike. What happens when you activate one? Well...that's both simple and a little complicated.

Basically, Skyloft and the smaller islands elsewhere in the sky are full of chests. Some are hidden, some are in plain sight, but none of them can be opened at the beginning of the game. You can only open these chests, called goddess's treasure chests, once you've used a Skyward Strike to activate the Goddess Cube in the surface world that corresponds to it. In short, the Goddess Cubes are very large keys that unlock a series of chests waiting for you in the sky.

Searching for hidden items is a staple of *Legend of Zelda* games, but in older games the search was mostly a matter of poking into every nook and cranny in the game and using every tool at Link's disposal. Searching for the Goddess Cubes is very different. You usually find them in areas that are very easy to see but tricky to actually reach. Some you will see dozens of hours before you have the right tools necessary to reach them.

The goddess's treasure chests in the sky work similarly. After you strike a Goddess Cube, the goddess's treasure chest you've activated is automatically marked on your in-game map. Finding the chest is simply a matter of checking to see whether it's on one of the sky's minor islands or somewhere in Skyloft itself (or just checking the maps in this guide). Just because you know where a chest is doesn't mean you can reach it, though. Some chests require you to approach them in a certain way while others absolutely cannot be reached until you've acquired a tool or story-related item that gives Link the abilities required.

Despite this, getting all of the Goddess Cubes is relatively easy and highly recommended, since you find a few unique and very useful items this way. It helps to remember that you only ever find Goddess Cubes in overworld areas, which in game terms means areas where you can dowse. As you'll discover in the game's next section, you cannot dowse in dungeons. So, basically, you don't have to worry about finding goddess's treasure chests in dungeons. In those areas, you can just focus on more traditional *Legend of Zelda* fare like finding hidden chests.

The maps in the walkthrough list all of the Goddess Cubes in a given area. The walkthrough will clearly point out which ones you can get in a given chapter. Others you won't be able to obtain until later in the game, when you re-enter an area with new tools at your disposal. The Goddess Cubes are all numbered. These numbers correspond directly to the numbered goddess's treasure chests listed on the map of the sky available in the "Getting Started" chapter.

The walkthrough covers how to get to the various goddess's treasure chests and recommends times to go and do this, typically when the game is making you return to the sky for a while anyway. Most of the stuff available in goddess's treasure chests you'll probably want to obtain earlier in the game, when it's more useful. Of course, if you like, you can simply skip over obtaining any Goddess Cube or chest. Nothing available in a goddess's treasure chest is required to finish the game. It's mostly stuff like helpful pouch items, Pieces of Heart, and extra Rupees.

As part of the tutorial, your Goron buddy asks you to activate the Goddess Cube right in front of him, which is Goddess Cube #1. Hit it with a Skyward Strike to activate it. We cover how to pick up the contents of goddess's treasure chest #1 a bit later. For now, move past the Goron and push over a shortcut log that'll be useful if you have to backtrack through this area. From there, you can hop down a series of platforms to emerge on the other side of the pit.

5. The Locked Temple

Turn to the right to spot and activate Goddess Cube #2. That's it for cubes you can activate in this area right now. Next, move toward the temple. This triggers a brief cutscene. Save your game at the bird statue. If you poke around the area around the temple, you'll discover some grassy areas. There's not much of interest to the building's left, but to its right there's a Deku Baba and a curious stone tablet.

The tablet gives a cryptic hint that describes how to open the temple's door. Tablets like this are scattered throughout the game's temples, containing hints that are indispensable (to players who are not proud owners of this fine strategy guide).

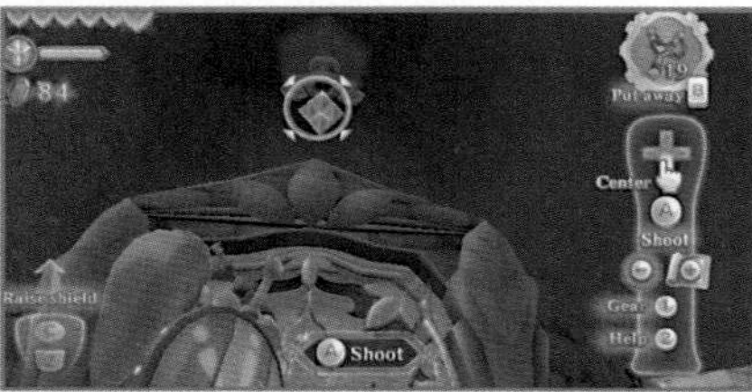

What the clue wants you to do is walk toward the temple's door. While you stand before it, use the Look command and see what's above Link's head. You should see a bright pink crystal. Crystals like this are switches that you can activate by hitting. It doesn't matter what you hit them with, a fact that will become extremely important in the next dungeon. This particular switch is best triggered by shooting at it with your Slingshot. This opens the way into the game's first real dungeon, Skyview Temple.

Goddess's Treasure Chest Pickups: #1 and #2

Chances are pretty good that you'll want to head back to Skyloft to resupply before you tackle Skyview Temple, so now's as good a time as any to recover the contents of the goddess's treasure chests you just activated.

Goddess's treasure chest #1 sits right next to the entrance of the Lumpy Pumpkin, a pub on one of the larger islands drifting in the sky. Inside is what will probably be the fifth pouch for your Adventure Pouch. This is the only Adventure Pouch slot you can obtain for free.

Goddess's treasure chest #2 is floating on a small island just south of Skyloft. It contains a Piece of Heart.

If you're having difficulty navigating to the goddess's treasure chests successfully, try using beacons. It's very easy to spot beacons from a distance while flying on your Loftwing, since the glowing light cuts through cloud cover.

A final note for those of you who might drop by the bazaar while you're flying around: Now that you have the Slingshot, Rupin's Gear Shop sells Seed Satchels, which let you carry more Deku Seeds. You shouldn't buy one now, though, since you can get one for free from a goddess's treasure chest if you're a little patient.

The Blue Birds

Now that you've got the Bug Net and you've messed with it a little, you can start preparing for the end of the game. There's a rare treasure that's necessary for making final upgrades to several pieces of Link's equipment. If you wait until the end of the game to grind for them, you may find the process quite annoying. It's much better to get started on obtaining Blue Bird Feathers now.

To get a Blue Bird Feather, you need to catch one of the small blue birds that occasionally appear throughout the Sealed Grounds, Faron Woods, the Deep Woods, and Skyview Spring in your Bug Net. Small blue birds are genuinely rare and are not guaranteed to appear in any area where small birds gather. Catching any type of bird in the Bug Net works like catching a bug, but the penalty for failure is a bit steeper—if you miss a swing of the Bug Net or let a bird get too close to you, all of the birds in a group will fly away.

What makes grinding for Blue Bird Feathers really annoying is that the game won't necessarily respawn blue birds if you leave an area and immediately return, either. You really need to run from bird spawn to bird spawn, seeing if you get lucky that time. This is really time-consuming and can be really frustrating if you get unlucky.

Instead, just keep your eyes peeled for small blue birds while you play through the game doing other things. Spending a few minutes here and there trying to catch small blue birds can pay off big and keeps failures from feeling too frustrating. You need at least one Blue Bird Feather to make equipment recommended by this walkthrough and four if you want to fully upgrade all of Link's gear.

It's worth noting that you can also catch the pink and yellow birds that spawn throughout the Deep Woods, Faron Woods, and the Sealed Temple areas to obtain a different treasure called the Bird Feather. You'll also need a fair number of these later in the game, but it's much easier to obtain these exactly when you need them.

The Lumpy Pumpkin

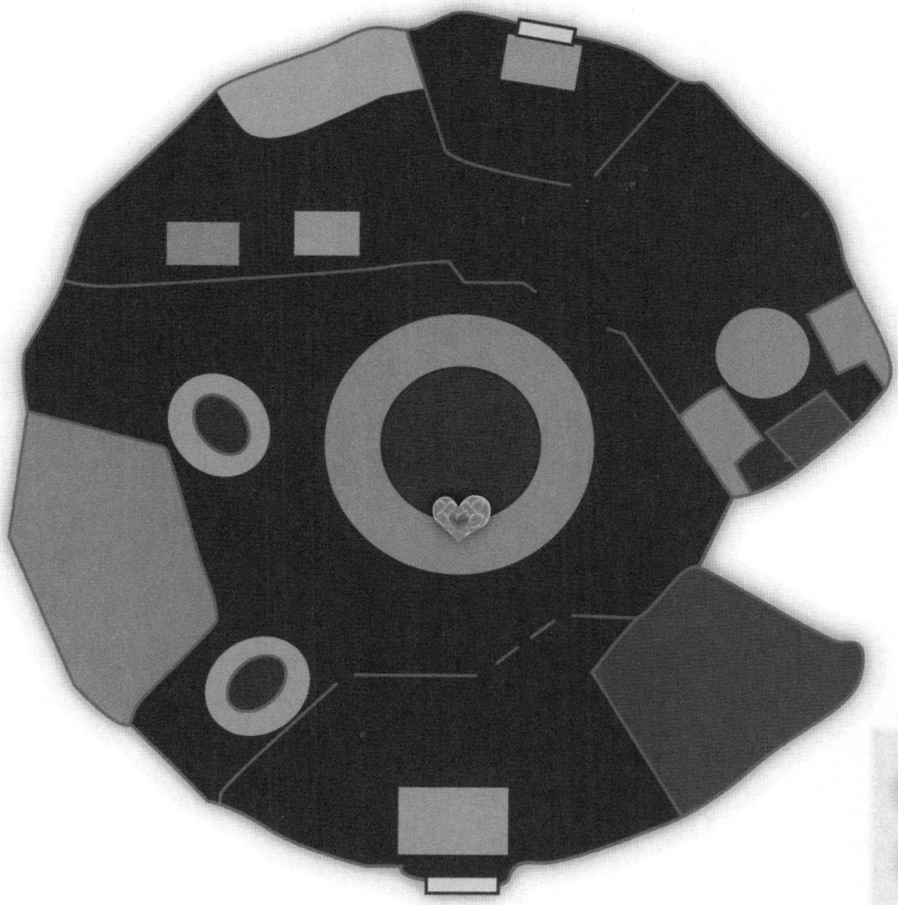

LEGEND

Piece of Heart

Goddess Cube

While you're hanging around the Lumpy Pumpkin anyway, go inside. You will immediately notice a chandelier conspicuously stuffed with Rupees and a Piece of Heart. There are signs around sternly warning any itinerant adventurers that they are not, under any circumstances, to smash up that chandelier so they can take that Piece of Heart.

You know what you must do.

Head up to the Lumpy Pumpkin's second level after you've talked to everyone. A balcony area lets you have an eye-level view of your inevitable and necessary foe, the chandelier. If you dash forward and roll into the balcony railing, it makes the chandelier rock a little. Dash-roll twice into the railing and that chandelier is going down.

Now, the guy who owns the Lumpy Pumpkin is, understandably, pretty mad that you trashed his chandelier. This initiates a chain of side quests you have to finish to pay the owner back. You can start the chain now if you like, by agreeing to fill an Empty Bottle with the pub's Pumpkin Soup and fly it over to the Knight Commander at the Sparring Hall in five minutes or less.

The catch is that you can't really get the chain of side quests any farther than that right now. Finishing the Lumpy Pumpkin side quests requires both progressing much farther in the plot and progressing through an entirely different chain of optional side quests. This guide recommends just ignoring the Lumpy Pumpkin's predicament for now and coming back to it toward the end of the game if you don't want to skip it entirely.

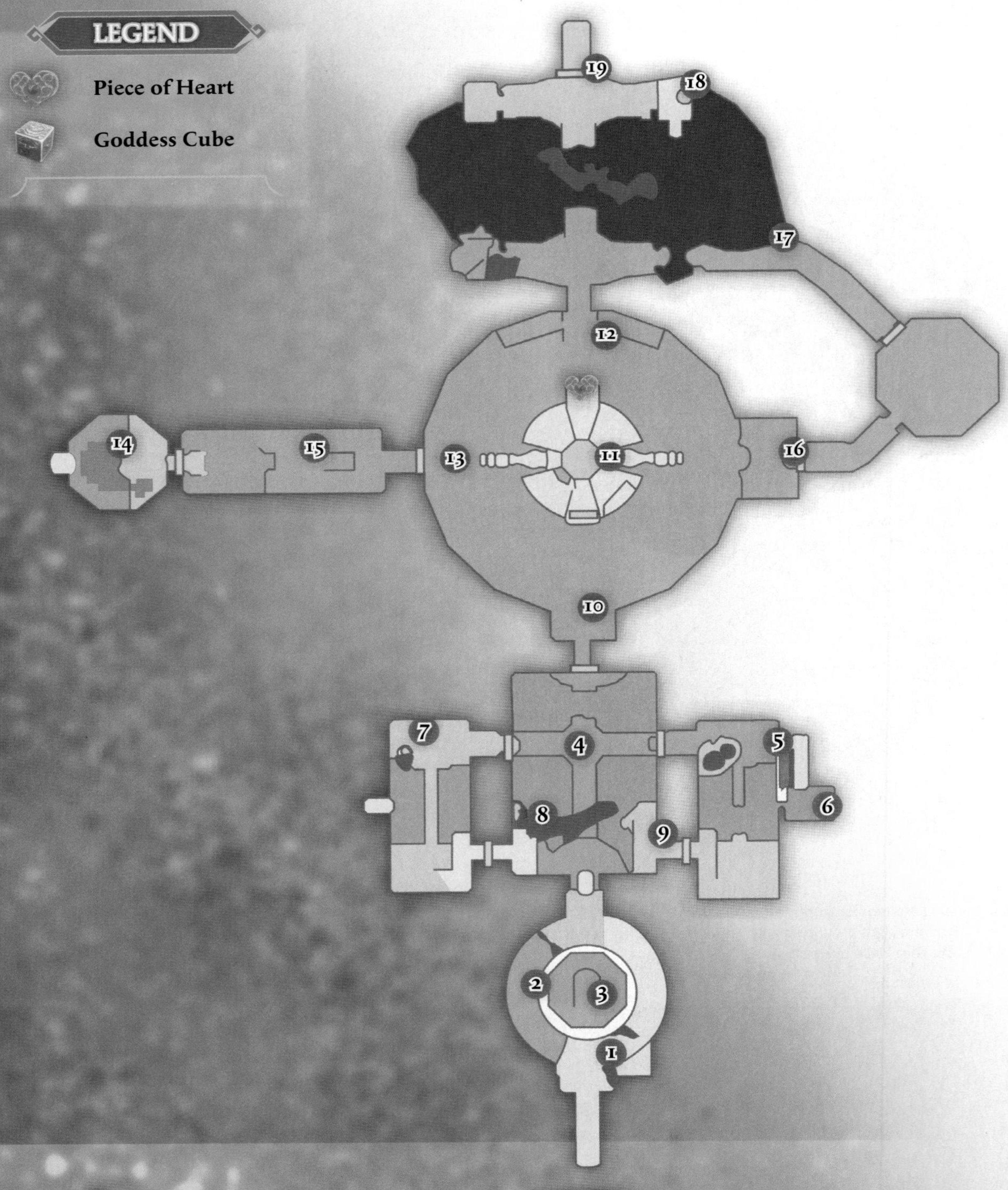

LEGEND

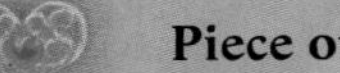

Piece of Heart

Goddess Cube

SKYVIEW TEMPLE

1. The Downward Spiral

Swat the Keese that attacks as you walk downward into the dungeon. Soon a large spiderweb blocks your path. Use your sword to slash through the strands and make an opening you can pass through. If you touch the web otherwise, you'll get stuck in it and have to shake the Wii Remote and Nunchuk to break free. Always make sure you break the strands at the bottom of the web, which can catch Link's feet as he tries to pass through.

You encounter more Keese as you make your way through the passage. Hack your way through another spiderweb and you come to an Amber Relic that's too high to be collected normally but can be nabbed with your Bug Net. At the end of the passage saplings block in a vine-covered wall. Hack down the saplings, then approach the vines with caution.

2. Plant and Switch

A Deku Baba waits at the top. It's close enough to the vines that it can attack you while you're still climbing. Back away just far enough that you can shoot the Deku Baba with your Slingshot from the lower level. This dazes it just long enough to let you get up the vines. After that, defeat the Deku Baba normally.

Behind the Deku Baba is a crystal switch. This one you can just smack with your sword. This opens a barred door set into the interior shaft of the first circular chamber. Backtrack to the door and use it to enter a room that contains no enemies, though there's an Amber Relic on the wall you can snag by doing a dash roll to knock it down. This room's main feature is a barred door that you must pass through to get farther into the dungeon.

3. The Sentry

If you step up to the top of the stone viewing platform at the center of the room, you'll see an eye-shaped sentry mounted on the door. It acts as the door's control switch. So long as you stand on the stone platform, which makes you level with the sentry, the eye will open to observe you. Your first impulse is probably to try to shoot or stab the eye out, but that's futile. The sentry's stone eyelid always closes before you can damage it.

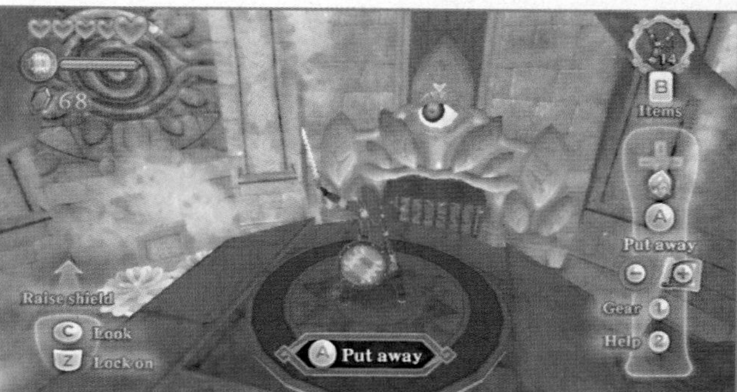

Instead, use your sword to trick the sentry. Watch the eye's behavior carefully. When your sword is sheathed, it watches you. When your sword is unsheathed, it focuses on the tip of your sword. Move your Wii Remote in a circle, such that Link moves his sword in the same way in the game. If you do this correctly, the sentry follows the point of your sword in the circle and its eye goes from blue to red. The sentry shudders and dies from dizziness, and the bars blocking the door it guarded rise.

4. The Central Chamber

Pass through the door into a hallway. The floor is thick with burrs, and two Deku Babas dangle from the ceiling. Move forward and attack the Deku Babas as you normally would. Fighting them with spin slashes helps eliminate the burrs around your feet, too. From the hallway you emerge into a large room with multiple doorways leading out of it. Save at the bird statue nearby before you begin exploring. Head to the area where the stone pathways cross to encounter a new enemy.

ENEMY: GREEN BOKOBLIN

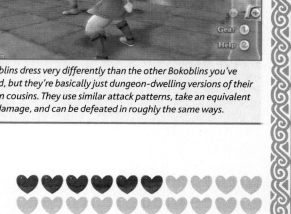

Green Bokoblins dress very differently than the other Bokoblins you've encountered, but they're basically just dungeon-dwelling versions of their Red Bokoblin cousins. They use similar attack patterns, take an equivalent amount of damage, and can be defeated in roughly the same ways.

The doors leading out to the left and right of this room are barred, but there's a switch above the door on the right. Fire your Slingshot to trigger it. The door that leads out at the far end of the room is closed with a padlock; you must explore the two nearby rooms to find a Small Key that opens it. Turn around and examine the area near the room's entrance; the walls are covered with vines and patrolled by another new enemy.

ENEMY: WALLTULA

Walltulas are the juvenile form of a race of monstrous spiders. Since they're too young to spin their own webs, they live on vine-covered walls and attempt to leap onto any prey that might pass by. They can't do much damage to you, but having to shake them off drains your stamina. On a long wall climb, this can tire you out and cause you to fall.

Walltulas aren't very tough. If you knock them off of their vine walls, say with a shot from your Slingshot, the fall immediately kills them. You can also kill them with a single slash or thrust from your sword, provided one comes close enough for you to hit.

Climb up the vines to find a narrow, boarded-up hallway. Use your sword to smash the boards. This opens up a shortcut that lets you quickly pass back into the dungeon's first chamber.

5. The Spider's Parlor

After opening the shortcut, head through the door on the right that you can open. Right now, you want to find a way to open up the left-hand door, which is necessary to obtain the Small Key you need. As you enter, the passageway is blocked by a spiderweb. Hack your way through. On the other side is a long stone walkway with a stone tablet waiting at the end. Look above it to see a new enemy lying in wait for you.

ENEMY: SKULLTULA

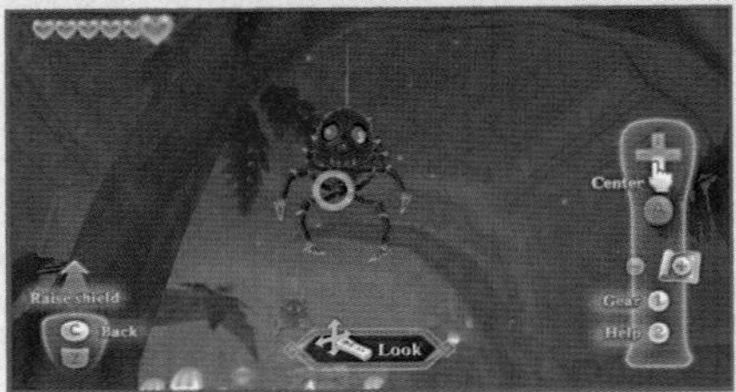

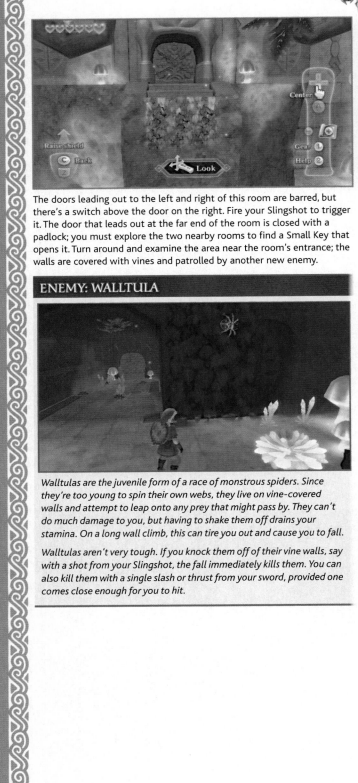

Skulltulas are what happen when Walltulas grow up. These enormous spiders dangle at the ends of their silken threads and wait for unlucky adventurers to pass beneath them. They descend quickly to take their prey by surprise. Other Skulltulas wait on webs and crawl onto the ground to attack once the web is disturbed. These Skulltulas try to entangle their would-be prey in webbing, then leap onto them and begin biting. A Skulltula's body is heavily armored, making it totally impervious to the strikes of even the strongest sword.

There's only one way to kill a Skulltula—by hitting the weak spot located on the underside of its body. A dangling Skulltula can be spun around with a horizontal slash or spin slash. One coming at you on the ground needs to be flipped over by any type of ascending sword strike (though ascending diagonals seem to work best). That lets you hit the weak point by locking on and performing a Fatal Blow. Skulltulas are extremely dangerous to you at this point in the game and should be approached with caution.

CAUTION

If you hit a dangling Skulltula with a thrust or vertical slash, it will simply swing back—and then ram you when it swings forward, dealing a full heart of damage. Try not to do this.

The tablet mentions a set of jewels where one is high and the other is low. You need to hit the low switch to get into the left-hand chamber. For now, look around this chamber to try and find the high switch.

6. The Hidden Chamber

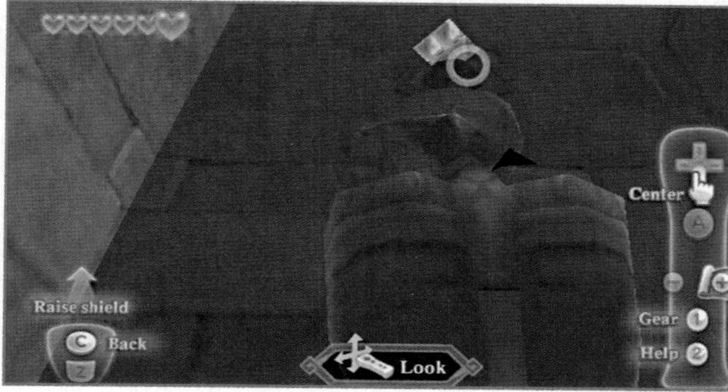

Jump down into the pit beneath the stone tablet. Look around for a small tunnel located in the pit roughly where the map indicates there should be some sort of passage into another room. Crawl into it and you'll emerge in a very small room. Walk up the stairs toward the large bird statue. Look up and you'll see a switch waiting above its head.

Hit the switch with your Slingshot to flood this chamber and the one next to it with water. Now you can swim over to some vines growing on a wall and climb up into a small, winding passageway. This shortcut takes you back to the room's entrance. Head back to the central chamber.

7. The Bridge of Doom

Walk underneath the stone walkway beneath the door that leads to the left to find the low switch the stone tablet was talking about. Climb up some vines to get back up on the stone walkway, then pass through the now-open door that leads into the left-hand chamber. A Green Bokoblin patrols the area just inside.

After you defeat the Bokoblin, take a moment to examine the room. You're on a high stone platform. A stone bridge extends across a pool of water to another high stone platform on the other side. Each end of the stone bridge is blocked by a spiderweb with a Skulltula lurking on it. You must find some way to cross to the other platform.

You probably think you need to fight the first Skulltula head-on, hack through the web after you've killed it, then go fight the second one. You can try that, but you'll probably take a lot of damage. There's a much simpler way to take care of these enemies, if you don't mind being sneaky.

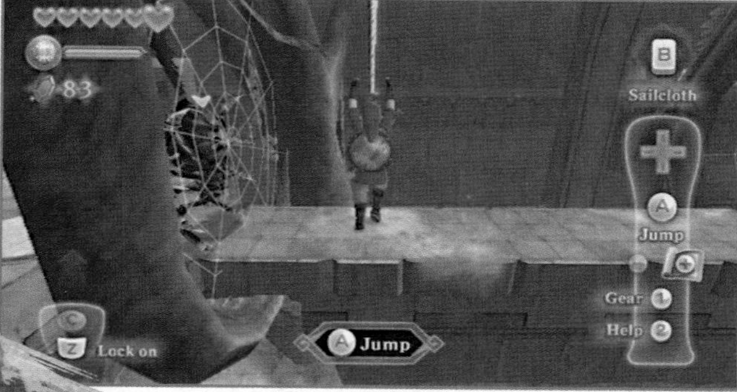

Examine the area to the right of the stone bridge, where two coiled vines dangle from the tree branches. You can knock down the one that's close to you with your Slingshot. Jump onto it and use your control stick to point Link toward the part of the stone bridge that's between the two Skulltulas. Swing over to this part of the bridge and you'll be standing right behind the first Skulltula, with its weak point pointed right at Link's face. A pair of quick thrusts will bring you an easy victory.

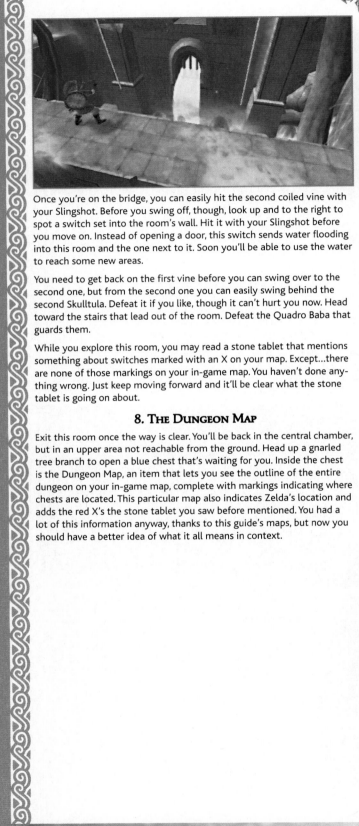

Once you're on the bridge, you can easily hit the second coiled vine with your Slingshot. Before you swing off, though, look up and to the right to spot a switch set into the room's wall. Hit it with your Slingshot before you move on. Instead of opening a door, this switch sends water flooding into this room and the one next to it. Soon you'll be able to use the water to reach some new areas.

You need to get back on the first vine before you can swing over to the second one, but from the second one you can easily swing behind the second Skulltula. Defeat it if you like, though it can't hurt you now. Head toward the stairs that lead out of the room. Defeat the Quadro Baba that guards them.

While you explore this room, you may read a stone tablet that mentions something about switches marked with an X on your map. Except...there are none of those markings on your in-game map. You haven't done anything wrong. Just keep moving forward and it'll be clear what the stone tablet is going on about.

8. The Dungeon Map

Exit this room once the way is clear. You'll be back in the central chamber, but in an upper area not reachable from the ground. Head up a gnarled tree branch to open a blue chest that's waiting for you. Inside the chest is the Dungeon Map, an item that lets you see the outline of the entire dungeon on your in-game map, complete with markings indicating where chests are located. This particular map also indicates Zelda's location and adds the red X's the stone tablet you saw before mentioned. You had a lot of this information anyway, thanks to this guide's maps, but now you should have a better idea of what it all means in context.

9. Hiding in Plain Sight

Once you're in the central chamber, look around for a particular log floating in the water. You might have noticed logs sitting in the bottom of the pit in the central chamber while exploring that area before. Now that this particular log is floating, you can climb up on it to reach an area of the right wall of the central chamber that's covered in climbable vines. Climb to an entrance that takes you to the previously unreachable stone platform that stands at the far end of the right-hand chamber.

A Skulltula guards the room. Defeat it so it's not in your way as you try to solve the room's puzzle. The blue chest you want stands behind a set of iron bars that is controlled by two sentries. They're placed much lower to the ground than the one you dealt with before, so you can trigger them while just standing on the floor. You need to get both sentries to look at your sword while you circle it, so you dizzy them both simultaneously. This knocks them both out, which causes the bars to rise. Snag the Small Key and return to the central chamber.

10. The Crumbling Dome

Pass through the locked door into a massive domed room. The area is full of dangling Skulltulas, Green Bokoblins, and swarms of Keese. Avoid needless battles where you can, but defeat enemies quickly once they're advancing on you. Even if you hear the game's "combat music" begin playing, you can still pass by enemies in the area if you just move away from them quickly enough. You shouldn't have to fight anything in this room unless it gets directly in your way.

11. The Trap

Both of the doors that lead out of this room are locked or barred. You need to enter the door in the dome's interior chamber, which you can open by hitting the switch above it with your Slingshot. Don't enter this room unless you're ready for a fight.

SUB-BOSS: STALFOS

This enemy occurs only in dungeons, usually as the guardian of an important item or room. Stalfos's bones assemble into a menacing skeleton wielding two scimitars the moment you step into the room. As with other sub-bosses, you cannot retreat from a battle with Stalfos once you've stepped into his territory.

Stalfos attacks by swinging his massive scimitars at you. You can shield-bash this attack, which causes Stalfos's arms to briefly fall off. This leaves him completely helpless for a few seconds, giving you plenty of time to damage him. Be careful when Stalfos rearms himself (pun intended), as he enters an attacking stance immediately after. You can choose shield bashing as the center of your strategy for battling Stalfos, but if you do, it's a good idea to upgrade to a Banded Shield before this fight.

You can also opt to take a more aggressive approach. You can successfully attack Stalfos while it advances on you, provided you read its guard correctly. Stalfos approaches you while holding its two swords up in a guarding stance. There's always a gap in Stalfos's guard you can exploit. If Stalfos holds its swords up vertically, you damage it with a vertical slash. If it's holding its swords horizontally, you can use a horizontal slash. Sometimes Stalfos will hold the swords perpendicular to each other, which means you can use a rising diagonal slash from the appropriate direction.

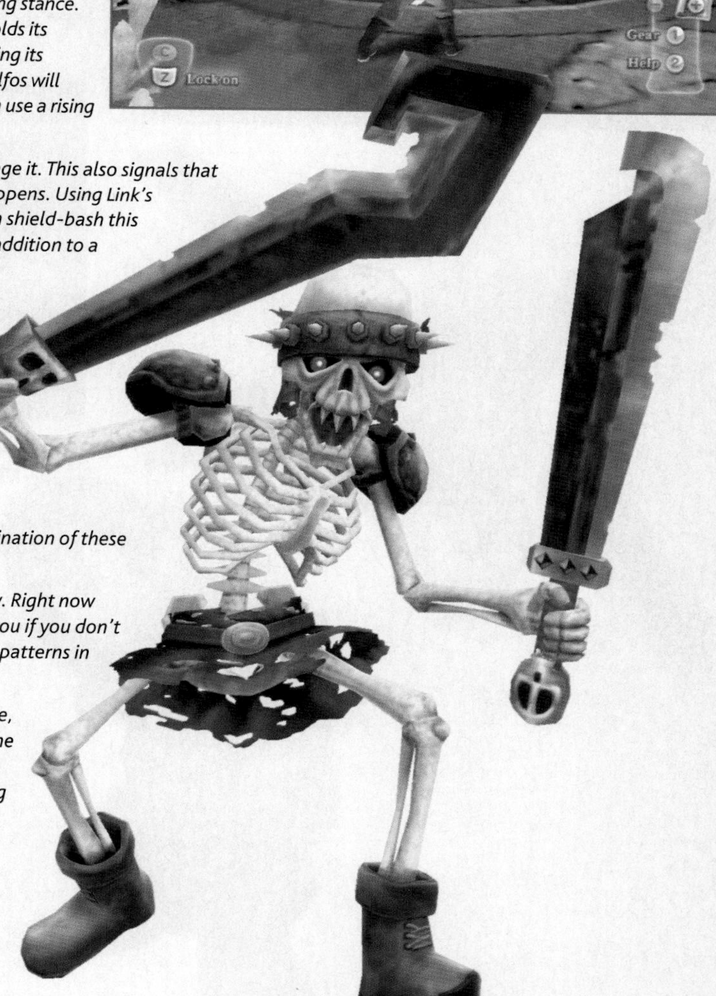

When Stalfos crosses its swords across its chest, you cannot damage it. This also signals that Stalfos is getting ready to attack. Back away rapidly when this happens. Using Link's backward backflipping dodge move should get you clear. You can shield-bash this attack, but the timing is very tight. If this attack hits you, then in addition to a full heart of damage it'll knock you over.

Finally, you can opt to play a game of keep-away with Stalfos. Make sure you're locked on to Stalfos and keep holding down Ⓩ. If you do this, then when he attacks, you can dodge rapidly in any direction by holding down Ⓐ and moving the control stick in a desired direction. If you dodge to the right or left while Stalfos attacks, you'll escape with no damage and be in an excellent position to take advantage of the opening with your own attacks. You can also use any combination of these techniques.

The important thing with fighting Stalfos is not to flail at it blindly. Right now you've got a pretty small health meter and Stalfos can easily kill you if you don't focus to some extent on dodging or defense. If you keep Stalfos's patterns in mind as you fight it, then you should win easily.

If you're having trouble fighting Stalfos and taking a lot of damage, don't forget that there are hearts scattered around the inside of the room. Stalfos is not very fast and it's easy to dash away from him, pick up some health, and then return to the fight. Your Revitalizing Potions may be called for here, both for healing and to keep your shield from breaking.

After you defeat the Stalfos, it turns into a blue chest. Open it to receive a tool you'll need to get through the rest of this dungeon.

THE BEETLE

The Beetle is an unusual but extremely useful tool. The Beetle is basically a small flying drone Link can control remotely. You can use the Beetle to explore areas you can't reach, including small passages and areas high in the air. The Beetle can also interact with small objects, striking switches and snapping ropes by bumping into them. It can also pick up small objects like hearts and Rupees. While you can use the Beetle to strike enemies, this is not really recommended. It has no effect on anything but very small enemies and is much slower than just using your Slingshot.

You control the Beetle using Wii MotionPlus's sensitivity to tilting. This means the Beetle can't fly directly up or down, but instead moves a lot like your Loftwing. It needs to make banking turns, slow ascents, and angular dives. Your Beetle also has limited stamina. It can't fly too far from Link, and banging into things drains its energy. Be sure to practice flying the Beetle for a bit in this dungeon to get the hang of using it. Sometimes it's helpful to use the Beetle purely as a scout, to find out what lies at the end of passages or on distant platforms before you send Link in himself.

Now that you have the Beetle, you can solve all of this dungeon's puzzles. Begin with the puzzle of how to get out of this room. While killing an enemy usually opens a barred door automatically, that is not the case here. Instead, you need to open the door yourself using the Beetle. Look up to see an area where chunks have fallen out of the room's domed ceiling, letting you see a dangling Skulltula in the outer room. Guide the Beetle successfully through this opening, then use it to trigger the switch outside that you used to enter the room in the first place. Bank the Beetle to the right once you've flown it out of the inner dome to find the switch.

12. Looting the Room

Once you're out, have some fun with the Beetle by using it to knock down the boxes suspended from the ceiling in the outer dome. They all contain Rupees, including a lot of Red and Blue Rupees. You can also use the Beetle to pick up a Piece of Heart, which is locked behind a series of iron bars set into the side of the inner chamber. Back up a few paces and launch the Beetle, then fly it up following the curve of the inner dome. If you go up high enough, you'll find a switch that's impossible to see from the ground but easy to hit with the Beetle.

13. The Well-Hidden Switch

Now it's time to move deeper into the dungeon. Head in front of the barred door that has a red X marked behind it on your map. That's a switch that you need to hit with the Beetle to unlock the door for Link. It's hidden in the small, tunnel-sized passage that's above the door. You can fire the Beetle into either of the entrances that appear above the door to reach it. There are passages like this all over the upper area of the central dome, actually, and you can ferret a lot of Red and Blue Rupees out of the rest of them. This is the only one you need to explore to advance, though.

14. The Dangling Block

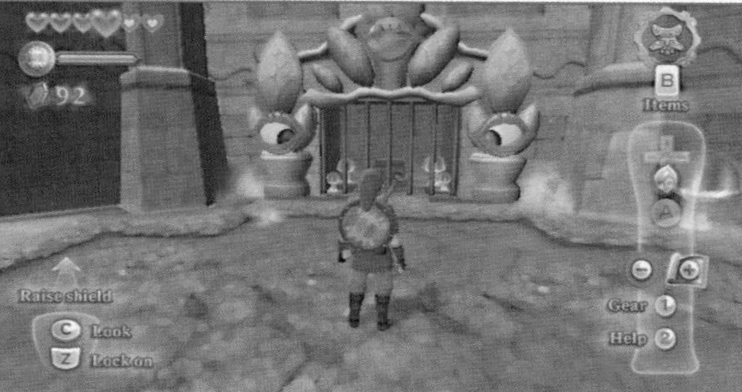

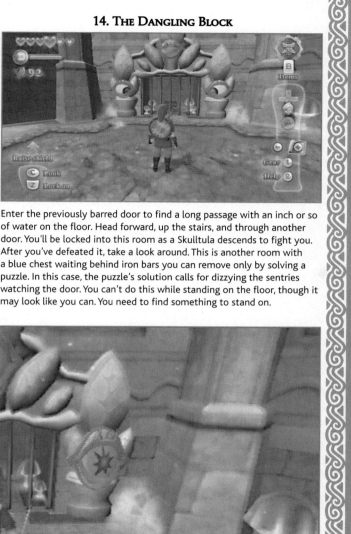

Enter the previously barred door to find a long passage with an inch or so of water on the floor. Head forward, up the stairs, and through another door. You'll be locked into this room as a Skulltula descends to fight you. After you've defeated it, take a look around. This is another room with a blue chest waiting behind iron bars you can remove only by solving a puzzle. In this case, the puzzle's solution calls for dizzying the sentries watching the door. You can't do this while standing on the floor, though it may look like you can. You need to find something to stand on.

Go stand in front of the iron bars and then examine the area just above the entrance. There's an iron block that's perfect for standing on dangling from the ceiling. Use the Beetle to sever the spider silk holding the block up, then climb up the vines so you can push it down to the lower level. Once you're there, push it to an area where you can stand on top of it and get all three sentries to look at you. Dizzy all three eyes at once to raise the iron bars and claim the Small Key in the blue chest.

15. Insufficient Water

As you head back down the corridor, there's a bit of a problem: You can't actually get out of this passage the way you came in. The stairs don't go down far enough and there are no ledges you can grab. Instead, launch the Beetle and fly it down the passageway to find a switch at the end of the passageway that the Beetle can hit, which raises the water level in the passageway. Now swim to the broken staircases.

At the top of them, you'll find a Skulltula that's much easier to kill than usual, since you can just knock it into the water to drown it. Head to the end of the passageway and climb the stairways to the area just above the switch. A tunnel leads out of the area, but it's blocked by saplings. Hack down the saplings and then crawl through the tunnel to emerge back into the dome.

16. The Perilous Door

Now you can unlock the door at the far side of the room. Head over there and you'll find an incredible five Deku Babas dangling from the ceiling above a rope bridge. You cannot possibly make it across until you defeat at least the three in the center. If you try to cross the rope and get knocked down, you'll have to fight a couple of Quadro Babas before you can get out. Instead of losing a lot of health fighting the Deku Babas, take care of them with the Beetle. You know how you can use the Beetle to sever ropes? Well, that trick also works on the vines that tether the Deku Babas to the ceiling.

Once you pass through the locked door, bars drop down to keep you from retreating. Head forward, smash down the boards, and prepare to encounter a new type of enemy.

Enemy: Staldra

The ancient three-headed Staldra patrols dungeons, using its three cyclopean eyes to watch its surroundings for signs of adventurers. When Staldra spots you, its three eyes burn red and it attempts to hit you with a triple headbutt. If you destroy one of its heads with a sword slash, it will simply grow back.

The only way to truly defeat a Staldra is to destroy all three of its heads simultaneously. The easiest way to do this is to wait until it has them lined up horizontally or diagonally, then try to destroy all three with a single strike. You can also try to hit all the heads individually, but this must be done very quickly.

17. The Chasm

Head into the next passageway and battle a Green Bokoblin. Next, use the Beetle to drop the dangling Skulltula up ahead into the abyss. Once the Skulltula is out of the way, jump over the pit. Eventually, the narrow passages open into a much wider room, rent in the middle by a bottomless pit. Hit the switch over the door to your left to open up a shortcut that leads back to the dome.

To proceed, you have to cross a rope bridge guarded by a Green Bokoblin on the far side. Hit him with a shot from your Slingshot to goad him into trying to cross the bridge toward you. Shoot him again once he's on the rope and he'll topple into the bottomless pit below.

18. The Canopy

Once on the other side, examine the door before you. It's locked and requires you find the (probably very odd-looking) key that opens it. Head to the left and pick up a Red Rupee from a small chest. Next, head to the right. There's a wall covered in vines you can use to climb up into the tangled canopy of branches that spans the top of the room. From here, you can cut down a fern to release a rope you can use to swing across part of the pit to a platform.

The platform is part of a winding tree branch you can walk across to find a pair of coiled vines. Knock them down with your Slingshot, then use them to swing across to the tower where a jeweled chest awaits. Inside this chest is the Golden Carving, which acts as the key to the dungeon's final locked door.

19. The Final Door

Climb up the vines on the far wall and then backtrack across the rope bridge to return to the final locked door. Be sure to save before you open it. If necessary, return to Skyloft and make sure you're supplied for a boss fight. Definitely get a shield if you've somehow lost yours. You use carvings to open doors by tilting them with the Wii Remote until they fit into the lock's shape.

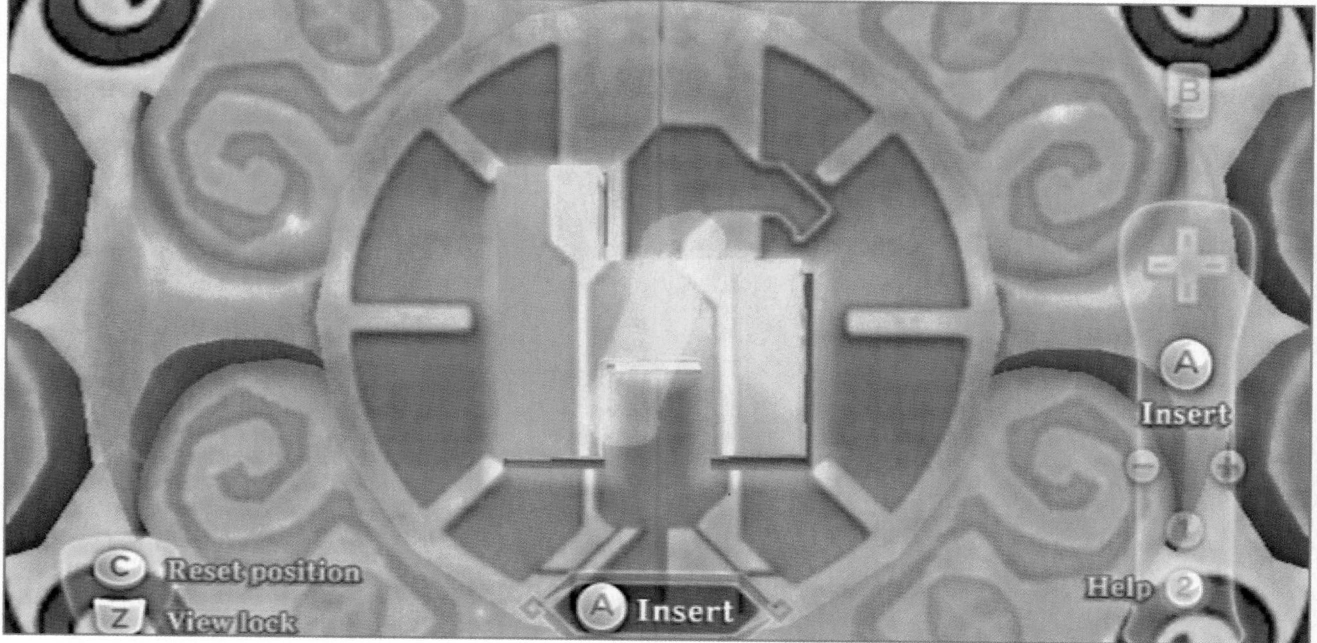

BOSS: DEMON LORD GHIRAHIM

It's not clear who Ghirahim is or where he came from, but it is clear that he wants you to be on the receiving end of a savage beating. Success in this battle is a matter of being careful and taking advantage of the handful of opportunities you'll have to attack. Also make sure you stay locked on to Ghirahim as much as possible, as that ensures you hit him when you create an opening.

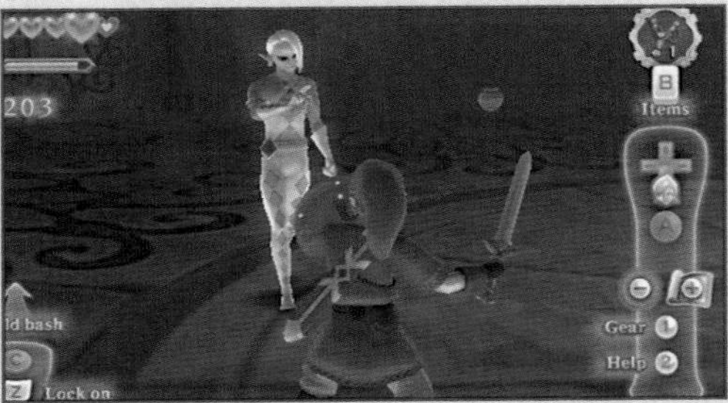

In the first phase of the battle, Ghirahim approaches you slowly with his right arm outstretched. You may be tempted to Skyward Strike him, since he gives you plenty of time to charge the move, but you'll find he teleports automatically out of the way of these attacks.

Ghirahim's main attack in this phase involves counterattacking by catching your sword when you try to attack him. If this happens, swing the Wii Remote up to get your sword free. If you fail, Ghirahim takes your sword out of your hand and begins swinging at you with it. The idea here is that you need to hit Ghirahim with blows that aren't telegraphed. Try leading Ghirahim's arm with the point of your sword, as you could lead the sentry's eyeball. If you hold still for a long time, until he's nearly on top of you, he relaxes his guard somewhat. That's when you need to strike with your sword, as quickly as you can.

The second phase of the battle begins when Ghirahim licks his lips and summons a sword. He becomes more aggressive in this phase. It helps to have a shield at this point, since most of his attacks can be shield-bashed. His most common attack pattern is lunging forward at you and rapidly swinging his sword in a wide horizontal arc. If you shield-bash when he begins to move, you can stagger him and land a few blows before he teleports away. You can also dodge around him and get a few hits in that way, but this window of opportunity is a bit shorter.

If too much distance opens between you and Ghirahim, he may summon a series of five floating diamond-shaped projectiles. If you shield-bash these the way you'd shield bash an Octorok's rocks, they'll bounce back at Ghirahim and inflict a little damage. Alternatively, Ghirahim may teleport just behind or in front of you and attack with a powerful descending vertical slash. Generally it's best to dodge out of the way of this, especially if Ghirahim is behind you. If he's in front of you it is possible to shield-bash this move, but the timing is tight.

If you take a lot of damage in the battle, remember that the pots that stand against the far wall of this boss room contain hearts. Ghirahim moves fairly slowly in this fight and you should be able to dash away from him long enough to top up your health. Just try not to let him out of sight for too long, or you might turn around and find he's teleported right on top of you.

After you defeat Ghirahim, he teleports away and leaves a Heart Container behind. Obtaining a Heart Container adds one full heart to your health meter, while also completely restoring your health. This is your usual reward for defeating a boss in *Skyward Sword*.

20. Skyview Spring

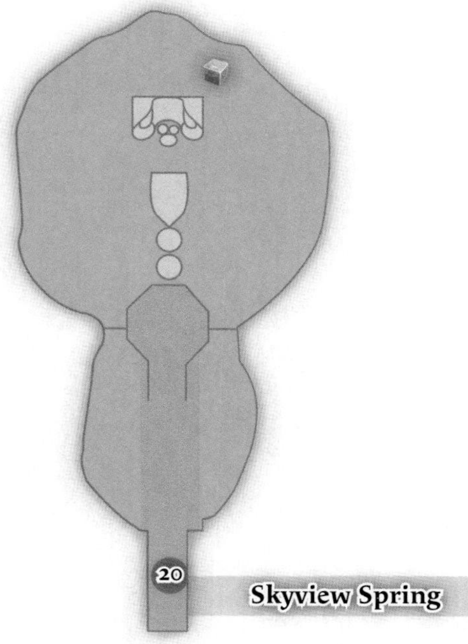

Approach the now-activated door on the other side of the boss room to access the enemy-free Skyview Spring area. You can send the Beetle up to the top of the pillars near the entrance to grab a Red Rupee. Instead of launching a Skyward Strike at the crest at the end of the platforms, hop into the water and run around to the rear of the altar. You'll find Goddess Cube #3 hidden there.

Once you hit the crest on the altar with a Skyward Strike, the dungeon is effectively over. You receive the next piece of the Ancient Tablet, the Ruby Tablet, and instructions to go seek out the Earth Temple. After the cutscenes end, you're returned to the dungeon's entrance. Save at the bird statue and then return to Skyloft. You're finished with this area for now.

Skyloft

Return to the room in the base of the Statue of the Goddess. Step up to the Ancient Tablet's pedestal and examine it to automatically insert the Ruby Tablet. This opens up a red pillar of light in the sky that leads to the Eldin Volcano area, where the Earth Temple is located.

While you're heading away from the Statue of the Goddess, a cutscene cues up. One of the Skyloft villagers, a little girl named Kukiel, has gone missing. This is the beginning of the game's optional Gratitude Crystal series of side quests. Turn to the "Secrets and Side Quests" chapter for information about completing these quests, which you can do at any time before the end of the game.

These quests are completely optional, despite this cutscene being mandatory. That said, collecting Gratitude Crystals is the only way in the game Link can acquire bigger wallets that can hold more Rupees. This walkthrough recommends spending some time progressing the Gratitude Crystal quests whenever you've maxed out Link's wallet in your game and can't afford (or have already bought) all of the Extra Wallet slots. Otherwise, it's easiest to complete the Gratitude Crystal quest chains toward the end of the game, when you have all the tools you need for them.

Resupply before you set out for the Eldin Volcano. When it comes to potions, you now have enough health for buying Heart Potions to be worthwhile. If you still have your Wooden or Banded Shield from your time in Faron Woods, take it to the Item Check girl and leave it there. You should instead pick up an Iron Shield from Rupin (if you can afford it), or simply tackle the next area with no shield at all. While Faron Woods was loaded with enemies that called for shield-bashing, Eldin Volcano can easily be cleared with a playing style that relies purely on dodging and offense.

Goddess's Treasure Chest Pickup: #3

The Goddess Cube you activate in Skyview Spring activates another goddess's treasure chest located on the Lumpy Pumpkin's island. This chest is on the left side of the roof area directly over the Lumpy Pumpkin's entrance. You can get up there, but doing so involves diving. You need to have your Loftwing fly you directly over that part of the island, then jump off and try to land on the roof next to the chest. This chest contains a Gold Rupee that's worth 300 Rupees. It can be a very good idea to go buy your first Extra Wallet at Beedle's before you open this chest.

Eldin Volcano

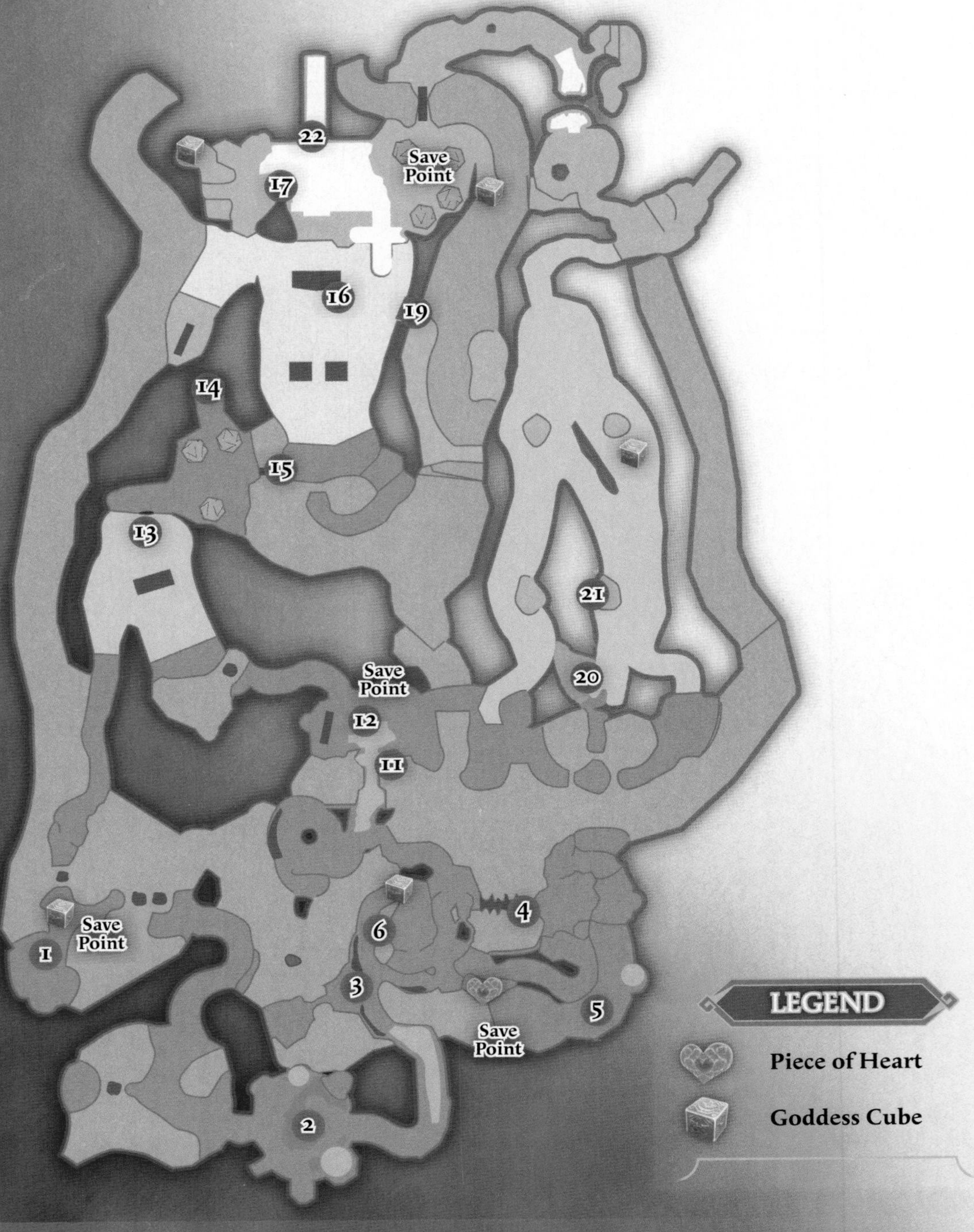

22
Save Point
17
16
19
14
15
13
21
Save Point
20
12
11
4
6
Save Point
1
3
5
Save Point
2

LEGEND

Piece of Heart

Goddess Cube

ELDIN VOLCANO

1. Meet the Mogmas

Eldin Volcano is an area thick with lava flows, inhabited by creatures that have adapted to the harsh environment and developed abilities that let them live comfortably in high heat. Link is not one of these creatures. In fact, he has a disconcerting tendency to burst into flames while exploring Eldin Volcano. This usually happens if Link is attacked by a fiery creature or if he falls into a pool of lava. Sometimes it happens because he stepped into the wrong room. Remember that when Link is burning, you can act quickly to extinguish it by dash-rolling, spin-slashing, or sliding. This can keep Link from taking a half-heart of extra fire damage.

Dowse for Zelda so you have a rough idea of what direction to go in. Head toward the two rock platforms floating in lava. Stop just to the right of them and drop down to activate Goddess Cube #4 before moving on. Once across the lava flow, you encounter a pair of friendly NPCs from the mole-like Mogma race, who confirm that Zelda passed by earlier. Continue down this path and fight your way through groups of new enemies.

ENEMY: RED CHUCHU

Red Chuchus are much like their green cousins, but they thrive on lava, whereas their cousins in Faron Woods thrive on moisture. They occur around lava flows in Eldin Volcano, often in groups and sometimes at enormous sizes. Defeat them the way you'd defeat any other Chuchus, but be ready to spend longer hacking them into bits. You must also try harder to keep an eye on all the Chuchus in a group, as these are more aggressive about attacking you.

ENEMY: FIRE KEESE

This is not merely a Keese that's on fire, it's a Keese that's made of fire. They gather in swarms throughout every region in the Eldin Volcano area. Their attack pattern is basically the same as that of the normal variety of Keese, but if their diving attack connects there's a chance that it will set Link on fire. Fight them using the same tactics you apply to the non-flaming variety of Keese, since nothing about a Fire Keese is especially dangerous until an attack connects.

2. Bomb Flowers and You

Head through an area where the lava surges and recedes, moving carefully. Simply touching the lava in this room can damage you and it's easy to misjudge its level. You encounter another Mogma in a chamber where large bulb-like blue flowers grow in abundance. The Mogma calls them Bomb Flowers, and they explode when picked. The Mogma explains how to use Bomb Flowers. Pick one up and roll it toward the cracked wall just behind the Mogma. It's generally better to roll than to throw Bomb Flowers at this point in the game, since a rolled Bomb Flower can go much farther than a thrown one.

Bombing the wall opens the way into a long, winding stone tunnel. Pass through it, fighting a pack of Fire Keese as you go. Save your game at the bird statue. Move beyond until the path branches and you can see a cave in a high stone pillar surrounded by a moat of lava. Go down the left branch of the path to find a dead end where Goddess Cube #5 is hidden.

3. The Cave and the Lava Moat

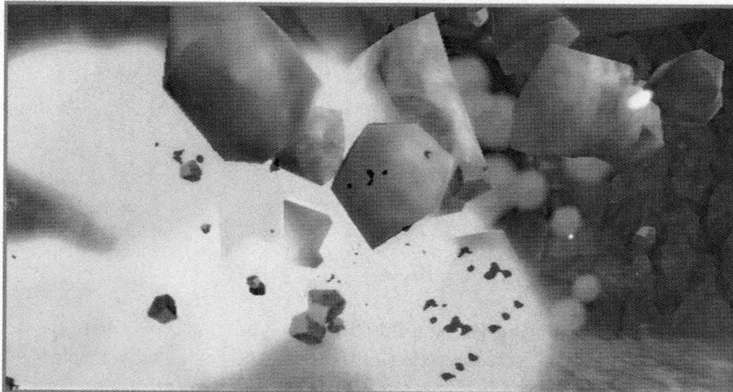

Speak to the Mogma who's in front of the cave's entry. This Mogma confirms that someone dressed in black did, in fact, pass through the area earlier. That doesn't exactly sound like Zelda, but it's a lead worth following anyway. You need to find some way to get into that cave, but you'll have to follow a circuitous route to do it. Walk past the Mogma and follow the path until it leads down into a pit. A cutscene introduces a new enemy that you must defeat before you can move on.

ENEMY: PYRUP

Pyrups are cowardly enemies you can't really fight head-on. When they see you, they immediately crawl into the nearest small cave or other protective object. From there, they breathe a steady stream of flame at you whenever you draw near. They're easy to avoid, but they tend to occupy areas that you have no choice but to pass through.

Bombs are really the best way to kill them. You can roll bombs into the small caves where Pyrups like to hide. Sometimes Pyrups hide in skulls, which have openings in the tops perfect for throwing bombs into. You should be able to find Bomb Flowers near any area where Pyrups are present.

4. The Skeleton Bridge

For this particular Pyrup, look for the Bomb Flowers near the edge of the pit. Once you've detonated the Pyrup, proceed down the path it blocked previously. You encounter a Red Bokoblin leader and a couple of its followers as you approach the crest of a hill. Continue down the path until you reach another drop-off that leads to a pit. The bottom of this pit holds a few Bomb Flowers, some hiding places for Pyrups, and a curious skeleton bridge. Drop to the lower area and first take care of the Pyrups.

Dash across the skeleton bridge next. When you reach the other side, you speak with a Mogma who points out that there's a plug nearby that's damming up the lava flow, sinking a nearby road beneath lava. That road leads toward the cave you want to get into, so you must find some way to get rid of the plug. Go back across the skeleton bridge.

5. The Back Way

There's a bit of exploring you should do before you deal with the plug. When you head back across the skeleton bridge, notice a series of platforms leading up off the bridge's left. Climb up them to reach a path that winds back into the stony foothills at the base of the volcano. Fight your way past a Red Chuchu and then emerge into a wider pathway patrolled by Pyrups. Beyond the Pyrups, look down to see a Piece of Heart waiting on a ledge. Simply drop down to claim it.

6. Beyond the Lava Plug

To get rid of the lava plug, roll a bomb across the skeleton bridge. You must roll the bomb straight enough that it makes it all the way across the bridge without bumping into either side of the bridge, which would cause the bomb to stop prematurely. If you roll the bomb straight, it automatically rolls down to the left and destroys the plug once it reaches the other side. Don't try to carry a bomb across the bridge, as you can't run fast enough while carrying something to get across before it blows up.

Once the lava plug is gone, the lava around the base of the cave recedes. You can enter the cave by dropping to a lower area and then riding a geyser up to the cave entrance. Once inside the cave's mouth, you'll see it's actually a platform that you must dive off of to enter an interior area of Eldin Volcano.

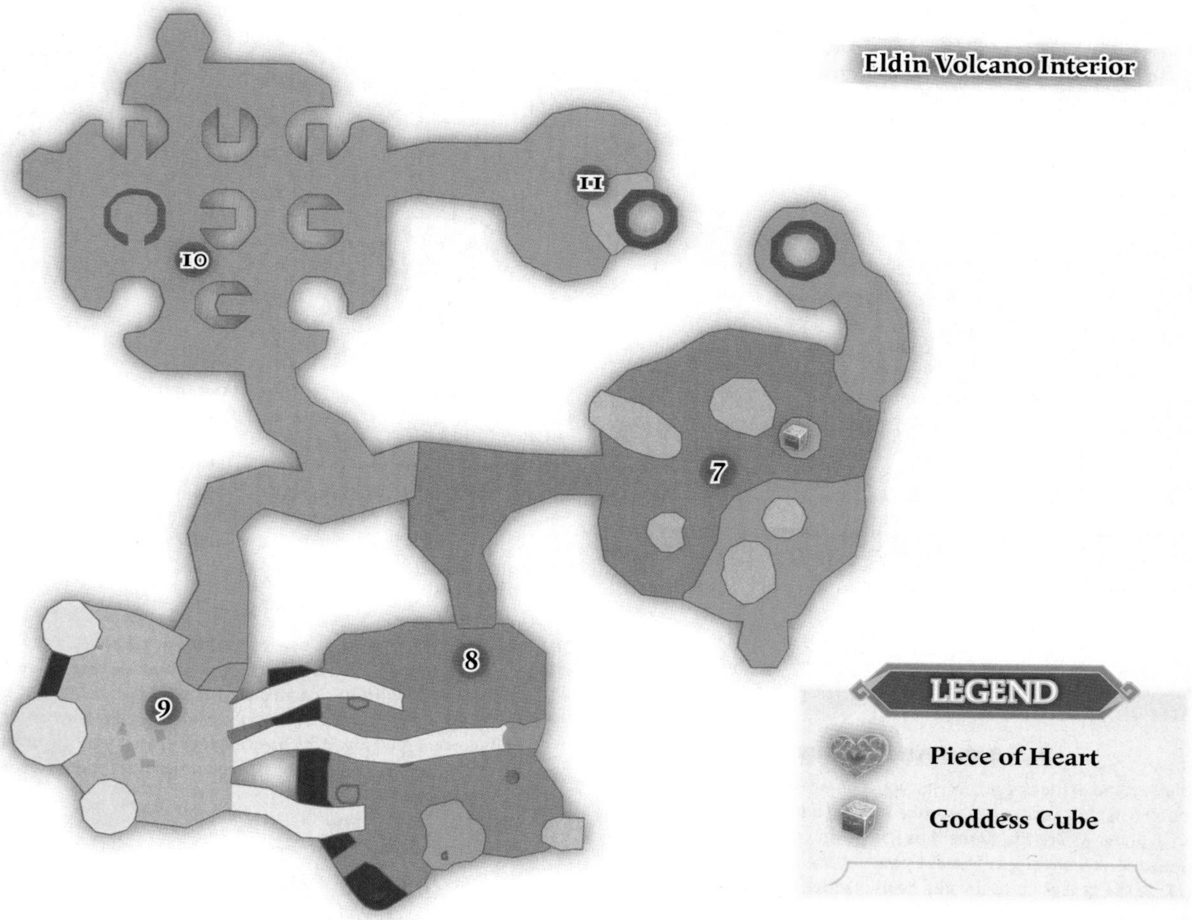

Eldin Volcano Interior

11

10

7

8

9

LEGEND

Piece of Heart

Goddess Cube

7. The Big Dive

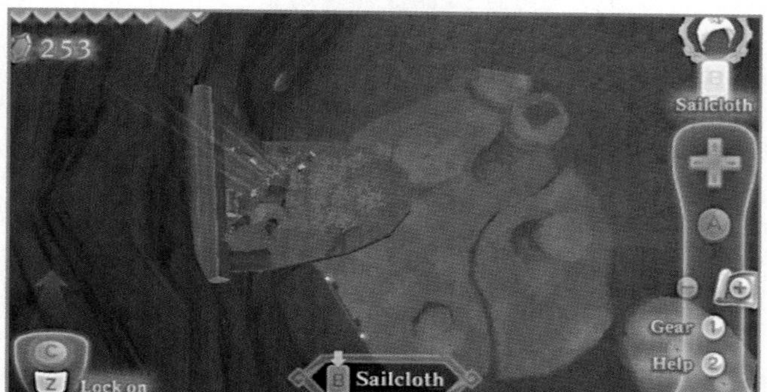

Once you dive, you'll see that there's a lot of loot you can nab on the way down. There's a blue chest containing a random treasure to your left, Goddess Cube #6 to your right, and a tall pillar where Bomb Flowers are growing. If you land on the platform with the Bomb Flowers, you can use them to bomb a cracked area along the south wall that reveals another blue chest containing a random treasure.

You'll probably miss most (or all) of this treasure on your first dive, which is fine. Once you land at the bottom of the entrance to Eldin Volcano, head toward the passage that branches off the room to the northeast. At the end of that passage is an Amber Relic, along with a massive geyser that launches you back outside. Use this massive geyser to repeat the dive as many times as necessary. There's no trick to controlling Link's dive, just tilt the Wii Remote appropriately.

Random Treasure Chests

Sometimes in Skyward Sword, blue chests contain treasures you can use to upgrade equipment. All of the contents of chests that contain treasures in this game are completely random. You might get a rare Goddess Plume or you might get your 27th Jelly Blob. It will be different every time you play the game.

An enterprising player might think, "Wait, does that mean I can save before I open one of these blue chests and just reset the game until I get the type of treasure I want?" In theory, yes. If you save your game before you open a chest containing a random treasure, you can load your game endlessly and get a different treasure each time.

In practice, though, trying to get a specific treasure out of each random chest is extremely time-consuming. It's actually more time-consuming than just getting the treasures you need by going out and hunting for them. In light of that, save-scumming random treasures is not recommended. Just think of the random treasures from chests as bonuses and hope you get lucky.

8. Burly Bokoblin Brawl

Once you're done diving for treasure, save at the bird statue and then move on to trigger a cutscene involving a Mogma. After that, head into the room full of Red Bokoblins. The trick of this battle is that the Red Bokoblins on the ground will respawn infinitely until you get rid of the Red Bokoblin leader up on the wooden catwalk. Once you've defeated every Bokoblin in the room, return and speak with the Mogma again. You receive a reward for your efforts.

DIGGING MITTS

Digging Mitts let you dig whenever you stand near a patch of dirt marked with a cross. You can dig in a dirt patch multiple times, until there's nothing left but a dark hole in the ground. Most dirt patches contain handfuls of Rupees or hearts, but several in the Eldin Volcano area contain the treasure Eldin Ore. You can also occasionally turn up a Fairy by digging in just the right place.

TIP

If you're using an Iron Shield in this area, then you really want to get your mitts (pun intended) on Eldin Ore. You need two Eldin Ores, two Ornamental Skulls, and two Monster Claws to make the Reinforced Shield, which is the best shield you can carry in this part of the game.

9. Sliding for Treasure

Now that you have the Digging Mitts, you can move forward by digging at a dirt patch that conceals a geyser. Ride it up to enter an area of tunnels you can explore. Where the tunnel forks, head down the branch immediately ahead of you and dig at the dirt patch at the end to reveal another geyser. Ride the geyser up to an area near a ladder. Climb up the ladder to explore a ramshackle village the Bokoblin invaders have set up. Defeat the Bokoblins in the area, then go down the center tunnel slide to claim a random treasure from the blue chest in the room where you fought the respawning Bokoblins before.

10. The Pyrup Maze

Backtrack to the area where the tunnel forks and head down the tunnel to the right this time. This brings you into a maze consisting of seven round rock pillars, six of which play host to flame-spewing Pyrups hiding in tiny caves. Pick your way through the pillars while avoiding the Pyrups' fire breath and looking for areas where Bomb Flowers grow. You can't eliminate every Pyrup in the maze, but you can eliminate the ones that block your way to the room's exit with Bomb Flowers. Be sure to search along the north and west walls for patches of cracked rubble you can blast away with Bomb Flowers. One contains Rupees, the other a blue chest containing a random treasure.

11. Going Back Outside

At the end of the next tunnel is another dirt patch you can dig at to reveal a small geyser. Ride the geyser up to a platform where an enormous geyser that leads to the surface is located. You emerge on a new rocky area. Speak to the Mogma just outside the area and he points out that the bridge to the temple is knocked out. A cutscene ensues and suddenly you have a bridge to cross. Before you move on, use a nearby Bomb Flower to clear away some rocks blocking a path. Now you can use the open path to backtrack quickly to the area around the skeleton bridge.

12. The Fallen Tower

Cross the bridge to enter the upper half of Eldin Volcano. On the other side of the bridge, you'll find a long bridge-like wooden structure. There's nothing you can do with this particular structure, but examine it carefully. It's actually a guard tower that was clearly knocked down when one of the Bomb Flowers growing at its base exploded. So if you see any towers standing upright in the near future, you could convert them into bridges by bombing their bases.

13. The First Climb

Save at the bird statue. Head up the path nearby and fight the swarm of Fire Keese you encounter. You emerge at the bottom of a steep, sandy slope. You can get up it, but you have to dash. If your stamina runs out while you're dashing, you'll immediately slide uncontrollably down the slope. To get up this one, first dash to the wooden platforms halfway up. They're patrolled by Red Bokoblins, but you should defeat them easily. Once you're standing on the platforms, your stamina gauge can refill.

Next, dash across to a stone platform with two patches of digable dirt and a Bomb Flower. While standing on this platform, look down to see the beginning of a stone path blocked by rubble. Roll the Bomb Flower down to blast the rubble away and open a shortcut that leads back down to the bottom of Eldin Volcano.

Return to the wooden platforms and look up at the top of the sandy slope. You'll see a Red Bokoblin holding up a boulder that it's clearly ready to roll down at you. Stay on the platform and equip your Slingshot. If you hit the Bokoblin with a Deku Seed while it's holding up a boulder, it'll lose its grip and be crushed to death. You have just enough stamina to dash up to the area it was guarding. Once there, head right and fight your way through the Bokoblins in the village. Once in the village, roll a Bomb Flower toward the cracked wall behind the Bokoblin huts on the left. This leads to a new minigame.

14. Thrill Digger

The Beginner course has less spots to burrow into, but it's great for first-timers!

The Thrill Digger is a minigame you can play to earn Rupees. Each level is a grid where Bomb Flowers, Green Rupees, Blue Rupees, and Red Rupees are placed in a semi-random configuration. On higher difficulties, the dreaded Rupoor also appears. Generally, Bomb Flowers and Rupoors are most likely to be adjacent to valuable Red Rupees, while dirt patches near Green Rupees tend to be safer. Your game ends whenever you pick up a Bomb Flower, with the goal of the game to pick up as many Rupees as possible.

Thrill Digger has three difficulty levels: Beginner, Intermediate, and Expert. A Beginner round costs 30 Rupees and you dig on a 5 x 4 grid of dirt patches, while Intermediate costs 50 Rupees and you play on a 6 x 5 grid. Expert rounds cost 70 Rupees but you play on an 8 x 5 grid. The idea is that the higher difficulties offer the prospect of greater riches, since there are more spots to dig, but are also riskier. Your chances of picking up a Bomb Flower or Rupoor also increase along with the total number of dirt patches.

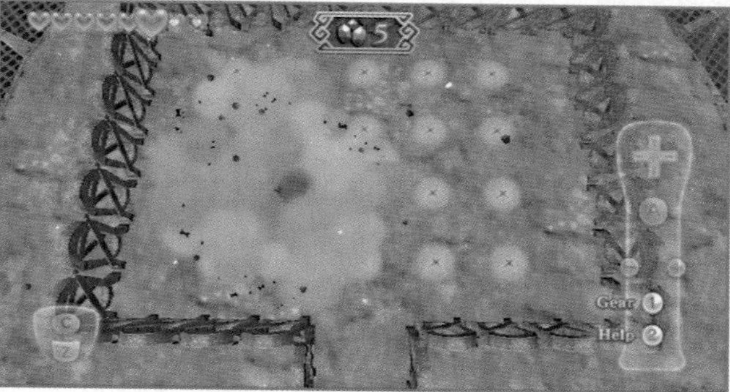

So how worthwhile is Thrill Digger for a player who wants to turn a profit? Not so good. On all of the courses, you'll have to play extraordinarily well just to make back your initial investment. The more difficult courses are actually less lucrative, since Rupoors increase the likelihood that you'll lose money. You're most likely to turn a profit on the Beginner course, but about the best you're likely to do is double your money. Thrill Digger is fun to play around with if you have money to burn, but look elsewhere for ways to earn fast cash.

> **TIP**
>
> Before you leave the Thrill Digger room, examine its walls. You should see that it's lined with great chunks of Rupee ore. Shoot at the appropriate chunk of ore to knock down some Rupees. This is actually a better source of fast cash than playing Thrill Digger, provided you don't shoot at the black Rupoor ore.

15. Make Your Own Bridge

Explore the Bokoblin village a bit more. A wooden guard tower stands near a gap. There's a Bokoblin leader standing atop the tower, but by now you've probably put any other Bokoblin he could summon to the sword. You can see a path on the other side and the gap isn't very wide...actually, it's about as wide as the guard tower is tall. Knock this tower over by throwing a Bomb Flower toward its base. Use the patch of Bomb Flowers that grow near the entrance to Thrill Digger.

Now you can proceed by using the tower as a bridge. At the end of the passage, vines cover a wall. Climb up to find a narrow stone pathway patrolled by an enormous Red Chuchu. Follow the path to find yourself at the bottom of another sandy slope patrolled by Red Bokoblins. Dash up to the wooden platforms located halfway up the slope. Quickly defeat the two Bokoblins that guard them. Keep an eye out for boulders, which the Bokoblins farther up the slope try to roll down at you.

16. The Second Climb

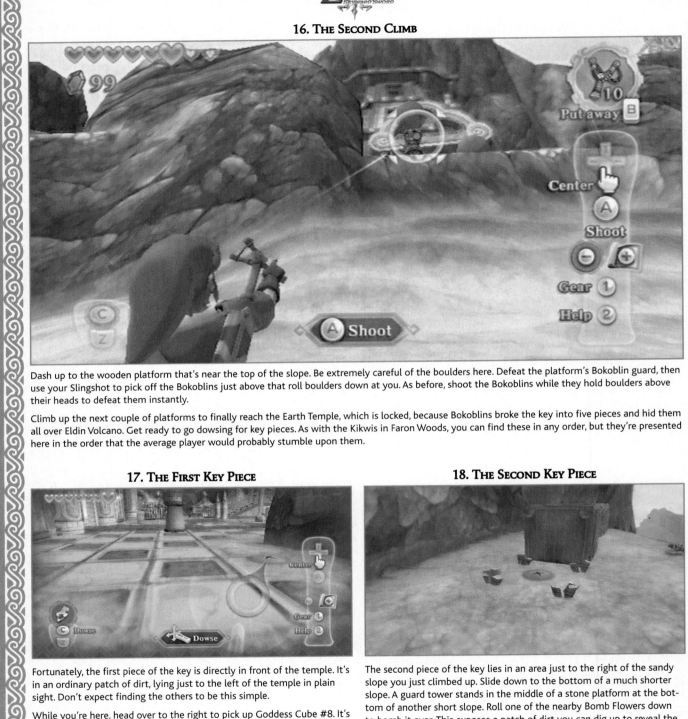

Dash up to the wooden platform that's near the top of the slope. Be extremely careful of the boulders here. Defeat the platform's Bokoblin guard, then use your Slingshot to pick off the Bokoblins just above that roll boulders down at you. As before, shoot the Bokoblins while they hold boulders above their heads to defeat them instantly.

Climb up the next couple of platforms to finally reach the Earth Temple, which is locked, because Bokoblins broke the key into five pieces and hid them all over Eldin Volcano. Get ready to go dowsing for key pieces. As with the Kikwis in Faron Woods, you can find these in any order, but they're presented here in the order that the average player would probably stumble upon them.

17. The First Key Piece

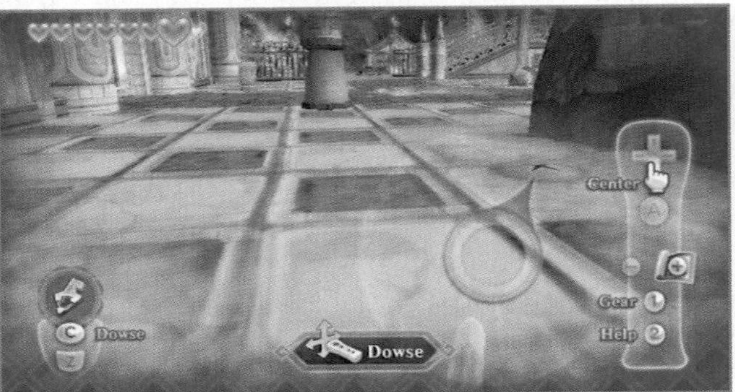

Fortunately, the first piece of the key is directly in front of the temple. It's in an ordinary patch of dirt, lying just to the left of the temple in plain sight. Don't expect finding the others to be this simple.

While you're here, head over to the right to pick up Goddess Cube #8. It's on a high stone platform that you can't reach, but there should be a patch of dirt where you can dig nearby. This reveals a steam geyser you can ride up to the platform so you can activate the Cube.

18. The Second Key Piece

The second piece of the key lies in an area just to the right of the sandy slope you just climbed up. Slide down to the bottom of a much shorter slope. A guard tower stands in the middle of a stone platform at the bottom of another short slope. Roll one of the nearby Bomb Flowers down to bomb it over. This exposes a patch of dirt you can dig up to reveal the piece of the key. Backtrack up to the temple after you claim it.

NOTE

Yes, there's a big pinwheel lying on the ground next to the guard tower. No, you can't do anything with it right now. Yes, you'll want to come back to get it later as part of the main quest.

19. The Third Key Piece

You can find the third piece of the key just below you, along the big sandy slope. Don't go after it just yet. Instead, walk over to a pair of Bomb Flowers growing on a ledge that overlooks the slope. Roll or throw one down to blast away a patch of rubble along the left-hand wall. This reveals a small cave that contains a dirt patch where you can dig. Slide down there to obtain the key piece.

20. The Fourth Key Piece

Head back up to the area in front of the temple, then head right into another Bokoblin village. Take out the Bokoblins in the area, then blast down the guard tower at the back of the village. Before you cross the bridge, follow a path that leads down to a small stone platform just beneath the village. There you can find and activate Goddess Cube #6.

Cross the bridge and enter a winding cave path. Fight off the swarm of Fire Keese that attack as you pass through. Check behind a large rock in your path to find an Amber Relic. At the end of the tunnel, the bridge you need to proceed is out. This time, you won't get it replaced for you in a cutscene. Instead, take another way around. Check along the left-hand wall and find a narrow ledge that winds around to a rocky path. At the end of the path is a patch of vines you can climb on to reach the area at the far side of the missing bridge.

Pass through the stone archway to enter a large cave. Step on the switch just inside to cause the missing bridge to slide back into place. Follow the stone path out of this first cave and toward a chamber so hot that just stepping into it makes you burst into flames. You want to pass through here. While you can't survive long enough to make it to the upper-left area, you can dash into a tunnel that lets you slide down a long, sandy slope.

This slope is basically a giant slide, with a few stone platforms you can maneuver Link toward with the control stick. There's a lot of loot stuffed into the platforms there, including Goddess Cube #7, but you may have to slide down several times to get it. For now, when you get to the bottom of the slide, follow the path that leads away from it. A lava plug dams up some lava that's blocking your path. Roll a nearby Bomb Flower toward it to clear the way.

Now, roll a Bomb Flower across to blast the rubble remaining after the lava recedes. This reveals a small cave with a single patch of dirt inside it. Dash across using the sandy slope nearby and dig to receive the fourth piece of the key. Backtrack to the stone platforms at the base of the big slope. Take the other branch to reach an area with an enormous geyser you can ride up to the very top of Eldin Volcano. There's also a pile of rubble you can bomb to create a shortcut back to the area with the first fallen guard tower.

21. The Fifth Key Piece

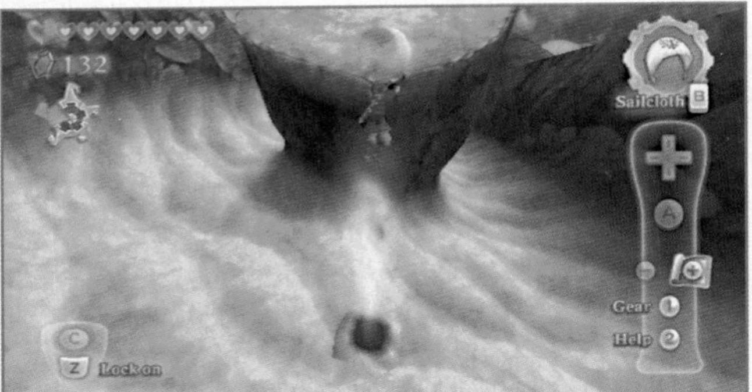

Now you can slide back down and try to get Goddess Cube #7 and the remaining piece of the key. To get it, veer to the left once you emerge from the slide's first tunnel. Aim yourself at the geyser and ride it up to the top of the platform, where you can dig up some Eldin Ore. Then drop to the platform just beneath that one to reach and activate Goddess Cube #7.

You'll need to take another slide down to get the fifth piece of the key. This time veer to the right and ride the geyser up to the first platform. You can dig here to find a Fairy. Hop down from this platform and veer down the right branch, but hug the left wall of it. This lets you land on another stone platform.

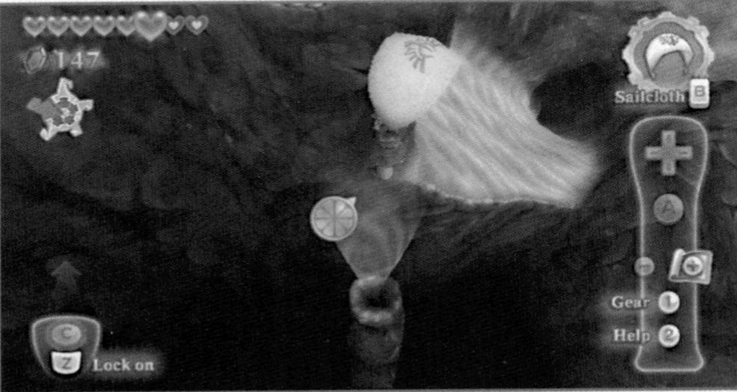

Walk to the left edge of that platform to see a couple of hot air geysers. These geysers are timed, so you don't want to try to move across until both geysers are active at the same time. Use the geysers to leap across to a stone platform that overlooks the left branch of the big slide but can't be reached from it. The fifth piece of the key is buried here.

22. Into the Earth Temple

Slide down to the bottom again and ride the enormous geyser back up to the top of Eldin Volcano one last time. Now you can quickly backtrack to the Earth Temple's entrance. Insert the key and your way into the game's second dungeon opens.

Goddess's Treasure Chest Pickups: #4, #5, #6, #7, #8, #9

Goddess's treasure chest #4 is on a small island to the southeast of Skyloft. It looks like nothing but stone if you approach it from Skyloft, but if you approach it from the opposite direction, you'll find a grassy area that contains the chest. Inside the chest is a Small Seed Satchel.

Goddess's treasure chest #5 is on a small island at the very northernmost area of the sky. Open it to obtain a Silver Rupee worth 100 Rupees.

Goddess's treasure chest #6 is located in Skyloft, in a storage shed that you can't get into right now. We'll come back to this chest later in the game, once you've obtained the item you need to reach it.

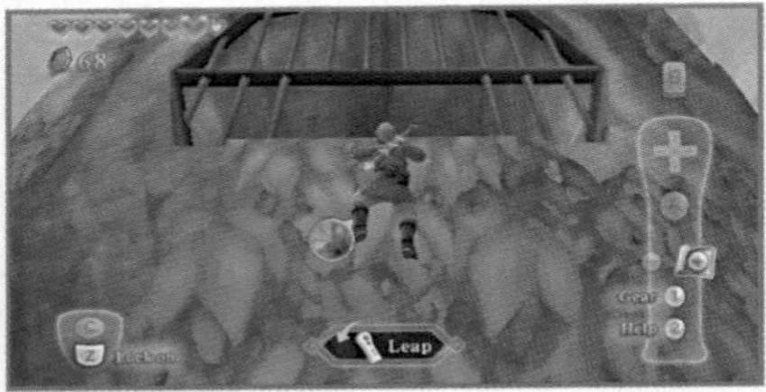

Goddess's treasure chest #7 is on a small island northeast of Skyloft. It's a bit tricky to reach, but you can get it now. Have your Loftwing drop you on the island's upper area and then climb down the vines that dangle off the island's edge. Follow the vines to the left and then climb up into an area that's behind iron bars. Open the goddess's treasure chest there to find a Treasure Medal.

Goddess's treasure chest #8 lays on a round island near the entrance to the Eldin Volcano region. When you dive onto the island, you should see the entrance to Peater's Clean Cut minigame. To find the chest, walk around the minigame's building. On the rear of the island, on a tiny strip of grass, you should find the activated chest. Open it to receive a Gold Rupee.

To get goddess's treasure chest #9, you need to have the Bomb Bag. You won't acquire that until after you've cleared the Earth Temple, so you'll have to wait a bit to pick up this loot.

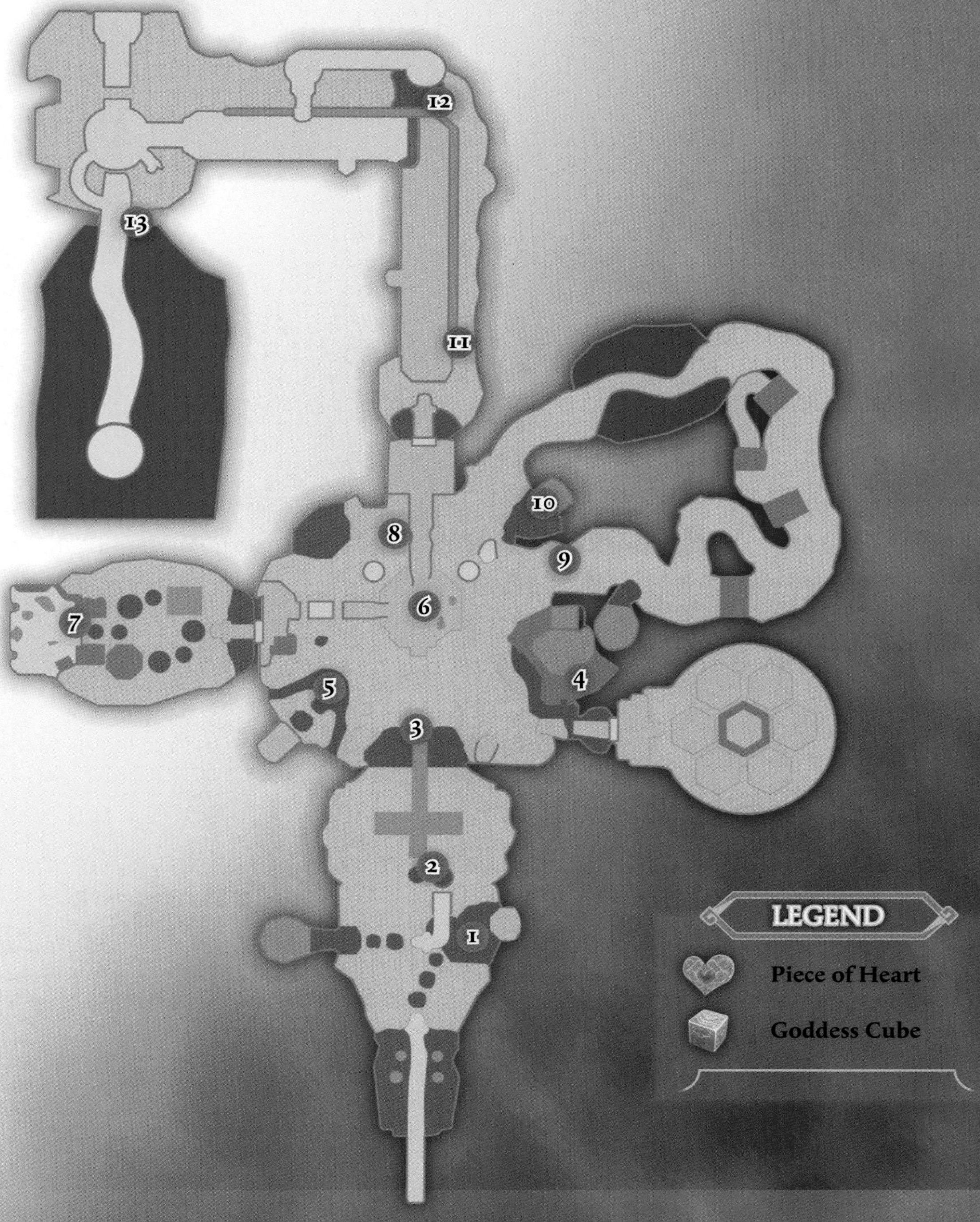

LEGEND

Piece of Heart

Goddess Cube

EARTH TEMPLE

1. Forgotten Riches

This temple is dominated by massive flows of magma. Moving around often involves hopping precariously between platforms. It's incredibly easy to take damage from accidental falls into the magma around you. Always be sure to carry plenty of Heart Potions with you in here.

As you head into the temple, bear to the right. Dig at the first dirt patch you find after crossing the first set of floating rock platforms to reveal a geyser. Ride it up to find a small chest containing a Red Rupee. Next, cross the string of floating platforms that lead to the left into a small cavern. Speak with the Mogma who is waiting there and dig up the dirt patches. Be careful; the one farthest to the left holds a Red Chuchu, not loot.

2. The Burning Path

Head back to the solid stone island where you revealed the geyser earlier. Climb the stairs that lead north to discover a pair of stone platforms that ride up and down on gushing magma fountains. Defeat the Fire Keese that attacks you, then carefully make your way across. It's easiest to hop onto the first platform while it's floating on the magma's surface. To proceed, hop off the second platform while it's high in the air to land on top of a broken staircase.

3. Across the Bridge

Next you need to lower the drawbridge. Walk down to the platform below. Pulley systems are located to the left and right of you. Walk up to each of the pulleys and cut the ropes with your sword. This lowers the drawbridge partway. To lower it the rest of the way, send the Beetle to cut the ropes on a pulley system located on the wall just to the right of the drawbridge. The other side of the drawbridge is guarded by a pair of new enemies.

ENEMY: LIZALFOS

Lizalfos dwell in dungeons, where they guard passageways and important rooms. They're extremely capable fighters that rely on their spiked, clubbed tails to bludgeon their enemies. If that doesn't work, they also have the ability to breathe fire. Lizalfos are clever and breathe their flames in a wide arc in front of them. Every Lizalfos wears an enormous metal gauntlet over its arm, which it can expertly use to defend against an enemy's attacks. They are also nimble, so hold down Z as you fight one so you can stay locked on.

There are two ways you can fight a Lizalfos. The slow, patient way involves waiting for it to initiate its spinning tail-bash attack, then shield-bashing it. This staggers the Lizalfos, giving you an opening that lets you pelt it with damage. You only need to stagger a Lizalfos twice to defeat it.

The downside to this technique is that the Lizalfos may get irritated with you and start breathing fire, which even an Iron Shield won't block. Quickly dodge around a Lizalfos's flames. If you're nimble enough, you can get close to the Lizalfos and damage it from behind while it's exhaling fire.

The other way to fight a Lizalfos is to be aggressive. Pelt it with rapid sword strikes that force it onto the defensive. No Lizalfos has a perfect defensive stance. Once you've forced a Lizalfos to defend, you can then change up your attack pattern to hit the Lizalfos's weakness. If (for example) the Lizalfos is crouching and blocking high with its gauntlet, then you need to attack with ascending diagonal slashes that hit it from its unprotected side.

The danger of taking an extremely aggressive approach is the Lizalfos attacking unexpectedly while you're battering it with sword strikes. If it tries to breathe flame, you'll probably hit it before it can damage you, but if it tries to use its tail-bash attack you'll get damaged if you don't quickly dodge back. You usually won't have time to shield-bash if you're fighting aggressively.

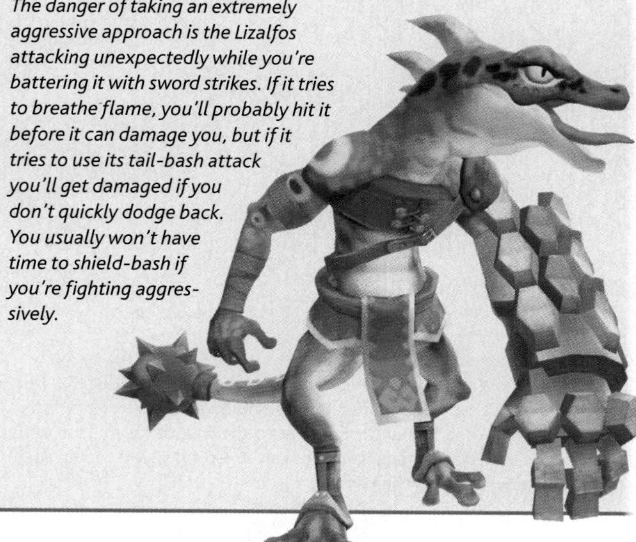

ENEMY: MAGMA SPUME

Magma Spumes are large, frog-like creatures that lurk in the Earth Temple's magma flows. If you pass too near to them, they begin hopping out of the water so they can spit bolts of fire at you. Once you obtain the Bomb Bag, you can easily defeat them by throwing bombs at them. For now, you have to settle for dizzying them with your Slingshot if you're forced to pass by one.

Once the Lizalfos is defeated, you can pick up an Amber Relic just to the right of the doorway. Then step forward and examine the area. Off to the right there's a Magma Spume you need to be careful around. In front of you is a curious-looking statue that has Bomb Flowers growing all over it. Launch the Beetle at the statue and have it crash into one of the Bomb Flowers. This destroys the statue and sends its stone eyeball floating through the magma, toward the platform where you're standing now. Hop onto the stone eyeball and use it to travel through the magma freely. Just move the control stick in the desired direction and Link starts rolling it with his feet. Don't roll too fast, or he might lose his balance.

TIP

Once you have the stone eyeball, you've got another way of killing Magma Spumes at your disposal. Roll toward a Magma Spume and it tries to retreat from you. If you can use the eyeball to force it into a wall or something else solid, you can roll over the Spume and kill it.

4. Bombs with Friends

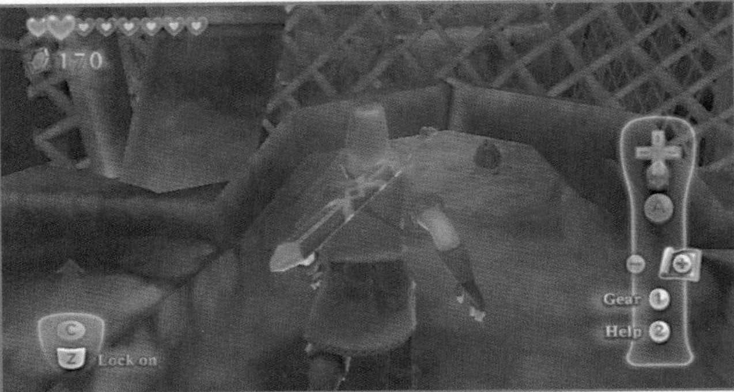

Roll over to the area just beyond the Magma Spume, where a Mogma is waiting. Talk to the Mogma, who's lamenting the loss of his Bomb Bag. He asks you to head into an area infested with Red Bokoblins and get it back. You can't bomb the cracked wall the Mogma points out to you, but you can crawl under a section of fence to get into the area where the Bokoblins are waiting. Kill the Bokoblin that's immediately in front of you, then roll a Bomb Flower under the fence and toward the cracked wall.

The blast exposes a door. Don't pass through it unless you're ready for a pretty tough fight. Once you step into this room, you're locked into a sub-boss encounter with two Lizalfos. There is no easy way to get through this fight beyond being able to kill a Lizalfos very quickly. Once you emerge victorious, a blue chest appears in the middle of the room. Inside the chest is the Mogma's missing Bomb Bag. The Mogma is so incredibly grateful that he just lets you keep his Bomb Bag.

The Bomb Bag

Now that you have a Bomb Bag, you can convert unstable Bomb Flowers into stable bombs that you can carry around with you. Pick up a Bomb Flower and press Ⓑ to stick it into your bag to make it into a bomb. Bombs let you open up hidden caverns, knock over structures, and even defeat enemies in certain cases. The biggest advantage to using bombs over wild Bomb Flowers is that bombs have a longer fuse, which gives you more time to get them into a desired position.

Walk around the top edge of the fence around the fenced-in area to a dirt patch; it turns up a Fairy when you dig into it. Bottle her up (if you can) before you return to your stone eyeball. Roll it through the magma over to the platform left of the chamber's entrance.

5. Rolling for Treasure

Once there, hop onto a stone platform that is riding up and down on a fountain of magma. Use a bomb to clear the rubble out of the pathway in front of it. Your best bet for doing this is to place a bomb at the far edge of the platform, then hop off and see if the timing is right for the bomb to clear out the rubble when it goes off. Once the rubble is gone, you can enter a small chamber and open a blue chest to claim a random treasure.

6. Rolling to Battle

Roll your stone eyeball toward the large stone platform at the center of this chamber. Save at the bird statue. Climb the stairs and detonate a bomb to clear the stone debris out of your path. Fight the Lizalfos waiting just beyond, once you can proceed. Open the door to emerge into a chamber full of magma fountains, rock platforms, and a Magma Spume sitting in the center of it all.

7. The Ancient Map

Sometimes you can grab an Amber Relic to your right. Dizzy the Magma Spume in the center of the platforms as you move around them. Bokoblins guard each of the larger platforms. Dispatch them quickly. The Magma Spume can take potshots at you while you fight. Once you're on the far side of the ring of platforms, hop onto the small rock platform located between the two large metal platforms. Wait a moment for a fountain of magma to carry you up to the top of the metal platform. Fight the Bokoblins waiting for you at the top. Open the blue chest they were guarding to get the Dungeon Map. Return to the platform where you left the stone eyeball.

8. Yes, That's a Switch

To clear the dungeon, you need to get through the door at the north of this area. Some platforms are going in the right direction, but at the moment they're too low. Stand on the middle platform and look down to see some curious metal protrusions, a bit like dumbbells, sticking out from either side of the platform. You need to press each of these by rolling the stone eyeball into them.

Getting the one on the left should be easy. Just roll the stone eyeball beneath the broken archway where you fought a Lizalfos earlier. It's the one on the right that will be difficult. Two broken pillars block you from simply rolling up to it. Instead, roll it over to the wall that's marked with a red X on your in-game map. If you look at it carefully, you should see some bombable cracks in the wall.

9. A River of Magma

Throw a bomb at the wall, then another bomb to finish the job. This opens up a long, winding passageway full of magma. Roll your way in and be careful to dodge the wall spouts. You eventually come to a metal platform that seems impossible to get around. Set off a pair of bombs at the nearby crack in the wall to open up a magma-filled passage that you can roll the stone eyeball around. Be ready to defend yourself against the swarm of Fire Keese that swoop out after you open the passage.

You come to a pair of metal platforms and an elaborate red gate that blocks your way. Examine the gate carefully to discover a pulley system on either side of it. You can easily use the Beetle to cut the rope on the pulley system that's on your side of the gate. The tricky part is getting the Beetle around to the pulley system on the gate's far side. You must navigate the Beetle through the passage that opens up just behind the bird statue on the high platform.

Once the gate is up, hop back on your stone eyeball and roll onward. You can stop at the metal platform just through the threshold to run back through the passage, defeat the Bokoblins patrolling it, and then save at the bird statue you could previously see but not reach. To move forward, you need to get past the spout on the wall that periodically spews magma. Wait for the spout to surge, then quickly roll through before the next surge begins.

Past the magma spout, you reach an unnerving area where magma somehow flows in a winding path through a yawning, bottomless chasm. Pause at the far end to fight the Fire Keese that swarm at you just before you pass through the room's exit. Finally, you emerge back in the dungeon's central chamber, but this time on the far side of the broken pillars that blocked you in earlier.

10. Some Pocket Money

Before you push the switch in, roll over toward the chamber's right wall to reach an area where a Lizalfos guards a small chest. Defeat the Lizalfos and claim the chest's Red Rupee. Next, push the switch in and head down the stone hallway that you can reach now. Sometimes there's an Amber Relic waiting just to your left, inside the threshold that leads to the next room.

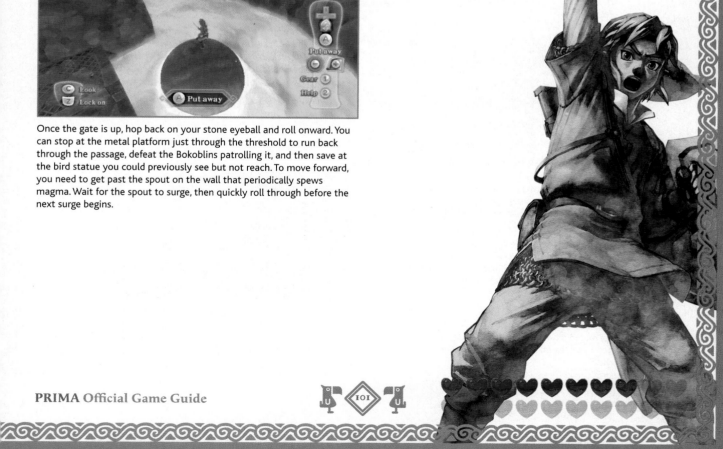

11. Hill of Death

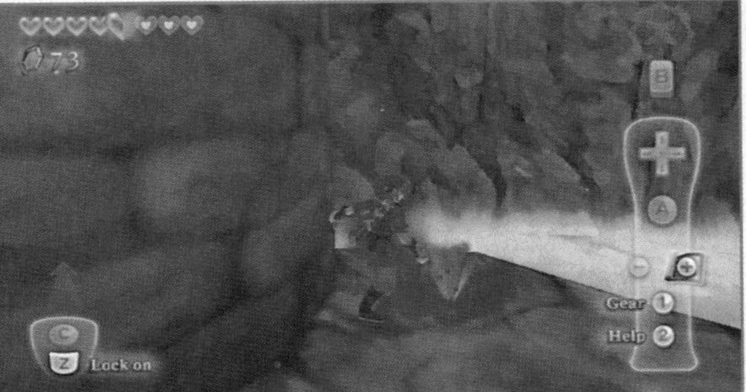

The next room is a tremendous upward slope. As you run upward, you trigger mechanisms that make boulders rain down on you. Take advantage of the alcove halfway up the slope to rest and avoid the wave of boulders. After a wave passes, hop out of the alcove and dash up. You come to the base of another enormous slope. On this slope, though, the alcove you'd need to avoid the boulders that rain down on you is blocked with rubble. Don't head up just yet.

12. Hill of Extra Death

Instead, crawl into a little tunnel that leads off to the right of the slope's bottom. Dig at a patch of dirt at the base of the massive stone pillar you find in this area. That reveals a geyser you can ride up to the top of the pillar. Once you're at the top, run up the stairs to find a platform that overlooks the second slope. From here, you can toss a bomb down to blast away the rubble blocking the entrance to the alcove. Throw your bomb up the slope a little from the alcove, so it goes off as it's rolling down the slope.

13. Raider of the Lost Key

Now that you've found the dungeon's final door, it's time to go hunting for the jeweled chest that contains the key carving. Head up the winding staircase that leads to a long, suspiciously sloping stone pathway. At the top of it is the jeweled chest. Open it to receive the Dragon Sculpture that opens the dungeon's final door.

After you take a few steps back down the way you came, a boulder drops down and rolls toward you. To outrun it, dash all the way down the slope and into the stairwell as soon as possible. Grabbing the Stamina Fruits on the pathway is very helpful. If the boulder hits you, it's an instant Game Over.

If you do manage to dodge the boulder, it'll block the flow of magma that's cutting you off from the dungeon's final door. Save your game one last time. If you're prepared for a boss battle, then go ahead and use the Dragon Sculpture to unlock the door. If you're not, then now's a good time to backtrack to Skyloft.

BOSS: SCALDERA

To initiate the battle with Scaldera, walk toward the top of the sloping path in the boss room. Dodge to the side as Scaldera's boulder-like form initially rolls down at you. Once Scaldera is beneath you, the battle can begin. Scaldera is an enormous demon of rock and fire, with a single eye leering at you from its boulder-like body. It moves with disconcerting speed on its six spindly legs.

Scaldera's attack pattern is extremely simple and exploitable, if you're brave enough to get close to it. Scaldera periodically opens its mouth, inhaling an enormous amount of air, before it breathes a hail of fireballs upward at you. You want to interrupt this attack by getting close enough to Scaldera to throw a bomb at it while it's inhaling. If Scaldera swallows a bomb, it instantly detonates once it disappears into Scaldera's fiery gullet.

This staggers Scaldera, causing its body to slump and its single eye to sag toward the ground. You damage Scaldera by attacking its eye with your sword. Bombs by themselves do nothing but stun it. As you begin to damage Scaldera, your bombs start reflecting that by blowing off parts of its rocky hide. This isn't the bomb directly hurting Scaldera, it's merely the bomb showing you how much damage you've done with your sword.

You can easily evade Scaldera's fireballs by weaving back and forth as you run up the slope, or running to the top of the boss area and staying very close to either wall. The main danger in Scaldera's fireball attack is that you'll run out of stamina while running away from it, becoming an exhausted sitting duck.

After each attack barrage, Scaldera moves a little bit closer to the top of the boss area. This makes it easier to attack, if you're trying to play it safe and stick to the upper area. In its initial forms, Scaldera won't be able to move up any farther than the Bomb Flowers that grow near the top of the slope. Later in the battle, Scaldera will be able to chase you all the way up to the top of the boss room.

Any explosion drives Scaldera back down the slope, so you can always roll a bomb when it's getting too close for comfort. Generally, the closer to the bottom Scaldera is, the more risky it is for you to try and damage it. If you just stick to the safe area at the top, though, you'll never be close enough to get a bomb in its mouth and the boss fight will drag on forever.

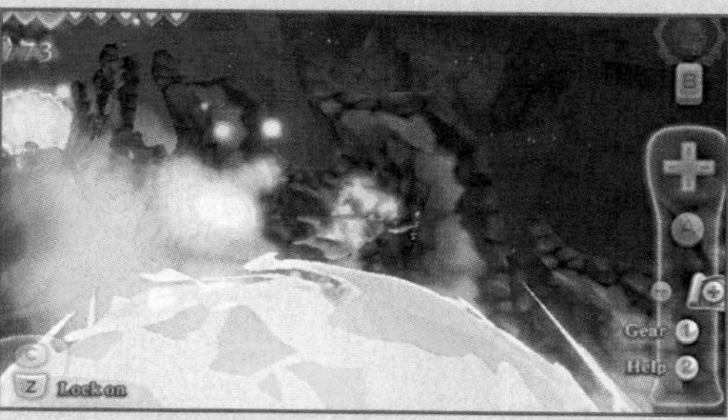

Once you've damaged Scaldera enough that all of the rock has flown off of its body, its attack pattern changes. Scaldera is mostly harmless early in the fight, but in this phase Scaldera can very easily kill you. Its body begins to glow white-hot and it becomes extremely fast. Now Scaldera charges at you, knocking you over if you can't get out of the way. If Scaldera gets above you, it will roll its burning body down at you like a fiery boulder. Its fireball barrage becomes more dangerous, the fireballs flying wider and able to hit the areas along the boss room's walls that were previously safe.

The window for getting a bomb into its mouth also grows shorter, which makes trying to damage it riskier. You want to use the same basic tactics to finish Scaldera off, but you can't afford to stay in the safe zone at the top of the boss area (which isn't very safe at this point, anyway). Stay near Scaldera and rely on being able to dodge through its fireball assault and its rolling boulder attack. As long as you don't let your stamina gauge run down and have some Health Potions or Fairies on hand, you should come through the battle fine.

This battle requires you to have plenty of bombs on hand. You can only carry 10, and if you're having difficulty with the timing required to get a bomb in Scaldera's mouth, you may run out. If this happens, run up to the top of the boss room and refill your Bomb Bag by picking Bomb Flowers. You can also refill your life with hearts here, which can help you get farther in the fight while using fewer Health Potions or Fairies.

Your reward for defeating Scaldera is a Heart Container. You're going to need it. You can pass through the door at the top of the boss area now and activate the crest in the next room with a Skyward Strike. This triggers a cutscene where you receive the last fragment of the Ancient Tablet, which is called the Amber Tablet. After that, you're automatically taken back to the beginning of the dungeon.

Skyloft

Return to the base of the Statue of the Goddess in Skyloft. Set the last piece of the tablet in place to open the pillar of light that lets you dive into the game's next region, Lanayru Desert. Resupply your Health Potions and invest any spare Rupees you have in Beedle's Extra Wallets and Adventure Pouch slots.

If you used an Iron or Reinforced Shield in this area, visit the Item Check girl and leave it with her. Lanayru Desert's enemies tend to use electrical attacks that a metal shield cannot defend against. You'll want to take a Banded Shield into Lanayru Desert with you instead. If you haven't made the Banded Shield yet, do so before moving on.

Also, Rupin is now selling the Small Bomb Bag, which lets you carry extra bombs. As with the other ammo bags, it's not recommended that you buy this. You can get one for free out of a goddess's treasure chest, so you're better off saving your Rupees for other things.

Lanayru Desert

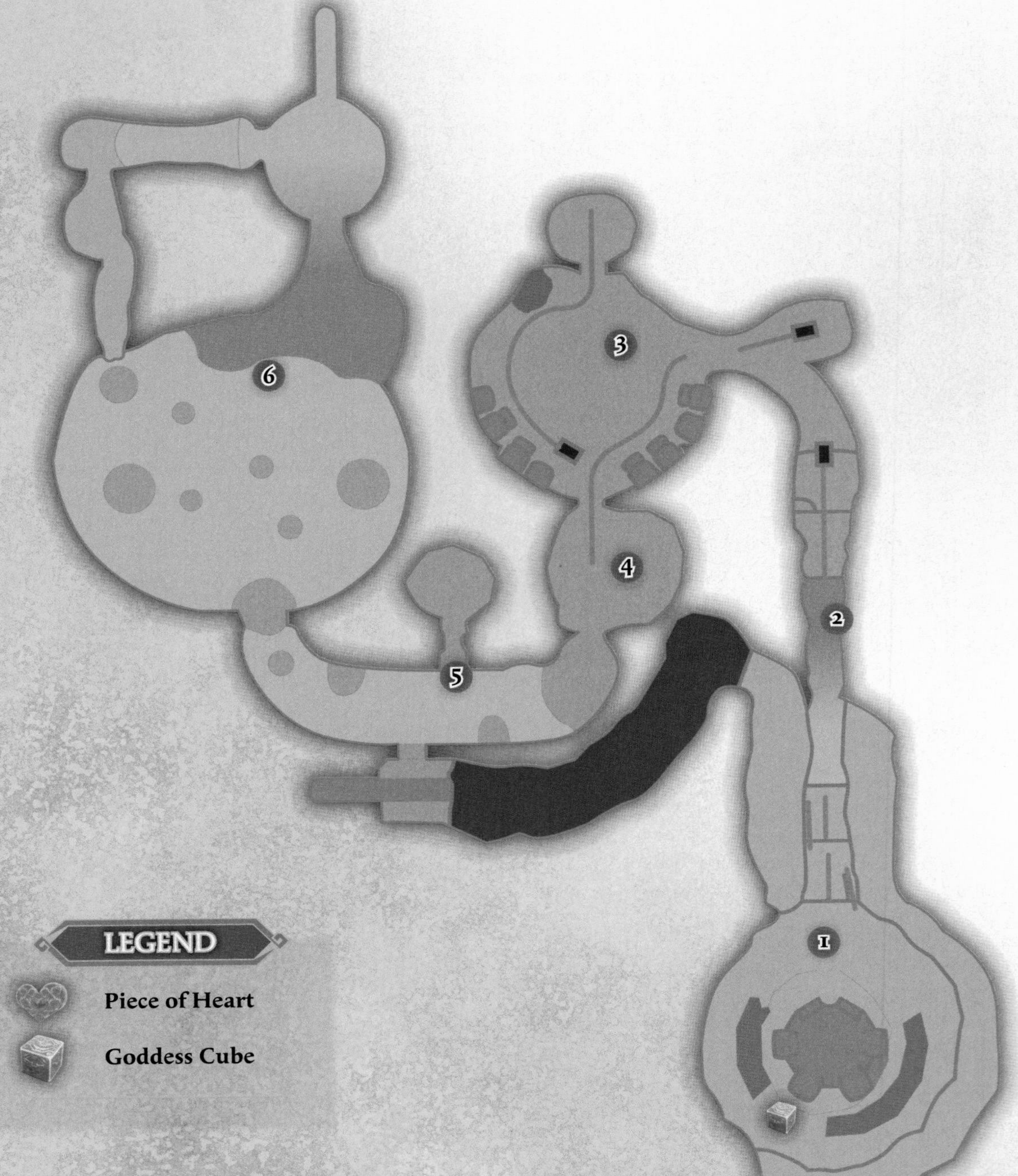

LEGEND

Piece of Heart

Goddess Cube

Lanayru Mine

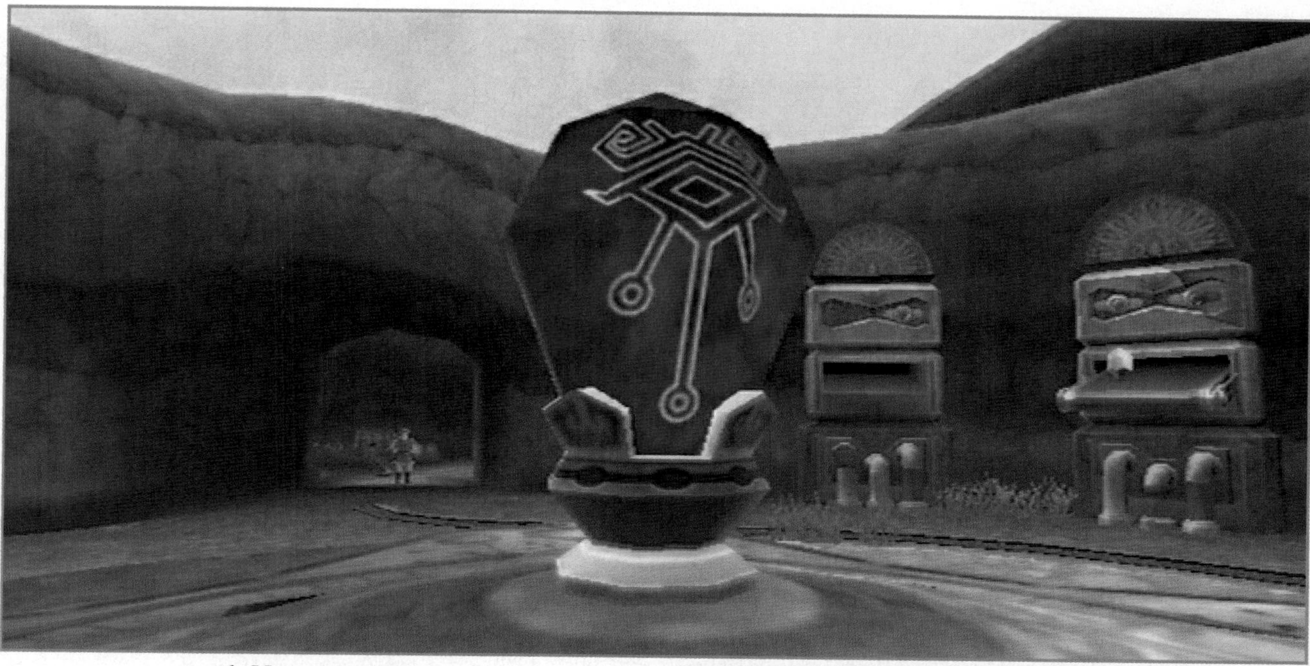

1. High and Dry

Lanayru Mine is the doorway to the much larger and more challenging Lanayru Desert region. Think of Lanayru Mine as a tutorial area that introduces you to the dangers (and riches) you can expect to find in *Skyward Sword*'s desert areas. Proceed forward to start tracking Zelda and solving some very unusual puzzles.

You land on a tall stone pillar. Don't hesitate to drop to the bottom area. Just northeast of the base is Goddess Cube #10. If you investigate the base of the pillar more thoroughly, you'll find small piles of rubble that look thoroughly bombable. Most of the rubble piles you encounter throughout this area just contain Green or Blue Rupees. The walkthrough will point out any you need to bomb to advance. Fortunately, there are plenty of Bomb Flowers throughout this area, so it's not hard to keep your Bomb Bag full. Save at the bird statue at the entrance of this area before you move on.

2. Mine Carts

Head down the long, descending passage into the mine. Eventually you come to a long-abandoned mine cart that's blocking the path. Push it forward along the track to an area where the path ahead drops sharply, causing a break in the track. Push the cart down into the pit and then move it against the far wall. You can stand on it to climb the far wall. While you're in the pit, you encounter the first of an irritating new type of enemy.

Enemy: Yellow Chuchu

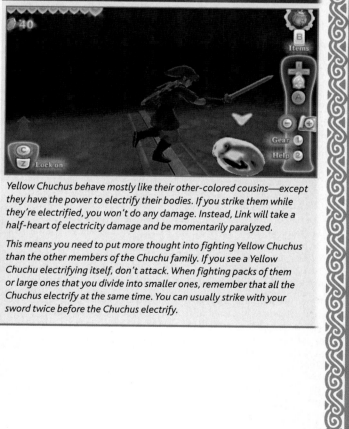

Yellow Chuchus behave mostly like their other-colored cousins—except they have the power to electrify their bodies. If you strike them while they're electrified, you won't do any damage. Instead, Link will take a half-heart of electricity damage and be momentarily paralyzed.

This means you need to put more thought into fighting Yellow Chuchus than the other members of the Chuchu family. If you see a Yellow Chuchu electrifying itself, don't attack. When fighting packs of them or large ones that you divide into smaller ones, remember that all the Chuchus electrify at the same time. You can usually strike with your sword twice before the Chuchus electrify.

3. Back in Time

TIP

Deploy the Beetle to grab the Rupees on the conveyor belts.

Go right at the end of the passage to enter a small cave filled with piles of rubble, a mine cart, and a pair of Yellow Chuchus. Step into the large round room just beyond to see your first Timeshift Stone. These mysterious objects are a major fixture of dungeons in the Lanayru Desert region. If you strike one with your sword...well, just do it and see for yourself.

Suddenly the brown, drab desert is an explosion of color. The broken-down robots are functional again, grass and flowers grow everywhere, and the mine cart system glows with power. By striking a Timeshift Stone, you transport the areas nearby back in time 1,000 years, to a period when Lanayru Desert was the home of a thriving, highly industrialized civilization.

The time shift that restores power to the mine carts also restores power to the automatic doors, which you can use to move deeper into the mine. Before you leave, though, be sure to grab the Ancient Flower that appears over by the conveyor belts on the right. This treasure appears only in time-shifted areas of Lanayru Desert. You need one to progress the game's story and five more if you want to upgrade all of Link's equipment.

When you jump into a powered-on mine cart, it moves automatically and won't stop until it reaches the end of its track. If you leap into it again, it'll go back where it came from. Jump into the one that's floating in the round room to enter a cave that holds a small chest, some piles of rubble, and a pair of busily working robots. Open the small chest to receive a Red Rupee.

Head back into the small cave where you fought the Yellow Chuchus earlier. While the mine cart in this room is too far from the Timeshift Stone to be time-shifted, you can physically push and pull it into the round room's time-shifted area. Then once the cart powers back on, you can ride it into the next room.

4. Bomb Toss

Hop out of the mine cart to enter a room that's halfway time-shifted into the past and halfway in the present. You can snag an Ancient Flower in the time-shifted part of the room. Bombing the pile of rubble right along the dividing line between past and present exposes a small, hidden Timeshift Stone. Hit it with your sword to create a new time shift field. Note that doing this cancels out the one you activated in the round room. Only one Timeshift Stone can be active in an area at a time.

Once you've time-shifted the room, head over to the large statue that resembles a giant worker robot holding a basket. Throw a bomb into the basket. The explosion topples the statue forward, revealing a passage into the next room.

5. Basketbomb

This room introduces you to the most omnipresent hazard in Lanayru Desert regions: sinksand. Link cannot move normally in sinksand, and if he tries, he will only sink. Link can dash across sinksand areas, but if he runs out of stamina, he slowly sinks into the sand and eventually dies. Dying in sinksand is like falling down pits: It doesn't reduce your health, but it's frustrating and forces you back to the last solid area you were standing on.

Here, you need to find a way to pass through the long stretch of sinksand that's guarded by the four basket-holding statues. You can dash to a stone platform that's nearby, but you don't have enough stamina to reach the stone platform on the other side of the statues. To proceed, bomb these statues the way you bombed the one in the previous room. Think of it as a game of exploding basketball.

Bomb the statue nearest to you first, then begin bombing the others you can reach. You want to bomb all four of them. Bomb the statue across from the first one you bombed to reveal a Green Rupee and a small tunnel. Hop across and crawl through the tunnel to emerge in a hidden area. A small chest here contains a Red Rupee. From this statue, you can bomb the one next to it. Once all four statues are bombed, you can easily move on to the next stone platform and into the next area.

6. More Sinksand

ENEMY: ELECTRO SPUME

These electric members of the Spume family dwell in sinksand the way their heat-loving cousins dwell in magma. Whereas Magma Spumes spat fire, Electro Spumes spit bursts of paralyzing electricity. As with the Magma Spumes, you do not yet have any tools that will let you defeat them. The best you can do for now is to dizzy them with your Slingshot and otherwise avoid them as much as you can.

The next area is a sea of sinksand dotted with small islands of stone. Dash carefully from island to island to pick your way across the room. While you make your way, you must avoid an annoying new enemy.

You can clearly see a blue chest standing on a tall pillar in the sinksand sea, but you can't reach it. Instead, cross the sea to the area that slopes upward. Enter the small round room at the top of the area and then make a left turn. You'll come to a long passage full of sinksand and containing a Bomb Flower. Roll a bomb toward the pile of rubble that sits in the sinksand. Then roll a second bomb toward the rubble piles at the far end of the passage.

The blast reveals a Timeshift Stone, though it's too far away to hit with your sword. That's no problem. You can use the Beetle to activate Timeshift Stones from afar. Once the area is time shifted, the sinksand in the passage becomes solid ground and you can simply walk to the other side. Be sure to defeat the Quadro Baba that appears and pick up the Ancient Flower on the far side of the passage. Follow the path around toward the blue chest, making sure to fight another Quadro Baba that blocks your way. Open the blue chest to receive a random treasure.

The parts of the sinksand sea in the time-shift effect's range are now solid ground, so simply walk back to the slope that leads up into the round room. When you return to the area at the base of the slope, a Quadro Baba awaits you. The time-shift effect you triggered to get the blue chest extends as far as the old mine cart's track, which now runs all the way up the slope. Push the old mine cart forward on the track until it's time shifted and it powers up. Head back up to the round room and bomb the rubble blocking the track. Now ride the mine cart out of this area and into the next one.

Goddess's Treasure-Chest Pickups: #9, #10

Now that you have the Bomb Bag, you can pick up goddess's treasure chest #9. Return to the island where you picked up chest #7. Drop down on the lower level of the island and then bomb the rubble you see in front of you. Walk inside the cavern to open the goddess's treasure chest and receive a Silver Rupee worth 100 Rupees.

Goddess's treasure chest #10 lies on an island near the Lanayru Desert entrance that's mostly rock. Fly over it with your Loftwing and dive toward the north side. The treasure chest sits there on a small, grassy outcropping just big enough to stand on. Open it to receive a Heart Medal.

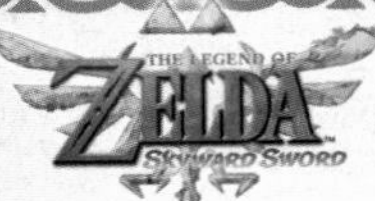

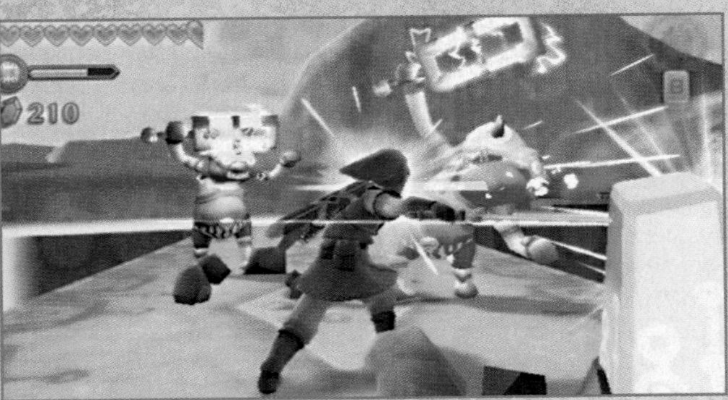

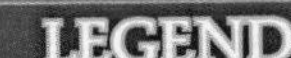

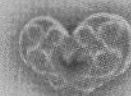 Piece of Heart

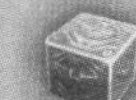 Goddess Cube

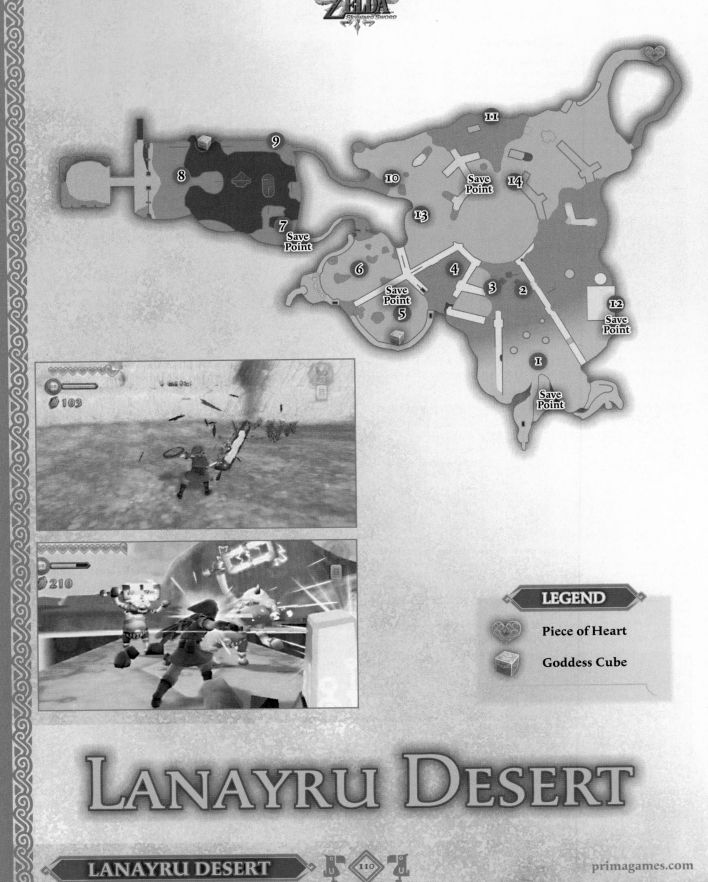

Lanayru Desert

1. The Shocking Sands

Lanayru Desert can be overwhelming at first, because it's such a big area. The way to tackle it is to focus on exploring areas you can reach and disregarding the ones that are, for now, a bit out of your reach. Head immediately down the slope to get acquainted with one of this area's major enemies.

ENEMY: AMPILUS

This enemy is one of the major reasons why you were urged to bring a good Banded Shield into Lanayru Desert with you. Ampiluses are enormous hermit crabs that wander the desert. When danger draws near to one, it hides in its massive spiral shell and electrifies it. The Ampilus has the uncanny ability to rev its electric shell like a tire and use it to run down anything that intrudes into its territory.

Defeating Ampiluses is about how to deal with this damaging ability. You can try sneaking up behind them, striking at their vulnerable heads quickly three times. An Ampilus won't attack what it can't see and gets locked up by hit-stun after a single blow. Another option is to get an Ampilus to charge at you, then climb up on one of the small stone platforms scattered throughout this area. Crashing into the side of a platform staggers the Ampilus, giving you ample time to run in and attack.

The quickest way to defeat an Ampilus, though, is to wait until it charges at you and then shield bash it. This staggers the Ampilus just the same as if it bangs into the side of a platform. Once an Ampilus is staggered, it's easy to pick it off with quick sword strikes to the head. The timing for this is fairly generous, so it shouldn't be hard to do, but if you have a Braced Shield you'll have more margin for error as you learn the timing.

Note that after you defeat an Ampilus, its shell lingers for a time before disintegrating. You can use this to your advantage a bit later on.

CAUTION

Try not to accidentally hit any of this area's tall cacti with your sword. Doing so causes the cactus to rebound back at you, which inflicts a quarter-heart of damage.

On Tumbleweeds

As you explore the initial area of Lanayru Desert, you see a lot of tumbleweeds bouncing around. These tumbleweeds spawn randomly and can't damage you. If you hit one with your sword, it just disintegrates. Believe it or not, these tumbleweeds are treasures you need to forge a surprisingly wide array of equipment. To harvest the tumbleweeds and make them Tumbleweeds, just chase them down and catch them in your Bug Net. This is much easier than catching actual bugs.

TIP

It takes only two Tumbleweeds, three Amber Relics, two Monster Claws, and one Ornamental Skull to upgrade your Banded Shield into the Braced Shield, the game's best wooden shield. This is the ideal shield to use in this area and it's highly recommended.

Climb up one of the short platforms in this area to snag the Amber Relic on top. Feel free to explore if you like, but there's not a lot you can get to right now besides different patches of sand with different Ampiluses patrolling them. To open up more of the desert, head through the initial patch of desert wasteland to find an area where a broken chunk of wall overlooks three cages.

2. Time Trapped

Examine the cages carefully. One holds a broken-down robot and another contains a pile of rubble that looks very bombable. Look up and examine the cage's roof. There's a fair-sized hole in it, sufficient for throwing a bomb through. To get in the right position for this, climb up the section of wall that overlooks the cages, then leap onto the roof of the cage that's nearest to the wall.

Inside the rubble pile is a Timeshift Stone. Activate it with your sword, by thrusting it through the bars of the cage. Once the area is time-shifted, the robot awakens and begs for you to help save him from his captors. You're about to meet a dangerous new enemy that only occurs in time-shifted areas.

ENEMY: TECHNOBLIN

In the ancient past, Bokoblins had access to high-tech weapons and sweet goggles. If you time-shift an area where any suspicious skeletons are lying, you may find yourself suddenly fighting Technoblins. They behave like ordinary Bokoblins, but the electrified clubs they wield make them much more dangerous to fight. If a Technoblin uses the club to guard against one of Link's blows, it delivers a powerful electrical shock to him.

This means Technoblins can damage you passively while guarding if your attacks are sloppy. Be really careful when fighting Technoblins. Make sure you're damaging them with thrusts or strikes that target only areas they're definitely not guarding. You can also shield bash their attacks, which staggers them and gives you a brief opening where you can attack freely. Be extra careful when fighting more than one at once.

Once you've defeated the Technoblins, set the worker robot free and speak with him. The worker robot notices that you're using a Beetle that's primitive by the standards of his ancient civilization. To show his gratitude, the worker robot gives your Beetle a free and extremely useful upgrade.

THE HOOK BEETLE

Add massive pincers to the Beetle and you have the Hook Beetle. It works mostly the same way, but the pincers let it carry objects through the air with it—large, round objects, like, say, Bomb Flowers. When you're flying the Hook Beetle while it's carrying a bomb, hold down Z to get a view of what's beneath it and tap Ⓐ to have it drop its payload. When the Hook Beetle carries a Bomb Flower, it won't go off until the Hook Beetle crashes into something or runs out of stamina. After it's dropped, the Bomb Flower detonates immediately upon hitting something. You sadly can't get the Hook Beetle to carry around the bombs you carry in your Bomb Bag, though. A bomb you've placed on the ground goes off before you can aim and launch your Hook Beetle.

3. Bombs Away

Test out your new Hook Beetle in an area just to the left of the cages. Aim it at the Bomb Flower growing atop the tree and then launch it. Fly your Hook Beetle over the basket-holding statues and drop the Bomb Flower into one of them. Bombing the statue only reveals Blue Rupees, but now you're ready for more serious exploring. Head back to your left, to another sinksand area patrolled by an Electro Spume.

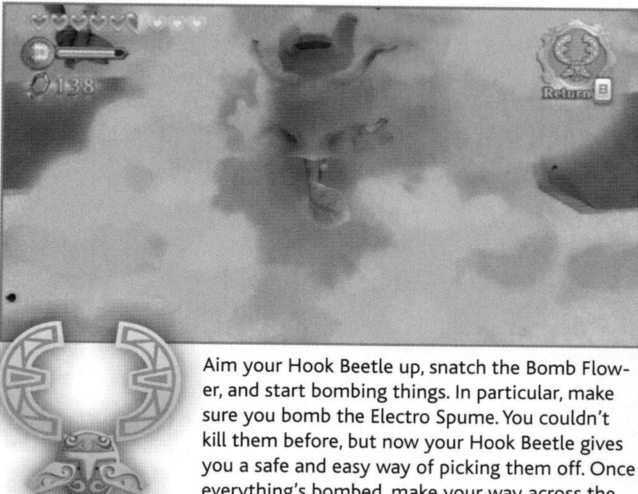

Aim your Hook Beetle up, snatch the Bomb Flower, and start bombing things. In particular, make sure you bomb the Electro Spume. You couldn't kill them before, but now your Hook Beetle gives you a safe and easy way of picking them off. Once everything's bombed, make your way across the sinksand by using the fallen statues as places to rest and regain your stamina. Investigate the area just behind the statue on the right to pick up an Amber Relic.

4. Boulder-Dropping Bird

Be extremely careful as you pass by here. Stepping too far into the area on the right rouses the wrath of an enemy that can absolutely destroy you at this point in the game.

ENEMY: HROK

The Hrok is a foe that's positively deadly at this point in the game. Hroks roost on the tall, twisted white trees that dot the Lanayru Desert area. Stepping into a Hrok's territory causes it to fly into the air toward you, slowly, inexorably. If you dash far enough you might escape a Hrok, but they can fly incredibly far from their roosts if they want to hurt you. A Hrok attacks by flying slowly through the air, waiting until it's above you, and then hroking—er, that is, horking—a boulder down at you.

If you're lucky and realize the Hrok is over you, it is possible to dodge the boulder. Most of the time, though, the Hrok catches you flat-footed and you get squashed. Even if you do dodge the boulder, the Hrok just keeps following you and horking boulders at you until it gets a hit. Only then does the vengeful Hrok fly back to its roost, satisfied that it's taught you the meaning of pain. Right now, the only way you can kill a Hrok is from afar, by using your Hook Beetle to drop a Bomb Flower on it.

So if you see a Hrok's silhouette on the ground beside you, run. Run as far and as fast as you can. Once a Hrok knows where you are, it will not rest until you're absurdly far away or it's horked a boulder on you. The best you can manage for self-defense is maybe using your Slingshot to make it prematurely cough up its boulder. If you do manage to kill a Hrok, it always drops a Red Rupee, so it's at least worth your trouble.

5. Burning Sands

To proceed toward Zelda, you need to cross the ocean of sinksand just beyond the vicious Hrok's territory. Take advantage of the Bomb Flower growing on the tree just in front of this area to help create some stepping stones for yourself. Fly the Hook Beetle over the Ampilus patrolling the area near you and bomb it. Dash toward the shell it leaves behind, pause just long enough for your stamina to refill, then dash toward the nearest stone platform.

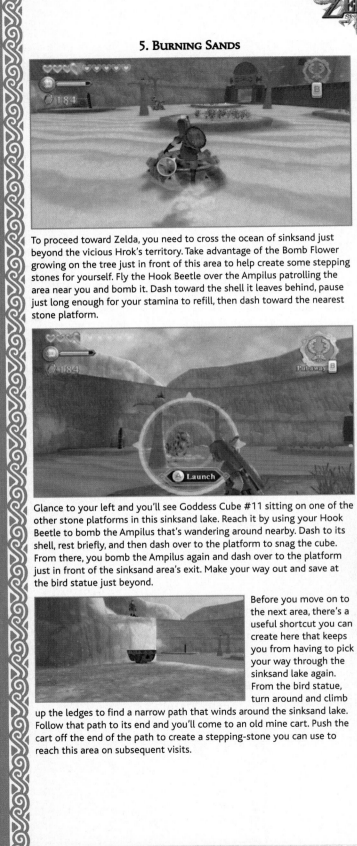

Glance to your left and you'll see Goddess Cube #11 sitting on one of the other stone platforms in this sinksand lake. Reach it by using your Hook Beetle to bomb the Ampilus that's wandering around nearby. Dash to its shell, rest briefly, and then dash over to the platform to snag the cube. From there, you bomb the Ampilus again and dash over to the platform just in front of the sinksand area's exit. Make your way out and save at the bird statue just beyond.

Before you move on to the next area, there's a useful shortcut you can create here that keeps you from having to pick your way through the sinksand lake again. From the bird statue, turn around and climb up the ledges to find a narrow path that winds around the sinksand lake. Follow that path to its end and you'll come to an old mine cart. Push the cart off the end of the path to create a stepping-stone you can use to reach this area on subsequent visits.

6. Flowing Sands

Now you need to cross a second sinksand lake that's right beside the first one. Use the same basic methods to make your way from platform to platform. There's a Bomb Flower growing on a cactus near the area's entrance that you can use to bomb the Ampiluses that roam the sinksand lake. Once you climb on an Ampilus shell, though, it should be obvious that the sinksand in this particular lake is flowing downward. Take advantage of this and ride Ampilus shells closer to stone platforms.

Ride over to the platform adjacent to the wall that separates the two sinksand lakes to dig up a patch of dirt that contains a Fairy. Head to the centermost platform in this sinksand lake when you're ready to leave. From there, you can easily dash toward the area's exit. As with the last area, you can set up a shortcut to make backtracking easier before you move on. Climb up the platforms to your left and head all the way down to the end of the narrow pathway.

There you find a sinksand "waterfall" with a series of small stone platforms jutting out of the area near the top. Move carefully across them. On the far side of the sinksand falls, you find an old mine cart. Just as with the last shortcut, you can push this down to create a stepping-stone you can use to reach this area easily from the ground. After that's done, head back to enter a passageway that leads into a strange plateau.

7. Riding the Rails

This plateau is the entrance to the Temple of Time, where Zelda awaits. Save your game at the bird statue before you get to puzzle-solving here. You clearly need to use Timeshift Stones to turn this area of crumbling mine tracks into something you can use to cross the bottomless pit that separates you from the Temple of Time's interior. Begin by activating the stone nearest you. This awakens a Technoblin; kill it quickly. You can also pick up an Ancient Flower here.

Ride the mine cart across to the central stone platform. To find the next stone you need to activate, face the enormous structure in the center of the plateau. Examine it with the Hook Beetle to find that it's actually an enormous tree stump, left over from a time in the distant past when Lanayru Desert was less arid. Inside the stump's hollow is a Timeshift Stone. Fly your Hook Beetle over the stump and drop a Bomb Flower down in the hollow to activate the stone.

Before you hop in the mine cart and ride across, launch your Hook Beetle down the cart's track. A Deku Baba is growing inside the stone the massive tree grew around, dangling from the ceiling. Use the Hook Beetle to cut its vine. Return the Beetle to Link's wrist, then launch it again. Fly it down the cart's track again and hit the crystal switch on the left side of the tunnel. This raises bars blocking the tunnel's exit. Now you can ride safely through the area. Once you reach the other side, grab an Ancient Flower to your right.

8. No Entry

Now head toward the Temple of Time's courtyard area. Ready your shield to take care of a group of Octoroks hiding around the entrance area. As you draw closer to the temple, it's obvious something's wrong. What should be the entrance is nothing but a pile of massive stones. Your Goron pal fills you in on what happened: A massive explosion collapsed the temple's entrance, cutting you off from Zelda.

Now you need to find some sort of alternative entrance into the Temple of Time's courtyard. Start by backtracking out of this area. Bomb the piles of rubble sitting atop the tall pillars to the right of the temple's collapsed entrance. Use the Hook Beetle and the Bomb Flower growing on the cactus nearby. This reveals a Timeshift Stone. Hit the stone to activate the worker robot in front of the mine cart. You also raise a pair of Technoblins, which you must defeat quickly.

After the Technoblins are gone, the worker robot tells you that you can get into the Temple of Time by passing through the Lanayru Mining Facility. The worker robot goes to mark the location of the mill's entrance on your map and then does something kind of alarming to it. He "fixes" your map by changing it completely into a map of what Lanayru Desert looked like 1,000 years ago.

This map does contain information that becomes useful to you shortly, but it can also be difficult to use. It doesn't clearly indicate sinksand areas, stone platforms, and other major features of how Lanayru Desert appears in the present. You really need to combine the information from both maps to get through the next area. So at the beginning of this chapter, both maps are presented side by side with identical labels. Consult them together.

9. Riding More Rails

The worker robot agrees to move off the tracks, which clears your way forward. Launch the Hook Beetle at the Timeshift Stone you can see if you stand directly in front of the mine cart. Even from this distance, you can tell that Goddess Cube #12 is just ahead. To activate this one, charge a Skyward Strike while you're in the cart and release it at just the right time.

Push the mine cart forward a few paces to get it completely inside the time shift effect, then hop in and ride it up. Leave the mine cart behind and move forward, through an area infested with Octoroks. Exit through the tunnel entrance just before you. It is possible to backtrack around to the way you came in (and pick up an Ancient Flower while you do so), but right now you don't really want to go that way.

10. Finding the Generator

You emerge into an area that is clearly a Hrok's territory. Use your Hook Beetle and a nearby Bomb Flower to get rid of it before you begin exploring. Something to keep in mind as you move through this area is that not all of the sinksand is as it appears. Study the past version of the map to see a network of roads that once crisscrossed this area. The roads aren't simply gone; instead, they've sunk beneath the sands.

So you can walk through the sinksand in this area, provided you're following one of the ancient roadways. Eventually you'll memorize the patterns, but for now, it helps to mark out nearby roads with beacons that remind you where it's safe and where it isn't. Slowly work your way toward the red X on your in-game map, dispatching any Hroks you spot on the way over. There are plenty of Bomb Flowers growing on trees and cacti in this part of the desert.

You arrive at some sort of ancient structure, long since deactivated. Bomb the piles of rubble nearby to turn up a Timeshift Stone. Activate it so you can talk to the worker robot nearby. Be sure to defeat the Technoblins who appear just beyond the Timeshift Stone first.

The robot gives you your next task. The structure at the red X on your map is, in fact, a generator that powers the entrance to Lanayru Mining Facility, but right now it won't operate. The generator has three remote power nodes scattered throughout the Lanayru Desert area, which you must activate before you can switch on the generator. You can locate the power nodes by dowsing. As with other missions like this, you can activate the power nodes in any order, but they're presented here in the order a player would be most likely to stumble upon them.

11. The North Node

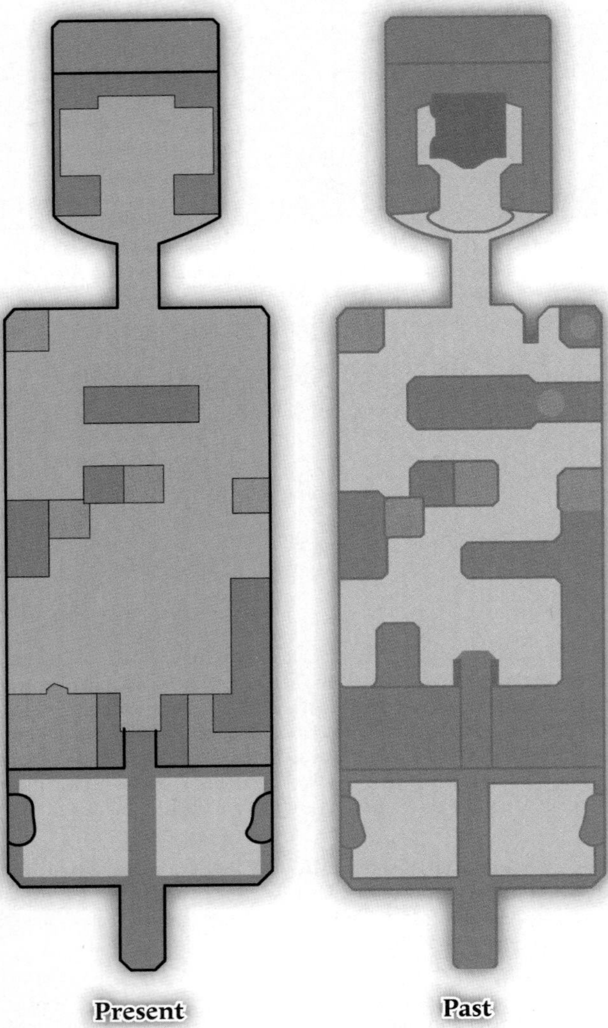

The first of the power nodes is nearby. Study the past map provided in this guide and it's obvious a building is just north of your current location. Head there in-game to find a cracked sandstone wall. Bomb the wall to open up the first of the two generator buildings.

When you enter the first generator building, it appears to be a wasteland of sinksand, patrolled by a pair of Ampiluses. Don't defeat the two Ampiluses if you can help it. Instead, move along the metal platforms to the center of the room. Bomb the pile of rubble there to reveal a Timeshift Stone.

Activating the Timeshift Stone transforms the interior of the generator building into an ancient industrial center, patrolled by Technoblins. The Ampiluses shrink down into their ancient egg forms. First, eliminate all of the Technoblins nearby so you can move around freely. A small chest in the building holds a Blue Rupee.

Next, find the deactivated generator located toward the back of the building. Right now the building's generator doesn't have power, either, but you can cheat your way around that. The solution is the Ampilus eggs, which emit periodic surges of electricity. Stand on the pressure plate in front of the generator, which opens a small internal chamber.

Launch the Hook Beetle from there. Have your Hook Beetle pick up the nearest Ampilus egg and fly it into the generator's internal chamber. This powers up the generator, causing the barred door at the rear of the building to open. Head into the rear room where the power node is located.

To activate the power node, lock on to it and thrust your sword forward. Once it's inserted, turn the power node's dial as far to the left as it will go. This makes the lightning bolt sigil on the main generator glow. One down, two more to go.

12. The Southeast Node

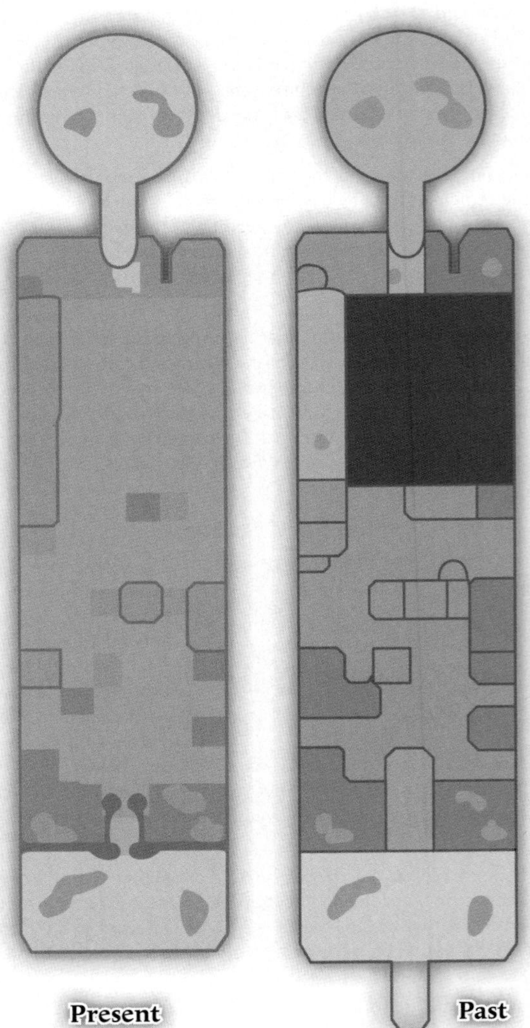

The second of the power nodes is far to the southeast, in the second generator building. Slowly make your way in the correct direction, picking your way through Hrok territories along the ancient roads beneath the sinksand. Once you've gone far enough south, as the present map indicates, you reach an area of solid rock.

Head south, through an area full of Ampiluses. This generator building is completely above ground and easy to enter. There's even a bird statue where you can save your game before you enter. On the inside, though, this building is quite a bit more treacherous than the first one. Fight the Yellow Chuchus that attack you as you draw near to the sinksand that fills the building.

Just as in the other generator building, you want to find a pile of rubble in the center of the area and bomb it to reveal a Timeshift Stone. Don't activate the stone yet. Instead, find a way to get over to the generator in the present. If you shift the area into the past, it becomes completely impossible to get close enough to the generator to stand on its pressure plate.

Unlike in the first building, the sinksand in this building flows rapidly toward the north. To get over to the generator, defeat the Ampilus that patrols the area near the Timeshift Stone. Dash onto its shell and ride it across the sinksand to the generator.

Once you're on the metal platforms at the far side, climb up the stack of metal crates that's now on your right. There's a blue chest at the end of the crate pathway, guarded by a Yellow Chuchu, that you can open to get a random treasure. While you're up there, push down the metal block to create a shortcut, in case you ever want to backtrack into this area.

Now activate the Timeshift Stone from the top of the crates, using the Hook Beetle. Head over to the generator, stand on the pressure plate, and send the Hook Beetle over the gap to fetch one of the Ampilus eggs. Use it to power up the generator, just as you did in the other building, and gain access to the power-node room.

Open the blue chest in this room to find another random treasure, then open the small chest to get a Blue Rupee. Next, activate the power node just like you did last time.

13. The West Node

The third power node isn't in a building. Instead, it's hidden out in the desert itself. To get to it, head right out of the generator building and search the wall to find a switch that controls a gate set into the wall. Pull it down to lift the bars covering the gate. Now you can easily pass through to the beginning of the area if you like.

To get to the third power node, circle back around to the main generator and then head west, into Hrok territory. The area you want appears on your map as a road running under the sinksand that leads to a dead end. Make your way carefully through the sinksand to an area alongside a wall that you can't climb yet. You're looking for an area where two basket-holding statues stand next to one that's already toppled over. The wall behind it is damaged. Bomb the wall to reveal a Timeshift Stone.

Now that you've got solid ground to stand on, you can easily toss bombs into the other two statues. The power node is behind the statue in the middle. Strike the Timeshift Stone and then activate the power node the same way you activated the first two.

14. Activating the Generator

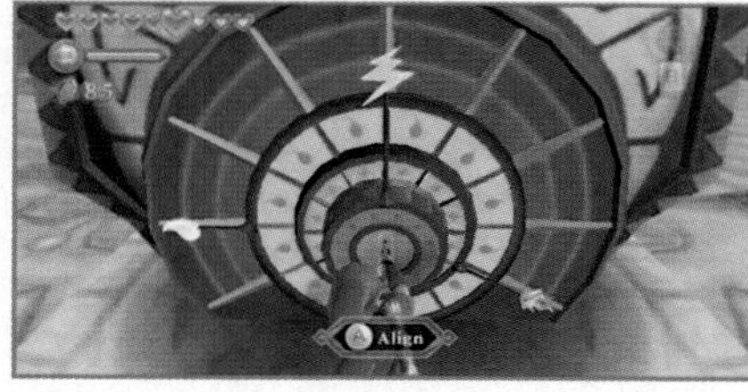

Head back to the main generator and activate the Timeshift Stone. Now you can activate the main generator—after you solve a little puzzle. You need to align the main generator's three dials correctly to turn it on. Each dial is marked by a symbol that corresponds to one of the power nodes you just activated. The correct alignment for the dials arranges the symbols based on how they appear on the circular center area of the desert in your map. Align them exactly as you see in the picture and the generator will activate, raising the Lanayru Mining Facility's entrance from the sands. Prepare yourself to explore a dungeon and then head inside.

Goddess's Treasure Chest Pickups: #11 and #12

To get goddess's treasure chest #11, dive onto the highest point of an island in the far northeast of the sky. Ignore the strange-looking wooden scaffolding on the island's lower level (for now). The chest is sitting out in the open on the top of a small plateau, waiting to be claimed. Open it to receive a Piece of Heart.

To get goddess's treasure chest #12, head for the Isle of Songs. Fly over the main island with the tower and have Link dive off. You want him to land on the grassy area that rings the tower's outside. The activated chest is waiting for you there. Open it to receive a Gold Rupee.

Ancient Circuit

LEGEND

Piece of Heart

Goddess Cube

Save Point

11

Save Point

9

8

10

7

Gust Bellows

2

4

Save Point

Small Key

6

3

5

1

12

Save Point

LANAYRU MINING FACILITY

1. The Factory Foyer

Lanayru Mining Facility is the factory where the ancient civilization of Lanayru Desert once produced its Timeshift Stones. Abandoned for centuries, it's now decrepit and infested with monsters. You need to use the Timeshift Stones scattered throughout the factory to activate its machinery, while finding ways to evade and destroy the factory's ancient security mechanisms. In this first room, though, you encounter a new enemy that's no more than an annoyance.

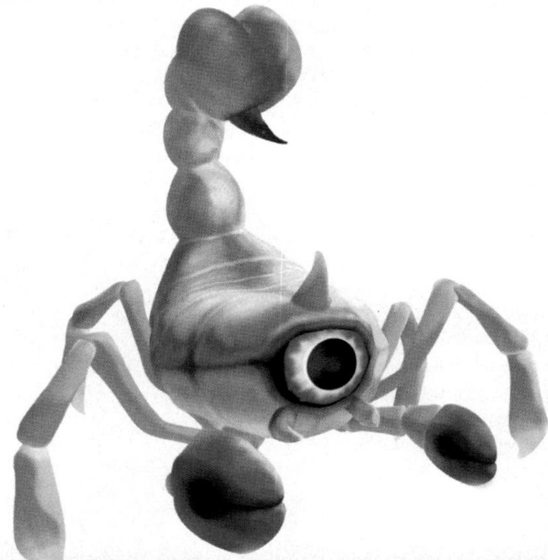

ENEMY: ARACHA

These small enemies are no more than larvae, easily dispatched with a single blow from your sword. They tend to appear in swarms, though, so sometimes one can attack you while you're dealing with another. Arachas attack by leaping onto you, similar to Walltulas. You can break free by shaking your Wii Remote and Nunchuk.

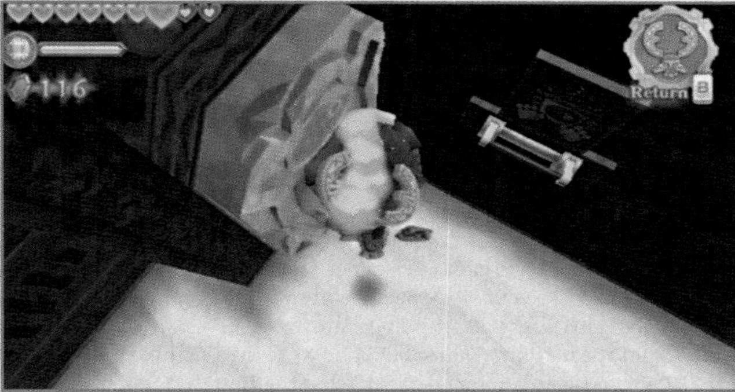

Investigate a hidden chamber to find a small chest that holds a Red Rupee. Use the Hook Beetle and the nearby Bomb Flower to defeat the Electro Spumes that lurk in the sinksand. Once the Spumes are cleared out, head in to pull down the two switches along the rear wall. You can get to the one on the right using stone platforms. The one on the left you can reach by bombing the basket-holding statue. Once you've pulled the left switch, you can pass into the next room.

Here you immediately encounter a pair of Staldras. After you defeat them, examine the doors they guard. The one on the right is padlocked and requires a Small Key. The one on the left is barred, so you'll have to find the right switch to open it. For now, head forward into the facility. Use the boxes to make it possible to climb up to this room's exit. You'll return here later.

2. The Lost Key

When you reach the end of the platform, you find a gap. On the other side, four wooden crates are stacked. You need to eliminate the boxes before you can leap the gap. Use the Hook Beetle and a Bomb Flower that's nearby to blast the crates away. Once the crates are gone, throw a bomb on the boxes across the gap, then leap over and climb the ladder once they're gone. If you don't have any bombs, make use of the Hook Beetle to carry a Bomb Flower to the boxes. At the top of the platform you'll find a blue chest containing a Small Key. Backtrack into the previous room and unlock the door to proceed. For once, there's not a sub-boss battle waiting for you on the other side.

ENEMY: THUNDER KEESE

Thunder Keese can electrify their bodies, just like many of the other creatures native to the Lanayru Desert region. Their attack pattern is fundamentally the same as that of an ordinary Keese, but they electrify themselves when diving. Just as with the Yellow Chuchus, attacking a Thunder Keese when it's electrified can damage you. The best way to handle Thunder Keese is just to defeat them as soon as you see them.

Throw a bomb on the boxes across the gap, then leap over and climb the ladder once they're gone. At the top of the platform you'll find a blue chest containing a Small Key. Backtrack into the previous room and unlock the door to proceed. For once, there's not a sub-boss battle waiting for you on the other side.

3. Conveyor Belts

Head toward the platform on the upper right. You need to get up to the top of it, but if you try to climb the ladder now, you find a wooden crate blocking the top. Use your Hook Beetle and snag the Bomb Flower that's growing nearby to blast the offending crate away. Now that you can get to the top of the platform, you should find a pressure-activated switch there. While you stand on it, the bars around the Timeshift Stone at the center of the room rise. While standing on the switch, launch the Hook Beetle at the Timeshift Stone to activate it. This turns on the room's conveyor belts and summons some dangerous new enemies.

Head down from the switch platform and toward the nearest conveyor belt. You can fight or just dodge around the Beamos you encounter on your way. Dash across the conveyor belt and climb up the platform just beyond it. At the top, you find a switch you can pull to raise the bars blocking in a door on the other side of the room. Inside is a chest with a Red Rupee.

Now you need to cross over to the other side of the room to move on. There is exactly one way to do this right now: by attempting to run to the other end of the conveyor belt below you. The belt runs in the opposite direction and there's a grate of lasers at its far end, so you take damage if you attempt to make the crossing and fail. The trick to getting across is to dodge the ore deposits while collecting the Stamina Fruits.

Climb up the platform with the door you unbarred to find a Red Rupee. After that, drop down and cross to the far side of the conveyor belt. Head up the stairs on the opposite side to find the door that leads to the next area. It's barred right now. To find the switch that unbars it, dash across the conveyor belt that's off to the door's right. This switch is guarded by a Beamos that you probably need to defeat.

4. Exploding Frogs

The next room is filled with tiny platforms arranged in a grid pattern. Much of the room is covered in piles of sand and rubble. If you drop down to the floor level, there are areas where spikes shoot up from the floor if you try to pass by. Your goal in this room is to pick your way over to a blue chest that contains a tool you need to solve some upcoming puzzles. You must combine moving over the upper platforms with a little bit of moving through the floor. The area above the platforms is patrolled by a new enemy.

ENEMY: BEAMOS

A Beamos is an automated guardian designed to keep meat-based intruders like yourself out of his territory. A Beamos's head spins on his pillar-like body, his camera eye searching for intruders. If a Beamos spots you, he fires a scorching electric laser at you. He is perfectly capable of tracking your movements and can shoot his laser surprisingly far. Once you've caught a Beamos's attention, he won't stop firing at you until you're dead, he's dead, or you're out of range.

Right now, it's possible to just dodge around Beamos. They usually protect small areas you can dash through quickly. Eventually, though, you have to start destroying them if you want to move on. You destroy a Beamos by slashing horizontally to chop his body down, then using a thrust to put out his camera eye. You must do this smoothly and quickly, since a Beamos is alerted to your presence the minute you start attacking him.

ENEMY: FROAK

Froaks inflate their bodies with superheated air and drift around their territories. If one spots you, damaging spikes erupt all over its body and it begins slowly drifting toward you. This makes a Froak into more of an obstacle than an attacker. Right now, you can shoot them down using the Slingshot, provided they don't have their spikes out.

Remember that when you shoot a Froak, it explodes like a bomb. You can take advantage of this to clear some of the rubble out of this room, but you also need to make sure you're never too close to a Froak when you shoot it. Once a Froak has its spikes out, you can't detonate it without pushing it into something solid.

Start shooting down Froaks with your Slingshot, both to clear your way and to start blasting the rubble piles on top of the platforms. Once all of the Froaks are gone, use your own bombs to blast away any rubble that's left. A blue chest in the floor area contains a random treasure you may want to snag. Once you make your way there, climb the ladder on the large platform at the rear of the room. Defeat the Arachas and then claim your new item.

THE GUST BELLOWS

The Gust Bellows is a magical device that can exhale infinite amounts of wind. It's only rarely useful for attacking enemies, but it's extremely useful for blowing away piles of sand. You can also use it to force light-weight enemies like Froaks and Arachas away from you.

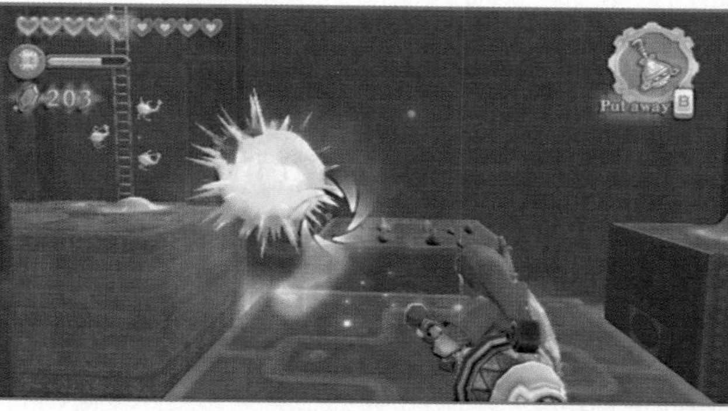

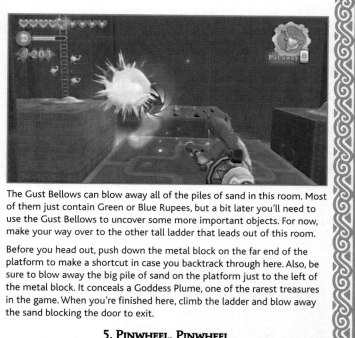

The Gust Bellows can blow away all of the piles of sand in this room. Most of them just contain Green or Blue Rupees, but a bit later you'll need to use the Gust Bellows to uncover some more important objects. For now, make your way over to the other tall ladder that leads out of this room.

Before you head out, push down the metal block on the far end of the platform to make a shortcut in case you backtrack through here. Also, be sure to blow away the big pile of sand on the platform just to the left of the metal block. It conceals a Goddess Plume, one of the rarest treasures in the game. When you're finished here, climb the ladder and blow away the sand blocking the door to exit.

5. Pinwheel, Pinwheel

You emerge above the area where you found the Small Key earlier. Move the metal block aside to create a shortcut for future use. Backtrack to the room patrolled by Staldras. Now that you have the Gust Bellows, you can open up the barred doorway. Walk to the area full of crates just to the right of the room's north exit. Use the Gust Bellows to blow away sand that's covering up a pressure-sensitive switch (and the Aracha guarding it). Push the block onto the switch to raise the bars. Now you can enter the left-hand room.

Head into it to find an area full of sand, Froaks, and strange platforms. Make your way across the sinksand by dashing from platform to platform. When you get to the area with the barred doorway, take a left and make your way to the platform in the corner. Blow away all of the sand (and the Froak) to reveal a Timeshift Stone. Hit it to activate the metal platforms. Now you can manipulate them with the Gust Bellows.

Get on the platform near the Timeshift Stone. Use the Gust Bellows to spin the vanes on top of the platform. This lets you move the platform along its track and ride it back to the barred doorway. Before you open up the door, head to the right. Use the Gust Bellows to move the platform toward you, then ride it over to the blue chest in the center of the room. Open it to receive a random treasure.

Examine the barred door carefully. Above it, you should see a pinwheel. Use the Gust Bellows to turn the pinwheel. This acts like a crank, slowly raising the bars. Defeat the Beamos that waits just inside, then drop to the next level. A new enemy awaits you down there.

ENEMY: SENTROBE

Sentrobes serve the same basic function as Beamos, but evading them is usually impossible. Fighting a Sentrobe is not difficult but demands patience. Shield bash the missiles the Sentrobe fires at you, then wait for it to release its two mini-drones. If you can't defeat the mini-drones, they bump into you and explode. To defeat them, let the mini-drones close in on you. You destroy them by using the appropriate slash on them.

One always demands a horizontal slash, the other a vertical slash. You can tell a mini-drone's weakness by the glowing blue line that appears on its body. Once you've destroyed the mini-drones, the Sentrobe attacks you with missiles again. Shield bash another missile at the Sentrobe to defeat it. Every time you defeat a Sentrobe, it drops lots of Green, Blue, and Red Rupees.

Once the Sentrobe is defeated, use the Gust Bellows to move the vane platform far enough down the track that you can step onto it. Stand at the edge of the area where you are now and you'll still be close enough for the Gust Bellows' wind to turn the platform's vane. Once you can step onto the vane platform, move it back to the left and hop onto the platforms at the other side of the room. Climb up the ladder and defeat the Beamos that waits at the top. Finally, use the Gust Bellows to open up the room's exit.

6. The Hopping Guardian

Battle the Staldras guarding the next room, then push the metal block to the end of the track in the ground. Now you can use it as a stepping stone to get up to the top of the next level. If you like, use the Gust Bellows to blow the Arachas off the tops of the metal blocks that run down the right-hand side of the room (from your current vantage point). Hop across them and blow away the sand pile on the last block to pick up an Amber Relic.

To proceed, use the Gust Bellows to blow away the sand inside the small barred area. This reveals a Timeshift Stone. Hit the Timeshift Stone with a Skyward Strike or the Slingshot. This activates the room's guardian, who you must defeat to exit this room. Once it is defeated, the bars will raise and you can retrieve the Dungeon Map from the blue chest.

ENEMY: ARMOS

This drone is designed to keep intruders away from important doors. When you step into the area it guards, the Armos hops rapidly toward you. In the Lanayru Mining Facility, this territory is always clearly indicated by a semi-circle on the floor. In encounters in future dungeons, this won't be marked out for you. Also keep in mind that an Armos can hop briefly out of its territory in order to attack you.

To defeat it, you need the Gust Bellows. When the Armos heads toward you, employ the Gust Bellows to spin the vanes on its head. This forces the Armos to open its mouth. Once it's open all the way, quickly put away the Gust Bellows and thrust at the power core the Armos has revealed to you. Wait for the Armos to reveal its other face to you, then repeat the process. Once both of its power cores are destroyed, the Armos is defeated.

7. Hidden Roads

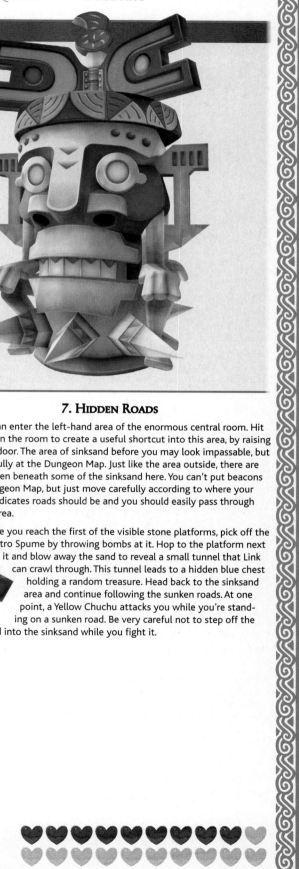

Now you can enter the left-hand area of the enormous central room. Hit the switch in the room to create a useful shortcut into this area, by raising the barred door. The area of sinksand before you may look impassable, but look carefully at the Dungeon Map. Just like the area outside, there are roads hidden beneath some of the sinksand here. You can't put beacons on a Dungeon Map, but just move carefully according to where your map indicates roads should be and you should easily pass through this area.

Once you reach the first of the visible stone platforms, pick off the Electro Spume by throwing bombs at it. Hop to the platform next to it and blow away the sand to reveal a small tunnel that Link can crawl through. This tunnel leads to a hidden blue chest holding a random treasure. Head back to the sinksand area and continue following the sunken roads. At one point, a Yellow Chuchu attacks you while you're standing on a sunken road. Be very careful not to step off the sunken road into the sinksand while you fight it.

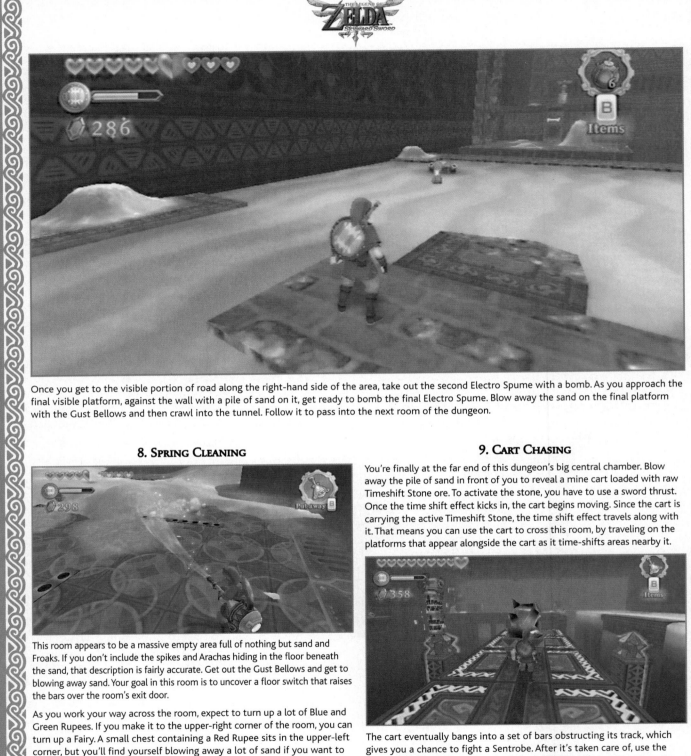

Once you get to the visible portion of road along the right-hand side of the area, take out the second Electro Spume with a bomb. As you approach the final visible platform, against the wall with a pile of sand on it, get ready to bomb the final Electro Spume. Blow away the sand on the final platform with the Gust Bellows and then crawl into the tunnel. Follow it to pass into the next room of the dungeon.

8. Spring Cleaning

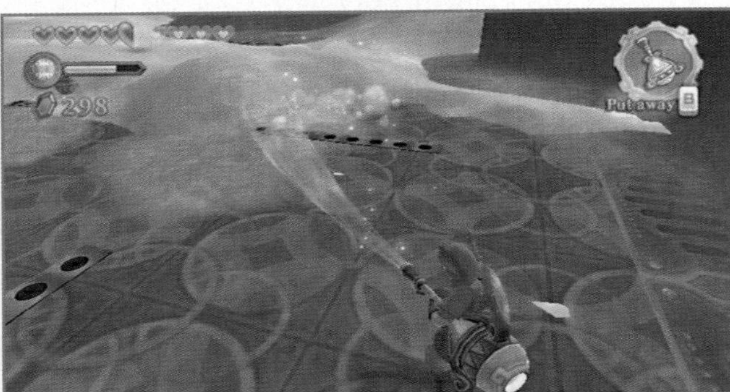

This room appears to be a massive empty area full of nothing but sand and Froaks. If you don't include the spikes and Arachas hiding in the floor beneath the sand, that description is fairly accurate. Get out the Gust Bellows and get to blowing away sand. Your goal in this room is to uncover a floor switch that raises the bars over the room's exit door.

As you work your way across the room, expect to turn up a lot of Blue and Green Rupees. If you make it to the upper-right corner of the room, you can turn up a Fairy. A small chest containing a Red Rupee sits in the upper-left corner, but you'll find yourself blowing away a lot of sand if you want to reach it.

9. Cart Chasing

You're finally at the far end of this dungeon's big central chamber. Blow away the pile of sand in front of you to reveal a mine cart loaded with raw Timeshift Stone ore. To activate the stone, you have to use a sword thrust. Once the time shift effect kicks in, the cart begins moving. Since the cart is carrying the active Timeshift Stone, the time shift effect travels along with it. That means you can use the cart to cross this room, by traveling on the platforms that appear alongside the cart as it time-shifts areas nearby it.

The cart eventually bangs into a set of bars obstructing its track, which gives you a chance to fight a Sentrobe. After it's taken care of, use the Gust Bellows to spin the pinwheel above the bars. The cart moves automatically once it can. The next set of platforms is patrolled by Beamos that you can only fight using Skyward Strikes, since they're too far away for conventional sword strikes. If you want, you can just pass by them by using the mine cart to provide cover. If you keep the cart between you and the Beamos, its lasers can't hurt you. Dash around and quickly defeat the Beamos that blocks the track. The mine cart finally comes to a stop just behind the barred door you saw when you entered this chamber for the very first time. Now you can use the Gust Bellows to spin the pinwheel above the bars, creating a shortcut. Next, head right from this area to find another mine cart loaded with Timeshift Stone ore. Activate it as you did the last one and get ready to follow it to your destination. You can dodge or defeat the Beamos that materializes halfway through the trip, since it's guarding a door you need to pass through eventually.

Your goal here is to use the Gust Bellows to spin a pinwheel that's only active when the mine cart is passing by. If you miss this the first time, just deactivate and reactivate the cart and pass by again. Once you've defeated the Beamos, you can really take as many tries at this as you like. Once you've spun the pinwheel, you can pass through the door the Beamos guarded.

10. More Conveyor Belts

You're in another production area full of conveyor belts. For now, you don't want to time shift this area. Instead, cross the dormant conveyor belt, being careful not to run into the hot jets of steam. At the end of the conveyor belt, begin climbing up the vines. Be very careful of the steam jets in this area, as well as the Arachas that patrol the area. Once you come to the top of the wall, two Thunder Keese attack you. Walk to the left, pulling the switch at the end of this platform.

This sends a vane platform sliding over to you. Before you can use it, you need to time shift the area. Run down to the opposite end of the upper platform. You find a series of basket-holding statues and a suspiciously large pile of sand sitting on a tall platform across the room. Bomb the statues so you can use them as stepping-stones to move across to the other side of the room. Blow away the sand to expose a Timeshift Stone and strike it. Head back the way you came.

To get back to the platform, you need to dash across the three moving conveyor belts between you and the vane platform. The penalty for failing at this is to be dashed down onto the conveyor belt below, hurled into lasers, and forced to backtrack all the way back around the room to try again. There's no trick to this—just plow ahead and veer Link to the right as much as you can. Now you can pull the switch and activate the vane platform.

Ride across the room on the vane platform. On the other side, you have to fight a Sentrobe. Next, bomb down the basket-holding statues. What you reveal by doing this is actually a cryptic clue that applies to something you have to do once you move on. Remember the numerical sequence revealed here: 2-3-1. Next, stand with your back toward the basket-holding statues. You should see a vane platform all the way to the right that you need to move down. Then use the vane platform you rode over to this side of the room to hop onto the vane platform you just moved into position.

Ride the new vane platform all the way down to the platform at the far north of the room. Here you should glimpse the jeweled chest, behind two sets of bars. You need to find a way to raise the bars now. While you're here, pull the metal block to the right to create a shortcut for use in any backtracking you might end up doing. Then move on to the other side of the room, where a vane platform is waiting.

Bomb the basket-holding statues to the left of the vane platform to expose a set of crystal switches. Remember the numerical sequence you revealed before: 2-3-1. Mirror the sequence hinted at on the other wall by hitting the switches in the order of left first, then right, then middle. You can easily do this by moving the vane platform back and forth with the Gust Bellows and hitting the switches with the Hook Beetle. When you've done it right, the first set of bars near the jeweled chest rises.

Head into the room behind the bars. Now you see the jeweled chest behind a second set of bars, which two Armos are guarding. Be careful to battle the Armos one at a time. If you do, then they're no tougher than usual. Fighting them both at once is significantly more challenging. Once both are defeated, open the jeweled chest to claim the Ancient Circuit, the key to this dungeon's puzzle door.

Now backtrack to the previous room. The easiest way to do this is to climb down the ladder and use the shortcut to quickly get back to the lower of the two conveyor belts. Instead of crossing it and climbing the ladder across from it, dash across this conveyor belt. Be careful not to barrel into the steam jets here while trying to make your way forward, and be sure to grab every Stamina Fruit you can.

11. One Last Puzzle

Finally, you can pass back into the far side of the main chamber. Climb up the ladder to the left first, so you can grab the dungeon's last bit of loot. Fight your way through the Thunder Keese that appear along the upper passage and you can grab a Red Rupee that appears at the end. Go a little beyond it, fight more Thunder Keese, and pull the metal block to the right to open up the dungeon's final shortcut.

Next, head to the right and save your game. Activate the mine cart carrying Timeshift Stone ore. You can't follow the cart directly this time, so instead hop onto the vane platform next to the cart that's activated now. Use the Gust Bellows to follow the mine cart as it goes across its track. Hot steam jets fire at you as you go across, so be careful and quick. As the mine cart comes to a stop at the next platform, the time shift effect removes the barbed wire that was covering up the dungeon's puzzle door. Insert the Ancient Circuit and then you're ready to face the boss.

BOSS: MOLDARACH

If you've felt a little guilty about all the Arachas you've killed in this dungeon, don't be. If any one of those Arachas reached maturity, it would become something known as a "Thousand-Year Arachnid," like the boss you face now.

Moldarach is an enormous scorpion, its body so heavily plated with armor that your sword is useless against it. The only way to damage Moldarach is to strike its eyes, its only vulnerable points. Begin with its two claws; each has an eye rooted at the base of it. When a claw is closed, you can't attack, but when Moldarach opens a claw you can strike.

Carefully observe the angle of Moldarach's claws. When you attack, you must use a strike that passes through Moldarach's claw cleanly. If Moldarach holds his claw at an angle, for instance, then you must attack with a diagonal strike. Damage a claw enough, and eventually you'll cut it off completely.

Once Moldarach loses both claws, its combat style changes. Instead of trying to grab you with its claws, it switches over to trying to head butt you. Now the only way to damage it is to draw close to it and thrust at the only eye Moldarach has left, in its forehead.

Periodically in this phase of the fight, Moldarach digs into the thick layer of sand that covers the boss room's floor. When this happens, force him out with the Gust Bellows. Otherwise Moldarach burrows through the sand, trying to get under your feet so he can attack you from below.

Keep up a strong offense against Moldarach and he won't last long. If you take a bit of damage, don't forget that the edge of the boss room is loaded with pots stuffed with hearts. After Moldarach expires, grab the Heart Container he leaves behind. You really earned this one.

12. Victory Lap

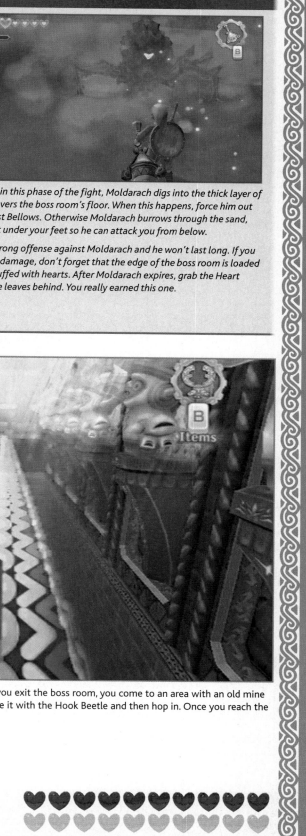

You have a little bit of traveling left to do before this dungeon is completely over. After you exit the boss room, you come to an area with an old mine cart. High, high up at the top of the hallway is the Timeshift Stone that activates it. Strike it with the Hook Beetle and then hop in. Once you reach the far side of this hallway, you can emerge into the Temple of Time.

Return to the Sealed Grounds

Walls and Stones

After the cutscenes end, talk to your Goron pal. He's discovered that there are "walls and stones that respond to beautiful tones." He's talking about Gossip Stones and goddess walls. After you acquire the Goddess's Harp, try playing it in areas where three Blessed Butterflies gather. In many (but not all) of these places, playing your harp activates either a Gossip Stone or goddess wall. You'll encounter walls more frequently in dungeons and stones more frequently in the overworld.

Gossip Stones give advice while goddess walls let you request an item by drawing an image on the wall. Once a goddess wall is used, there is a timed reset for it to become reactivated. The Gossip Stones give you a random treasure as a gift when you first summon them. Keep an eye out for likely areas, but don't sweat searching for goddess walls and Gossip Stones the way you should sweat getting all of the Goddess Cubes.

TIP

You can obtain Rupees, bombs, arrows, and hearts from goddess walls by drawing the appropriate shapes. One of the most useful things to draw is the image of the Triforce. This lets you summon three Fairies, perfect for bottling!

The Piece of Heart in the Wall

Most of what you get from goddess walls are common items, but there is one very special thing you can get just once. It is possible to get a Piece of Heart out of a goddess wall by helping your Goron pal Gorko solve riddles. Basically, talk to Gorko after you've revealed the goddess wall in the Sealed Grounds. He tells you a riddle that relates to something you can draw to get an item from a goddess wall. If he mentions an "arrow in repose," for example, draw an arrow.

You have to do it at this particular goddess wall, where Gorko can see it and be amazed. Goddess walls have a timed reset after you use them, so after you solve a riddle you need to go do something else in the game for a while before you can summon it again and solve another Gorko riddle. After you solve enough of Gorko's riddles, he mentions wanting to see a "crimson source of life". Draw a heart on the goddess wall. This completes Gorko's research and makes him so happy that he gives you a Piece of Heart in gratitude.

Harping

GODDESS'S HARP

Hey, remember that harp Zelda tossed you a couple cutscenes ago? It's about to become really important. When you want to play the harp, press ✚ to summon it. Then hold down Ⓐ and slowly wave the Wii Remote back and forth to strum it. Rhythm is very important to playing the harp. You have to play the harp at points to advance the story, but you can also play it whenever you like in the overworld or dungeons. If you play it in the right places, you can make interesting things happen.

Head into the temple area of the Sealed Grounds immediately after you touch down. This triggers a cutscene where the old priestess teaches Link how to use the harp he just acquired. Expect to be using the harp frequently to progress the plot during the rest of the game. When the tutorial ends, you are awarded the first of the harp's five songs, the Ballad of the Goddess.

A Terrible Resonance

You also get your next goal during this sequence: to open the Gate of Time in the Sealed Temple by undergoing a series of spiritual and physical trials. The moment the Gate of Time emerges, the Sealed Temple shakes. The evil force Link sealed so easily in his first visit to the Sealed Temple is awakening. This time, it's going to put up a lot more of a fight. Save your game immediately after the Sealed Temple cutscenes end and get ready for a boss fight.

BOSS: THE IMPRISONED

The moment you set foot in the bottom of the pit outside in the Sealed Grounds, The Imprisoned awakens. It's not entirely clear what this creature is at this point, but it's clearly very old and very evil. Link must stop it by any means necessary. In this particular fight, that means a desperate battle with The Imprisoned's massive toes. The Imprisoned summons rings of deadly red energy with every titanic step, which makes even approaching it risky.

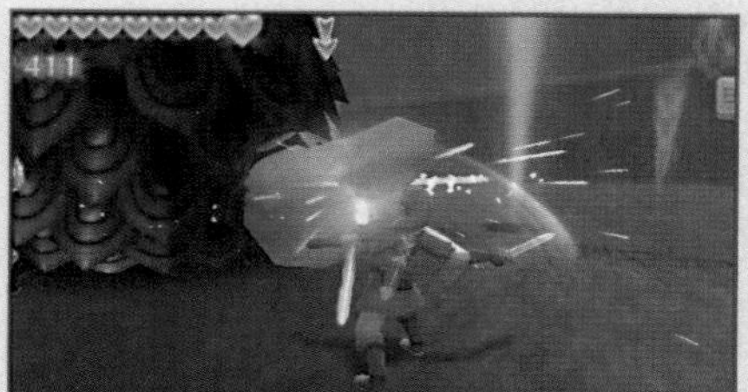

It's easiest to begin by getting behind The Imprisoned and destroying its back toes first. After that's done, sweep around to the left. The best time to strike at the toes on The Imprisoned's left foot is when it's moving its right foot forward. This means the monster is putting all of its weight on its left foot and can't move it. For now, you're out of the reach of the deadly red energy ripples.

If you hold Z, you can use the autolock and rapid sword slashes to help destroy The Imprisoned's toes faster. If you're quick, you can wipe out the front toes of a foot with one flurry of blows. Once all of the toes are off of a foot, The Imprisoned begins limping. If you take damage here, remember that The Imprisoned's toes often drop hearts after you destroy them.

After you've removed all the toes from both of The Imprisoned's feet, it topples over backward. Quickly dash around it by running beneath its slightly upraised leg. Lock on to the stake sticking out of The Imprisoned's snout and hit it with a series of ascending vertical strikes. After you drive the stake in, The Imprisoned roars and begins slithering rapidly up the slope.

There are two ways to lose the fight with The Imprisoned. You can get killed by losing all of your health the old-fashioned way, or The Imprisoned can reach the Sealed Temple at the top of the pit and destroy it. You need to catch up with The Imprisoned quickly after it slithers. The easiest way to do this is often to ride a geyser up with the Sailcloth. You can also track the location of The Imprisoned on your in-game map.

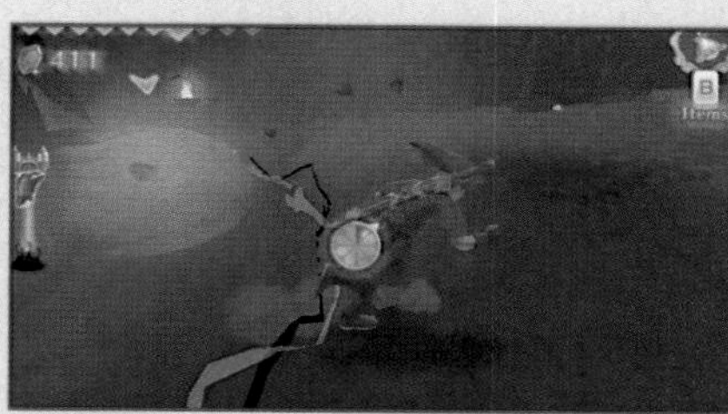

You have to repeat the entire damage cycle on The Imprisoned two more times to defeat it. Once you have the basic pattern down, you should find it easy to take out all of The Imprisoned's toes quickly a second and third time.

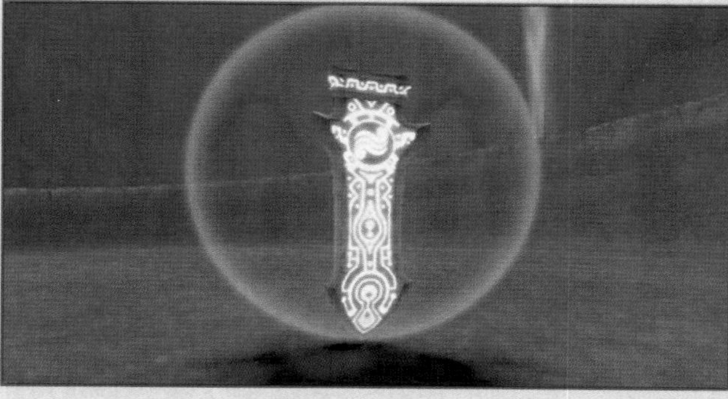

In this encounter, The Imprisoned isn't likely to get very close to the Sealed Temple. Of course, at the end of this battle, you haven't really defeated The Imprisoned, just sealed it once again. The Imprisoned has already escaped once...so it's probably just a matter of time until it gets out again.

Back Outside

Before you backtrack to Skyloft as instructed, step back out into the area behind the Sealed Temple. Your Goron pal has discovered a trio of Blessed Butterflies. Walk up to the Blessed Butterflies and strum your harp a little. If you're close enough, then after a moment or two you should go to a cutscene. This particular trio summons a Gossip Stone.

Skyloft

Once you're back in Skyloft, head to the Knight Academy and speak with Headmaster Gaepora. Get him to give you the lyrics to the Ballad of the Goddess. The lyrics are a clue indicating what you need to do next. The "whirling sails" lyric refers to the island's two enormous windmills. You have to align them so they point at the Light Tower. Start by visiting the one that's just south of the plaza. Have the Gust Bellows ready.

Work the Gust Bellows to spin the pinwheel at the windmill's base, which lets you turn the windmill slowly around in a circle. Note that the windmill picks up a lot of inertia as it turns and can't stop on a dime. When you've lined up the windmill correctly, a symbol at the base of it flashes brightly.

The other windmill that's over by the graveyard is a problem. The pinwheel that should be at the base of it is missing, so you can't use the Gust Bellows on it. Jakamar says he could fix it if someone could retrieve the pinwheel propeller from somewhere beneath the clouds, but it's not very likely you can do it without some help.

Next, talk to Gondo at the Scrap Shop. He has one of the little worker robots you saw all over the place in the past in Lanayru Desert, but of course it's broken now. Gondo says he could fix it with the oil from an Ancient Flower. If you took this guide's advice, then you have one to hand over right now.

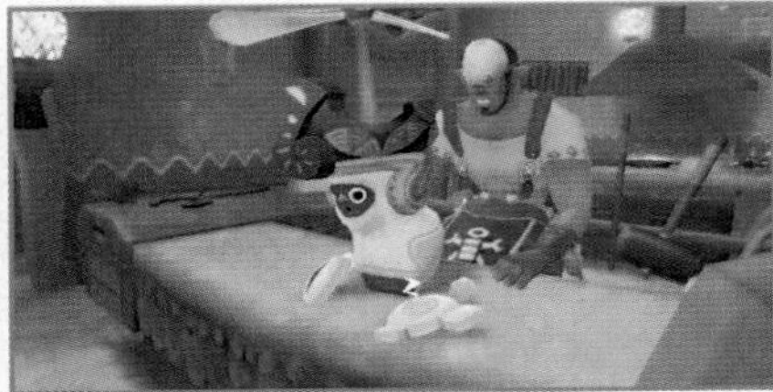

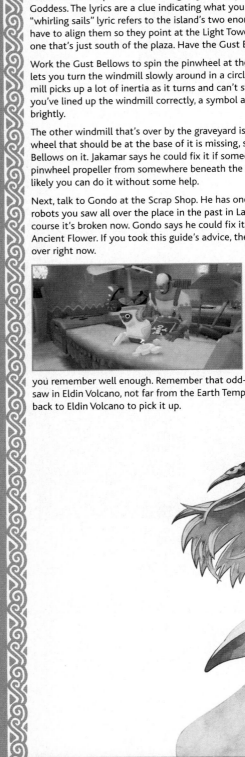

Once the robot (called Scrapper) is fixed, it eventually agrees to carry the propeller back once you've found it. Gondo advises you to talk to the fortuneteller about where it's located, but chances are you remember well enough. Remember that odd-looking pinwheel you saw in Eldin Volcano, not far from the Earth Temple? That's the one. Head back to Eldin Volcano to pick it up.

From the temple's entrance, it should be just a quick dash back to this area. If you flip back to the Eldin Volcano map, it's waypoint 18. Slide down the slope and examine the propeller to initiate a cutscene. Scrapper appears and carries the propeller back to Skyloft. Save your game at the bird statue outside the temple, then quickly return to Skyloft.

Talk to Jakamar and he fixes the windmill. Now you can get out the Gust Bellows and align the windmill so it's pointing toward the Light Tower in the plaza. After the cutscene ends, head to the Light Tower in the plaza and climb to the top. Stand in the center of the stone circle, get out your harp, and start strumming. Play in rhythm with the circle of light.

When this sequence is done, a beam of light points to the thunderhead in the northwest corner of the sky and makes a portal in it. Now you can fly your Loftwing into the thunderhead through the portal. Do so to reach your next destination, the Isle of Songs. Be sure to avoid the strange creatures that fly through the thunderhead's skies as you fly to the isle.

The Isle of Songs

Drop down in the Isle of Songs' courtyard. You have to solve one puzzle before you can go inside, but it's a pretty big puzzle. Right now there's no bridge connecting the courtyard to the small tunnel that lets Link enter the island's tower. Pieces of the bridge instead point out from different points of the courtyard at random.

Examine the three concentric rings that mark the courtyard. Each ring corresponds to a different part of the missing bridge. The smallest ring is the first part, the second ring the middle part, and the outer ring the third part. A stone node sits on each of the rings. The node indicates where that ring's piece of bridge projects. So to construct the bridge that leads into the Isle of Songs, you have to align the three nodes.

This sounds simple, but there's a complication. In addition to the node, each ring has two small segments of stone wall that rise whenever you activate a certain ring. You can't move a node past a wall. You can take advantage of the walls to align the nodes, but the walls make getting the aligned nodes pointed toward the tower a bit difficult.

You move the nodes by pushing the giant stone paddle at the center of the island. You can't move the nodes one at a time. Until a node hits a wall, moving the paddle moves all of the nodes on the circle. You control the walls by using your sword to hit the crystal switches on the control panel that stands to the left of the stone paddle.

To solve the puzzle, you must first manipulate the switches so that you slowly move all of the nodes into alignment. Next, manipulate the switches so that you can move the nodes together without a wall knocking a node out of alignment with the others. Note that you can only move nodes clockwise; you can't go backward.

The top switch controls these two walls.

The right switch controls this wall.

The left switch controls these two walls.

Once you can enter the tower on the Isle of Songs, save your game at the bird statue and then Skyward Strike the crest at the end of the long stone walkway. A cutscene ensues, you get more details about your current mission, and you also get the second harp song, Farore's Courage. Get ready to return to Faron Woods.

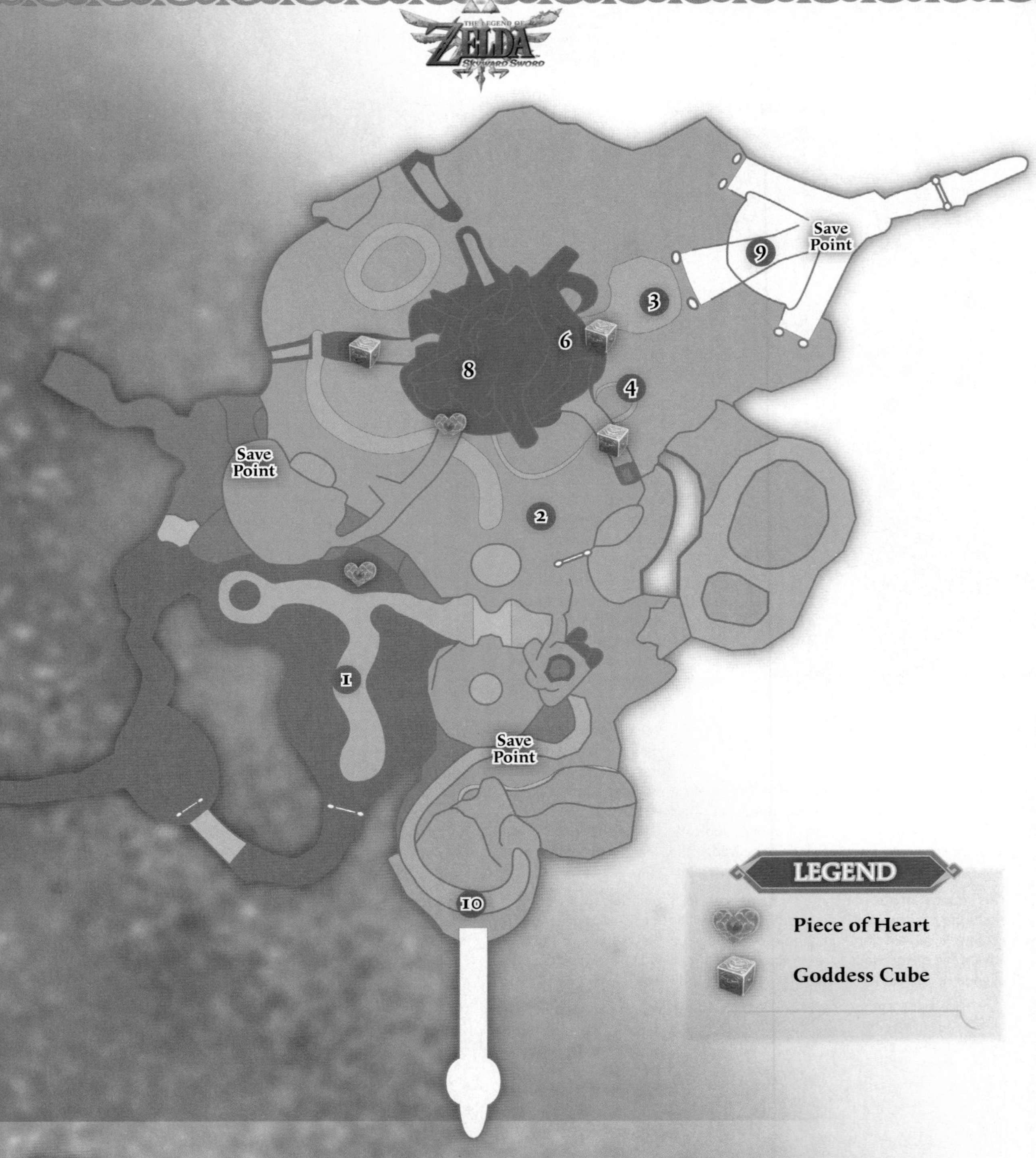

Return to Faron Woods

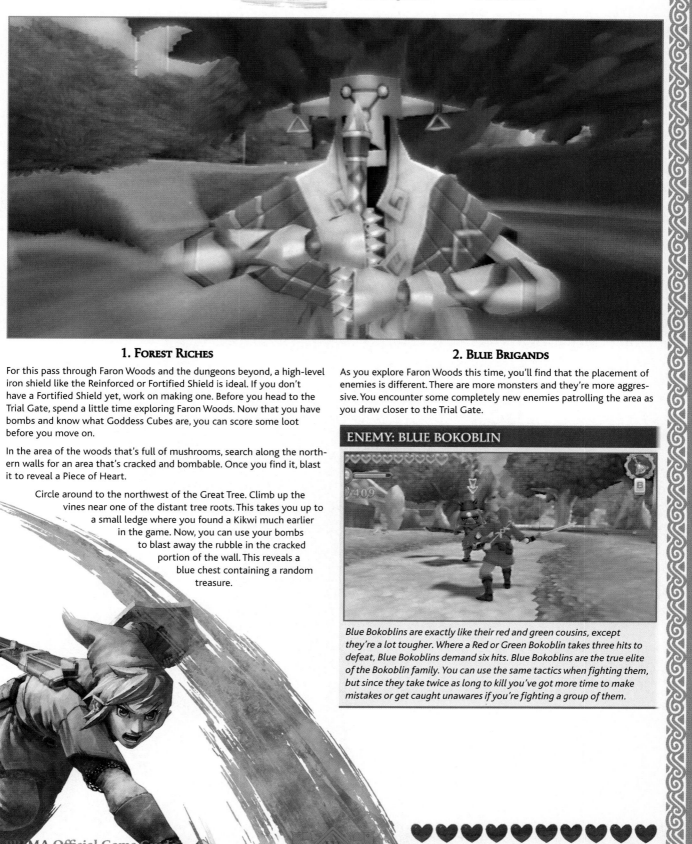

1. Forest Riches

For this pass through Faron Woods and the dungeons beyond, a high-level iron shield like the Reinforced or Fortified Shield is ideal. If you don't have a Fortified Shield yet, work on making one. Before you head to the Trial Gate, spend a little time exploring Faron Woods. Now that you have bombs and know what Goddess Cubes are, you can score some loot before you move on.

In the area of the woods that's full of mushrooms, search along the northern walls for an area that's cracked and bombable. Once you find it, blast it to reveal a Piece of Heart.

Circle around to the northwest of the Great Tree. Climb up the vines near one of the distant tree roots. This takes you up to a small ledge where you found a Kikwi much earlier in the game. Now, you can use your bombs to blast away the rubble in the cracked portion of the wall. This reveals a blue chest containing a random treasure.

2. Blue Brigands

As you explore Faron Woods this time, you'll find that the placement of enemies is different. There are more monsters and they're more aggressive. You encounter some completely new enemies patrolling the area as you draw closer to the Trial Gate.

ENEMY: BLUE BOKOBLIN

Blue Bokoblins are exactly like their red and green cousins, except they're a lot tougher. Where a Red or Green Bokoblin takes three hits to defeat, Blue Bokoblins demand six hits. Blue Bokoblins are the true elite of the Bokoblin family. You can use the same tactics when fighting them, but since they take twice as long to kill you've got more time to make mistakes or get caught unawares if you're fighting a group of them.

3. Tears of Farore

You find the Trial Gate in the circular area just in front of the viewing platform. To activate it, take out your harp and strum it. When the circle of light appears, strum in time with it as best you can. As you play the song correctly, flower petals blossom along the circle of light. When the song is done, follow the on-screen instructions to thrust your sword into the Trial Gate. Once you thrust your sword into the gate, you're taken instantly into the Silent Realm.

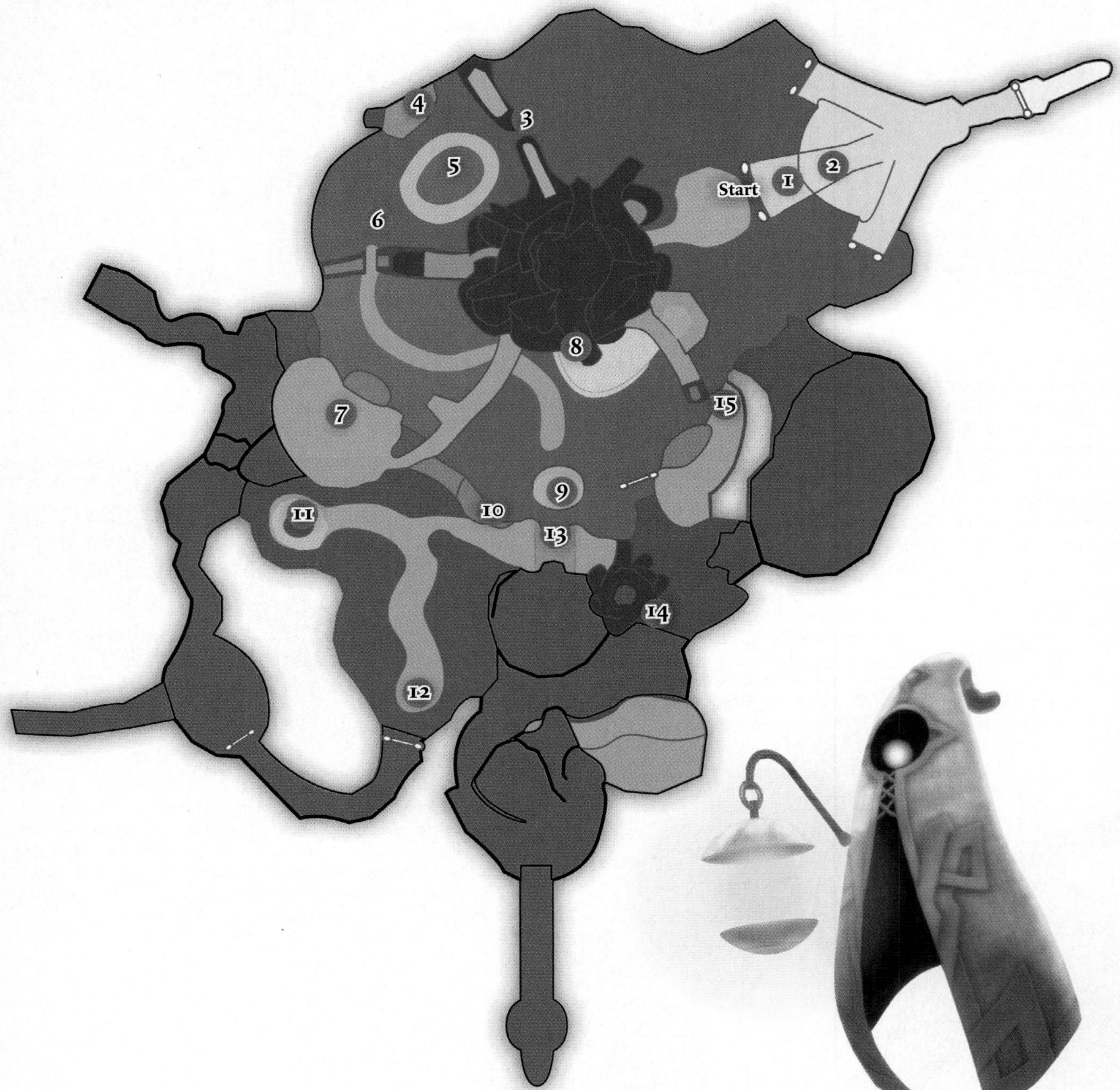

In a Silent Realm challenge, you're stripped of all your weapons and transported to an eerie mirror of the area where the Trial Gate was located. The enemies in this area are completely invincible and you have no defense against them. The twist to this is that the enemies in this area (Guardians) remain asleep as long as they don't notice you. They awaken the moment you step outside of the challenge's starting area but immediately return to sleep when you grab one of the 15 items you're gathering as part of the challenge. For the Faron Woods challenge, you're collecting Tears of Farore.

After you've grabbed a tear, the Guardians return to sleep for 90 seconds. You don't have an in-game timer, but as your time runs down the Spirit Vessel in the upper-left part of the screen begins to wilt. When it turns completely brown, the Guardians awaken and begin hunting you down. You can also awaken the Guardians if you're spotted by one of the roving Watchers or if you touch the Silent Realm's Waking Water. If you are attacked by the Guardians, note that you get to restart the Silent Realm challenge immediately.

If you accidentally awaken the Guardians, your goal should be immediately finding the nearest tear so you can grab it and put them back to sleep. In this particular Silent Realm challenge, you mainly need to focus on keeping the Watchers from noticing you. Since you're on a timer you may be tempted to dash everywhere, but if there's a Watcher nearby, dashing draws its attention. If you just move at a normal pace and give Watchers a wide berth, you should make it through the challenge safely. In general, the easiest way to beat Silent Realm challenges is to not panic and just do things at a steady, careful pace.

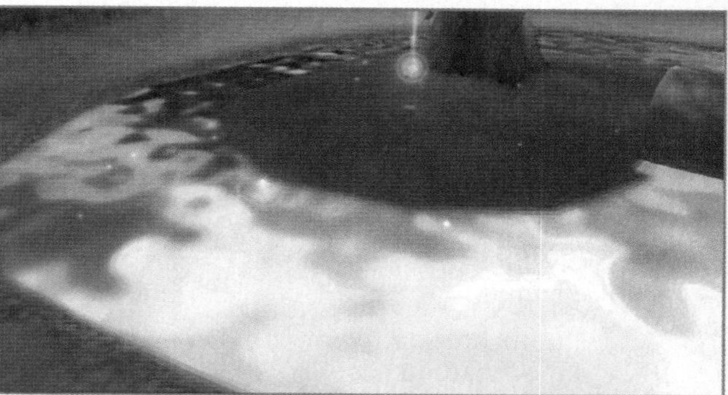

You can collect the 15 Tears of Farore in this Silent Realm in any order, but the numbers presented are a suggested order you might want to try. Silent Realms are dotted with white Light Fruit you can grab to make the tears shoot beacons into the sky, which can help you orient yourself if you've gotten lost looking for one. After you collect the 15th tear, you have to return to the start point to finish the challenge.

This can be the most dangerous part of any Silent Realm challenge, since if you awaken the Guardians you have no way to put them back to sleep. You just have to make a mad dash for the start point. If you gather the tears in a pattern that lets you circle around the area, then you can make your trip back to the start point just a little bit shorter. Note that there's a treasure worth collecting in the Silent Realm besides Tears of Farore.

Dusk Relics

A treasure you need for upgrading certain equipment in Skyward Sword *is the Dusk Relic. You can only acquire Dusk Relics in Silent Realms and from blue chests that contain random treasures. If you want to fully upgrade all of Link's equipment, you need 13 Dusk Relics. Even if you want to make only recommended equipment upgrades, you'll need 11 Dusk Relics.*

The Faron Woods Silent Realm is the easiest of the four you visit in the game, so it can be useful to pick up lots of Dusk Relics here while you're learning the ropes. Once you have at least 13 Dusk Relics, you can forget about collecting them in Silent Realms and just focus on passing the challenges.

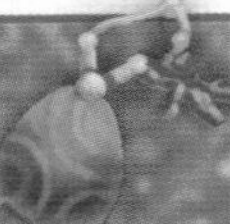

THE WATER DRAGON'S SCALE

Your reward for clearing this Silent Realm trial is the Water Dragon's Scale, which lets Link swim deep underwater. To swim, just hold down Ⓐ and tilt the Wii Remote. Like flying your Loftwing or the Beetle, controlling Link underwater uses Wii MotionPlus sensitivity. While you're underwater, you can shake the Nunchuk to make Link do a spinning attack that also lets him pass through small tunnels. Note that while swimming your stamina meter becomes your air meter, which indicates how long you can stay underwater without drowning.

4. Inside the Great Tree

Now that you have the Water Dragon's Scale, head to the pool of water that's just to the left of the Great Tree in the center of Faron Woods. Dive deep within the water to find the entrance to a long tunnel that runs through the roots of the Great Tree. Swim inside the tunnel to enter the next area you must explore. Don't worry about running out of air; there are plenty of air bubbles for Link in just about any area where he can swim for long.

5. Red Herring

At the end of the tunnel you come into a hollow area inside the Great Tree's trunk. Climb the nearby vines out of the water. Above you are two platforms that seem to lead to the exit. The far platform is patrolled by a Blue Bokoblin. In this room, you can easily take him out by using the Gust Bellows to blow the Froaks drifting around at him. The Froak explosion is powerful enough to kill the Blue Bokoblin in one shot.

Then use the Gust Bellows to set the platform you're on in motion, by blowing air at something else solid (like, say, the other platform). Making the jump from the second platform to the door is very difficult. It's faster to instead swing your platform at the solid area to your left. From there, you can follow the small platforms around the wall and then drop down right over the door on the other side.

Before you leave, you can follow the platforms farther up in the tree to find some hidden loot. The route up is guarded by a dangling Quadro Baba, but you can use the Beetle to cut it down. Once you reach the top of the root-platforms, you should find a blue chest containing a random treasure.

6. Tree Trunk

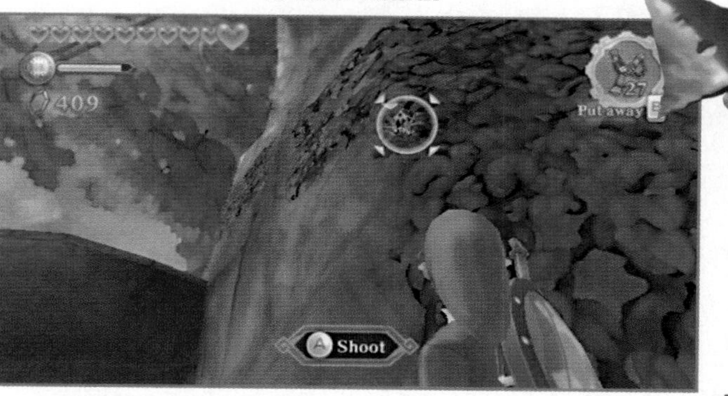

After you exit the tree interior, climb up a series of platforms that grow on the outside of the Great Tree's trunk. At the final platform, you come to a patch of vines patrolled by Walltulas. Clear out as many Walltulas as you can with your Slingshot and then start climbing. Be sure to stop and rest at the platform halfway through the vines, so you can get rid of more Walltulas and regain your stamina. At the far end of the vines is another entrance that leads inside the Great Tree.

7. Back Inside the Great Tree

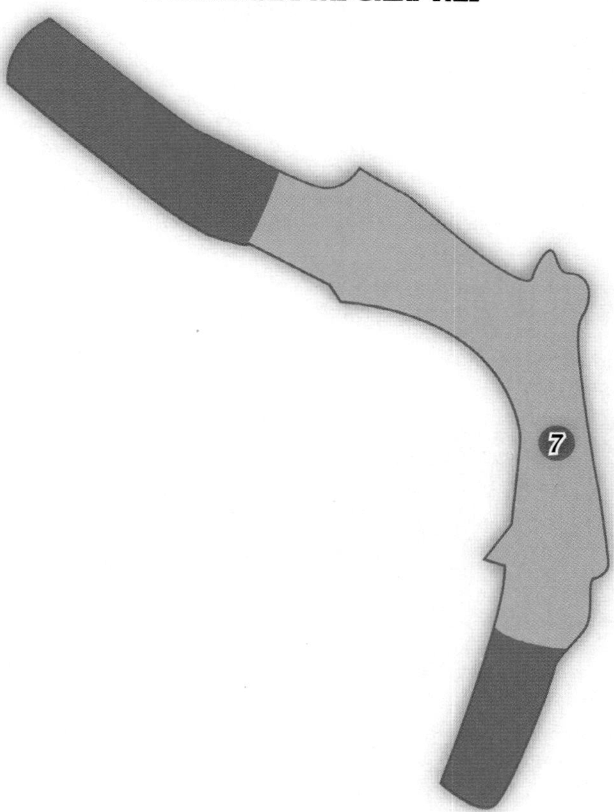

Follow the passage to enter a chamber of the Great Tree that's nothing but a single gnarled branch. This narrow passageway is patrolled by a new foe that's one of the toughest common enemies you can fight in the game. Actually, at this point, this enemy is going to be tougher than any of the sub-boss fights you've been in so far.

ENEMY: MOBLIN

One of the original Legend of Zelda *enemies is back in fine form in* Skyward Sword. *Moblins are the enormous, muscle-bound cousins of the Bokoblins. They are absurdly tough, taking well over a dozen strikes from your sword to defeat. Even when you do manage to defeat one, it can damage you in its death throes by falling on you.*

Moblins typically carry spears and either wooden or iron shields. You can destroy a wooden shield with your sword's blows, but when a Moblin has an iron shield there's nothing you can do about it. The ideal way to damage a Moblin is either to get behind it and attack it (which is difficult) or to shield bash its spear thrusts (which is surprisingly easy).

The most effective way to fight a Moblin, though it demands patience, is to wait for it to attack, shield bash to stagger the Moblin, and then hit it with a flurry of attacks. You can repeat this three or four (or more) times to defeat the Moblin as needed. If you destroy a Moblin's shield, its attack pattern changes. Instead of thrusting its spear, it becomes more of a wide sweep. You can still shield bash it, but the timing is different and a bit trickier.

At this point in your game, a Moblin is so ridiculously tough that if you can weasel out of fighting one, you should do so. Most Moblins are slow and can be dashed around. When a Moblin is guarding a narrow passage as it is in this room, though, escaping may very well be impossible.

You can sometimes evade the Moblin in this room. If it starts turning around, keep pressing your advantage, moving forward and attacking it. You might get lucky and get to slip behind the Moblin. If so, then dash out of the room and save. You get no particularly interesting rewards for defeating a Moblin. Once you've defeated or evaded the Moblin, head out and save your game at the bird statue high up in the Great Tree.

8. Back Outside

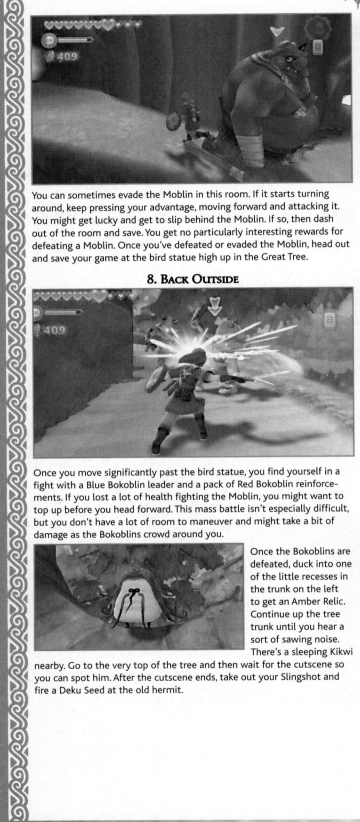

Once you move significantly past the bird statue, you find yourself in a fight with a Blue Bokoblin leader and a pack of Red Bokoblin reinforcements. If you lost a lot of health fighting the Moblin, you might want to top up before you head forward. This mass battle isn't especially difficult, but you don't have a lot of room to maneuver and might take a bit of damage as the Bokoblins crowd around you.

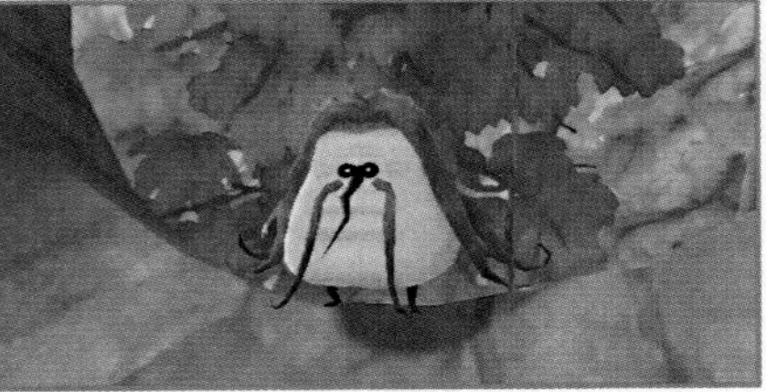

Once the Bokoblins are defeated, duck into one of the little recesses in the trunk on the left to get an Amber Relic. Continue up the tree trunk until you hear a sort of sawing noise. There's a sleeping Kikwi nearby. Go to the very top of the tree and then wait for the cutscene so you can spot him. After the cutscene ends, take out your Slingshot and fire a Deku Seed at the old hermit.

Tell the old Kikwi, named Yerbal, about your quest and in turn he tells you that the sacred flame you're looking for is in the possession of the Water Dragon, Faron. Even more helpfully, he shows you which part of Faron Woods you need to visit to begin making your way to the Water Dragon's domain. To pass through the gate, you must make the symbol you see in the picture here complete.

Now that you can climb up to the top of the Great Tree, you can snag some Goddess Cubes by diving off of it. Begin with Goddess Cube #13. To get this one, go back to the vine-covered area on the outside of the tree. When you get to the Stamina Fruit, drop down. You should find yourself on one of the small platforms growing on the outside of the tree's trunk. Look beneath you and you should be able to see the curling root you want to leap onto below. Jump down onto the root to activate the Cube.

Head back up the tree and use a similar method to claim Goddess Cube #14, which sits on the curling root that grows over the pool of water at the tree's base. Use the Look command to confirm when you're on a platform that overlooks this root, then jump off to reach and activate Cube #14.

Back up the tree one more time. You also get to Goddess Cube #15 by leaping off the tree, but this time you need to go up high enough that your fall becomes a dive. You can't land directly on the area where the Cube is located, but there's a little platform nearby that you can land on instead. From there, cross the tightrope to reach and activate Goddess Cube #15.

You're done in the Great Tree for now. Feel free to make your way down by jumping right off of it, wherever you please.

9. Return to the Viewing Platform

Head over to the viewing platform and fight the Blue Bokoblins that patrol the area now. Next, head to the top of the viewing platform, between the entrance to the Deep Woods and the bird statue. Look at the ground to see the completed symbol you must create. Once you're satisfied that you're familiar with it, go find the door to the Water Dragon's domain.

10. Return to Spiral Hill

Go back to the top of the spiraling hill that's at the southernmost point of Faron Woods. Defeat the Octoroks that still infest the area. Once the area's safe, approach the stone wall bearing the incomplete symbol. Charge your sword to do a Skyward Strike in front of the symbol and you get a prompt to draw on the wall, just as if you were standing before a goddess wall. Move Link's sword into the desired position and then hold down Ⓐ on your Wii Remote to have Link put the tip of his sword into the wall, to carve the stone. Draw a circle in the center of the innermost crescent. (As you can see from the picture, it doesn't necessarily have to be a very good circle.)

After you successfully draw a circle, the wall turns into a pair of double doors that open inward. Run down the long stone hallway behind them if you're ready to enter Lake Floria.

Goddess's Treasure Chest Pickups: #6, #13, #14, #15

Now that you have the Water Dragon's Scale, you can pick up goddess's treasure chest #6. If you've searched around the shed the chest stands in with the Beetle, you may have noticed a pool of water in it. You can get into the shed by leaping into the river in Skyloft and looking for an underwater stone passageway along the eastern side of the river's flow. When you find the entrance, just follow the passage until you come to the top. Climb out of the pool inside the shed to open goddess's treasure chest #6 and pick up a blue chest that contains a random treasure.

Goddess's treasure chest #13 is on Skyloft. Dive into the Knight Academy courtyard and exit as if you were going to the plaza. Eventually you should come to a wooden diving platform on your right. Stand at the end of it and Look down to see that there's a pier holding the activated goddess's treasure chest just below you. Leap off of the diving pier and you should have no trouble landing on the platform. Open chest #13 to receive a Silver Rupee.

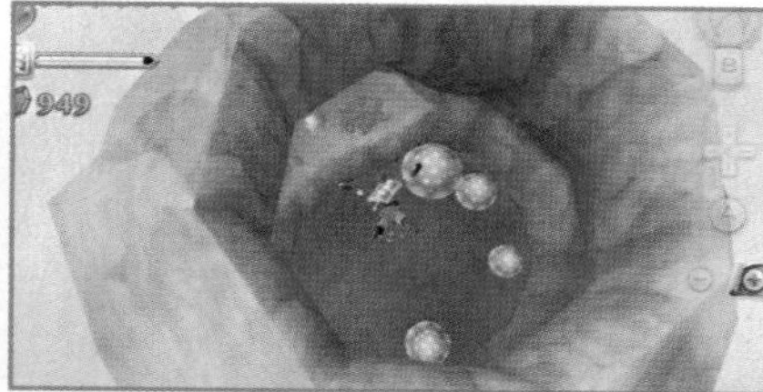

Goddess's treasure chest #14 is located on the curious island near the Lanayru Desert entrance where you grabbed chest #10 earlier. This time, you need to dive into the hollow center of the island to grab the activated chest. Open this chest to obtain a Piece of Heart.

To get goddess's treasure chest #15, head into the thunderhead. This chest lies on a tiny speck of an island that's just to the northeast of the Isle of Songs. Despite how small this island is, it's packed with treasure. First, dig in the dirt patch to reveal a steam geyser. Ride it up to a blue chest that contains a random treasure.

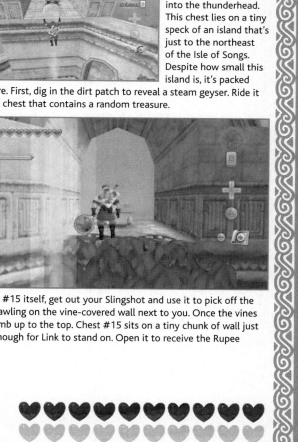

To get chest #15 itself, get out your Slingshot and use it to pick off the Walltulas crawling on the vine-covered wall next to you. Once the vines are clear, climb up to the top. Chest #15 sits on a tiny chunk of wall just barely big enough for Link to stand on. Open it to receive the Rupee Medal.

1

2

3

4

5

LEGEND

Piece of Heart

Goddess Cube

LAKE FLORIA

1. Break On Through

After a long, long dive you find yourself in an enormous pool of water. Swim north, toward where the lake becomes more of a river. Keep going until you come to a rather panicky-looking Parella. Like the Kikwis you met earlier in the game, he mistakes you for some sort of predator and runs away. Chase him. When he disappears into a boarded-up tunnel, do a spin attack to break through.

Of course, only people with Water Dragon's Scales can do spin attacks, so the Parella is quite impressed when he sees you break through. Realizing you're an emissary of the goddess, he asks you to help the Water Dragon with a problem she's having. Let the Parella lead you into a large chamber. It's not completely underwater, but you can't do much more at the surface besides get a breath of air.

2. Swimming Bombs

The usual exit to this chamber is blocked by a massive boulder. You can't remove it, so instead you need to take the long way around. Swim toward a tunnel in the north part of the room to proceed. If you want to explore a little, note that this area is full to the brim with Froaks and cracked, bombable walls. To make the underwater Froaks explode, just spin-attack them. Be sure not to get too close before you start your spin attack, or the Froak defends itself with its damaging spines. Opening up the bombable walls reveals hearts and Red Rupees. Save your game before you move on.

3. Amphibious

To enter the next room, you have to master the art of leaping out of the water so you can get over the iron gate that bars the way. Swim toward the gate, angle Link up at the surface of the water, and shake the Nunchuk just before you reach the surface of the water. Link leaps out of the water like a dolphin. If he hits a solid surface, he makes a rolling landing. If he hits water, he just dives back in.

Continue to follow the Parella. When he passes through a narrow crack between two blocks of stone, leap after him. This time Link hits solid ground. Save your game at the nearby bird statue and then explore the area above it. Open the blue chest there to receive a random treasure. Cross the room and defeat a few Green Chuchus that spawn on the way. Use your Slingshot to knock down the Green Chuchu that lies in wait for you on the ceiling.

Go back in the previous room and walk over the arch above the iron gate you jumped earlier. On the other side of the arch is Goddess Cube #16. Just beyond it, pick up an Amber Relic. You can find another in an alcove in the same room—one you can only reach by jumping into the water and then jumping onto it. Rejoin the Parella in the water on the other side when you're ready to move on.

4. Finny Fiend

Follow the Parella down a deep underwater tunnel full of burrs. You can spin-attack to destroy burrs safely or just evade them. Leap over the next iron grate. The next area features one of the "scary fish" the other Parellas have been talking about. If you swim near it, it turns red and charges you. Direct a spin attack at the cross-shaped scar on its forehead to defeat it. After that, follow the Parella to an underground doorway. The Water Dragon is in the next room.

5. The Water Dragon's Test

The Water Dragon is not entirely convinced that you are who you say you are, whether you've got a Water Dragon's Scale or not. She proposes a test to see if you're really a hero and tasks you with fi nding more sacred water for her tub. Fi sets the sacred water as a dowsing target. Make sure you've got an Empty Bottle and then prepare for a bit of backtracking through a dungeon. Leave the Water Dragon's room the way she directs and save at the bird statue outside.

> **NOTE**
>
> While there is another Goddess Cube in Lake Floria, you can't get it right now. You can pick it up later in the game, when you've acquired a necessary tool.

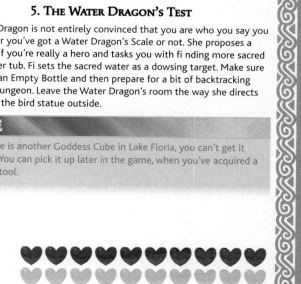

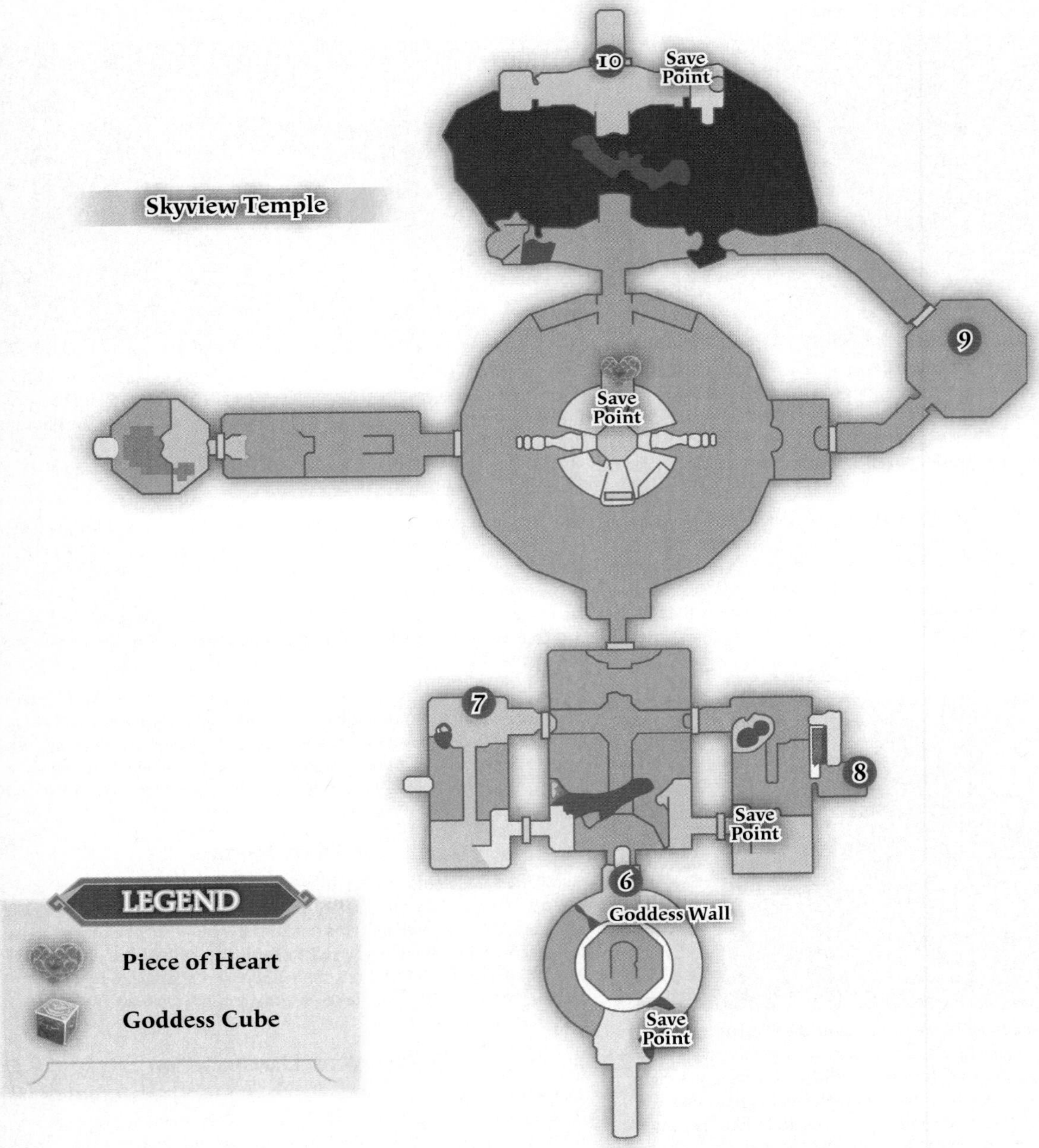

Skyview Temple

10 Save Point

9

Save Point

7

8

Save Point

6 Goddess Wall

Save Point

LEGEND

Piece of Heart

Goddess Cube

6. Return to Skyview Temple

Dowsing for sacred water leads you inexorably toward Skyview Temple. This only makes sense; you can pass through it to reach the surely sacred Skyview Spring. When you reenter the temple, though, you find this is no quick backtracking mission. Powerful monsters have anticipated the Water Dragon's needs and taken over the temple. Expect to fight your way back into Skyview Spring.

For now, though, start by fighting your way past a Quadro Baba back to the shortcut you created in your last trip here. Three Blessed Butterflies are now gathered around the opposite wall. Approach and strum your harp to summon a goddess wall. The music catches the attention of an unlikely visitor, one of the Mogmas you met earlier in Eldin Volcano.

7. The Missing Key

Use the shortcut to enter the next room, which is now patrolled by a Staldra and a throng of Froaks. Once you defeat the Staldra, examining the north door reveals that you've got something of a problem. The monsters have relocked the door, forcing you to go find the Small Key for it again. The two adjoining rooms are still unlocked, so you'd better start looking around for it.

Head into the left-hand room and you meet another one of the Mogmas. He gives you a valuable clue: He says that he swiped the Small Key from a monster, but then lost it in a "hole somewhere." What's the closest thing to a hole you've encountered in this dungeon? The area you can only get into through a tunnel in the right-hand room, of course.

8. Out of the Way

Spin-attack into this area, then grab the vines and climb up. Now there's a patch of dirt at the end of the small passageway. Dig in it to retrieve the Small Key. Head back into the central chamber and proceed.

9. Dragon Heads

As you head toward the entrance to Skyview Spring, you get locked into another sub-boss encounter in this area. This time it's a pair of Staldras instead of just the one. By now, you should have enough experience fighting Staldras that both go down quickly.

10. The Gauntlet

ENEMY: BOKOBLIN ARCHER

Bokoblin archers are perhaps the most deadly of the Bokoblins you fight in this game. Regardless of skin color, they all behave roughly the same way. Bokoblin archers raise the alarm when they spot you, like Bokoblin leaders do, and can also attack you from far distances with their bows and arrows. Right now you have no good way of damaging them short of rushing up to them with your sword at the ready—which isn't an option when they're on the other side of a rope bridge. If you can get close to a Bokoblin archer, it goes down in a single blow.

The Bokoblin archers here can be a real pain. The only way to deal with them now is to launch the Hook Beetle and start looking around for a Bomb Flower. Dizzying them with your Slingshot is useless because Bokoblin archers never, ever move toward you. Fortunately, a Bomb Flower is now growing from one of the curling vines in the canopy, just above the archers.

What makes Bokoblin archers so much more dangerous than other Bokoblins is that, well, they aren't stupid. The Bokoblin archers are definitely going to try to shoot down the Hook Beetle before it can drop bombs on them. If they land a shot on the Hook Beetle, it automatically detonates the Bomb Flower and counts as a crash. The Hook Beetle goes back to Link's wrist launcher and you have to try again. Just keep at it until the way is clear. If you can get the Hook Beetle close to a Bokoblin archer before it's shot down, the explosion may take out one of the archers, too. You can also try sneaking the Hook Beetle in just behind the archers, so they have a hard time targeting it.

Once you make it past the archers, well, you should know better than to expect the boss room to be unoccupied. The minute you step inside, you're locked into a sub-boss encounter with three Stalfos. You absolutely can't get through this fight using defensive techniques. You can't even get very far dodging and counterattacking, since the three Stalfos are all agile and stagger their attacks so they aren't all striking at the same time.

The secret to getting through this sub-boss encounter is bombs. Instead of the usual hearts, the pots in this boss room are full of bombs. The easy way to beat these Stalfos is to plant bombs in the room and then lure the Stalfos onto them. The bombs only stagger them, but the bombs can stagger all three of them at once (if you're lucky) or stagger one and give you a chance to damage it without the other two dog-piling you. Once bombs help you whittle the Stalfos' numbers down to something manageable, you can dispatch the last of them with your usual preferred tactics.

Once the Stalfos are defeated, enter Skyview Spring. There's a lot of water here, but not all of it counts as sacred. Dowse in the Spring until you come to a waterfall where Fairies gather. Only water taken from the base of this particular waterfall counts as sacred water. Just stand near this area with the Empty Bottle in hand to get the prompt to scoop some water into it. After you've gotten the sacred water, the game automatically takes you back to the entrance to Skyview Temple. Head back to Lake Floria as quickly as you can to see the Water Dragon. Simply stand in front of her tub and talk to her with the sacred water in your Adventure Pouch to trigger the series of cutscenes that eventually reveal the Ancient Cistern to you. Gear up for a dungeon crawl.

Goddess's Treasure Chest Pickups: #16

To get goddess's treasure chest #16, you need a tool that you don't have yet. Come back to get this one later.

LEGEND

Piece of Heart

Goddess Cube

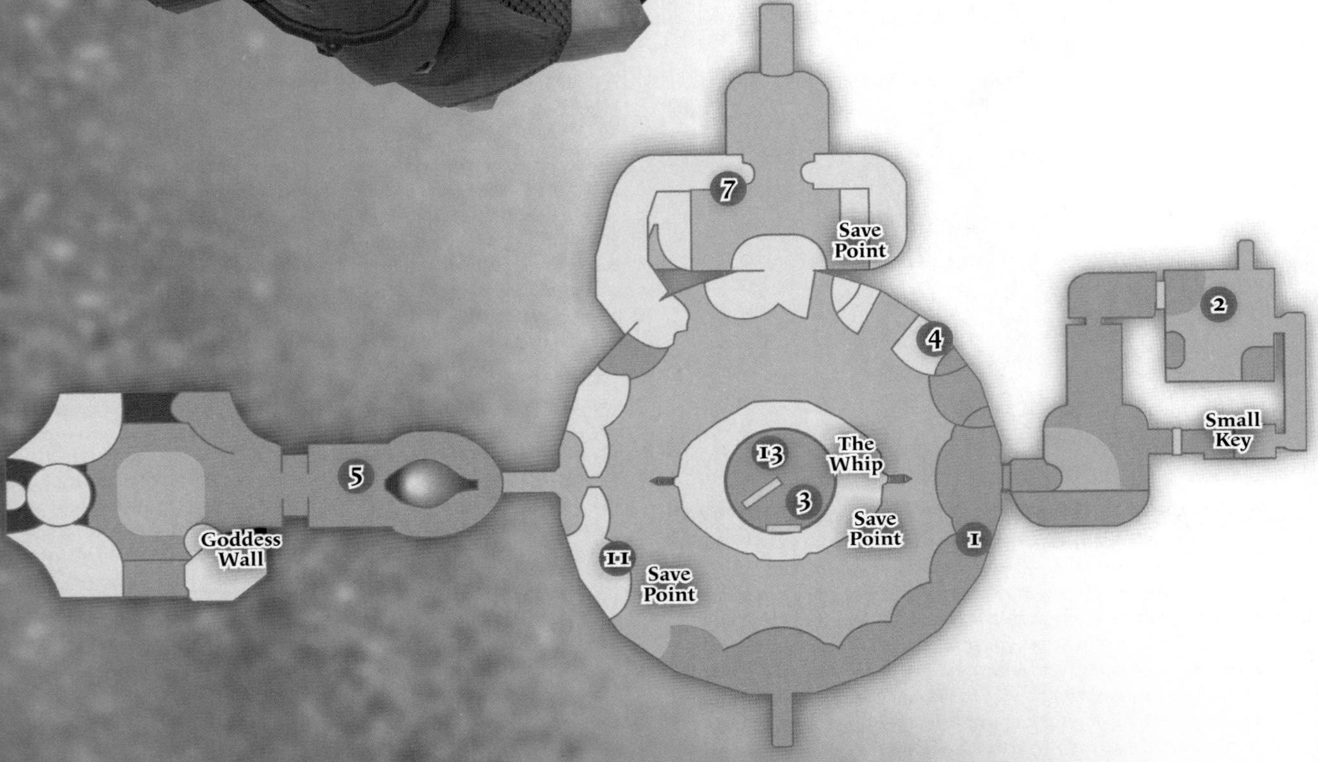

Save Point

Small Key

The Whip

Save Point

Goddess Wall

Save Point

The Ancient Cistern

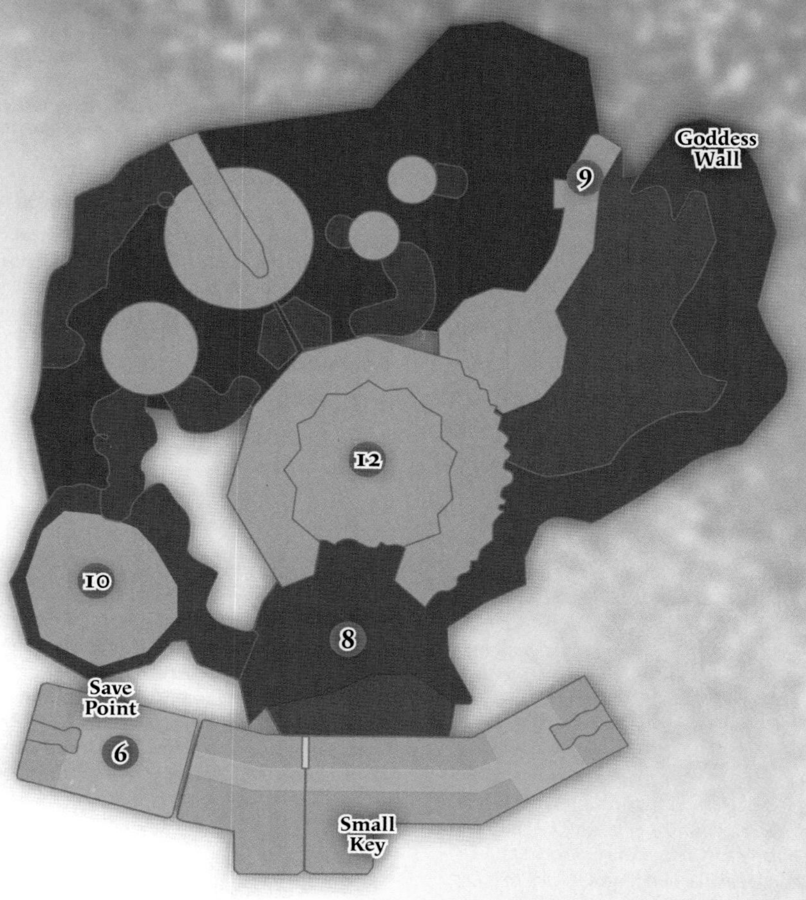

1. Consider the Lotus

Begin by heading around to the right, fighting the groups of Green Chuchus that spawn in your path. Pull the switch to raise the bars blocking the door leading into the right-hand chamber. Dive off the platform and splash down in the pool. Follow the room's walkways around to the left. Fight or sneak your way past the Skulltulas until you come to a door sporting an unusual floral lock. Read the stone tablet next to it for the clue that tells you how to unlock it.

Return to the central chamber and examine the enormous statue there. If you leap from the water onto the solid platform that runs around the statue's back and sides, you can read another stone tablet that contains another important clue. You need to examine spots on the upper back, lower back, back of the right palm, and back of the left palm. A red arrow points in a certain direction on each spot. For the impatient, the order of the arrows is up-down-left-right. This indicates the order you should strike the "petals" on the floral lock: the top one, the bottom one, the left one, and then the right one.

TIP

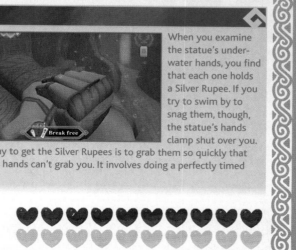

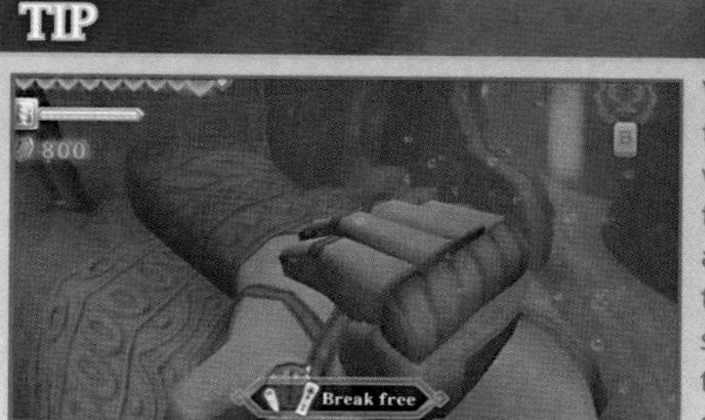

When you examine the statue's underwater hands, you find that each one holds a Silver Rupee. If you try to swim by to snag them, though, the statue's hands clamp shut over you. The only way to get the Silver Rupees is to grab them so quickly that the statue's hands can't grab you. It involves doing a perfectly timed spin attack.

2. Thorny Situation

You're in a room full of water and lily pads. Before you try to explore the room, look up. There's a pair of dangling Skulltulas lying in wait for you. Use the Hook Beetle to cut their threads and drown them. Next, go examine the room underwater. A lily pad with especially thorny roots is blocking the underwater tunnel that leads out of this room.

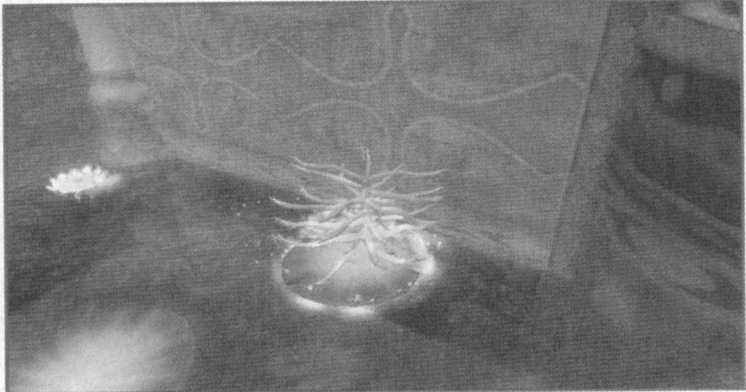

When you jump onto a lily pad, notice that it shifts quite a bit under your weight. If you leap onto a lily pad from a high enough height, you can actually overturn it. This is how you clear the thorny roots out of your way. There's a tall platform you can climb onto using vines right next to the lily pad you need to flip. Leap from the top of this platform onto the thorny lily pad to overturn it. Next, follow the passage to its end and claim a Small Key.

3. Give Me the Whip

Head back into the main room and save at the bird statue. Next, leap across the two lily pads and unlock the door that leads into a room inside the massive statue. At the very top of this chamber is a puzzle door, but there's no indication of a jeweled chest around and no way to move up. Instead, walk forward and drop down into the hole in front of you. Bear in mind that you're jumping into a sub-boss battle.

SUB-BOSS: STALMASTER

A Stalmaster is a four-armed, armored Stalfos that's harder to kill and a more dangerous attacker. It wields four enormous weapons but uses only two swords in the first phase of the battle. In this phase, you can fight the Stalmaster as if he were an ordinary Stalfos. shield bash his sword attacks to stagger him or dodge around him to inflict some damage while he's extended. You can also get some extra damage in when the Stalmaster approaches while guarding with his swords, since he always leaves an opening.

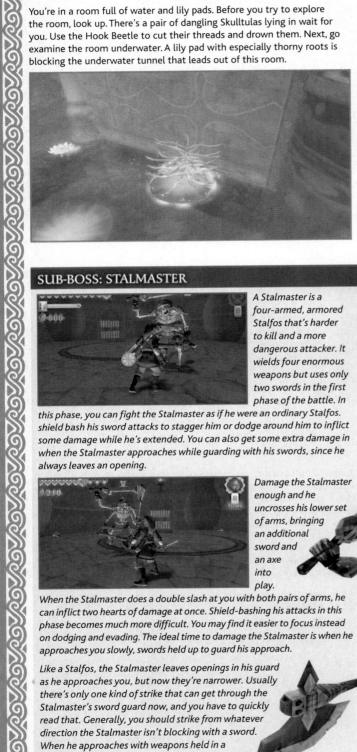

Damage the Stalmaster enough and he uncrosses his lower set of arms, bringing an additional sword and an axe into play.

When the Stalmaster does a double slash at you with both pairs of arms, he can inflict two hearts of damage at once. Shield-bashing his attacks in this phase becomes much more difficult. You may find it easier to focus instead on dodging and evading. The ideal time to damage the Stalmaster is when he approaches you slowly, swords held up to guard his approach.

Like a Stalfos, the Stalmaster leaves openings in his guard as he approaches you, but now they're narrower. Usually there's only one kind of strike that can get through the Stalmaster's sword guard now, and you have to quickly read that. Generally, you should strike from whatever direction the Stalmaster isn't blocking with a sword. When he approaches with weapons held in a rectangular pattern, you can damage him with a thrust.

When both sets of swords are crossed, the Stalmaster is planning to attack. Prepare to dodge away from him. It's difficult in this phase to dodge around to attack him while he's locked in his attack animation, but not impossible. If your attack misses while the Stalmaster is approaching you, expect a counterattack and try to dodge quickly. Patiently stick to hit-and-run tactics and eventually you should defeat him. Once the Stalmaster is defeated, a door containing a blue chest opens. It holds a valuable new tool.

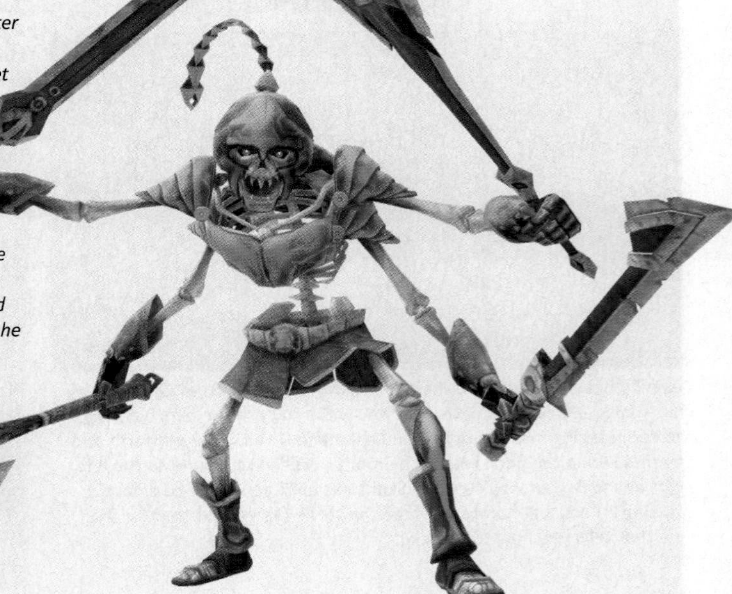

THE WHIP

The whip opens up new areas, both in this dungeon and in the places you're about to explore. You use it by snapping the Wii Remote sharply forward, as if cracking a real whip. You can use the whip to grab onto hooks and similar objects. Once you've snagged something with the whip, you can yank it toward or away from you if it's a switch. On solid hooks, you can swing from them as if the whip was one of the ropes and vines you used back in Faron Woods. Finally, you can use the whip to steal from certain enemies.

No doors lead immediately out of this room, so try using your new whip on the four-ringed metal knob you find when you examine the place. Hold Z to lock onto it, then snap the Wii Remote back sharply after the whip has snared it. The knob twists up, turning on a huge, high-pressure jet of water. Ride the water jet up to the next level of the area inside the statue. If you turn on all of the other water jets inside of the statue, you can ride them all the way up to the dungeon's puzzle door. A stone tablet beside the puzzle door mentions that its key lies "beneath the earth."

4. Platform Swings

Head back into the central chamber and leap up the platforms to the left of the door you initially entered. Now you can pass through this area by using your whip to swing from the hooks. Once you reach the platform on the far side, you come to a barred door with a blue chest containing the Dungeon Map to its left. You may also encounter a new enemy in this area, if you get unlucky.

Once you see the bars blocking your way, it should be clear you can't enter the room from this platform. You need to get over to the next set of platforms somehow. Circle around to the left to find the switch pictured here. You need to pull it, but a lily pad's thorns are blocking you. The thorn at the top is hook shaped, so try using your whip to grab it. Flick the whip to yank the lily pad over, then stand on it and use the whip to pull the switch.

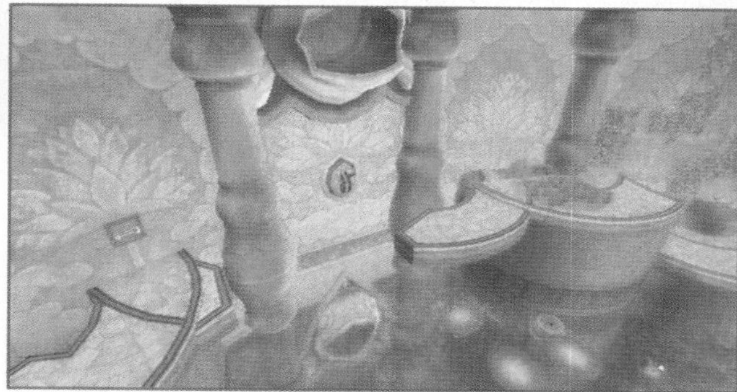

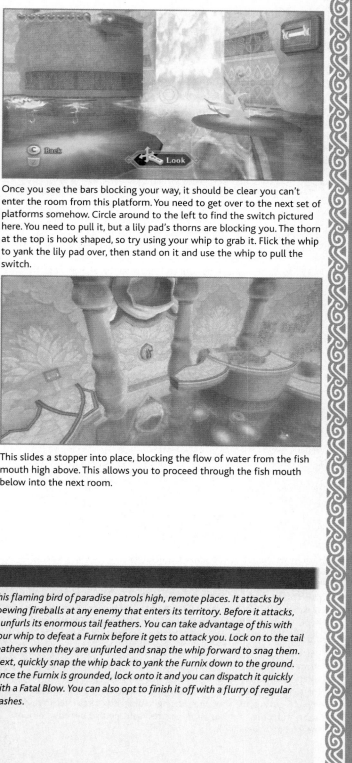

This slides a stopper into place, blocking the flow of water from the fish mouth high above. This allows you to proceed through the fish mouth below into the next room.

ENEMY: FURNIX

This flaming bird of paradise patrols high, remote places. It attacks by spewing fireballs at any enemy that enters its territory. Before it attacks, it unfurls its enormous tail feathers. You can take advantage of this with your whip to defeat a Furnix before it gets to attack you. Lock on to the tail feathers when they are unfurled and snap the whip forward to snag them. Next, quickly snap the whip back to yank the Furnix down to the ground. Once the Furnix is grounded, lock onto it and you can dispatch it quickly with a Fatal Blow. You can also opt to finish it off with a flurry of regular slashes.

5. Down the Hole

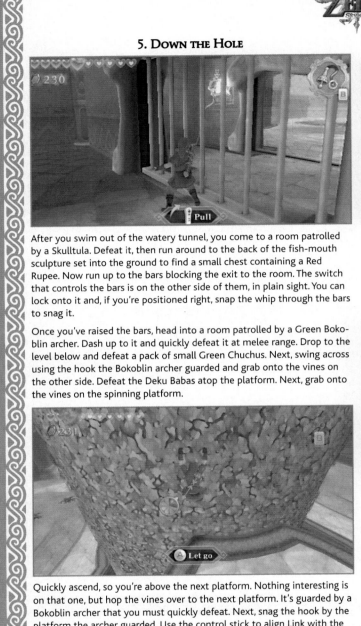

After you swim out of the watery tunnel, you come to a room patrolled by a Skulltula. Defeat it, then run around to the back of the fish-mouth sculpture set into the ground to find a small chest containing a Red Rupee. Now run up to the bars blocking the exit to the room. The switch that controls the bars is on the other side of them, in plain sight. You can lock onto it and, if you're positioned right, snap the whip through the bars to snag it.

Once you've raised the bars, head into a room patrolled by a Green Bokoblin archer. Dash up to it and quickly defeat it at melee range. Drop to the level below and defeat a pack of small Green Chuchus. Next, swing across using the hook the Bokoblin archer guarded and grab onto the vines on the other side. Defeat the Deku Babas atop the platform. Next, grab onto the vines on the spinning platform.

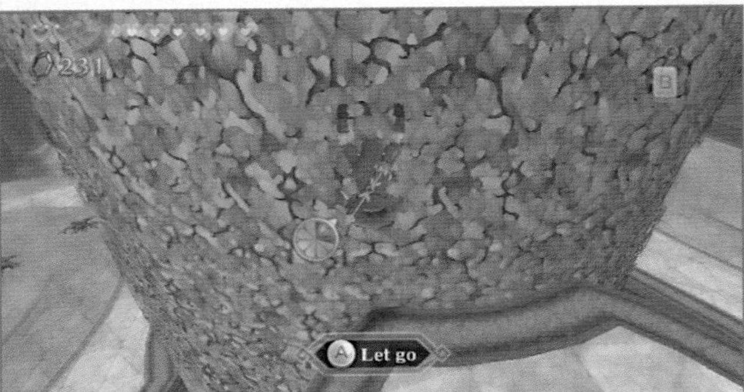

Quickly ascend, so you're above the next platform. Nothing interesting is on that one, but hop the vines over to the next platform. It's guarded by a Bokoblin archer that you must quickly defeat. Next, snag the hook by the platform the archer guarded. Use the control stick to align Link with the switch on the far wall, rather than the patch of vines directly opposite the hook. Swing over the switch and leap onto it to pull it. The switch raises the bars blocking you off from the top platform.

Once you drop to the area below the switch, get out your Slingshot and shoot the Walltula off the vine patch. Backtrack up onto the platform where you fought the archer. Now swing onto the vines and climb up to the top of the platform. Defeat the three Deku Babas there, then use the whip to yank up the knob they were guarding. This turns a nearby pool into a whirlpool. Step out onto the small balcony that directly overlooks the whirlpool and dive in.

6. The Prisoner

The whirlpool sucks you down to the Ancient Cistern's basement level. Save your game at the bird statue, then snag the Amber Relic nearby. Three Skulltulas dangle from this room's ceiling, directly over three lily pads. Use the Hook Beetle to cut their threads and drop them, flipping over the lily pads and drowning them in the pool below. This reveals a tunnel you can use to swim under the bars and pass into the next area.

In the next room, you find a padlocked door on the left. In front of you are bars and beyond them is a Green Bokoblin guard. Get out your whip and snag the Bokoblin's belt. Snap the whip back and it drops the Small Key you need, right into your hands. Now you can pass into the next room and defeat the Bokoblin. A cutscene shows you that the jeweled chest is waiting at the bottom of a deep pit to your left, one you can't reach yet. Swim into the pipe at the end of the passageway to return to the cistern's first floor.

7. The Crossing

You come out in the room to the cistern's north you couldn't get into before. Swim until you find an upside-down lily pad beneath a patch of vines growing on a wall. Leap onto the platform nearby and use the whip to flip the lily pad back over. Follow the stairs up and fight the Quadro Baba at the end of the platform. Dive off the platform to flip over the lily pad below you. This opens up an underwater tunnel you can swim through.

Snag the Red Rupee at the bottom of the tunnel, then swim through a long tunnel populated by Froaks. When you spin-attack these Froaks, they drop air bubbles that help you top up your air gauge. Follow the water tunnel to its end, then walk up the stairs. Defeat the Deku Baba hanging from the ceiling at the top of the staircase. Beyond the Deku Baba, there's a knob you can spin up with your whip.

This sends a massive water jet shooting up beneath the lily pad you flipped earlier. You're on the far side of the chamber now, so jump back in the water and swim across to the vines you climbed up earlier. Head up the stairs and use your whip to flip the lily pad over. Now you can use it as a platform to cross the gap. Ascend the stairs at the other side and pull the switch at the end of the hallway. Battle the Furnix (or Furnixes) you encounter at the other side.

Climb down the vines to a platform holding a small chest containing a Red Rupee that's beneath the platform you were on previously. Then use the vines to cross over to some platforms before you. Walltulas lurk on these vines, but they're relatively easy to outrace. Once you're there, use the whip to spin up the knob before you. This opens up a useful shortcut. Then head over to the hook at the end of the platform. Yank it down. This causes something fairly unexpected.

The statue at the center of the room descends, its feet touching down in the basement level. Head back into the statue and drop all the way down.

8. Abandon All Hope

ENEMY: CURSED BOKOBLIN

Cursed Bokoblins were once ordinary Bokoblins, but they've succumbed to the influence of evil powers. Now they shamble about in a terrible unlife, seeking to spread their curse to others. Cursed Bokoblins try to jump onto you, similar to Walltulas and Arachas, so they can drag you down by sheer force of numbers.

The quickest way to defeat them is to use the Fatal Blow. Either pummel them with three-hit combos or use Link's jump attack to knock them over, then quickly follow up with a Fatal Blow. If you simply knock them over, they can get back up a couple times. Cursed Bokoblins often appear in positively huge groups, so every fight against them is an exercise in crowd control.

As soon as you step foot in the basement area, you're attacked by a horde of Cursed Bokoblins. Once you thin out their numbers, head down the only passage that leads away from this area. More Cursed Bokoblins wait for you there. Cross the moat of polluted water on the lily pads. Use your whip to flip the last one over, so you can reach the opposite shore. Head down the stone walkway to an area where a hook overlooks a platform that's blocked by a cracked stone.

CAUTION

The thick purple-black water beneath the lily pads is so polluted that it actually does a half-heart of damage and curses you if you fall into it. While cursed, you can't attack, use items, or wield any of your tools.

You need to bomb the cracked stone and clear the platform before you can proceed. You can't throw or roll a bomb over to the stone; you instead need to find a Bomb Flower growing somewhere in the area so you can use the Hook Beetle to do the job. Head back across the lily pads and down the long, winding pathway where you can summon a goddess wall at the end. Battle a swarm of Fire Keese that attack you toward the end.

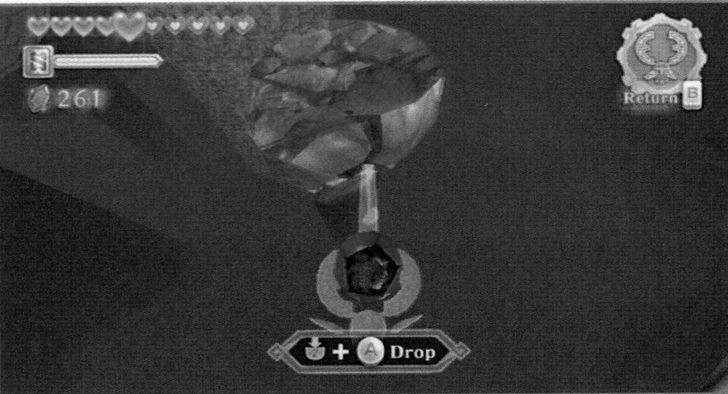

The Bomb Flower you need is at the end, growing next to a cryptic stone tablet. Follow the tablet's instructions. If you examine this area, you should find that the polluted waterfall is spewing from the mouth of a skull. Launch your Hook Beetle and guide it into one of the Skull's eye sockets to find a tunnel that hides a crystal switch. If you hit the switch, the polluted waterfall's flow stops. You can bomb the rock wall that lays beyond. Launch the Hook Beetle, snag the Bomb Flower, then fly it down the passage you've opened. If you want to do things the hard way, it's worth noting that your Hook Beetle just barely has enough stamina to get the bomb over to the stone if you fly it the long way around, too.

9. Deadly Towers

Now that the path is clear, swing across the gap. Swing across to a second platform, then grab onto the spinning vine-covered stone pillar beyond. Climb to the top of the spinning pillar, then leap to the vines on the next spinning pillar. Climb up the vines and then leap off so you get onto an area of solid stone on the other side. Follow the stones around to another vine-covered wall, which you can leap onto. Climb up to a narrow passageway next to rusted iron bars.

A hook there functions as a switch. Snag it with the whip and then yank it to your left, rather than toward your body. You may need to position Link very close to the bars to pull this off. Once you pull the switch, the stone pillar below you stops spinning counterclockwise, which would carry you toward deadly spikes, and instead spins clockwise, which takes you toward your goal.

Backtrack to the vine-covered spinning pillar you initially rode over. Use it to ride around to a small stone platform, which in turn leads to the spinning pillar you just reversed. Ride that pillar around to the base of a long stone pathway that slopes upward. Follow it, battling Cursed Bokoblins as you go. At the end of the pathway you come to a platform where you can see the exit area. You can't make the jump directly from your platform to the exit area, though.

Instead, jump onto the spinning cylinder covered in vines that's spinning clockwise next to you. Ride it around to a small area of stone platforms leading up to the other side of the rusted iron bars you saw earlier. Climb up to this area so you can reverse the switch you hit earlier. Reverse the switch. In addition to reversing the pillar below, it reverses the spin of all the pillars in the area. Backtrack to the vine-covered stone pillar you rode into this area. Now that it's spinning counterclockwise, you can grab on and ride it around to the area you couldn't reach before.

10. Day of the Cursed Bokoblin

Walk down the slope and battle the Fire Keese that roost there. At the end of the stone path, you overlook an area where sunlight pours down from above, with a single dangling rope leading out. Leap down and approach the rope. Grab onto it and begin climbing. After you've moved a little ways up, eight Cursed Bokoblins spawn. They climb up the rope after you, trying to grab hold of you and drag you back down.

To pass on to the next area, ignore the Cursed Bokoblins and just rush for the top as fast as you can. One of the Cursed Bokoblins will grab you, but if you quickly shake him off you can continue climbing. If you drop to the bottom of the area to fight the Cursed Bokoblins, another group of eight respawns the moment you begin climbing the rope again. That said, you can take advantage of this in one way.

When defeated, Cursed Bokoblins are very likely to drop a rare treasure called the Evil Crystal. They are the only enemy in the game that drops this treasure reliably and this is the only area in the game where you can easily get an infinite number of them to spawn. If you want to fully upgrade Link's equipment, you must acquire three Evil Crystals. It can be very wise to bring a Treasure Medal into this area and repeat the battle until you have all the Evil Crystals you will ever need.

11. The Final Switch

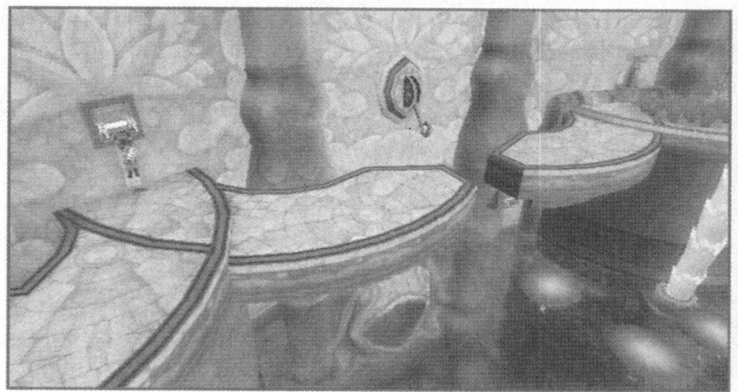

At the top of the rope, you emerge onto an otherwise unreachable platform in the Ancient Cistern's first floor. Save at the bird statue there. Read the stone tablet, which is basically telling you how to claim the jeweled chest. First, pull the switch on the right-hand side of the wall to extend a stone platform toward the hook switch on the wall. Next, use the whip to yank the switch back up. This raises the statue in the center of the area back into its original position.

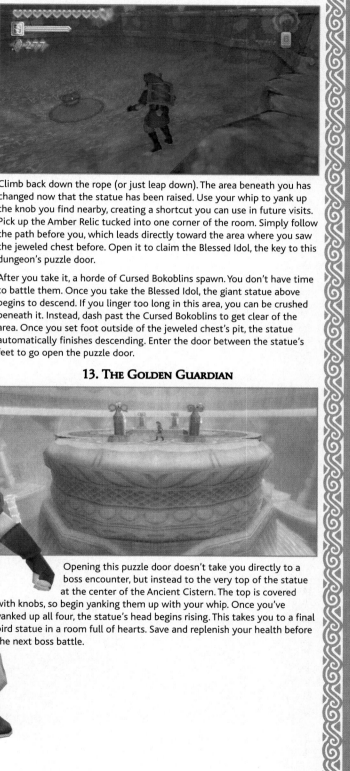

12. Give Me the Idol

Climb back down the rope (or just leap down). The area beneath you has changed now that the statue has been raised. Use your whip to yank up the knob you find nearby, creating a shortcut you can use in future visits. Pick up the Amber Relic tucked into one corner of the room. Simply follow the path before you, which leads directly toward the area where you saw the jeweled chest before. Open it to claim the Blessed Idol, the key to this dungeon's puzzle door.

After you take it, a horde of Cursed Bokoblins spawn. You don't have time to battle them. Once you take the Blessed Idol, the giant statue above begins to descend. If you linger too long in this area, you can be crushed beneath it. Instead, dash past the Cursed Bokoblins to get clear of the area. Once you set foot outside of the jeweled chest's pit, the statue automatically finishes descending. Enter the door between the statue's feet to go open the puzzle door.

13. The Golden Guardian

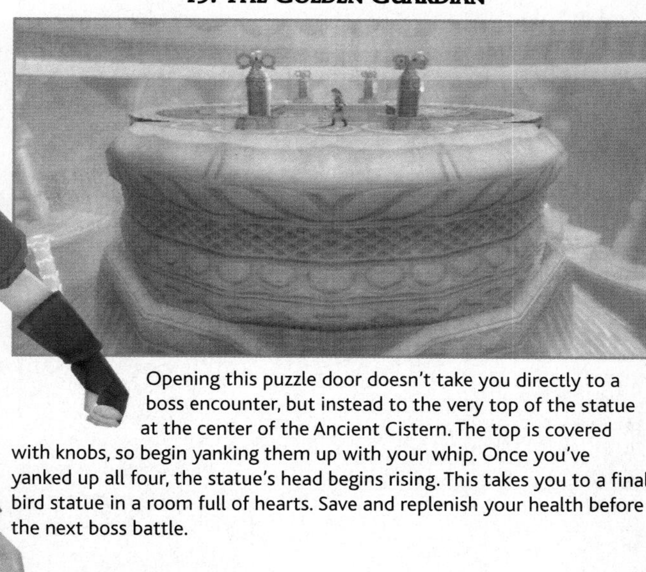

Opening this puzzle door doesn't take you directly to a boss encounter, but instead to the very top of the statue at the center of the Ancient Cistern. The top is covered with knobs, so begin yanking them up with your whip. Once you've yanked up all four, the statue's head begins rising. This takes you to a final bird statue in a room full of hearts. Save and replenish your health before the next boss battle.

BOSS: KOLOKTOS

Koloktos is a golden automaton created to help defend the Ancient Cistern, now corrupted by Ghirahim's magic. Your battle with him proceeds in phases, with his attack patterns changing in each. In the first phase, Koloktos remains stationary in the center of the room. Two of his six arms cross protectively over the weak point located within his chest, two more attempt to attack you when you close to melee range, while another pair wields throwing blades used to attack you from a distance.

The pillars in this room offer little protection. Instead, the easiest way to avoid the throwing blades is to lurk at the edges of the room and keep moving. Pause occasionally to see what Koloktos is doing. Periodically, his arms smash into the floor near him. When that happens, equip your whip and dash toward them. You can snag the golden loops at Koloktos's elbow joints with your whip and then yank them back to tear the arms off.

Once you pull off both of the arms he uses for melee defense, Koloktos raises the arms he usually keeps crossed over his weak point. That's your cue to dash in and start pummeling it with sword-strike combos. Hit it as rapidly and as fast as you can. Eventually Koloktos crosses his arms again to defend his weak point. Now that Koloktos has been disarmed (pun intended), he can only attack you at melee range by exposing his weak point.

Move a bit closer to Koloktos, but keep moving to make sure the throwing blades don't get you. When Koloktos reaches forward to try and smash you, dodge away and then get out your whip. Snag and yank at Koloktos's elbow joints to pull off the lower set of arms. Otherwise, circle Koloktos and wait for a moment when he's not protecting his weak point. When you have a clear shot at it, unsheathe your sword and do as much damage as you can before Koloktos begins guarding again.

Once all four of Koloktos's lower arms are torn off, he defends his weak point with the arms that hold his throwing blades and reassembles his destroyed arms from wreckage strewn about the boss room. At this point, he begins repeating his attack cycle. Deal with him the same way, tearing off his arms and damaging him whenever you get a clear shot at his weak point. The first phase of combat ends when you've damaged Koloktos's weak point enough that he drops his throwing blades and stands up.

In the second phase of this battle, Koloktos wields six gigantic swords and takes thundering steps across the boss area. Once again, the pillars are poor cover. In fact, Koloktos can destroy pillars and damage you right through them if you try to use them for cover. Instead, stay in the inner area of the boss room and keep moving. Koloktos can attack by slashing all six swords at you, a move you should simply evade.

Other times, Koloktos strikes down at you with all the arms on a given side so forcefully that the sword blades bury themselves in the floor. The elbow joints on one side of Koloktos's body are covered in golden hoops you can snag with the whip. Use this opportunity to tear at least one of Koloktos's arms off. This makes it collapse into a pile of rubble on the floor. You can now pick up Koloktos's own giant sword and attack him with it. Chop off all of his arms or just destroy his legs with a single horizontal slash.

Once Koloktos is immobilized, you have an opening to begin battering the weak point on his chest with slashes from the enormous sword. During this phase of the battle, Koloktos begins summoning Cursed Bokoblins. They are distractions you should ignore as much as possible. Frequently Koloktos ends up destroying them himself. You should focus on disarming and then damaging Koloktos by hammering at the weak point on his chest.

Each time you damage Koloktos's weak point in this phase, he reassembles his arms, reclaims all of his swords, and then repeats his attack cycle. You can make the battle quicker by going directly for Koloktos's legs once you steal one of his swords, but otherwise this phase of the fight demands patience. React to Koloktos's attacks in the correct way and pummel his weak point at every opportunity.

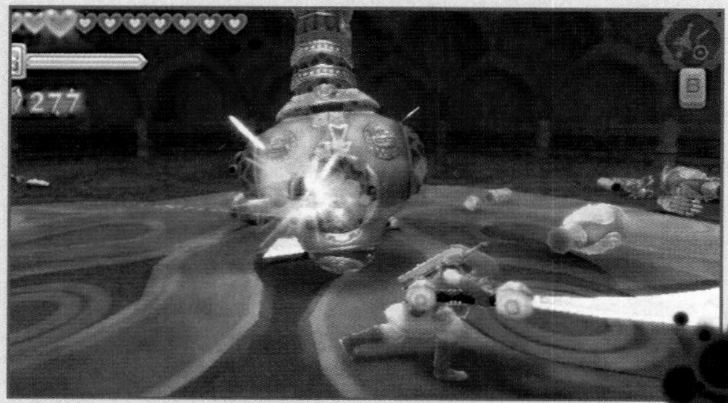

The third phase of the battle begins when Koloktos begins swinging his swords wildly in a rampaging battle dance. Get as far away from him as you can when he begins doing this. Otherwise, Koloktos repeats his second phase attack pattern, but a bit quicker and with briefer windows of opportunity for tearing off his arms or moving in to cut off legs once you've stolen one of his swords. Stay patient and look for chances to damage him. Once Koloktos has taken too much damage in this phase of combat, he explodes.

Claim the Heart Container that Koloktos leaves behind, then step into the next room and activate the crest with a Skyward Strike. That summons Farore's Flame, which ends this part of your quest and transforms Link's sword into something far more powerful.

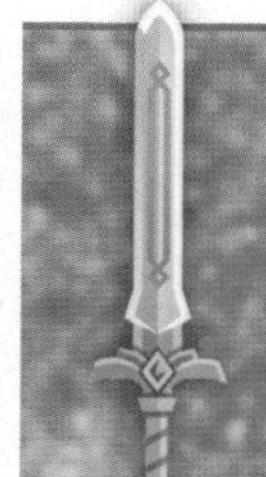

THE GODDESS LONGSWORD

Farore's Flame transforms the Goddess Sword into its next form, the Goddess Longsword. The slightly longer blade makes it easier to hit enemies. More importantly, the Goddess Longsword strikes with twice the power of the Goddess Sword. Enemies that once took two hits to defeat may now be struck down with one. Enemies that required an odd number, like three, now require only two.

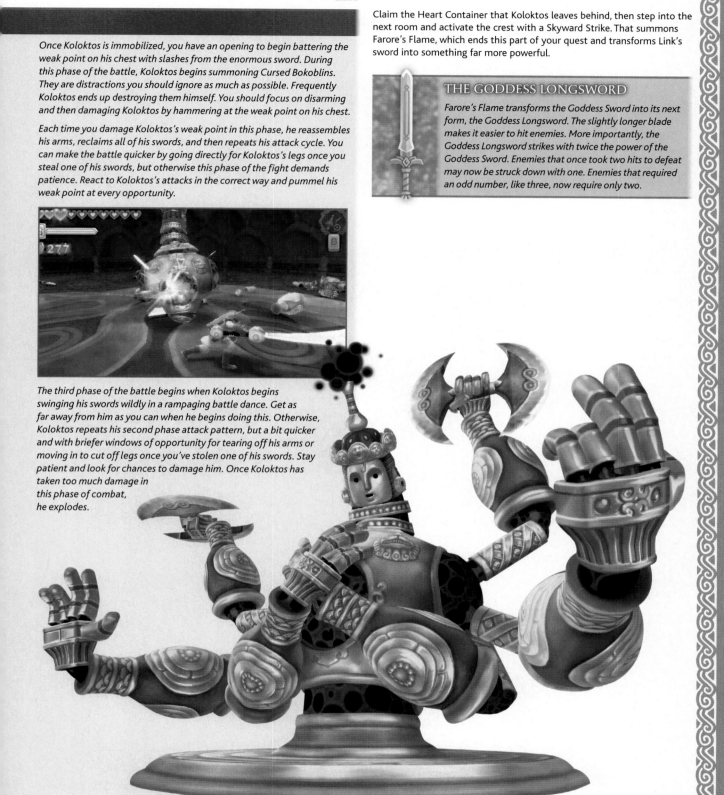

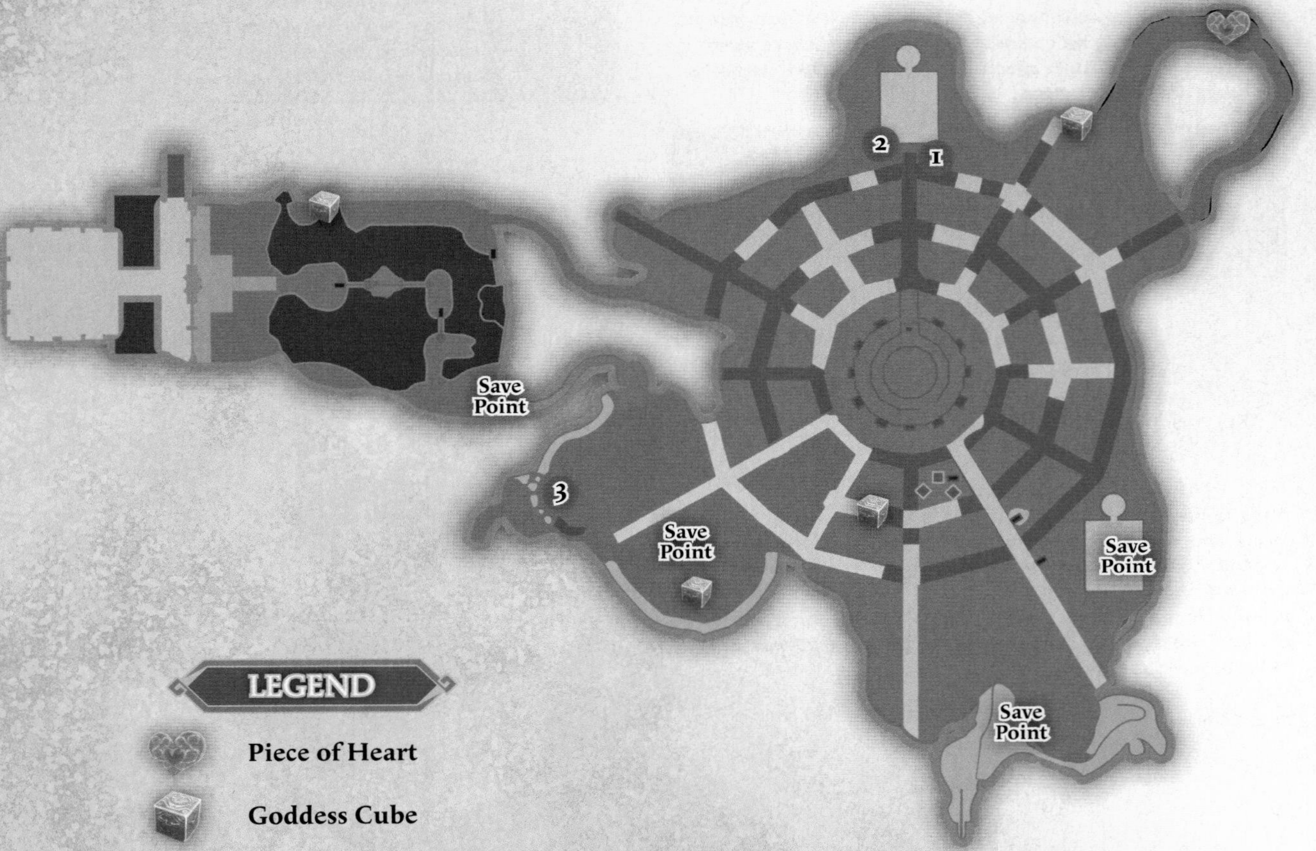

Save Point

Save Point

Save Point

Save Point

Save Point

LEGEND

Piece of Heart

Goddess Cube

Return to Lanayru Desert

1. The Trial Gate

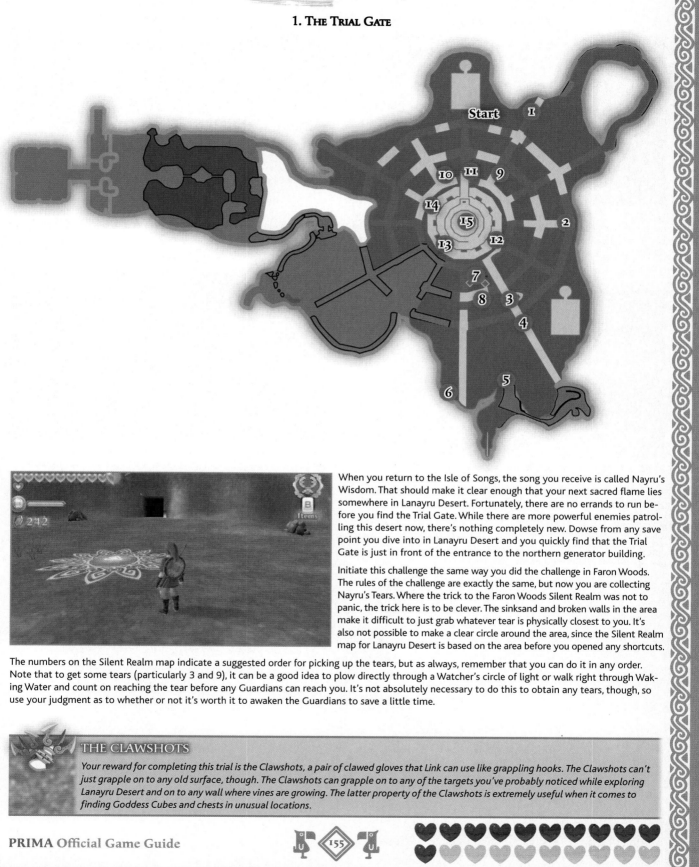

When you return to the Isle of Songs, the song you receive is called Nayru's Wisdom. That should make it clear enough that your next sacred flame lies somewhere in Lanayru Desert. Fortunately, there are no errands to run before you find the Trial Gate. While there are more powerful enemies patrolling this desert now, there's nothing completely new. Dowse from any save point you dive into in Lanayru Desert and you quickly find that the Trial Gate is just in front of the entrance to the northern generator building.

Initiate this challenge the same way you did the challenge in Faron Woods. The rules of the challenge are exactly the same, but now you are collecting Nayru's Tears. Where the trick to the Faron Woods Silent Realm was not to panic, the trick here is to be clever. The sinksand and broken walls in the area make it difficult to just grab whatever tear is physically closest to you. It's also not possible to make a clear circle around the area, since the Silent Realm map for Lanayru Desert is based on the area before you opened any shortcuts.

The numbers on the Silent Realm map indicate a suggested order for picking up the tears, but as always, remember that you can do it in any order. Note that to get some tears (particularly 3 and 9), it can be a good idea to plow directly through a Watcher's circle of light or walk right through Waking Water and count on reaching the tear before any Guardians can reach you. It's not absolutely necessary to do this to obtain any tears, though, so use your judgment as to whether or not it's worth it to awaken the Guardians to save a little time.

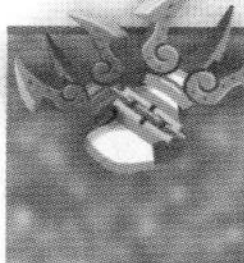

The Clawshots

Your reward for completing this trial is the Clawshots, a pair of clawed gloves that Link can use like grappling hooks. The Clawshots can't just grapple on to any old surface, though. The Clawshots can grapple on to any of the targets you've probably noticed while exploring Lanayru Desert and on to any wall where vines are growing. The latter property of the Clawshots is extremely useful when it comes to finding Goddess Cubes and chests in unusual locations.

2. Looting the Desert

Now that you have the Clawshots, do some exploring in Lanayru Desert before you move on. Now you can obtain every Goddess Cube and Piece of Heart stuffed into the area. Begin by grappling up onto this section of wall to open a blue chest containing a random treasure.

3. Petite Canyon

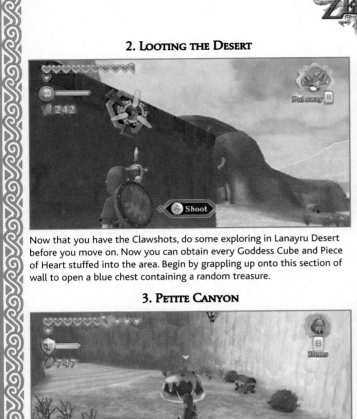

There's a bombable wall here, in what appears to be the middle of the empty desert. Blasting the wall reveals a narrow canyon teeming with enormous Yellow Chuchus. Fight your way through them to reach a blue chest that contains a Piece of Heart.

The canyon floor before you is an endless expanse of sinksand. Use the Clawshots to grapple along the walls instead, moving from wall-mounted target to wall-mounted target. At the end of the canyon, drop onto a high stone platform. From there, you can grapple over to Goddess Cube #17.

4. Wall-Climbing

Use the target above the sinksand pool to grapple up onto a section of wall you couldn't reach before. Simply walk over to Goddess Cube #18 to claim it.

5. Into the Caves

Once you're done exploring, head back to the sandfalls you explored much earlier in the game. Stand on the tallest rock in the middle of the falls and look up. There should be a target visible that you can ride up to enter a new area.

6. The Friendly Goron

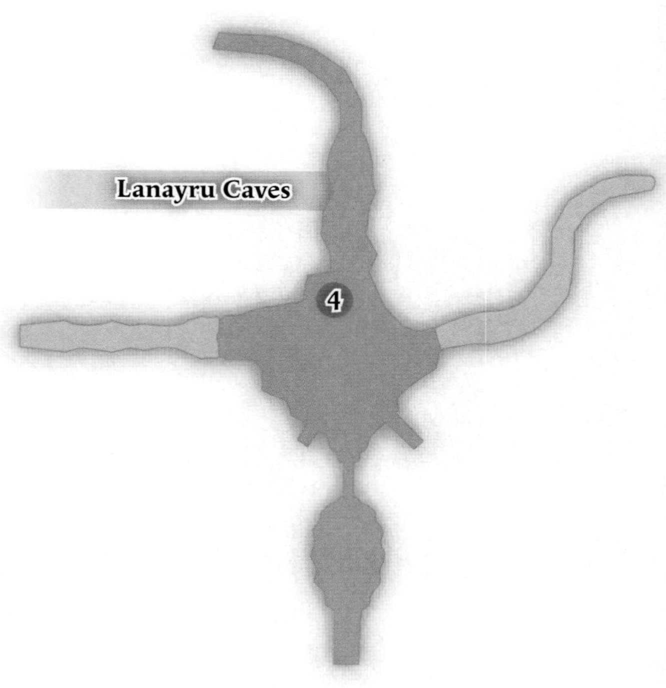

Once you enter the Lanayru Caves, speak to the Goron you see digging at a crack in the wall. His name is Golo and he's a scholar of ancient legends. Mention your quest to him and he tells you about the Lanayru Sand Sea, where Nayru's Flame is said to be kept. After you finish speaking he gives you the Small Key you need to unlock the door to the Lanayru Sand Sea. Before you leave, snag the blue chest in this area to get a random treasure. Next, grapple up to the door and pass through to begin questing for the next dungeon.

Goddess's Treasure Chest Pickups: #16, #17, #18

Now that you have the Clawshots, you can pick up goddess's treasure chest #16. Go to the area around the waterfall cave's entrance at Skyloft and grapple up to a nearby platform with a wall of vines dangling from it. You can't get directly to the platform with the chest from here, but you can grapple up to the top of the enormous waterfall that is the highest point in Skyloft. From there, you can leap off just above the platform where goddess's treasure chest #16 is located and dive down to it. Open the chest to claim a Gold Rupee.

Goddess's treasure chest #18 is on an island you've visited before, but this chest's in a tricky position. It's in a tiny alcove on the very bottom of the island. It's not possible to simply dive off from your Loftwing and get to it. Instead, drop into the area where you claimed goddess's treasure chest #4. Climb the vines leading down from this particular platform. Follow the vines down into the alcove where the chest lies. Open it to receive an invaluable Life Medal that adds one heart to your health meter.

Goddess's treasure chest #17 lies on the island where you claimed goddess's treasure chest #5. This time, drop down to the area below the chest you already opened. There's a pool of water there. Dive into the pool to find a small underwater tunnel that leads into the hollow rock. Hop up on the platform to open the chest and claim a Heart Medal. You can also find a Fairy here.

LEGEND

Piece of Heart

Goddess Cube

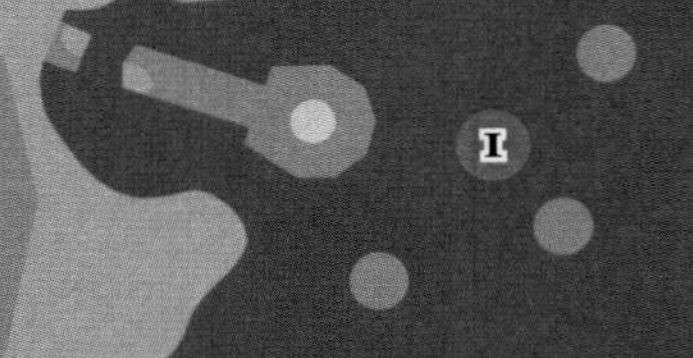

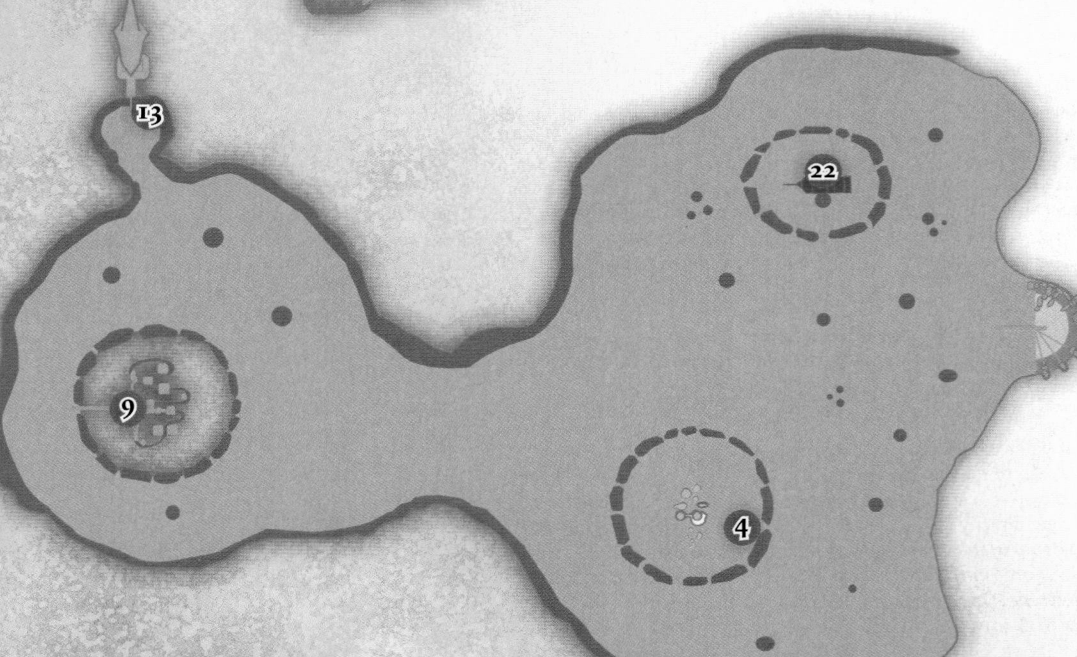

Lanayru Sand Sea

1. It Begins

The ideal shield for the challenges ahead of you is going to be something from the Sacred Shield line. Rupin should be selling the basic Sacred Shield at his Gear Shop by now. In the upcoming areas you have to deal with enemies that use fire attacks and enemies that use electric attacks at the same time. The Sacred Shield can defend you from both and also regenerates durability over time.

If you care to invest the time, you can easily upgrade a Sacred Shield to a Divine Shield or even a Goddess Shield at this point in the game. Once you've made a Goddess Shield, then you have the second-best shield in the game and one you can easily finish the game with.

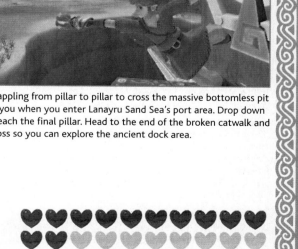

Begin by grappling from pillar to pillar to cross the massive bottomless pit that greets you when you enter Lanayru Sand Sea's port area. Drop down when you reach the final pillar. Head to the end of the broken catwalk and grapple across so you can explore the ancient dock area.

2. Dockside

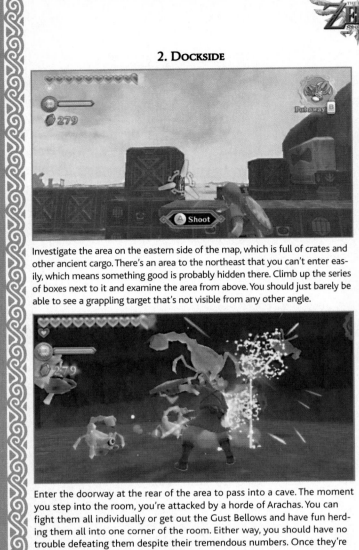

Investigate the area on the eastern side of the map, which is full of crates and other ancient cargo. There's an area to the northeast that you can't enter easily, which means something good is probably hidden there. Climb up the series of boxes next to it and examine the area from above. You should just barely be able to see a grappling target that's not visible from any other angle.

Enter the doorway at the rear of the area to pass into a cave. The moment you step into the room, you're attacked by a horde of Arachas. You can fight them all individually or get out the Gust Bellows and have fun herding them all into one corner of the room. Either way, you should have no trouble defeating them despite their tremendous numbers. Once they're cleared away, activate Goddess Cube #19.

3. Meet the Skipper

When you're done exploring, head down the old pier. At the end of it you find a deactivated worker robot and a tiny boat, sitting swamped in sand. There's a Timeshift Stone in the boat's rear. Strike it with your sword. Once the time shift effect is in place, go speak to the robot. He identifies himself as the captain of a ship that once carried Nayru's Flame. The ship was seized by pirates long ago, though, and the captain never found it or his captured crew. You can call him Skipper.

He believes the ship is out there somewhere in the Lanayru Sand Sea but also that the pirates have probably turned on its invisibility systems to hide it. Agree to help Skipper find his ship and he'll agree to give you passage on his little time-shifted boat. Your first goal is to acquire a sea chart from Skipper's old home. Naturally, this task is not going to be as simple or easy as it sounds.

My Sea Is the Sea of Sand

You travel the Lanayru Sand Sea by sailing in Skipper's little motorboat. Since it's powered by a Timeshift Stone, it time-shifts the entire area around it, which transforms modern-day sand into the water of a long-ago ocean. You control the boat with the control stick and can fight enemies by pressing Ⓑ to activate the ship's cannon. By pressing Ⓐ, you can speed up if you need to (and eventually you need to). You control the cannon with Wii MotionPlus input, which lets you move in one direction while firing in a completely different one.

There are no hazards in this portion of the Lanayru Sand Sea, but you eventually run into enemies. Common green Spumes spawn in the Lanayru Sand Sea and spit bolts of water at you. The water bolts do nothing if they hit the ship but can damage Link if they hit him. It's easy to pick them off with the cannon.

More-dangerous foes that lurk in the Lanayru Sand Sea are Bokoblin archers, who stand in groups on islands and take potshots at you with flaming arrows as you pass by. The arrows don't damage the boat, but if they hit Link he can take damage from the arrow plus additional fire damage. Your cannon's range is much larger than that of the archers' arrows, so it's best to pick them off as soon as you sight them.

Occasionally you find crates of explosives floating in the time-shifted areas of the Lanayru Sand Sea. Shooting them with cannonballs creates massive explosions. Take advantage of these when you find them near groups of inconvenient Spumes or potentially dangerous Bokoblin archers.

4. Skipper's Playhouse

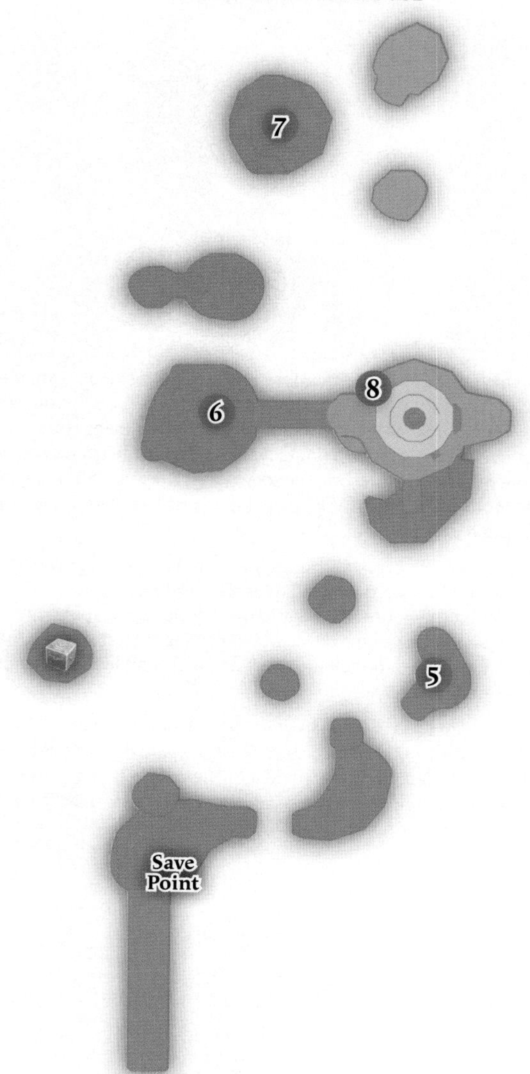

Skipper made his home in an area that is now little more than a collection of tall stone pillars, infested with hostile monsters. Save at the bird statue after your ship docks and then head into the area. Dash over the sinksand from the first stone platform to a second. Use the Hook Beetle and a Bomb Flower growing on a nearby cactus to bomb the Electro Spume at the end of the platform. Next, use the Clawshots to grapple to the plateau above.

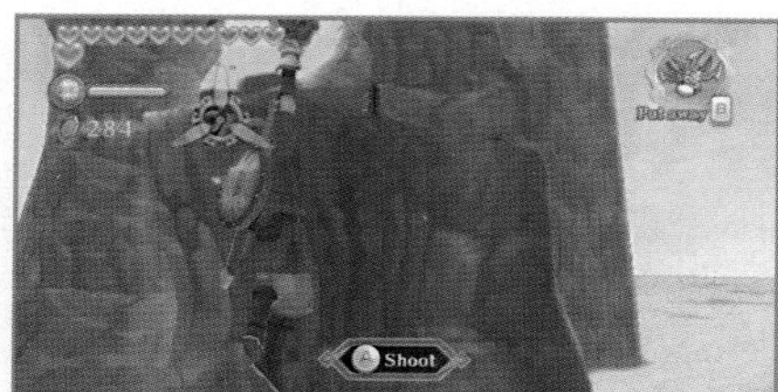

Defeat the Deku Babas and then examine the odd flying plant you see hovering in the air just beyond them. Although it doesn't look like it, as far as your Clawshots are concerned this is a grappling target. Use it as a stepping-stone to reach the next wall-mounted grapple target, which is otherwise up too high for your Clawshots to reach.

5. Needles and Shocks

At the next plateau you must face an enormous Yellow Chuchu in a very small area where two cacti are standing. The cacti are as much of a hazard as the actual enemy. It's incredibly easy to hit a cactus by accident when trying to slash at the Yellow Chuchu as it divides. Although the hits from the cacti only do a quarter heart of damage, that can really stack up if you're having bad luck or get flustered.

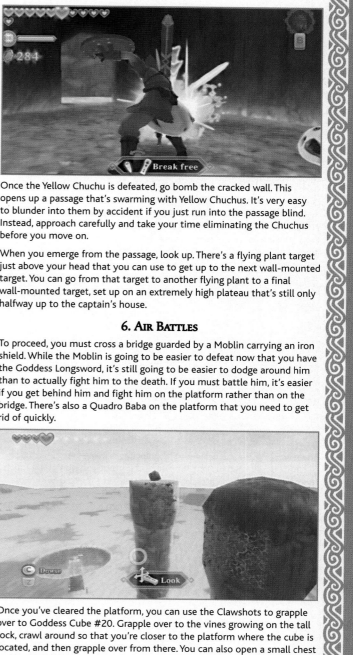

Once the Yellow Chuchu is defeated, go bomb the cracked wall. This opens up a passage that's swarming with Yellow Chuchus. It's very easy to blunder into them by accident if you just run into the passage blind. Instead, approach carefully and take your time eliminating the Chuchus before you move on.

When you emerge from the passage, look up. There's a flying plant target just above your head that you can use to get up to the next wall-mounted target. You can go from that target to another flying plant to a final wall-mounted target, set up on an extremely high plateau that's still only halfway up to the captain's house.

6. Air Battles

To proceed, you must cross a bridge guarded by a Moblin carrying an iron shield. While the Moblin is going to be easier to defeat now that you have the Goddess Longsword, it's still going to be easier to dodge around him than to actually fight him to the death. If you must battle him, it's easier if you get behind him and fight him on the platform rather than on the bridge. There's also a Quadro Baba on the platform that you need to get rid of quickly.

Once you've cleared the platform, you can use the Clawshots to grapple over to Goddess Cube #20. Grapple over to the vines growing on the tall rock, crawl around so that you're closer to the platform where the cube is located, and then grapple over from there. You can also open a small chest on the platform to receive a Red Rupee.

7. Unpleasant Surprises

Grapple over to another set of platforms, just to the north of you on the map. This area is patrolled by a very aggressive Furnix that won't hesitate to pelt you with fireballs if you take too long yanking it down with your whip. Once the Furnix is dispatched, then use your whip on what appears to be a very odd plant. When you yank it up, it becomes another plant target. Once it's moved into position, you can use it to reach the next wall target.

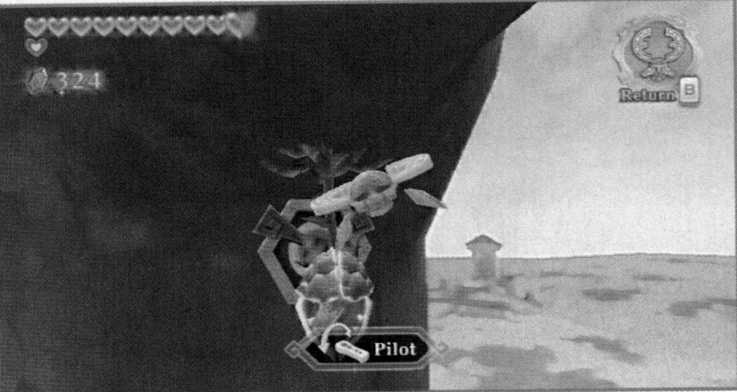

Once you're at the next platform, walk up to an area where a wall appears to have crumbled around the perimeter of the platform. Before you grapple over to the next wall target, examine it carefully. There's a Deku Baba growing above the target that knocks you to the ground if you try to grapple over while it's alive. Send the Hook Beetle out first to cut its vine and make the area safe to pass through.

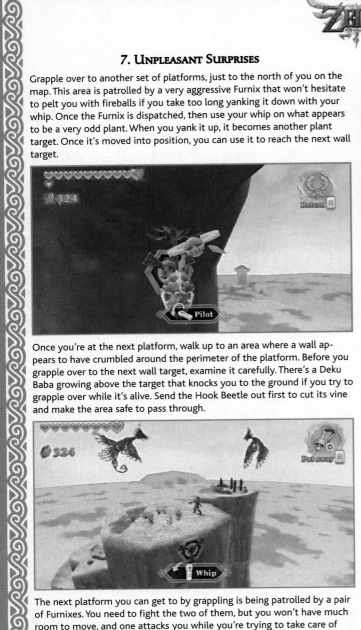

The next platform you can get to by grappling is being patrolled by a pair of Furnixes. You need to fight the two of them, but you won't have much room to move, and one attacks you while you're trying to take care of the other one. There is no easy way to deal with this situation. You can try dodging to avoid fireballs, but be careful you don't throw yourself off the platform by accident.

8. Up and Over

Proceeding beyond here to the captain's house is a little tricky. Grapple on to a plant target that's moving slowly up and down. On the other side of a massive rock, look for another plant target that's moving the same way. To get over to the captain's house, you need to move from one plant target to the other during the brief window when they're within range of each other. From there, you can finally grapple over to the very top of the area, the captain's house.

Once you go inside the captain's house, you find a massive buildup of loose sand. A thousand years of wind does that. Get out the Gust Bellows and start cleaning the house up. You uncover Green Rupees, pots, two Amber Relics, and finally a blue chest while blowing the sand away. The Ancient Sea Chart is within the blue chest and acts a bit like a Dungeon Map for the Lanayru Sand Sea.

You can ride the zip lines swiftly down to the bottom of the area. Once you're halfway down, you can dive the rest of the way to try to get the blue chest that's sitting out in the middle of the desert. It only contains a random treasure, though, so it's not a big deal if you miss it. Once you're done in this area, head back to Skipper.

9. The Shipyard

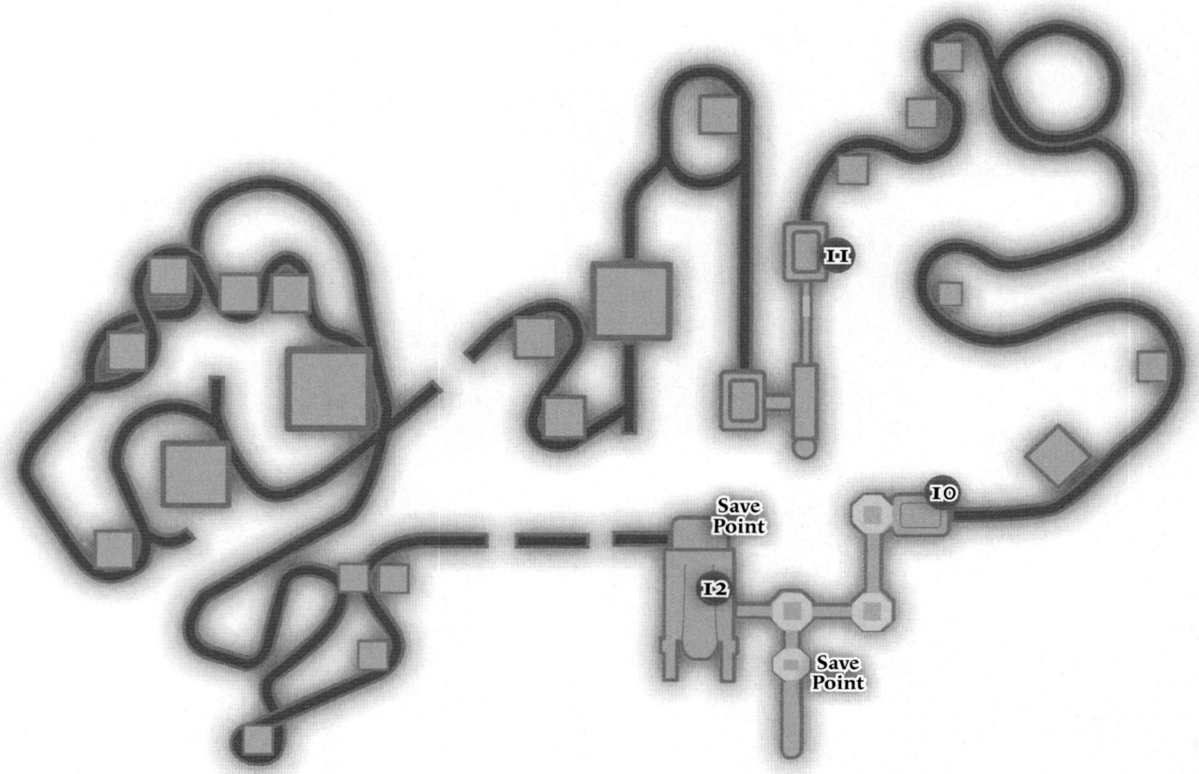

Skipper suggests heading to the Shipyard next and marks it on your map. After a short sea cruise, you arrive there. Save at the bird statue, then head toward the mine-cart station. Two Lizalfos guard the way in to the mine-cart station. Fight them using your preferred tactics.

10. Rickety Coaster

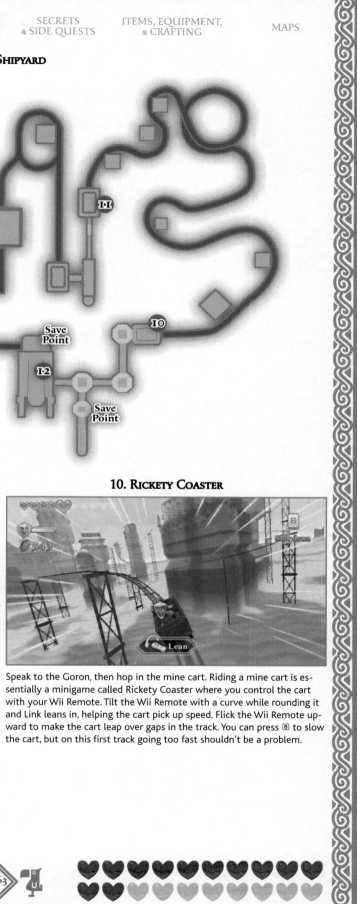

Speak to the Goron, then hop in the mine cart. Riding a mine cart is essentially a minigame called Rickety Coaster where you control the cart with your Wii Remote. Tilt the Wii Remote with a curve while rounding it and Link leans in, helping the cart pick up speed. Flick the Wii Remote upward to make the cart leap over gaps in the track. You can press Ⓑ to slow the cart, but on this first track going too fast shouldn't be a problem.

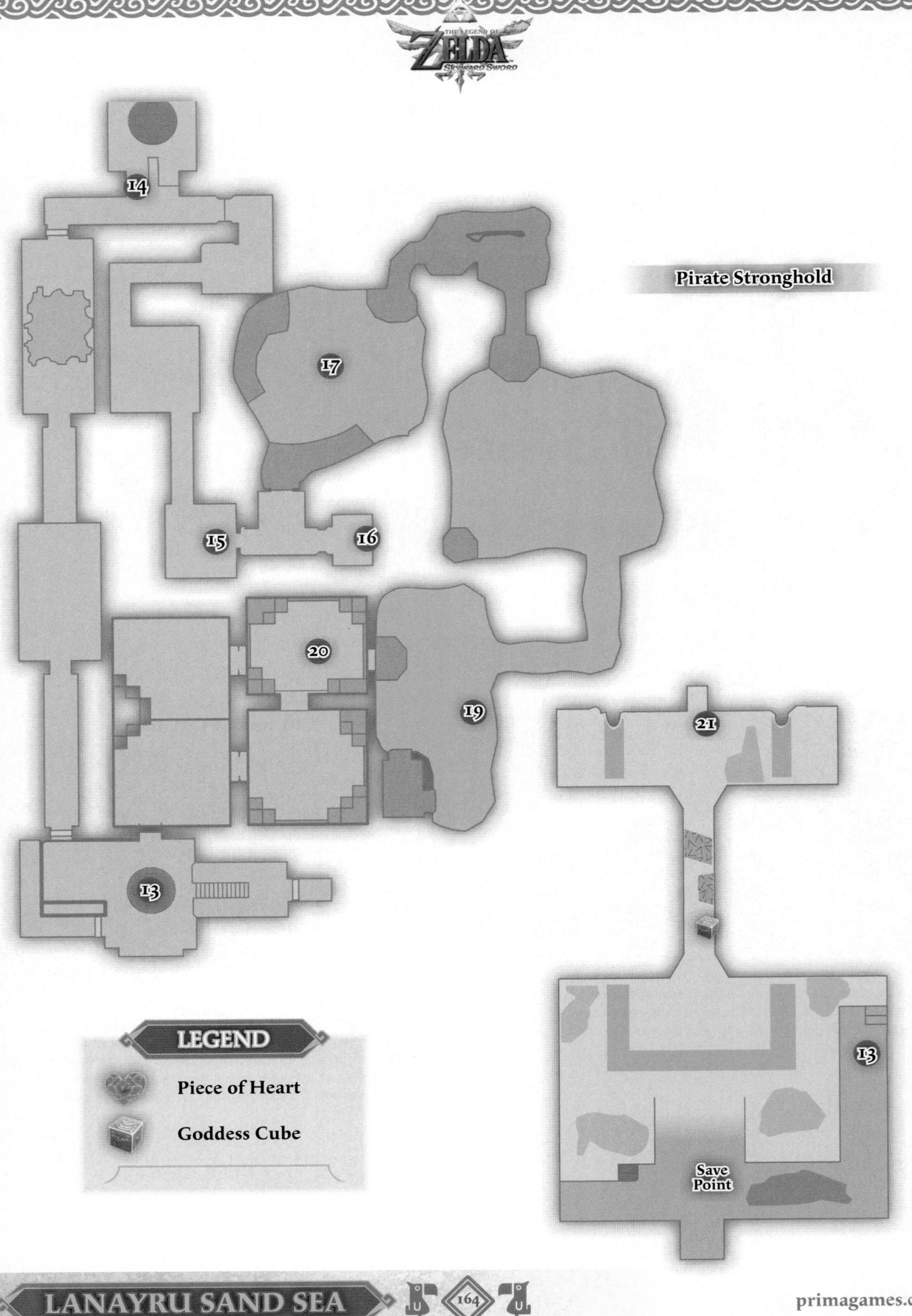
14
Pirate Stronghold
17
15
16
20
19
21
13
LEGEND
Piece of Heart
Goddess Cube
13
Save Point

11. Unsafe Coaster

Get out of the cart once your ride is over. Follow the pathway around to another mine-cart station. Fight your way through a small group of Arachas along the way. There's a zip line here you can grab to shortcut back to the beginning of the stage, but for now just move on to the next mine-cart station. Hop in and get ready to ride a much more challenging course. Some areas where the cart swerves rapidly back and forth are going to be easier to get through if you slow down a little. Make sure you're geared up for a sub-boss encounter before you hop on.

12. Too Much Sand

Now you can finally enter the Shipyard proper, which over the years has become a pit infested with Arachas and sand. Hop down with the Gust Bellows and start trying to clear the sand away. Instead of exposing a section of stone floor, blowing away the sand in this room only reveals more sand. When you get into the middle of the room, you find what initially looks like some rocks or maybe an ancient, broken machine hiding beneath the sand. Blow away more sand and...it's a Moldarach.

Surprise boss fight! The Moldarach probably takes you by surprise, but remember that your sword strikes do twice as much damage as they did before. Simply use the same tactics on this Moldarach that you used on the first one; their behavior is identical (though this Moldarach can do a bit more damage to you). The main danger posed by this boss battle is that you might show up unprepared or limping from encounters with the Furnixes and Moblins in the captain's quarters.

All you've found by exploring the Shipyard is that after a thousand years, it's become nothing more than a boss room. Exit once the barred door in the room unlocks. Now you're back at the beginning of the Shipyard area. Save your game at the bird statue and report back to Skipper. There's no trace of his ship here.

13. Shut Tight

There's nowhere else to look for the ship now besides the ancient Pirate Stronghold, the home base of the guys who stole it in the first place. Sail north until you reach the stronghold, then save your game at the bird statue as you enter the area. When you initially visit the outside area, it's shut tight. Start poking around the outside area, looking for a way in. This part of the stronghold is thick with Thunder Keese. You find the entrance around to the right of the outside area.

> **CAUTION**
>
> Be careful about stepping toward the "teeth" that are clamped shut over the entrance to the Pirate Stronghold. The area around them is sinksand. It's easy to dash off of it if you step on by accident, unless you're in the middle of a fight with a Keese swarm at the time. In that case, Link can be half-drowned in the sinksand before you realize what's happening to him.

14. Portable Generator

Once you step inside the stronghold, it's clear that the only way to open it is to install a Timeshift Stone in the empty holder that sits there. Examine the area carefully and you find it has two exits, but one is currently barred. Take the other one and see if you can find a Timeshift Stone somewhere nearby.

You first come to a room guarded by two Lizalfos. By now, you should be able to end a fight like this very quickly. Next you come to a small passage where a single Electro Spume guards a small patch of sinksand. Get close enough to the Electro Spume to toss a bomb at it. In the chamber just beyond that, you find a strange new type of Timeshift Stone sitting in a holder.

15. Ancient Enemies

This Timeshift Stone is a portable model called a Timeshift Orb. You can pick it up and carry it with you to create a sort of traveling Timeshift Stone effect, similar to the one that lets Skipper's boat travel the Lanayru Sand Sea. Note that the Timeshift Orb is very heavy, so you can't throw it or roll it very far. For now, pick it up and head toward the eastern exit from this room. It was covered in barbed wire before, but this disappears as you approach now.

Continue through the passages until you get to a room where your Timeshift Orb resurrects a group of Technoblins. Quickly set it down and battle the enemy. Be careful not to get too far from the Timeshift Orb while you fight. If you knock a Technoblin out of the time shift effect while you fight, it instantly reverts to an ancient skeleton. You just end up having to fight the Technoblin again after you pick up the Timeshift Stone and move forward a little.

Once the Technoblins are defeated, you come to a room where the Timeshift Orb resurrects a Beamos. The moment the Beamos is solid enough to fight, put down your stone and dash over to quickly defeat it. The rooms in this area are small and the Timeshift Orb slows you down, so evading the Beamos is never really going to be an option.

16. In Plain Sight

When you pass out of the Beamos room, you can see a blue chest sitting in a room at the far end of the hallway. If you approach it while carrying the Timeshift Orb, the time-shift effect summons barrier lasers that bar your path. Leave the Timeshift Orb in the Beamos room and you can just walk over to collect the blue chest, which contains a Silver Rupee.

17. Sudden Mountains

Pick up your Timeshift Orb and finally exit the winding interior pathways. Now you're in a series of caves filled with sinksand. As you walk across the area, the time shift effect around you turns the sinksand into solid ground. In the first cave you pass into, the time shift effect also abruptly raises huge rock platforms from the ground. Look for an Ancient Flower at the far side of the room.

To exit, raise the stone platform with the time shift effect and then climb up the slope nearby. Although it looks too far, it is possible to jump over to the platform. As you cross to the far side of the time-shifted rock with jumps, a second rock appears. Cross both of its platforms and a third rock appears. Continue jumping to reach the exit on the far side of the room.

18. Modern Switch

The next room you come to is a set of solid-stone passages. The larger passage is blocked by bars, but if you attempt to carry the Timeshift Orb down the smaller passage, the time shift effect summons a laser barrier. Put down the Timeshift Orb and run through the present-day version of the passage. When you reach the room on the other side, there's a switch you can pull to raise the bars. Go back for your Timeshift Orb and you can pass through this cavern.

19. Pressure Plate

First, collect the blue chest in this room's far corner. To get it, walk close enough that there's only a short area of sinksand to dash over and put down your Timeshift Orb. If you get too close to the blue chest while you're time-shifting the area around you, a massive rock platform springs up in your path. Inside the blue chest is a random treasure. Now you can simply walk through the rest of this room, though be ready to fight Deku Babas summoned into existence by the time shift effect.

The narrow passage you must pass through here becomes infested with enemies as you time shift the area. Be ready to fight a Quadro Baba flanked by two Deku Babas and a Technoblin in rapid succession. When you pass into the last of the cavern areas, first focus on clearing out the enemies that get summoned from the past by the time shift effect. You fight a Quadro Baba in the center of the room and a Technoblin flanked by a Deku Baba toward the rear. Tucked in the corners of the room in the present day are Electro Spumes you should clear out with bombs.

Once the room is enemy free, focus on solving its simple puzzle. At the southwest corner of the room is a small area that's solid stone even in the present day. You can't carry the Timeshift Stone into it because the time shift effect activates a laser barrier over the door. If you step into the chamber, you find a pressure plate that raises the bars over the room's exit door so long as it's pushed down. This also raises a set of bars that separates the room from the sinksand area in the center of the room.

Now you need to find something that can hold the switch down. Tucked into a corner of the pressure switch's room is a metal block that does the trick. Before you pull the block onto the switch, make sure you've left your Timeshift Stone near the entrance of the stone passage so you can retrieve it.

20. Guardians

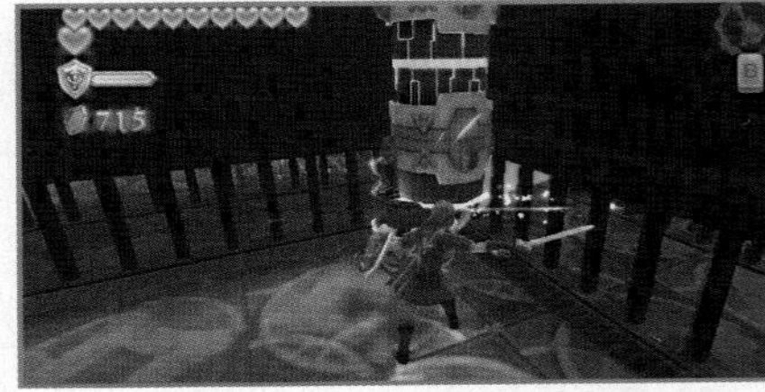

Now you've got to navigate one last sequence of rooms before you're finished here. You can't take your Timeshift Orb into the large room to the west, so go in while it's in the present day. Open the blue chest there to get a random treasure. Next, position the Timeshift Stone outside so that just the middle wall of this room is time-shifted into the past. Pull the switch there to bring down bars blocking the room's other entrance.

Double back, pick up your Timeshift Orb, then head into the room to the south. The time shift effect awakens a pair of Beamos in the room. Destroy them quickly. If you slowly edge into the room, you can wake them up one at a time and make them easier to handle. Once the Beamos are gone, take your Timeshift Orb into the next room through the doorway you just unbarred.

Be careful as you approach the Armos that guard this room's barred exit. Just as you did with the Beamos, edge toward them so you only wake up one at a time with the time shift effect. Set your Timeshift Orb down once you're in a good position and then battle the first Armos. Repeat the process to battle the other one. In this battle with the Armos, their movements are restricted by the size of the time-shifted area around your Timeshift Orb.

Once you've defeated both Armos, the bars blocking the doorway they guarded lift. Pick up your Timeshift Orb and head through to emerge back at the beginning of this area. Place the Timeshift Orb in the empty base to cause the "jaws" protecting the Pirate Stronghold outside to open. Go back outside.

21. Upraised Treasure

Once you step outside, you automatically gain the ability to dowse for Nayru's Flame. Before you leave, pick up Goddess Cube #16. It's high in the roof areas of the stronghold's exterior.

Turn and face the door you just exited. Examine the area above it to find a grappling target. Grapple up to it, then turn and grapple to a second target directly opposite the first one. Climb up to the area above this target. Walk to the end of the platform to find Goddess Cube #21, ready to be activated.

22. Ship Battle

You have one last task in the Lanayru Sand Sea: dowsing for the location of Skipper's ship and attacking it with your cannon to reveal its location. The ship can quite literally be anywhere and is constantly on the move. Locate the general direction it's moving in, then hold down Ⓐ to dash toward the location. When the size of the dowsing circle indicates that you're drawing close, prime the cannon and begin firing it in the longest arcs you can manage.

Once you've landed three shots on the Sandship, it comes to a final rest at this location. Note that while you go automatically to the beginning of the Sandship, you can leave by climbing down the ladder. It's probably a good idea to resupply at Skyloft and pick up your goddess's-treasure-chest loot before you start this dungeon.

Goddess's Treasure Chest Pickups: #19, #20, #21

To get goddess's treasure chest #19, head back to Skyloft and enter the bazaar. The activated chest should be sitting in a little alcove located between Gondo's Scrap Shop and Peatrice's Item Check. Open the chest to receive a Gold Rupee.

To claim goddess's treasure chest #20, head back to the island in the sky where you previously found chests #4 and #18. Chest #20 is in a cave behind the iron bars opposite chest #4. To get behind the bars, use the Clawshots to grapple onto the patch of vines growing on the cave's roof. This chest contains the Potion Medal.

To claim the goddess's treasure chest #21, head to Skyloft. Head to the waterfall cave area and use your Clawshots to grapple your way up to the highest point on Skyloft, the very top of the waterfall itself. Chest #21 waits for you up here. Open it to receive a Piece of Heart.

1F

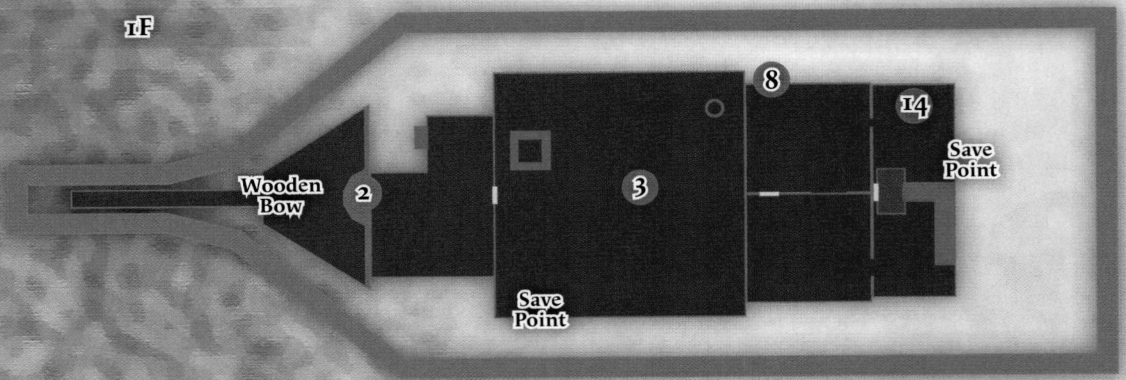

Wooden Bow

2

3

8

14

Save Point

Save Point

B1

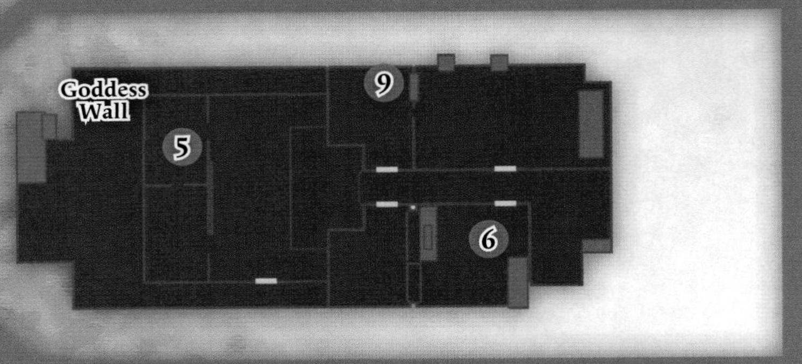

LEGEND

 Piece of Heart

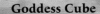

 Goddess Cube

THE SANDSHIP

B2

Small Key
Small Key
Save Point
1
4
13
15

B3

10
11
12

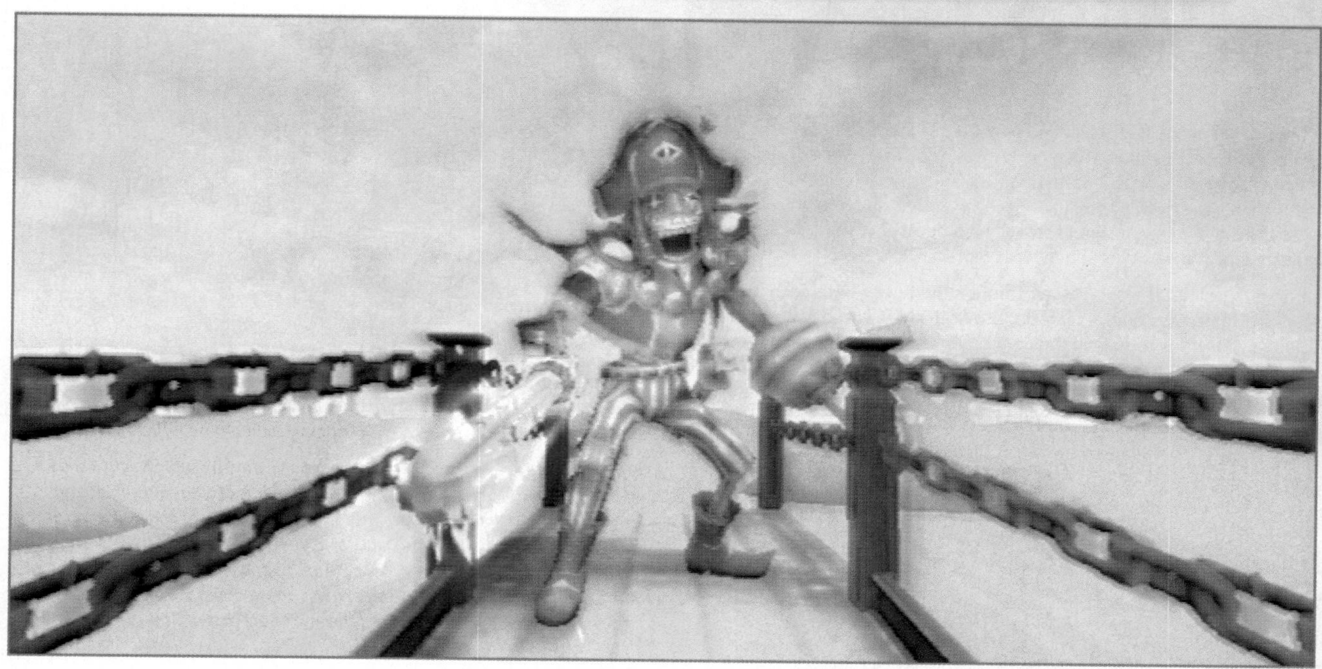

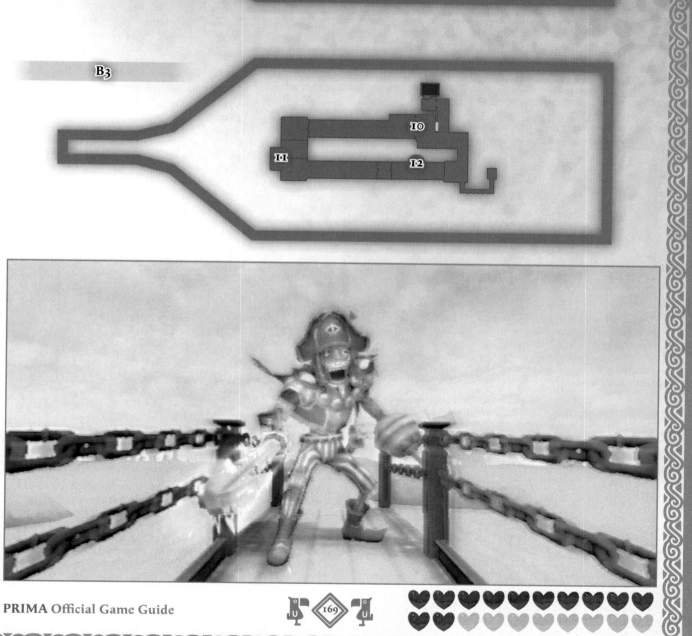

1. Unlocking

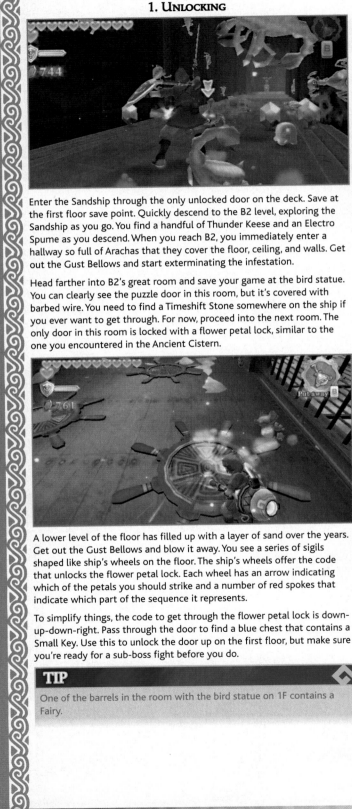

Enter the Sandship through the only unlocked door on the deck. Save at the first floor save point. Quickly descend to the B2 level, exploring the Sandship as you go. You find a handful of Thunder Keese and an Electro Spume as you descend. When you reach B2, you immediately enter a hallway so full of Arachas that they cover the floor, ceiling, and walls. Get out the Gust Bellows and start exterminating the infestation.

Head farther into B2's great room and save your game at the bird statue. You can clearly see the puzzle door in this room, but it's covered with barbed wire. You need to find a Timeshift Stone somewhere on the ship if you ever want to get through. For now, proceed into the next room. The only door in this room is locked with a flower petal lock, similar to the one you encountered in the Ancient Cistern.

A lower level of the floor has filled up with a layer of sand over the years. Get out the Gust Bellows and blow it away. You see a series of sigils shaped like ship's wheels on the floor. The ship's wheels offer the code that unlocks the flower petal lock. Each wheel has an arrow indicating which of the petals you should strike and a number of red spokes that indicate which part of the sequence it represents.

To simplify things, the code to get through the flower petal lock is down-up-down-right. Pass through the door to find a blue chest that contains a Small Key. Use this to unlock the door up on the first floor, but make sure you're ready for a sub-boss fight before you do.

TIP

One of the barrels in the room with the bird statue on 1F contains a Fairy.

2. Robot Skeleton Pirate

SUB-BOSS: SCERVO

Scervo is the robot skeleton pirate captain of the terrible crew that seized Skipper's ship and imprisoned his crew long ago. Once you face him, it's not so strange that Skipper is still scared senseless of him. For this battle you fight Scervo on a long gangplank. Taut iron chains keep you from moving much to the left or right. Behind you is a damaging gate made of spikes Scervo intends to impale you upon. Behind Scervo is a long fall into the sinksand below. Only one of you is walking away from this fight.

Your battle with Scervo proceeds in three phases. In the first phase, Scervo draws his saber and slowly advances on you, using thrusts to try and drive you back onto the spikes. When the battle begins, run as far as possible toward Scervo so you don't have to drive him back quite as far. You can shield-bash his attacks, creating an excellent opportunity for driving Scervo back with a sword thrust of your own. Scervo guards himself with his saber, but he leaves plenty of openings for you to keep hitting him with thrusts.

Drive Scervo back as far and as quickly as you can on the gangplank. If you press your advantage too far, Scervo may punish you with a quick swat of his sword. If you see him preparing this attack, dodge backward. The timing is most likely going to be too tight for you to shield-bash it. As you drive him toward the end of the plank, he may begin swatting at you with his hook arm. You can shield-bash this attack if you see him beginning the animation. Scervo also begins winding up a longer, more elaborate lunging thrust where he electrifies his sword. This attack knocks you back and inflicts paralysis.

The second phase of battle begins after you've driven Scervo back to the end of the gangplank once. Scervo drops his saber but catches himself. He pulls out another and the spiked gate moves up two lengths of chain. The battle begins again, with you moved back to an area just in front of the starting gate. Your basic strategy should be the same in this phase, but Scervo becomes a more dangerous opponent. He begins this phase doing the electrified thrust attack that he began doing toward the end of the first phase.

Scervo is also much faster to swat you aside if you press your advantage and attack too aggressively. In the second phase of combat, being able to shield-bash Scervo's attacks consistently becomes crucial to gaining ground. You can get in the odd thrust or two while Scervo tries to advance on you, but you can't go on an all-out offensive like you could in the first phase.

The battle enters phase three after you drive Scervo to the end of the gangplank a second time. Once again, he catches himself before falling, but this time you've driven him back so forcefully that he loses his second saber and his entire right arm. Scervo doesn't give up easily, though, and is perfectly willing to take you on again armed with nothing but his left hook (pun intended). The spiked gate slides up two more lengths of chain and the battle begins again.

Scervo's entire offense now consists of swiping and thrusting forward with his hook. Both attacks can be shield-bashed easily. When Scervo is reduced to only his hook, his ability to defend himself is severely compromised. If you can stagger him once, you can drive him nearly to the end of the gangplank by pummeling him with an all-out offensive of thrusts and slashes. As long as you slash from your left-hand side, he won't be able to block you consistently. Once you drive Scervo to the end of the gangplank a third time, he falls to his doom and you get a long-overdue reward.

THE WOODEN BOW

Now that Link has the Wooden Bow, he can attack enemies from a distance. To use this bow, press Ⓑ to bring up the Wooden Bow's targeting reticle. Once you've found your target, press Ⓐ to nock an arrow. Hold Ⓐ to slowly build tension in the string and close in on your target.

As the tension builds, a red tension guage fils up. Once you're at max tension, the entire gauge turns red. If you want to instantly charge your tension gauge, hold Ⓒ and physically pull back the Nunchuk. Releasing arrows at max tension causes your arrows to do more damage on impact. Most common enemies you'd want to attack with arrows die in a single shot.

Now you can quickly defeat lots of enemies like Spumes and Hroks that, up to now, you've had to slowly pick off with bombs or the Hook Beetle. You can also shoot arrows to activate certain switches that look like small, round blue targets. You can upgrade the Wooden Bow to the Iron Bow and then the Sacred Bow at the Scrap Shop to increase the damage you do with arrows. This is very highly recommended.

3. Mutiny

Save at the bird statue and then head out onto the deck. Break the barrels to fill up your quiver with arrows, then take aim at the arrow switch located just a little ways up from the deck. This causes a massive Timeshift Stone to slide up into position at the very top of the ship's mainmast. You can strike it by firing an arrow up at it. Striking this Timeshift Stone time-shifts the entire ship all at once, which is an important rule to keep in mind.

Activating the Timeshift Stone has the unfortunate side effect of bringing the ship's original pirate crew back to life. The second the stone is active, the ship's deck and masts are suddenly thronged with Bokoblins and, in particular, Bokoblin archers. Once the Bokoblins are summoned by the time shift, the one on the mast cranks a dial that causes a bronze cage to close around the Timeshift Stone and bars to drop over the door that leads into the ship. You need to clear the deck and masts of Bokoblins, climb up the mast, and open the cage around the Timeshift Stone before you can proceed.

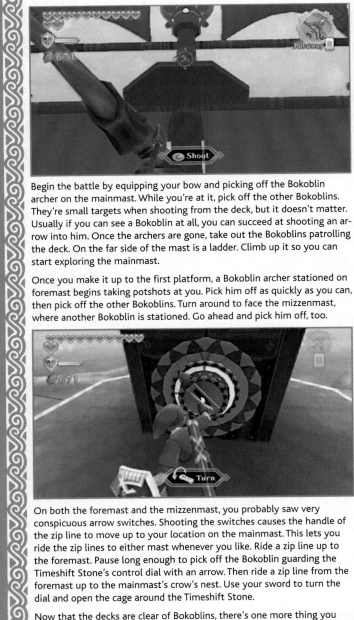

Begin the battle by equipping your bow and picking off the Bokoblin archer on the mainmast. While you're at it, pick off the other Bokoblins. They're small targets when shooting from the deck, but it doesn't matter. Usually if you can see a Bokoblin at all, you can succeed at shooting an arrow into him. Once the archers are gone, take out the Bokoblins patrolling the deck. On the far side of the mast is a ladder. Climb up it so you can start exploring the mainmast.

Once you make it up to the first platform, a Bokoblin archer stationed on foremast begins taking potshots at you. Pick him off as quickly as you can, then pick off the other Bokoblins. Turn around to face the mizzenmast, where another Bokoblin is stationed. Go ahead and pick him off, too.

On both the foremast and the mizzenmast, you probably saw very conspicuous arrow switches. Shooting the switches causes the handle of the zip line to move up to your location on the mainmast. This lets you ride the zip lines to either mast whenever you like. Ride a zip line up to the foremast. Pause long enough to pick off the Bokoblin guarding the Timeshift Stone's control dial with an arrow. Then ride a zip line from the foremast up to the mainmast's crow's nest. Use your sword to turn the dial and open the cage around the Timeshift Stone.

Now that the decks are clear of Bokoblins, there's one more thing you want to do before you move on. From the crow's nest where you should be now, turn and face the back of the ship. At the top of the mizzenmast, you should see an arrow switch. Trigger it. This brings the handle for a zip line that runs from the crow's next to the top of the mizzenmast over to you.

Once you're on the mizzenmast, drop down to the upraised rear deck area. Use your Clawshots to grapple up onto a pole that's behind the visible rear deck. Once there, point your free Clawshot down onto a grappling target mounted on a portion of the ship's hull that wasn't visible before. From there, drop down to find a hidden area of deck. On this low deck area is the blue chest you can see but not reach while on B2. Open the blue chest to receive a Piece of Heart, then grapple back up to the ship's main deck.

4. Jailbreak

Now that you control the ship, descend to B2 while the ship is time-shifted. You're going back to the room with the flower petal lock you visited before. On your trip through the time-shifted ship, expect to face Technoblins instead of Thunder Keese. A Beamos now stands in front of the puzzle door in B2's great room. When you get to the room with the locked door, which is in fact the ship's brig, fight a couple of Technoblins who are acting as prison guards.

You can't get into the cell while the boat is time-shifted, because a laser barrier blocks the door in. Talk to the captive crew robots through the prison's bars. They give you your next mission—to rescue them by opening a path from the cell to the outside through the engine room. To do this, you have to activate two power generators on the ship's B1 level. This task sounds simple but actually involves quite a bit of puzzle-solving. Head up to B1.

5. Trick Shot

In this room, there's a grate where light from outside filters in. If you stand beneath the grate and face in the correct direction, you can use arrows to strike the ship's Timeshift Stone from the inside. After you strike the Timeshift Stone, head into the adjoining room and claim the blue chest inside. It contains the Dungeon Map. Pull the switch on the wall to lift the bars in front of the blue chest to open up an exit from the room. Take note of this room's location, as time-shifting the ship while inside it is key to solving the next few puzzles.

6. Very Tricky Shot

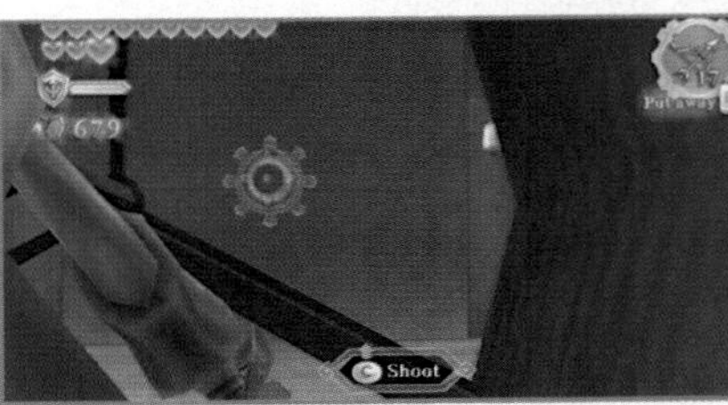

Head down this hallway and examine the fan set into the south wall. When the ship is time-shifted, it spins rapidly. When you bring the ship into the present day, the fan is still. Either way, you should see an arrow switch on the other side. Your bow is accurate enough to let you shoot through the gap created in the fan casings when the fan's blades aren't spinning. This raises the bars that were blocking your way.

Enter the room in the present day and fight the Thunder Keese roosting there. Move the metal block that's blocking another fan set into the wall that separates this room from the other one that leads off the south side of the hallway. This reveals another fan casing you can shoot through. When you stand on the pressure plate in this room, it opens the bronze casing that's blocking another arrow switch you need to hit.

Make the shot through the fan casing while standing on the pressure plate. It may look impossible, but you're completely capable of making this shot. Hitting this switch unbars the entrance to the room next door, which contains the generator. Exit this room and go time shift the ship into the past. Once you have, go enter the generator room and fight the Technoblin guarding it. Once the coast is clear, use your sword to activate the generator. One down, one to go.

7. Let a Little Light In

Getting into the next generator room is significantly trickier. First, enter the easternmost room on the north side of the hallway that separates the generator rooms in B2. Push the metal block onto the pressure plate in the room. This opens the portholes in the side of the room. For now, you're done here.

8. Over the Side

Now, head up on deck. Defeat the Bokoblins all over again, since they respawn every time you enter and exit the ship's interior. Make sure the ship is time-shifted into the past, so you can climb up the ladder that leads to a raised platform at the aft area of the ship. Defeat the Bokoblin archer that's guarding the area, then examine the rowboat hoisted along the north side of the ship. There's an arrow switch on the pulley holding the rowboat up. Shoot the switch to lower the rowboat. Then fire an arrow up at the Timeshift Stone to shift the ship back into the present day.

9. Power's On

Jump down onto the rowboat and then enter this room through the porthole. This is the only way to get into this room while the ship is time-shifted into the present day. Since the ship is in the present, the laser barrier over the door into the adjoining generator room is shut off. Step into the generator room and then look up through the grate in the ceiling. Fire an arrow through this grate to time shift the ship into the past and then activate the generator with your sword. When you're done here, there's a switch on the wall near the exit that raises the bars, letting you exit the generator room.

10. Descent

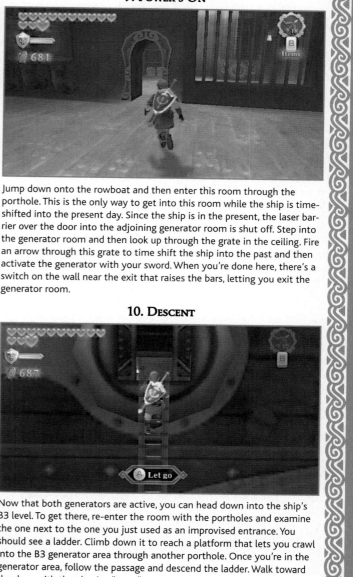

Now that both generators are active, you can head down into the ship's B3 level. To get there, re-enter the room with the portholes and examine the one next to the one you just used as an improvised entrance. You should see a ladder. Climb down it to reach a platform that lets you crawl into the B3 generator area through another porthole. Once you're in the generator area, follow the passage and descend the ladder. Walk toward the door with the glowing "eyes."

Pass through the door to reach an area where pistons thunder up and down. Wait until they're moving up and then dash under them one by one. Climb up the ladder at the end and then use your whip to snag the hook just above the high platform you should find yourself standing on.

11. Loot

Instead of swinging across the chasm, turn Link around with the control stick and point him at the alcove in the wall to your right. Swing over to it. Climb up the ladder here to reach a room in B2 stuffed with five Blue Chests. Two of the chests contain Silver Rupees while the other three contain random treasures.

12. Touch and Go

Hop down to the far side of the passage once you're done with the treasure room. You come to another hallway with crushing pistons but also a hook overlooking the hall. Get out your whip and use it to swing on top of one of the pistons. They don't go all the way up to the ceiling, so there's no chance that you'll be crushed. Dash-jump carefully from the top of one piston to the next. From the last piston, simply step off into the next metal hallway. Hit the switch on the wall to create a shortcut, then crawl into the small tunnel in the wall next to it.

13. Sneaking In

Climb up the ladder at the end of the tunnel to emerge into a new room in B2 that's behind the brig. Hit the switch on the wall to free the crew robots. In gratitude, they give you a Small Key before going to join the Skipper. Use your shortcuts to quickly return to the deck.

14. Trick Arrows

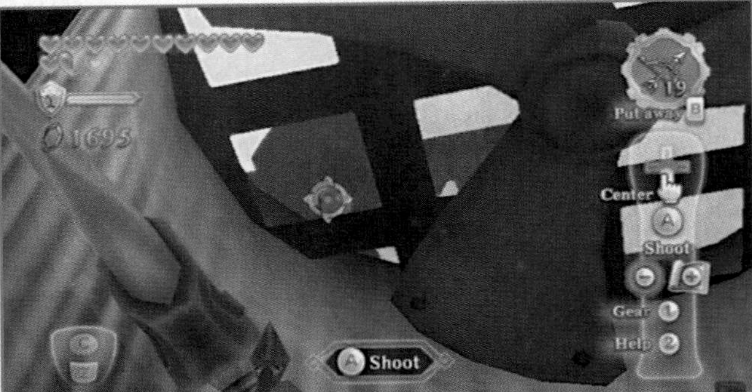

Climb up to the aft platform where you dropped the rowboat earlier. Now you can enter the locked door here. Save your game at the bird statue once you pass through. Make sure the ship is time-shifted into the past. Walk up to the room on the left with the barred entrance. Get out your bow and use it to defeat the Beamos by shooting through the bars. You can get one-hit kills on Beamos with the bow by shooting them directly in the eye.

Step outside, time shift the room into the present day, and then return. Enter the room on the right. Defeat the Arachas patrolling the room, then stand beneath the enormous fan that's letting sunlight into the room. You have to position yourself very carefully, but it is possible to strike the Timeshift Stone with an arrow while within this room. After you time shift the room into the past, dash over to the Beamos and quickly defeat it. Next, battle the Technoblin.

Once both enemies are defeated, stand on the pressure plate. This lifts a metal plate set into the wall dividing the two rooms. Now that all of the Beamos are defeated, you can shoot through the hole to trigger the arrow switch located in the other room. This raises the bars blocking the door that leads into the adjoining room. Quickly defeat the Beamos hiding in the corner of the adjoining room.

Once this final Beamos is defeated, the bars blocking in the jeweled chest rise. Open the jeweled chest to receive the Squid Carving. Now head back to the puzzle door on B2. As usual, be ready for a boss fight before you use the Squid Carving to open the puzzle door.

BOSS: TENTALUS

The minute you step into the control room, you're accosted by the tentacles of this massive squid-like creature. The first phase of battle is a mad dash to get onto the deck of the ship. When you reach a passageway with tentacles blocking your path, use Skyward Strikes to sever them. Dash toward the door out of the area, but stay just to the left of it. Occasionally barrels roll down the hallway from the door.

Dash up the stairs as the water level rises beneath you. Weave through the barrels as you dash through the next hallway. Getting hit by a barrel knocks you over and does one heart's worth of damage. When you pass the hallway, more tentacles smash through the boat to block your way. Use Skyward Strikes to sever them. If you accidentally run into one of the tentacles, it snares you and you're forced to repeat this sequence.

The second phase of battle starts once you're out on deck. Tentacles smash through the deck of the ship and Tentalus briefly reveals himself before diving beneath the surface of the water. More tentacles smash through the deck. Charge your Skyward Strikes while running around the deck. Don't stand in one place for too long or you'll get snared by a tentacle. Once a Skyward Strike is charged, fling it at a tentacle to sever it.

Once you've severed enough tentacles, Tentalus rises from the depths and tries to smash you with his tentacle-like arms. Equip your bow and prepare a shot at Tentalus's eyes. Shoot quickly, or Tentalus will attack and you'll miss your chance for a shot at him. If your shot hits true, Tentalus roars in pain and collapses to the deck. Dash toward him and rapidly slash at his eye, doing as much damage as you can. After Tentalus hits you or you successfully damage Tentalus, he may dive back under the surface of the water and repeat his attack pattern.

Once you've damaged Tentalus enough, the third phase begins. Tentalus begins to violently destroy the section of deck you're standing on. After you see a metal box fall to the deck in a cutscene, dash toward it and use it to climb up to the ship's stern. Tentalus looms over you and begins attacking with the tentacles on his head, which fly forward and bite at you with tiny tooth-filled mouths.

Don't try to dodge or shield bash or do anything else you'd typically do when a boss is attacking you. Instead, stand your ground and slash your sword vertically as rapidly as you can. This lets you slash through all of the attacking tentacles before they can damage you. If you're low on health, some of the tentacles drop hearts after you sever them. Tentalus looms toward you and roars between attack cycles, giving you a chance to shoot his eye again. This staggers him and gives you a chance to run toward him and damage him further. Once you've damaged Tentalus enough, he's defeated. Snag the heart container and Nayru's Flame in the aftermath.

THE GODDESS WHITE SWORD

Absorbing the power of Nayru's Flame has purified the Goddess Longsword further, turning its blade pure white. This doesn't make the sword a more powerful weapon, but it greatly enhances Fi's dowsing abilities. Once you have the Goddess White Sword, Fi has eight dowsing slots. In the next few hours of the game you can speak with NPCs you encounter in your travels to unlock new dowsing abilities for her. Among the items she can dowse for are Goddess Cubes, treasures, and many other useful things.

NOTE

Although it seems like Tentalus has completely destroyed the Sandship in the boss battle, this isn't the case. If you backtrack to the ship later, you will find it's completely intact. Don't underestimate Skipper and his crew.

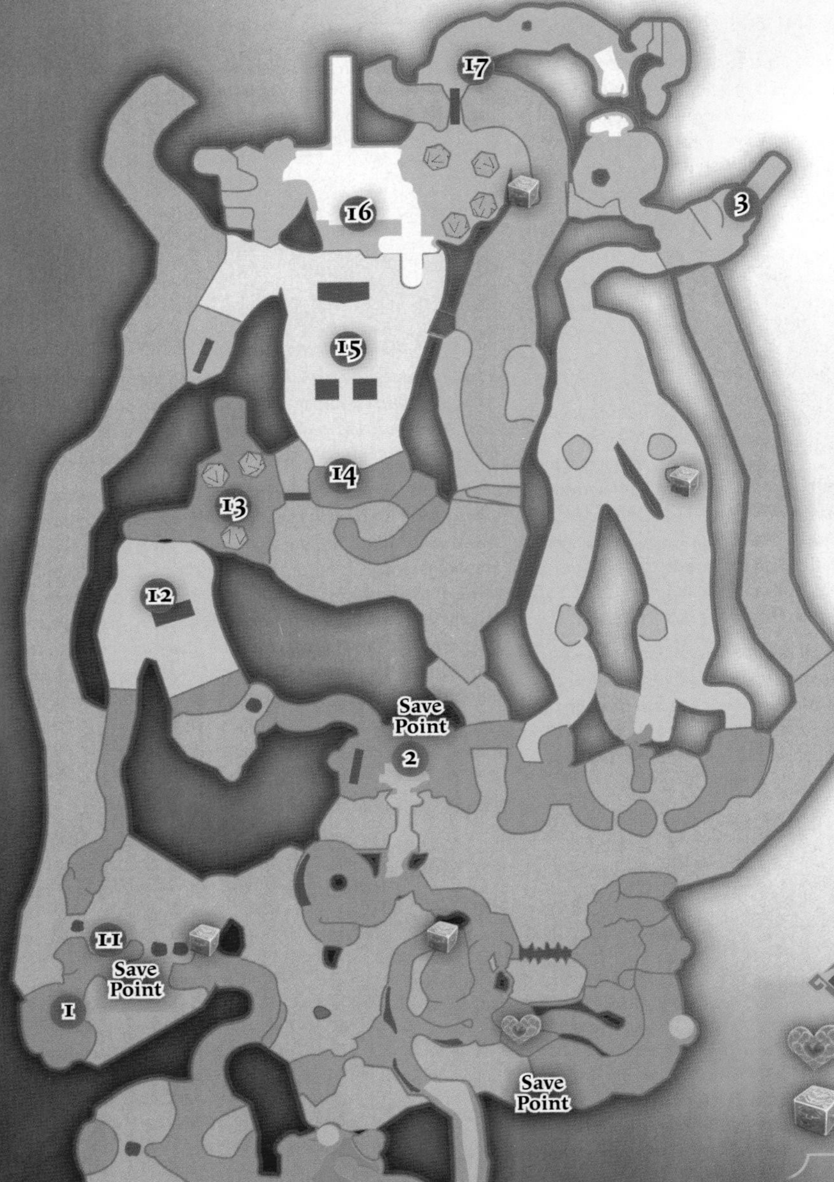

LEGEND

 Piece of Heart

 Goddess Cube

RETURN TO ELDIN VOLCANO

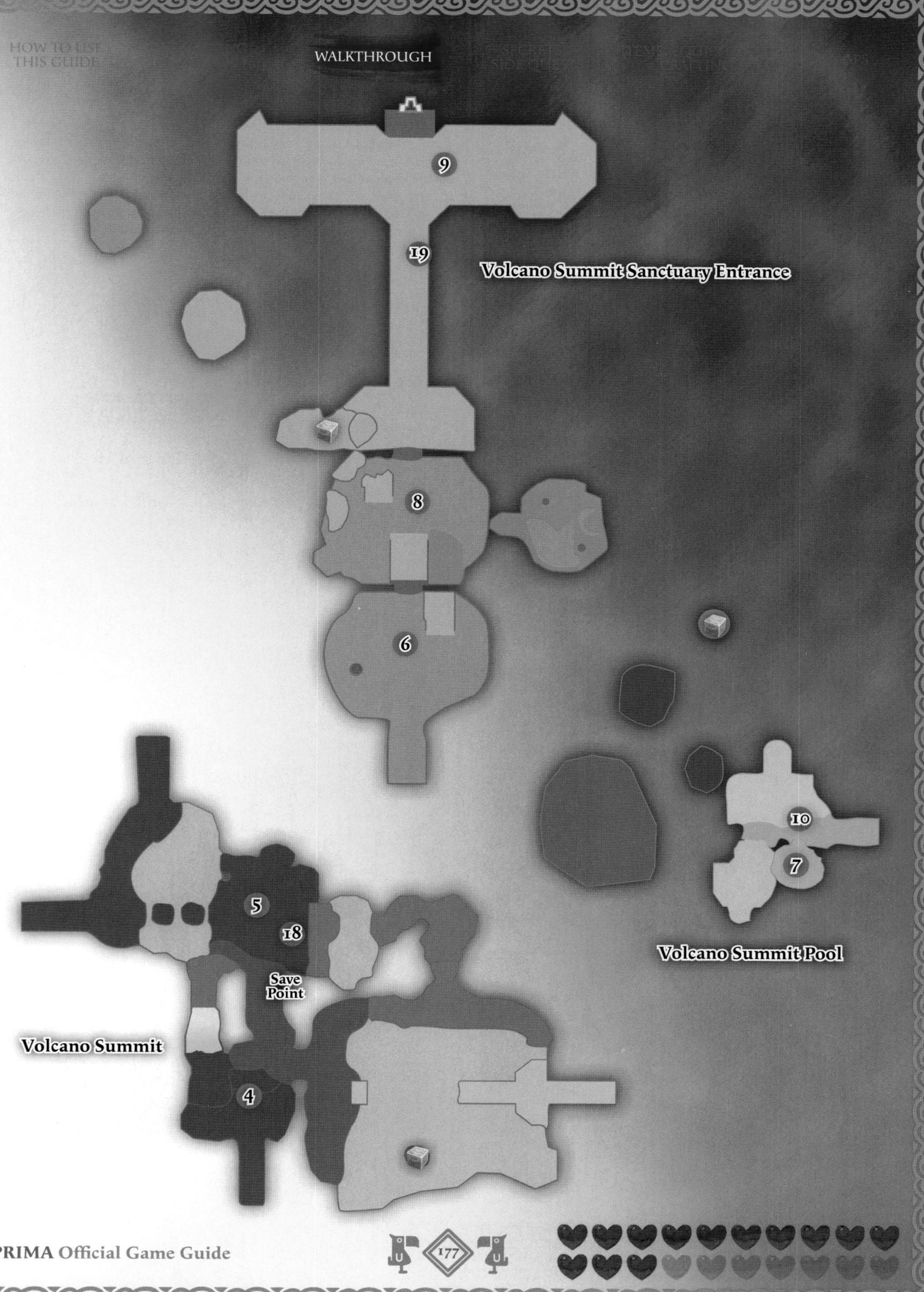
9
19
Volcano Summit Sanctuary Entrance
8
6
10
7
Volcano Summit Pool
5
18
Save Point
Volcano Summit
4

1. Your Goron Friend

The next tune you get from the Isle of Songs is a little ditty called Din's Power, so it's time to return to Eldin Volcano. Come down at the entrance to the area. Your Goron pal is there, talking about new Goddess Cubes in the area. He's referring to ones you can obtain in a new area you're about to discover, as you should already have activated everything in the immediate area. If you haven't, that's okay! This conversation causes Fi to unlock her extremely useful ability to dowse for Goddess Cubes.

2. The Trial Gate

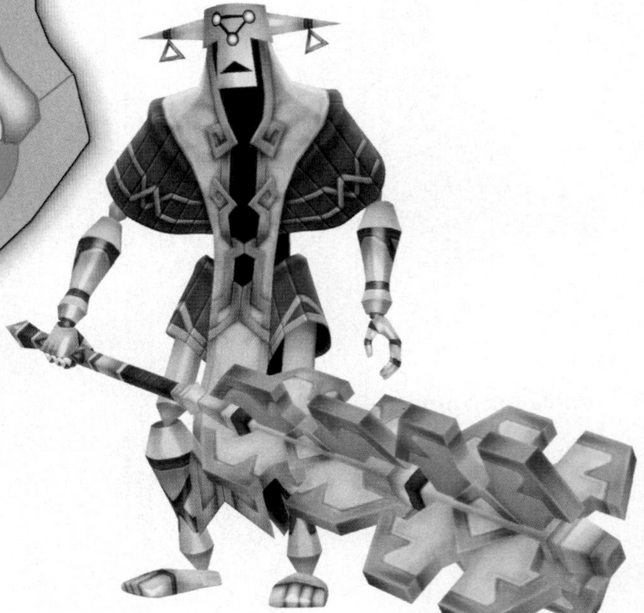

LEGEND

Piece of Heart

Goddess Cube

Return to this area to find the Trial Gate for your next trip to the Silent Realm. Eldin Volcano's narrow areas and rugged terrain make its Silent Realm a unique challenge. If you make a mistake that awakens the Guardians, it can be very difficult to run away from them. This Silent Realm challenge is a test of pure player skill, relying on your ability to move around the area with precision. As always, the numbers on the Silent Realm map indicate a suggested order for picking up Din's Tears, but you can grab them all in whatever order works best for you. Whatever order you decide on, it's generally best to go after the tears that are the most difficult or risky for you to reach first.

Since it's so difficult to retreat from Guardians in this Silent Realm and so easy to blunder into Watchers, keeping easy-to-grab tears on the map is the only reliable way you can save yourself after awakening them. This also means that there's a limited number of mistakes you can recover from in this Silent Realm. In some areas of the map, awakening the Guardians is a death sentence that's nearly inescapable due to a lack of places to run and a lack of any convenient tears to grab. Just be patient and repeat the challenge until you have the hang of it.

FIRESHIELD EARRINGS

Your reward for completing this trial is the Fireshield Earrings, an item that makes Link a noncombustible substance. You still take damage from fire attacks, but you no longer take extra damage from being set on fire. This means you can now walk through areas that were dangerously hot before.

3. At Long Last

Now that you have the Fireshield Earrings, you can explore this area without taking any damage. Enter the passage you find there, as it leads to an entirely new area to explore.

4. It's a New Frontier

Explore your immediate area. If you dash up the slope to your left, you battle some Fire Keese. If you head up the stone platforms just ahead, you fight Red Chuchus and can find a bird statue.

Before you move on, duck into the room on the right. Fight your way through some Fire Keese, then use your bow to carefully pick off the Cursed Spumes. Examine the right-hand side of the cavern to see Goddess Cube #25 sitting on a tiny island surrounded by magma. If you stand at the very edge of the solid area directly in front of the Cube, you can shoot your sword beam just far enough to activate it.

5. The Lurking Curse

Drop down into the large room to the north. A horde of Red Chuchus spawn immediately. Fight your way through them as fast as you can. When this many Chuchus are in an area, they can merge into a single large Chuchu if you don't pick them off quickly enough. When the Chuchus are taken care of, head toward the floating stone platforms nearby. There's a new enemy lurking there, waiting for you in the magma.

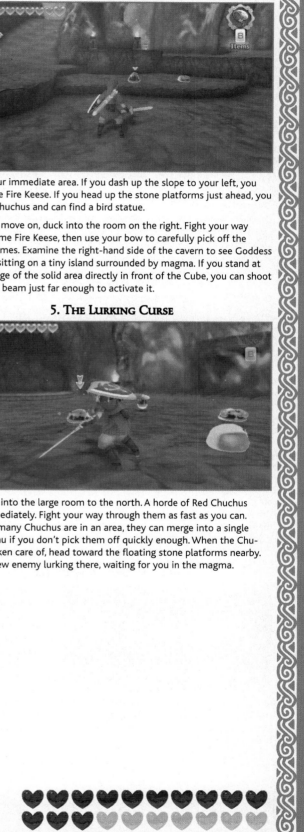

ENEMY: CURSED SPUMES

Cursed Spumes have spent too long soaking in the magma of evil. Now they spit malevolent bolts of cursed power at any creature that enters their territory. You can easily defeat them with your bow and should do so from a safe distance. You can protect yourself from curse attacks by shield bashing with any shield from the Sacred Shield line, but it's better to pick off enemies like the Cursed Spume before you can be cursed at all.

6. The Thirsty Frog

Hop across the stone platforms and head up the slope on the other side. Pause to fight the enormous Red Chuchu that ambushes you here. This brings you to a new area outside the entrance to your next dungeon: the Fire Sanctuary. Your path ahead in this area is blocked by flames. Examine the area. Take note of the frog's head idol mounted on the wall. Read the stone tablet next to it. Make sure you've got an Empty Bottle on hand, then head back down the slope. At the bottom, enter the area to your right.

7. The Unexpected Waterfall

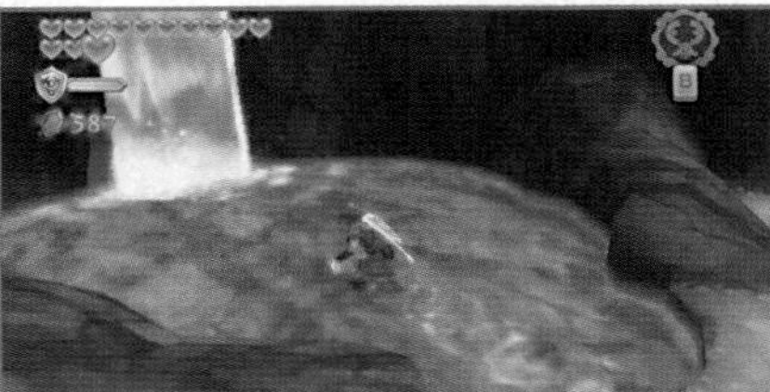

Scoop water from the pool in this area into your Empty Bottle. While you're here, you can also pick up a cleverly hidden Goddess Cube. Walk toward the platform that overlooks the deep bottomless pit at the north of this area. To claim the Goddess Cube, run and leap off into the bottomless pit. You begin diving. Move Link toward the left and back a little as he falls. Goddess Cube #22 is hidden behind a rock outcropping, but it's still possible to land on it.

Once the cube is activated, use the Clawshots to grapple back around to solid land. Find a pair of rocks covered in vines that you can use as stepping-stones to grapple on to a vine-covered wall you can climb to reach the top of the small waterfall that's filling this area's pool. Open the blue chest you find in this area to obtain a random treasure. Drop down and head back to the frog idol.

8. Another Thirsty Frog

Stand at the frog idol's mouth and pour the water in. This extinguishes the flames and allows you to pass through into...another room with an exit blocked by flames and a frog idol. In this room, the stairs leading up to the idol's head are broken. Once you've gone back to the pool and gotten more water, return here and examine the area. There's a platform near the frog's head you can stand on to pour the water in its mouth. To get up there, use the Clawshots to grapple onto the vines above the stone platform nearby.

9. A Really, Really Thirsty Frog

In the next area you find a really big gateway blocked by really big flames, with a truly gigantic frog's head idol above it. Save your game here at the bird statue. To proceed, you must backtrack out of this area entirely for a brief time. Before you go, there's a Goddess Cube in the area you can snag. Run over to the area on your left and climb up into the open window that overlooks the bottomless pit that drops off to your left.

From the window, you can use your Clawshots to grapple over to a vine-covered rock. From there, grapple up to a high stone platform guarded by a Lizalfos. In this fight, it's important not to let the Lizalfos damage you, because the knockback can throw you off of the platform completely. Once you've defeated the Lizalfos (or knocked him off the platform), you can grapple over to a high stone ledge above the entrance to this area. Goddess Cube #23 sits there, waiting to be activated.

10. Friendly Advice

When you revisit this area, one of the Mogmas is hanging out. Tell him about your problem and the Mogma mentions, in a roundabout way, that there was a lot of water in a big lake over in Faron Woods. He's talking about Lake Floria, where you saw the Water Dragon soaking in a huge tub earlier. Since her wounds are healed now, she can't need the tub anymore, right? Go pay her a visit and see if she'll let you borrow the tub and fill it with water from her domain. As for how to move the tub from Lake Floria to the Volcano Summit, well, that's what Scrapper is for.

11. The Water Escort

You don't get to select where you dive back into Eldin Volcano when you return, unfortunately. You end up diving down into the lower-left corner of Eldin Volcano due to a mistake on Scrapper's part. Now you must walk all the way back to the Volcano Summit entrance while keeping Scrapper safe from monsters. You can really use any route to do this, provided you're willing to fight every single monster along the way. More powerful monsters now infest Eldin Volcano, so almost any route you pick is going to force you to fight heaps of Fire Keese, Red Chuchus, Bokoblins, and probably a Moblin or two. The waypoints on the map indicate a suggested route that has the virtue of being very direct.

12. Sniping and Sneaking

Before you start forward on the suggested route, use your bow to pick off a pair of nearby Bokoblin archers. In general, on any route, you should use your bow to pick off enemies before they're in attack range whenever possible. On the suggested route, head through a narrow passageway. Pick off the archer at the end of the passageway, then battle a group of enormous Red Chuchus that spawn. Proceed through the passage to reach the bottom of a sand slope. Pick off another archer waiting on a stone just up the slope and then an archer camped on the wooden platform in the middle of the slope. Now it's safe to proceed.

13. Not Too Fast

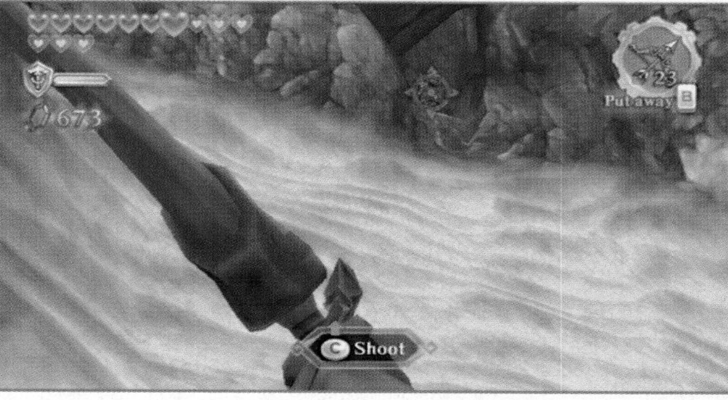

Dash halfway up the slope, then pick off the Bokoblin archer guarding the entrance to the top area. Next, dash up to the top of the slope. If you get too far away from Scrapper, he asks you to wait for him. You always should, since it's easier to defend Scrapper when he doesn't get too far from you.

14. Death Duel

To cross the bridge into the next area, you must fight the Moblin that guards the narrow bridge. Sneaking past him is impossible, since you need to get Scrapper through the area, too. It is possible to defeat him with Arrows, though it takes many shots to do this. It may actually be faster to battle the Moblin at melee range. Now that you have an upgraded sword, you do twice the damage per strike. If you fight the Moblin patiently, using your shield to parry its shield strikes, you should find you win relatively quickly. If you close to melee, be sure to dodge back when you hear the Moblins death cry. Once you cross, you should only have to battle another Red Chuchu before you come to the base of the next sandy slope.

15. Headshots

Start picking off Bokoblin archers on the wooden platforms halfway up the slope once you come to the base of it. Dash up to the platforms once the archers are gone and defeat the Bokoblins guarding them. From the middle platforms, you can pick off the Bokoblin archers at the top of the area. When you make it to the top wooden platform, pick off one last Bokoblin archer, hiding in a stone walkway above you.

16. Iron Death Duel

Climb up to the stone area at the top of the slope. You should be outside the Earth Temple's entrance now. Save your game at a bird statue and then start the second half of your climb. Head right into the Bokoblin village and defeat the Blue and Red Bokoblins waiting inside. To exit this area, battle the Moblin guarding the bridge that crosses the gap. This Moblin has an iron shield, but you have nothing to fear so long as you fight him carefully and patiently. If you get lucky, you may be able to turn him around and attack him from behind a few times.

17. The Last Bridge

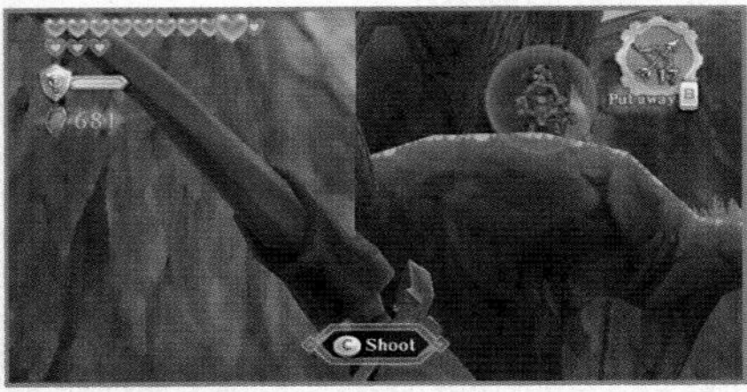

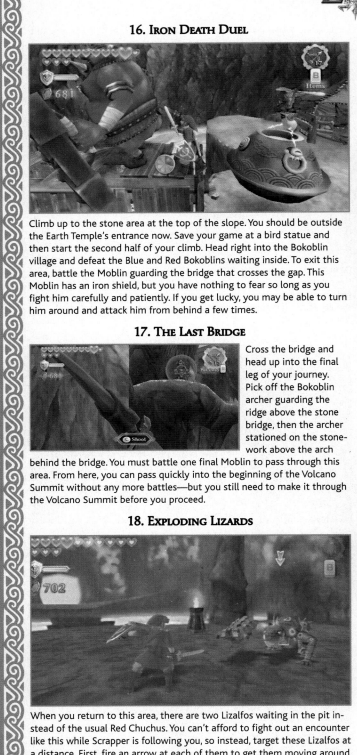

Cross the bridge and head up into the final leg of your journey. Pick off the Bokoblin archer guarding the ridge above the stone bridge, then the archer stationed on the stonework above the arch behind the bridge. You must battle one final Moblin to pass through this area. From here, you can pass quickly into the beginning of the Volcano Summit without any more battles—but you still need to make it through the Volcano Summit before you proceed.

18. Exploding Lizards

When you return to this area, there are two Lizalfos waiting in the pit instead of the usual Red Chuchus. You can't afford to fight out an encounter like this while Scrapper is following you, so instead, target these Lizalfos at a distance. First, fire an arrow at each of them to get them moving around and ready to fight.

Drop bombs down at them until you've picked one off. Lizalfos leap out of the way of bombs if they see them, but once they're looking for an enemy, they sometimes stop to use their fire-breath attack. This is a great opportunity to drop a bomb on them. Once one of the Lizalfos is picked off, wade in and finish off the other one at melee range.

Pick off the Cursed Spumes with your bow, then lead Scrapper up the slope. The giant Red Chuchu doesn't spawn here during this sequence.

19. Happy Frogs

Approach the enormous frog's head idol and Scrapper automatically pours the water into its mouth. Save your game at the bird statue and, if necessary, gear up for a dungeon crawl. The Fire Sanctuary awaits.

Goddess's Treasure Chest Pickups: #22, #23, #25

To claim goddess's treasure chest #22, you need to go to the island that eventually plays host to Strich's Bug Heaven. Run up to the castle tower that is the island's highest point, then drop down from the area in the accompanying screenshot. You land on a small wooden pier where chest #22 sits. Open it to receive a Piece of Heart.

Goddess's treasure chest #23 sits on the Isle of Songs in the thunderhead, high atop the tower you enter in order to receive new songs. You can simply dive onto it from your Loftwing. Open the chest to receive the Small Bomb Bag.

Goddess's treasure chest #25 can't be collected yet. Getting to it requires the Mogma Mitts, an item you won't acquire until you complete the Fire Sanctuary.

LEGEND

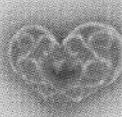 **Piece of Heart**

 **Goddess Cube**

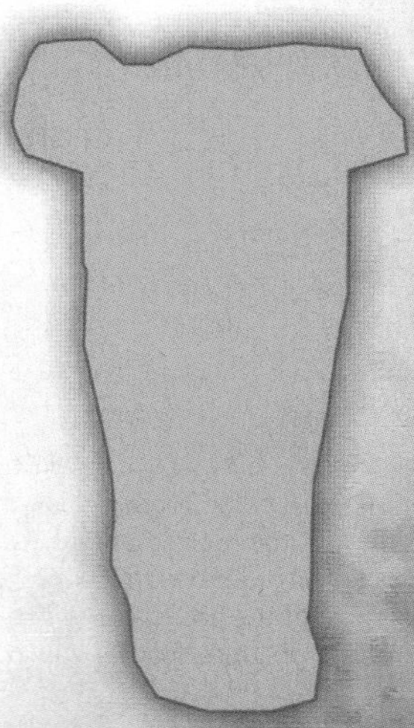

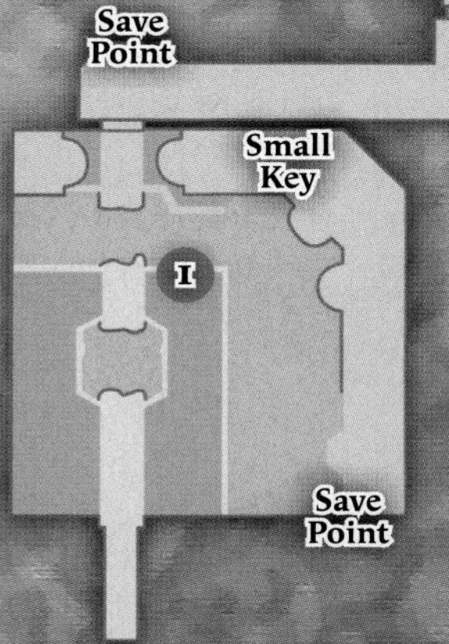

FIRE SANCTUARY

1. Just Add Water

At the entrance of the Fire Sanctuary, thorn-covered plant buds dangle from the ceiling. Hit one with something. It doesn't matter what, as any impact has the same effect. A suggested item to use is the Clawshots, which don't have ammo requirements and strike very quickly. Once hit, the bud peels open, sending a drop of water falling down. The bud promptly regrows, much like a Bomb Flower. These buds are key to solving many of the puzzles in this dungeon.

In fact, you can't even enter the dungeon without using one. When you walk up the stairs between the giant owl statues, you come to an impassable flow of magma. Hit the thorn bud above the magma flow. The drop of water that falls into the magma solidifies it briefly into a solid stone platform. Quickly leap across to the other side. Stationary platforms you create this way don't last long and may melt back into magma while you're standing on them.

The next magma flow you come to has a current, like a river. There's not a thorn bud growing above the gap in the magma where you'd like to cross, but glance to your left and you should see one. Hit it. Since the magma here has a current, the platform stays stable until it moves to the current's end. Create a platform. Before you cross to the other side, use the platform to ride over to the right-hand side of the room. Bokoblin archers you should pick off with the bow are stationed above you.

When you get to the end of the current, put your bow away and prepare to leap across to fight the Bokoblins patrolling the stone platform area to your right. If you don't make the jump fast enough, you end up riding the platform to its end and falling into the magma as the platform disintegrates. Defeat all of the Bokoblins patrolling the right-hand area. Once you have, bars blocking in a blue chest containing a Small Key automatically rise.

Collect the Small Key, and then leap down to the padlocked door that leads out of this room. Before you leave, you meet a new Mogma, the elder, Guld. He's in the Fire Sanctuary with his entire tribe, searching for a great treasure. Guld gives you a hint that becomes crucial much later on in the dungeon. Among his people, there's a legend claiming that the treasure of the Fire Sanctuary involves finding two statues that face each other and leaping into the "sleeping" statue's mouth.

2. Archery Contest

ENEMY: DARK KEESE

Dark Keese were once ordinary Keese, but now they've succumbed to dark forces. Dark Keese attack the way all other Keese do, but they have the power to wreathe their bodies in evil energy before they dive at you. If a Dark Keese damages you, you also become cursed for a brief time. Dark Keese aren't dangerous by themselves, but more dangerous enemies are usually just around the corner from one of their roosts.

Now you're in an exterior part of the sanctuary. Head down the narrow walkway before you and carefully battle the Dark Keese that roost here. Just beyond them is a Blue Bokoblin. Once he's defeated, move into a strange room with a grated iron floor. Beneath the grate is magma, but also something else that seems to move the magma through force of sheer malevolent will. Dash across the floor and stand on the stone platform there.

An enormous hand made of magma attempts to grab you whenever you stand still in this room. Since you're standing on the platform, all the hand can do is lift you up to a passage that leads out of the room. Hop off the stone platform and move into the room's upper passageway. Head down to the right and climb up the vines covering the wall. This takes you to another passageway patrolled by a Bokoblin.

Defeat the Bokoblin, then take cover behind a pillar. There's a pair of Bokoblin archers patrolling other sections of the room that you absolutely must pick off before you move on. You need to climb across a long section of vine-covered wall to reach the next part of the passage, and getting hit by an arrow knocks you back down to the iron grate, leaving you at the mercy of the giant magma hand.

At the end of this passage is a section of vines on the opposite wall that you can grapple to with the Clawshots. When you drop down, you face a red gate you can't do anything with just yet. Ignore it for now. Instead, save at the bird statue and move into the next part of the dungeon.

3. Bombing Run

ENEMY: DARK LIZALFOS

Dark Lizalfos are tougher and bluer than ordinary Lizalfos, though they use the same general attack pattern and can be fought with the same tactics. The main difference is that Dark Lizalfos breathe solid streams of cursed energy instead of fire. Getting cursed while fighting a Dark Lizalfos, especially in a narrow, locked-in area like this, leaves you totally defenseless. When you see a Dark Lizalfos getting ready to breathe evil energy at you, quickly get out of the way and roll or toss a bomb at it.

Once the Dark Lizalfos here is defeated, the doors in the area unlock. Cross to the other side of the narrow passage. Bars prevent you from going to the right, so instead just pass through the door. When you enter this room, begin by picking off the Cursed Spumes that dwell in the magma flows in this area. Head to the far end of the stone platform and battle a pair of Dark Keese. Finally, pick off a pair of Bokoblin archers on a stone platform at the far end of the room.

Once the room is clear of enemies, take a moment to examine your surroundings. You can use a thorn bud to create a stone platform, but it's not in a useful place. You need to do something to get the magma in this room flowing. On the south side of the room, magma flows out of sculpted dragon-head spouts. There's a dragon-head spout on the north side of the room, but its mouth is closed.

To open it, find a Bomb Flower to drop on it. Start exploring the room with the Hook Beetle. There's a long tunnel leading west near the closed dragon-head spout that your Hook Beetle should be able to get into. Pick up the Blue Rupee; just beyond there's a clump of hidden Bomb Flowers growing. Pick one up and carefully navigate your Hook Beetle into the tunnel just beyond the Bomb Flowers.

That tunnel should have your Hook Beetle emerging directly across from your bombing target. A basic Hook Beetle can make the trip if you're careful not to hit anything. If you're having a hard time navigating your Beetle through this sequence, you may want to consider backtracking out of the dungeon and upgrading it to the Quick Beetle or Tough Beetle.

Once the rubble blocking the dragon-head spout is blasted away, the magma flowing from its mouth creates a powerful current in this room. Hit the thorn bud to create a traveling stone platform. Hop onto it to ride over to the broken staircase at the base of the net platform. One of the doors here is locked, but you can pass through the other.

4. Uncomfortable Position

One of Guld's Mogmas has already gotten into trouble in this dungeon. He's held captive, dangling from a chain high above a pit of magma. You can't help him now, so move on through this room. Get out the Gust Bellows to blow away the patches of superheated rubble lying around. When you come to the blue chest, open it to get a Small Key. Backtrack into the last room and pass through its padlocked door.

5. Portable Water

Now you're in a stone area where the thorn buds grow low enough to the ground that you can lock onto them. To proceed through this area, you must chop some of them down. You may discover when you do this that if you thrust your sword through a thorn bud, the bud stays impaled there until you strike something with the sword. This property of thorn buds is essential to solving the next few puzzles.

Continue to explore the room to find a small chest that holds a Red Rupee. Chopping down one of the thorn buds next to the small chest reveals a Fairy. To exit the room, you must pass a wall of fire beneath a frog's head idol. Head up to the room's second floor. Defeat the Red Chuchus. Open the blue chest up here to find a random treasure. When you're done, impale a thorn bud on your sword.

Walk as close to the frog's head as you can, lock onto it, and thrust your sword forward. That should get enough water into the frog's mouth to make it happy. Drop to the bottom level and exit the area.

6. Turned to Stone

Defeat the Bokoblins and the Dark Keese waiting in the next room, then save at the bird statue. The next room is another iron-grated room. Two magma entities are active in it and two stone platforms lie at its bottom. One stone platform leads up to a small alcove where two thorn buds grow low to the ground.

Impale a bud on your sword and drop to the ground. If you strike at one of the magma hands while a thorn bud is on your sword, the hand solidifies into stone. Strike it with your sword and the stone hand falls apart, destroying the magma entity. Defeating both of the magma entities in this room lowers the magma level in this part of the dungeon, making it possible to free the imprisoned Mogma. It also raises the iron grate up to door level. Exit through the open door in this room to free the imprisoned Mogma.

7. Burrowing

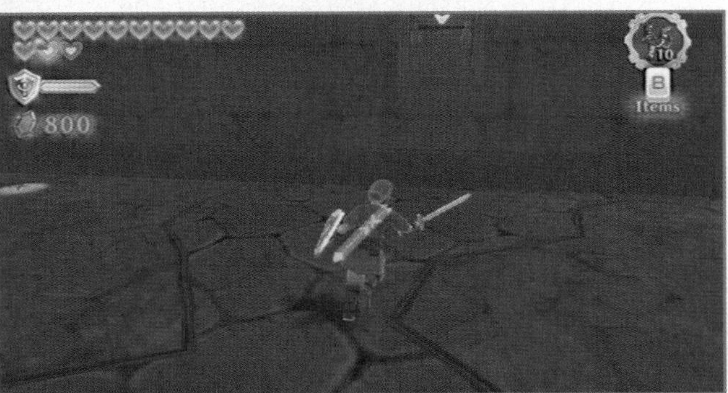

Now that the magma is drained from this area, you can hit a wall switch to lower the trapped Mogma to the ground. Once the Mogma is free, he shows his gratitude by giving you a much better pair of mitts than the busted old Digging Mitts you've been using awhile. Open the blue chest he gives you to receive the Mogma Mitts.

The Mogma Mitts

The Mogma Mitts boast longer, sharper claws than your old Digging Mitts. Not only can you use these to dig up dirt, but now you can even burrow underground like a Mogma. Look for burrow openings in patches of digable dirt. If you dig and see a hole there, you get the prompt to burrow. When you're underground, you can use your claws to attack enemies, smash boulders, or roll bombs by swiping the Wii Remote.

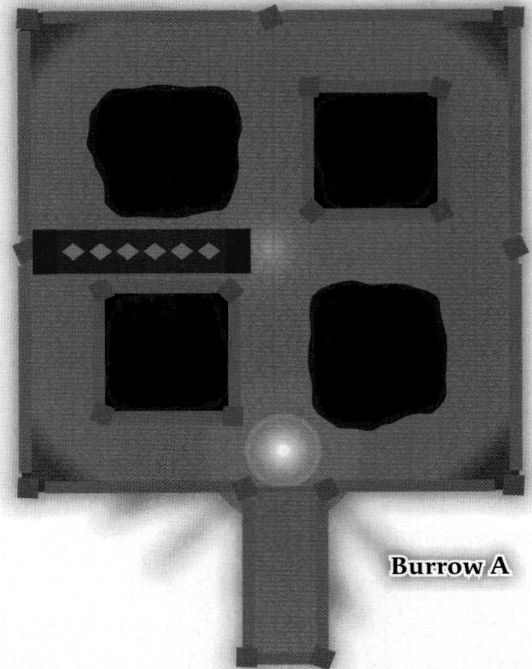

To exit this room, burrow underneath the screened-in area. Dig at the dirt patch nearest the screen to open the entrance to what we'll call Burrow A. Swipe to smash the boulders in your way. Collect all of the Blue and Red Rupees stuffed down here, as they're easy money. To exit the burrow, swipe at the Bomb Flower, rolling it toward a pile of rubble blocking your way. Once the way is clear, climb toward the exit to emerge on the other side of the screen.

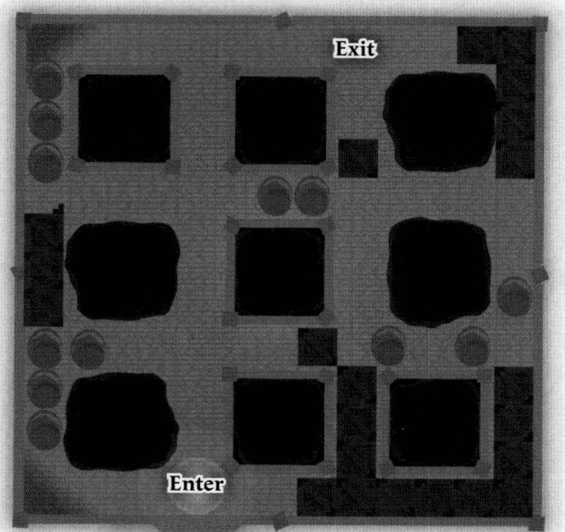

Burrow B

You emerge into the room where you fought the magma entities before, only now you're beneath the iron screen. Dig into another burrow here, Burrow B. Hit the switch that slides aside the red screen that's blocking an alternative way out of the room. Save at the bird statue before you leave. Right now you're looking for a Small Key to open the padlocked door here.

8. Underground Battles

Get out your bow and pick off the Bokoblins on the far side of the broken stone passageway. Step a bit closer to the edge of the passage and snipe the Bokoblin archer stationed high above on the other side. Drop into the pit, and check the area under the door to activate a goddess wall. Grapple out of and across the pit with the Clawshots and pass through the far door.

You find another captive Mogma in this room. Rescuing him involves passing through a door blocked by a flame barrier and a frog's head idol at the end of this room. To get water to the idol, you must thrust your sword through a thorn bud that's behind a screen and walk up a flight of steps. A red gate is blocking you from doing this.

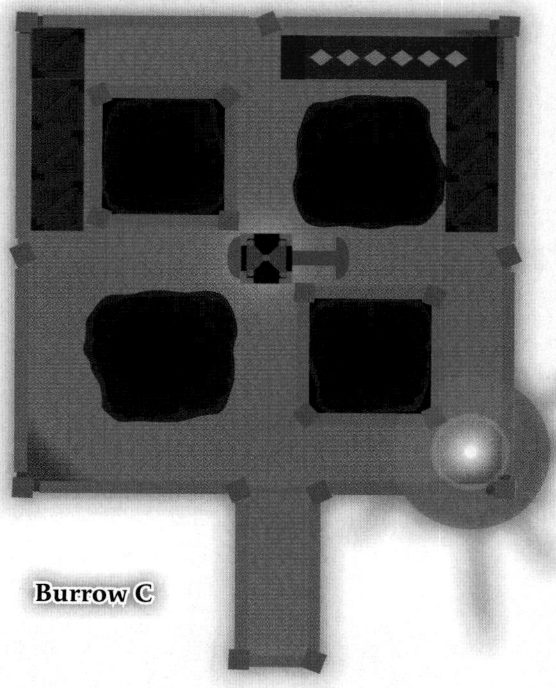

Burrow C

Pass through another red gate to find a burrow you can dig into, Burrow C, where the underground switches controlling the red gates lie. Hit both switches so the blue end is sticking out and then walk back to the thorn bud. Appease the frog idol and pass into the next room to rescue the Mogma. Once there, hit a switch that lowers the poor Mogma to the ground. This Mogma gives you the Dungeon Map as a token of his gratitude.

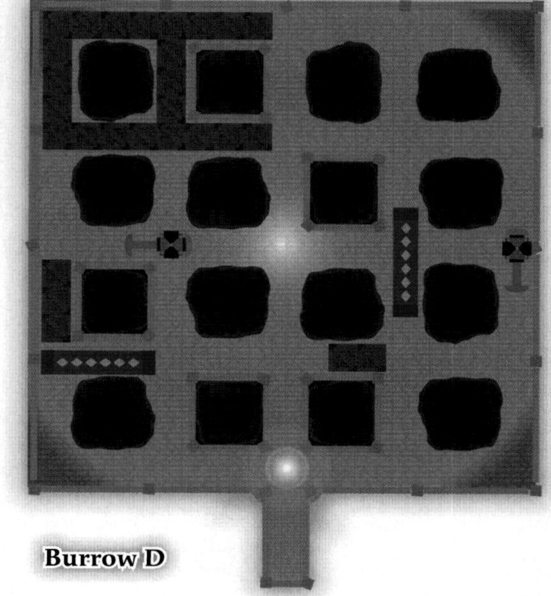

Burrow D

Study the map of this room and the location of the hidden room should be fairly obvious. Plant a bomb in the middle of the area's west wall. This reveals a small patch of dirt that's the entrance to what we'll call Burrow D. Simply move toward the exit. This area is patrolled by a centipede, the underground monster that the Mogmas warned you about. You don't need to fight it—just hurry on to the area's exit.

If you do want to fight it, then get behind the centipede and hit its orange tail with a swipe of your claws. Holding down Ⓐ to dash helps you catch up with the centipede. The centipede attacks by winding around a grid of the burrow, looking left and right when it comes to a crossing. If it sees you, it rushes toward you and tries to take a swipe at you with its pincers. If you trick it into rushing at a wall or box, it staggers itself. Burrow D's exit takes you to a room where a blue chest waits. Open it to receive a Small Key.

9. Bottling

Before you head through the padlocked door, backtrack to the first iron grate room to grab some loot. When you're heading back through the passageway with the broken floor, take a left before entering the door. Fight the Blue Bokoblin waiting there and then step on the floor switch. The bars ahead of you rise, creating a shortcut to the earlier parts of the dungeon.

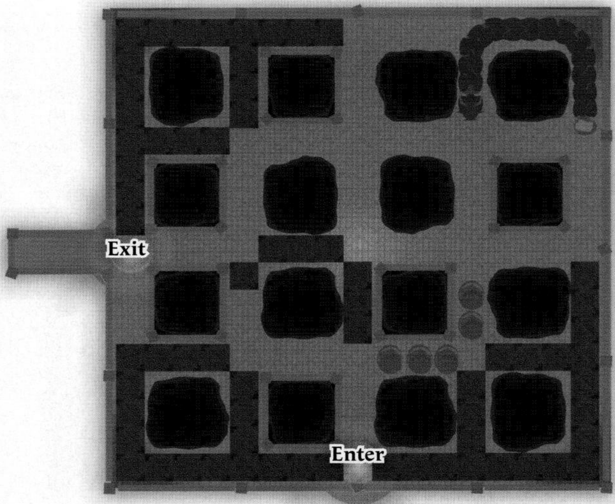

As you head back to the room with the iron grate, take a left to see the area blocked with the red gate. Dig at the dirt patch in front of it to reveal Burrow E. Hit the blue switch located behind the red gate to clear the way, then crawl back up to the surface.

Pass through a winding, descending stone passageway. Eventually you come to an area where thorn buds are growing. The way into the room with the iron gate is barred, but there's a floor switch you can hit nearby. Before you do this, circle all the way around to find a small chest holding a Red Rupee. Head back and get ready to battle the magma entity that dwells beneath the iron grate. You can use the same basic tactics on this one that you used on the others.

Destroying this magma entity drains the magma from this room. Now you can pass through a small passage that was previously blocked up with lava. Follow the passage to a door that leads to a blue chest. Open it to receive a third Empty Bottle, an extremely valuable find.

10. Lava Crossing

When you're done here, pass through the padlocked room. Bokoblin archers stationed high above immediately fire on you. Get out your bow and snipe at them. Your arrows, fortunately, have a longer range than theirs. At the bottom of the stairs, use your bow to clear away the Cursed Spumes lurking in the magma. Once the initial area is clear of enemies, hit a thorn bud above your head to create a stone platform. Hop across the lava flow to the other side.

11. Mogma Race

Head up the stairs toward an area to your left. Fight the Red Chuchus as you go. Once you're inside, battle a swarm of Dark Keese and a Green Bokoblin. Head around to a tall platform that overlooks a large magma flow infested with Cursed Spumes. Shooting them with the bow is difficult here because you have to stand close to the edge, where the Spume can hit you with its accursed spit.

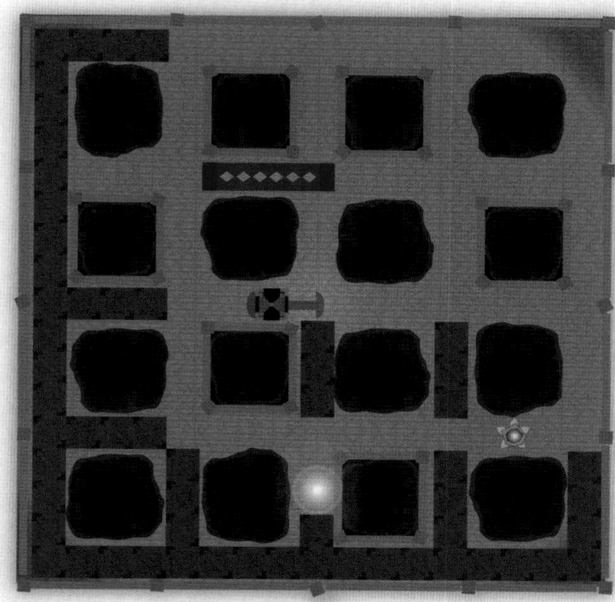

Burrow F

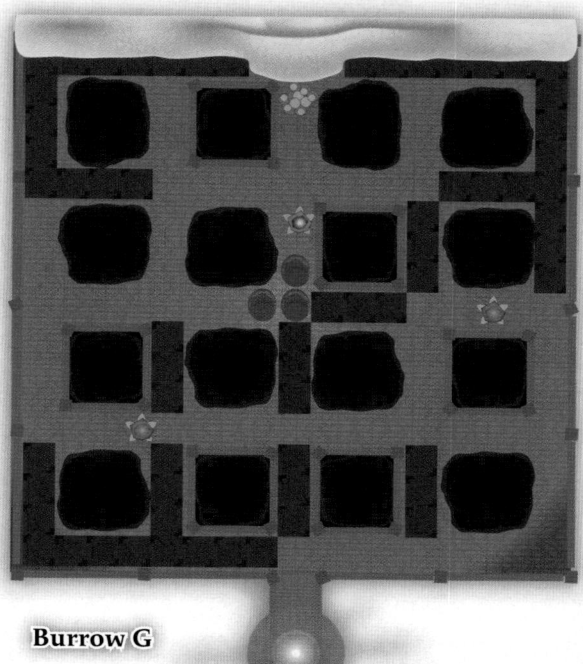

Burrow G

You need to work your way around the magma pool. Right now, your path is blocked by a red gate. Dig into a nearby burrow, Burrow F, to move it aside. When you hit the blue switch, though, a little Mogma crawls by to move it back. If you approach him, he mistakes you for a monster and panics. He says the only way to catch him is to block his path, but it's actually much simpler than that. You just need to get close enough to touch him, which you can achieve by dashing.

Once you get close enough to touch him, the Mogma speaks with you and sees that you have his brother's Mogma Mitts on. He apologizes for the switch shenanigans and moves the red gate over himself. He also gives you a blue chest containing a Piece of Heart.

Pass through the area once blocked by the red gate. Use your bow to pick off a Cursed Spume waiting for you in the magma on the other side, then battle a swarm of Dark Keese. Use a thorn bud to create a platform you can use to hop over to the other side. Absolutely make sure to save your game at the bird statue.

Dig and crawl into the burrow just in front of it, Burrow G. Work your way around to the Bomb Flower and attack it to send it rolling at the pile of rubble up above. This undams the lava the rubble was holding back, which begins flowing through the burrow. You need to get out of there, quick. Dash back the way you came, taking advantage of the Stamina Fruits to rapidly refill your stamina. If the lava touches you, it's an instant Game Over and you have to repeat the sequence. Save your game once you make it out of the burrow in one piece.

12. Leap of Faith

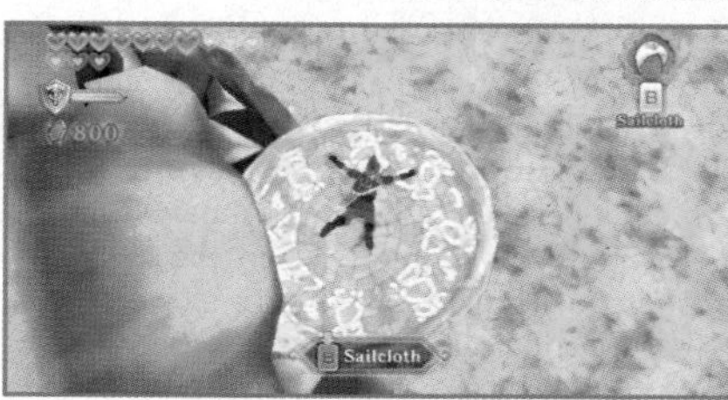

Now that lava is flowing from the dragon-head spouts, the lava river has a current. Head back down the stairs and use a thorn bud to create a stone platform. Now you can ride it over to the right side of this area. Head up the stairs and save your game at the bird statue. Note that this one you can use to go directly to Skyloft, rather than just to the start of the dungeon. So now it's also possible to dive directly into the dungeon, too.

Your goal over here is to try to obtain the key to the puzzle door, which you've finally reached. To get it, read the stone tablet that's just in front of the bird statue. Walk to the end of the long bridge behind it. You've come to the point in the game where you need to remember Guld's clue about the two statues. Look down while standing at each open side of the bridge's end. There's a statue on either side. The one to the right has open eyes, the one to the left closed ones.

Dash off the side of the bridge and dive into the sleeping statue's open mouth. During the dive, move Link forward and to the right a little. You want to land him on the glowing platform that appears in the statue's mouth as you fall. You immediately slide down the platform into the statue's mouth, which takes you into the Fire Sanctuary's hidden lower level.

13. Accursed Battle

Head down the passage you find yourself in. There's a goddess wall just before the first door you come to. When you pass through the door, you're locked into a sub-boss encounter with two Dark Lizalfos. There's a high platform on the other side of the room you can use for shooting arrows and throwing bombs at them. You can also use it as a retreat if you get hit by their cursed breath. This room isn't set up for a bombing strategy to be super-effective, so you may have to wade down into the room and battle both Lizalfos at once.

14. The Upward Spiral

After you defeat the Dark Lizalfos, move on to the next area. You enter a long passageway that leads to a tall, winding tower. There's a goddess wall on the bottom floor of the tower, so you can stuff Fairies into any bottles of yours that are now empty after fighting the Lizalfos. Once this is done, head up the tower. When you come to areas where the stairway has collapsed, use your Clawshots to grapple across to an area where vines grow on the walls. Expect to periodically battle Dark Keese in this room. About halfway up the tower is an alcove where a blue chest holding a random treasure is tucked away. To snag it, grapple over to a section of vines nearby and climb all the way to the left. Take aim with your Clawshots from this position and target vines growing on a wall just inside the alcove. Grapple over to claim the chest.

Exit the door at the top of the tower to return to the Fire Sanctuary's first floor, in a previously inaccessible area.

15. Light the Lights

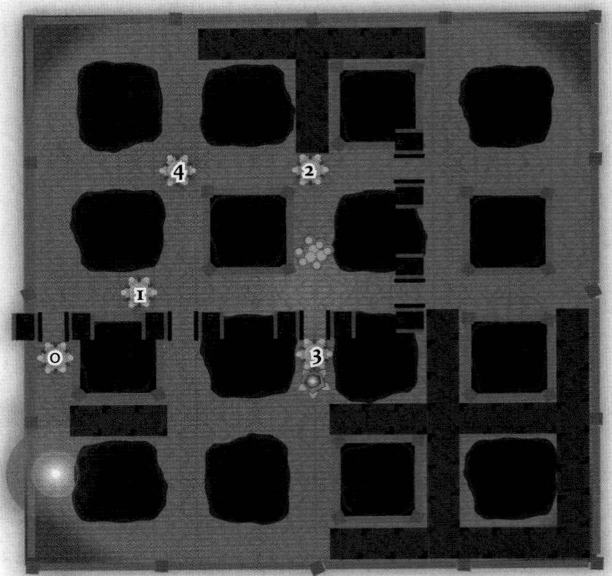

Burrow H

The jeweled chest holding the key to the dungeon's puzzle door is in this room, but you have to solve a puzzle to get it. Carefully examine the statues in the center of the room, then dig into the burrow in front of them. Each statue has a certain number of wings protruding from it (or in one case, none at all). This indicates the order in which you should light the statues. To light a statue, crawl over one of the orange circles in the burrow area. Be careful not to accidentally light the statues out of order. To see which circle corresponds to which statue, press Z to get a quick view of the surface above.

After you light all of the statues, you have to earn the right to exit the burrow by defeating the centipede that lurks in the area. When the centipede is at its full length, catching up to it and damaging it is easy. After you hit it twice, the centipede is small enough that catching up to it is a bit difficult.

To make landing the last blow easier, try to lure it into rushing into a wall or a crate and staggering itself. Once you've defeated the centipede, exit the burrow and open the jeweled chest to receive the Mysterious Crystals. Hit a switch on the way out of the room to unbar the area, so you can head back to the bird statue that's in front of the puzzle door. As always, don't open the puzzle door unless you're ready for a boss battle.

BOSS: GHIRAHIM

Ghirahim is back, and this time, he wants answers. You don't intend to tell him anything, so it's time for a fight. This time Ghirahim is more aggressive and uses more complex attack patterns. Where he only attacked you with one hand in the last battle, he uses both hands in this fight. This battle is a lot like your last battle with Ghirahim, a fight where patience and persistence pay off.

In the battle's first phase, Ghirahim advances on you with a pair of magical projectiles orbiting around him. So in addition to having to hit him quickly with a move that isn't telegraphed, the position of the projectiles dictates what kind of strike you can use. If they're orbiting with one on top of the other in a vertical pattern, for instance, you can only hit Ghirahim with horizontal strikes. Also, don't expect to get to hit Ghirahim more than once at a time during this phase. After taking damage, Ghirahim quickly leaps back from you. If it's too close to a wall for his leap, he teleports to a random point in the room.

In the second phase of battle, Ghirahim uses three or four orbiting projectiles at a time to guard himself. You can still damage him, but now only one or two strikes at a time is capable of getting through his guard. You can always use a thrust, as well as whatever type of slash can get through a particular configuration of the projectiles. Just stick to your usual tactics for getting Ghirahim to relax his guard and strike as fast as possible.

When Ghirahim licks his lips and summons a pair of short swords, the third phase of combat begins. Your opportunity to damage him is when he slowly advances on you holding both swords in a guarding position. Much like a Stalfos, the way Ghirahim holds his swords indicates how you should try to hit him.

Ghirahim attacks you in this phase by abruptly teleporting away and then dropping down on you with a killing strike from above. Dodge out of the way. When this attack misses, Ghirahim's swords are temporarily trapped in the floor. This gives you an opening to damage him.

He occasionally attacks you with a wide, arcing horizontal slash. You can shield-bash this attack to stagger him, just as you could in your last battle with him. Ghirahim still uses projectiles sometimes, too, this time summoning them in a ring around you. If you shield-bash at the right time, you can prevent yourself from taking any damage and do a little damage to Ghirahim. He also sometimes sends volleys of projectiles at you, three waves of five projectiles each that you can shield-bash to deal a little damage.

Eventually, you dish out more than Ghirahim can take and he retreats. Claim the Heart Container that he leaves behind. Head forward and strike the crest to claim Nayru's Flame.

With the power of all three flames, Link's sword is very close to complete. Now that you have the Master Sword, you can awaken the Gate of Time at the Sacred Temple. This upgrade has also increased your sword's attack power. A single strike from the Master Sword is three times as powerful as a strike from the original Goddess Sword. Now you can defeat a Red Bokoblin with a single blow.

Return to the Sealed Grounds

BOSS: THE IMPRISONED

As soon as you attempt to follow the priestess's instructions and activate the Gate of Time, The Imprisoned begins to break out of its seal again. When you go down to the bottom of the spiral pit to fight it, you see that now it has arms. Periodically during the fight, The Imprisoned stops walking up the spiral slope and instead starts trying to climb up to the next level. While The Imprisoned is climbing, you can't attack it and it puts itself much closer to the Sealed Temple.

Fortunately, you get a little extra help this time. Groose has built a giant catapult called the Groosenator and a track system that goes all the way around the top of the Sealed Grounds. The Groosenator can launch super-sized Bomb Flowers at The Imprisoned, staggering it. When Groose has a bomb ready to launch from his catapult, you hear him shout "Hey!"

Press ✚ to leave Link standing still and go up to control the catapult. You can move the catapult left or right with the control stick and aim its payload with the Wii Remote. Press Ⓐ to fire it. Use Groose to fire as many bombs as possible, but be careful never to miss a shot. Missing can lead to The Imprisoned gaining ground very rapidly. Two misses can easily lose the battle for you.

Link's part in the battle is exactly the same as it was the first time: to knock The Imprisoned over by destroying its toes and then drive the sealing spike back into its head. In this fight, The Imprisoned's every footstep sends energy shockwaves rippling around its feet. Approach with caution. You have enough time between footsteps to destroy one toe and then get clear. It might be tempting to wait for the Groosenator to stagger The Imprisoned before you attack its toes at all, but you can't afford to waste that much time waiting.

As in the other fights, it's easiest to go after The Imprisoned's back toes first and then work your way around either foot. Once you've removed all the toes from one foot, The Imprisoned slows down significantly. This is to your advantage, so focus on one foot at a time. When The Imprisoned begins climbing a wall, you have a brief but excellent opening to annihilate the toes on one foot. Once you can't attack it anymore, use the Groosenator to knock it back down the wall. When The Imprisoned is knocked out of a climb, you get another valuable opening to attack its feet.

When The Imprisoned falls over, you can't run directly up to its head anymore. The arms block your way. Instead, dash around the monster's left. If necessary, drop down a level and then ride back up a geyser to get at the monster's head. Hammering the spike back into its head works exactly as it did in previous battles. After each time you hammer the spike back into The Imprisoned's head, its walking speed when it gets back up becomes just a little bit faster and its toes are harder to attack. After the second time you knock it over, it slithers rapidly up part of the slope. A shot from the Groosenator can knock it out of this and force it back to its feet. After driving the stake into The Imprisoned's head three times, the battle ends—for now.

Beyond the Gate of Time

After you pass through the Gate of Time, save your game at the bird statue. Do as Impa instructs and enjoy the cutscenes. When it's all done, prepare to return to the present with a new mission—to seek out and use the Triforce to destroy Demise. You also return to the present with your final weapon.

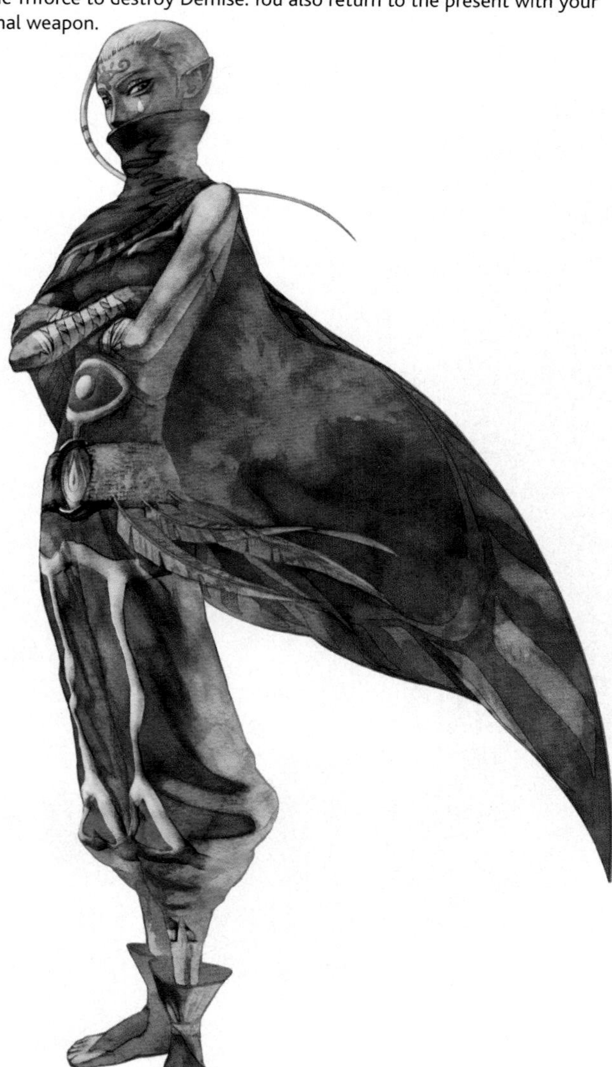

THE TRUE MASTER SWORD

A blessing from the goddess's own hand has given the Master Sword its complete and perfect form. It is the weapon reserved for the hero of legend who is tasked with seeking the Triforce. This version of the Master Sword is longer than the last blade, giving you a better attack reach. It's also far more stylish.

Skyloft

Begin your search for the Triforce here. First, head to the Knight Academy and speak to Headmaster Gaepora. He doesn't know anything about the Triforce himself, but suggests that Link go ask the great sky spirit Levias. Right now, it's believed that Levias is trapped somewhere in the thunderhead. Go speak to Instructor Owlan for more details. He's right next door.

Owlan says that Levias is not entirely in his right mind and that speaking to him now is dangerous. Of course, you want to do it anyway—you've got a world to save. Owlan reluctantly agrees to send you, but only after teaching your Loftwing a new ability, the Spiral Charge, which replaces your Loftwing's old dash. After you prove your skill with it, you can seek Levias.

Owlan's Test

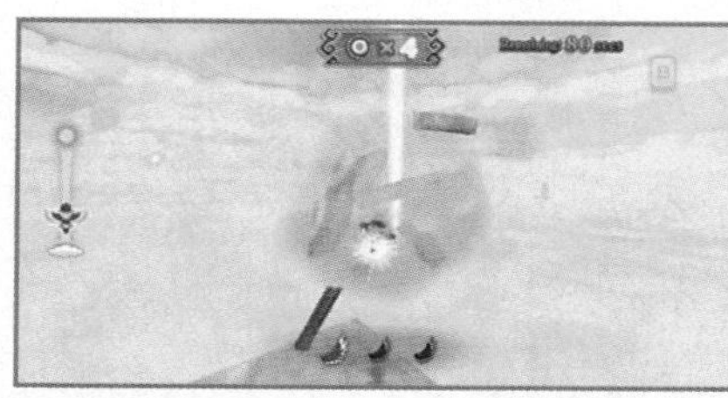

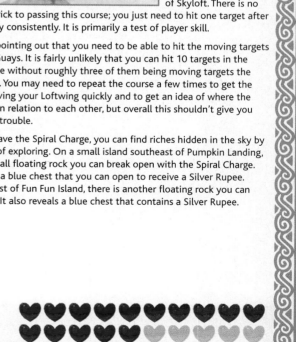

To prove you're ready to go after Levias, you have to hit 10 targets with Spiral Charges in 120 seconds in an obstacle course that Instructor Owlan summons up outside of Skyloft. There is no particular trick to passing this course; you just need to hit one target after another very consistently. It is primarily a test of player skill.

It is worth pointing out that you need to be able to hit the moving targets carried by Guays. It is fairly unlikely that you can hit 10 targets in the allotted time without roughly three of them being moving targets the Guays carry. You may need to repeat the course a few times to get the hang of moving your Loftwing quickly and to get an idea of where the targets are in relation to each other, but overall this shouldn't give you any serious trouble.

Once you have the Spiral Charge, you can find riches hidden in the sky by doing a bit of exploring. On a small island southeast of Pumpkin Landing, there's a small floating rock you can break open with the Spiral Charge. This reveals a blue chest that you can open to receive a Silver Rupee. Similarly, east of Fun Fun Island, there is another floating rock you can break open. It also reveals a blue chest that contains a Silver Rupee.

Pumpkin Soup

Once Owlan has cleared you to use the Spiral Charge, he tells you how to see Levias. It turns out that he, like every sophisticated being in the sky, really enjoys the Lumpy Pumpkin's signature pumpkin soup. Speak to the owner of the Lumpy Pumpkin and he prepares a massive pumpkin-shaped tureen for Levias. Scrapper carries it for you, so you won't need to prepare an Empty Bottle for it.

You need to take the soup tureen to an island in the thunderhead that's covered by a bright rainbow and fairly hard to miss. Unlike other pumpkin soup, the soup in the massive tureen won't go cold after five minutes. If you need to gear up for a boss fight after you put your soup order in with the Lumpy Pumpkin, you should have the time to spare.

BOSS: BILOCYTE

When Levias shows up to claim his soup, there's clearly something wrong with him. Terrible evil eyeballs trail off from his body. Once he passes by, leap off the island and summon your Loftwing. Pursue Levias and attack the eyeballs on his body with Spiral Charges. Once you destroy all of the eyeballs, the next phase of the battle begins.

Bilocyte reveals his main body after all the external eyeballs are gone. He extends himself on a stalk growing through Levias's blowhole. The area around Bilocyte's body is flat, and you can descend to it by diving off of your Loftwing. Bilocyte attacks by spitting noxious green projectiles at you. Shield-bashing these is quite easy, but for this battle you want to do something different.

Try attacking the projectiles with your sword. Use a slash to the left to bat the projectiles at Bilocyte's left eye-covered frill and slashes to the right to hit the right frill. After you've damaged both frills, Bilocyte slumps and his eye points downward. You can't hit it with a regular sword slash, but you can charge a Skyward Strike and hit it with a sword beam launched vertically. Bilocyte slumps down completely after that, letting you pummel his eye with a combo of sword strikes.

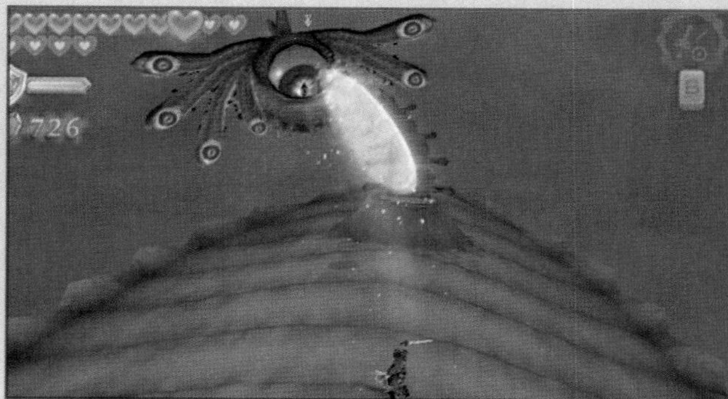

The third phase of battle begins when Bilocyte recovers from his first pummeling. It begins like the last phase, with Bilocyte spitting projectiles at you. Once you've taken Bilocyte's frills out, it slumps forward again—only it keeps spitting projectiles at you. You can momentarily stagger it by swatting a projectile directly into its eye with a vertical slash, which gives you an opening to hit it with another Skyward Strike. You can also pass on staggering it and just fling sword beams at Bilocyte until one finally connects. Once it does, Bilocyte shrivels and dies, restoring Levias to sanity.

Song of the Hero

Levias tells you that to find the Triforce hidden somewhere in Skyloft, you need to learn the harp's final song, the Song of the Hero. The Song of the Hero is divided into four parts. Levias knows one, and the other three are guarded by the dragons that guard the regions of the surface world below. If Link can get the song parts from each of the dragons, Levias can teach him the last part of the song.

Return to each of the three surface regions one last time to speak with the dragons that live there. You can make your farewell visits in any order, but a suggested order is provided in this guide.

It's worth noting that despite the three errands before you, the game only has one dungeon left. You will not pass through any new dungeons in the course of getting the three parts of the Song of the Hero. While you should prepare yourself for a journey before leaving Skyloft, think more along the lines of exploring than preparing to face massive combat challenges.

Farewell to Faron Woods

Prison Break

When you attempt to return to Faron Woods this time, Fi tells you that some force is preventing you from diving into the area. Land at the Sealed Grounds instead. Go inside the Sealed Temple to see what's going on. It looks like the seal is about to break again, so you've arrived just in time.

BOSS: THE IMPRISONED

The first phase of this now-familiar battle is roughly like your last encounter with The Imprisoned. It still has arms, and its every footstep still sends out deadly shockwaves. It still tries to climb up the sides of the pit and is still staggered by bombs flung by the Groosenator. For the first phase of combat, you can simply fight The Imprisoned as you did last time. The Imprisoned does move a little more quickly in this battle, but you have enough time to beat on its toes between footsteps. Take the extra speed into account when firing bombs at it, though.

When The Imprisoned rises again, disaster strikes. Part of the Sealed Temple has collapsed, blocking the route to the Groosenator's giant Bomb Flowers. Groose has no ammo, so it's time to improvise. Make your way up to the top of the pit and around to Groose's catapult as quickly as you possibly can. For lack of any other ammo, Groose is going to fire Link at The Imprisoned. Aim the catapult so that Link lands on The Imprisoned's head, then drive the sealing spike back in while it's in mid-flight.

After you knock over The Imprisoned once, it stands again and grows an enormous black halo. The Imprisoned is done with the slow trudging and is ready to just fly over to the temple. The only way to knock down The Imprisoned at this point is to hit it with one of the Groosenator's bombs. This sends it flying to the very base of the pit in the Sealed Grounds. Quickly make your way down to its head and drive the sealing spike back in.

Fastball Special

Go inside the Sealed Temple and talk to Groose and the priestess about what happened. The priestess explains that Faron Woods has completely flooded, which is probably why you can't dive into any of the bird statues there at the moment. She's also dammed up the entrance that usually leads from the Sealed Grounds to Faron Woods and admits that she has no idea how you're going to get into the woods to find the Water Dragon. Groose has an idea, which amounts to stuffing Link in the Groosenator and flinging him over the tree line. Remarkably, this actually works.

The Great Flood

The priestess wasn't kidding about Faron Woods being flooded. The water level is so high that areas of the Great Tree you could once only reach after a long climb through the trunk are now just at the water's surface. Go talk to the Kikwi elder who's nearby to find out what's going on. As promised, Faron Woods is completely flooded. The Kikwi elder says that the water came gushing out of the base of the Great Tree. Go visit the Great Tree, either by swimming back from the bottom or grappling up to the top from a lily pad using your Clawshots and some flying plant targets. Enter the topmost room, where you fought a Moblin last time.

This is where the Water Dragon is presiding over the flooded woods. Have a little chat with her. While she's impressed with your progress, she wants you to pass a test before she gives you a new portion of the Song of the Hero. She takes her portion of the song and splits it into a great number of Tadtones, swimming musical notes that she scatters throughout the flooded woods. Gather all of her Tadtones and you can have her part of the Song of the Hero. She even promises to drain the woods, as a little something extra.

Zelda
Skyward Sword

Gathering the Tadtones

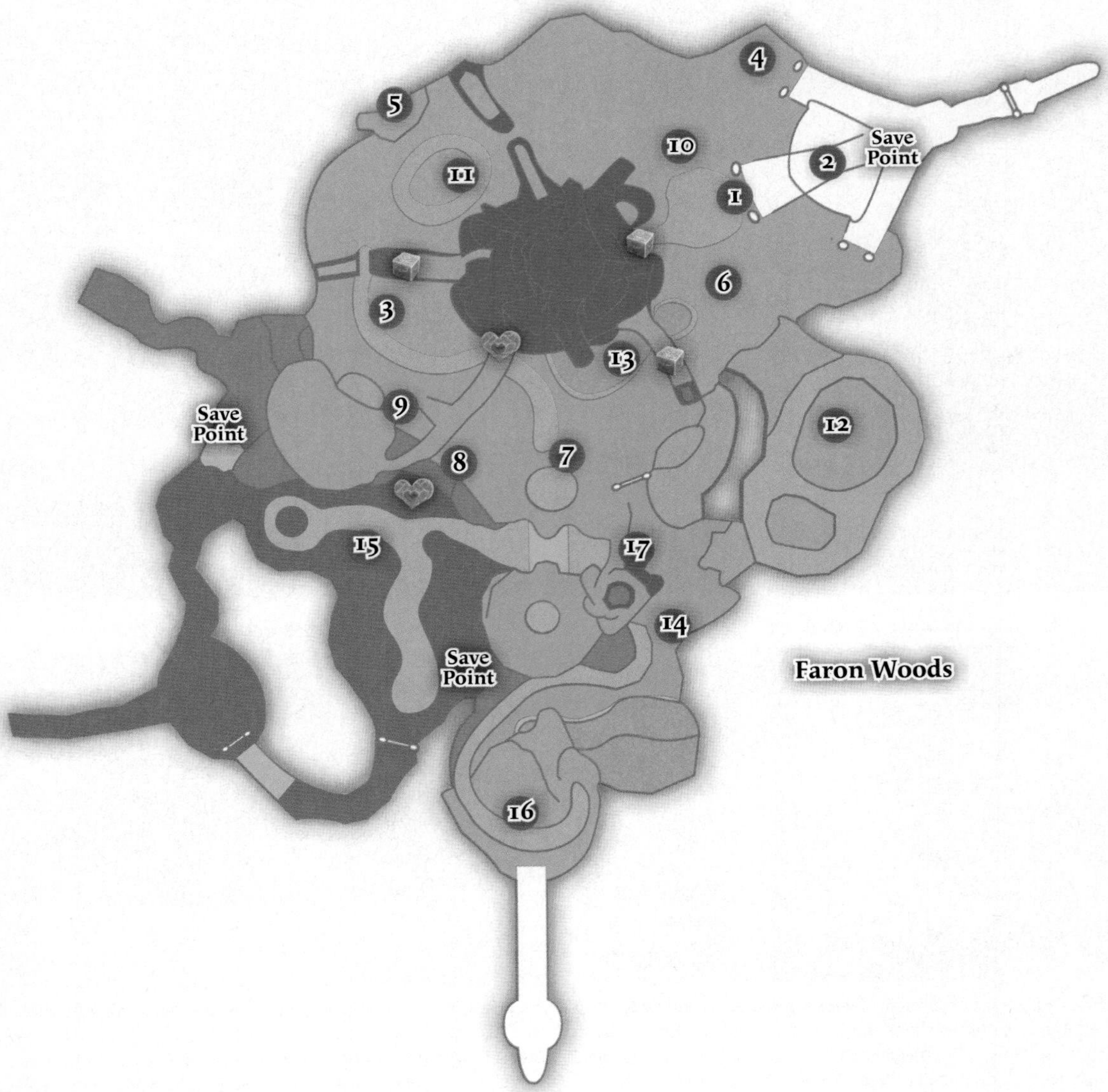

Save Point

Save Point

Save Point

Faron Woods

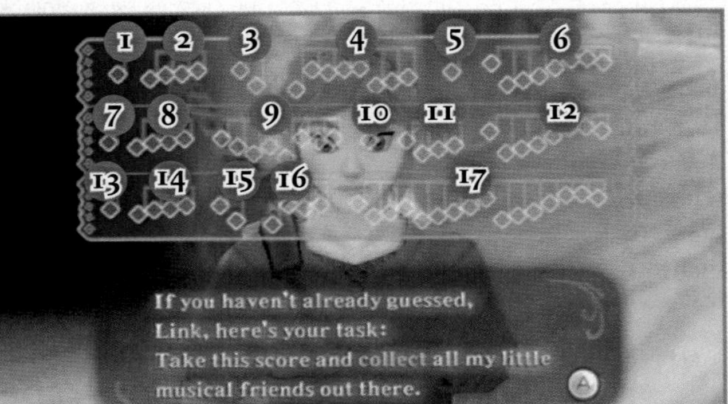
If you haven't already guessed,
Link, here's your task:
Take this score and collect all my little
musical friends out there.

Each group of Tadtones corresponds to a given note or group of connected notes on the musical staff in the picture. The map of Faron Woods is numbered with the location of each group, in the order they play their part of the song on the staff. You can collect the Tadtones in whatever order you please. The only thing you absolutely have to make sure you do is collect all of the Tadtones in a connected group quickly. If you don't get all the Tadtones in a group quickly, you lose the ones you have and are forced to start over.

To gather a Tadtone, swim near it and do a spin attack to draw it to you. When you're collecting Tadtones in a group, you can gather multiple notes to you at once. Note that Tadtone 5 is trapped behind a pile of rubble you must blast by spin-attacking a Froak. Tadtone 7 is in the tree hollow where the Kikwi elder used to stand. Tadtone 10 must be freed from thorns by diving onto a lily pad from the top of the Great Tree.

There are enemies in the flooded woods, but only one is new and none are especially threatening. It's primarily Froaks and the occasional Blue Chuchu, both easily defeated with your spin attack. While you work on the challenge, you can save your game at the bird statue located outside the exit of the Water Dragon's temporary residence in the Great Tree.

ENEMY: BLUE CHUCHU

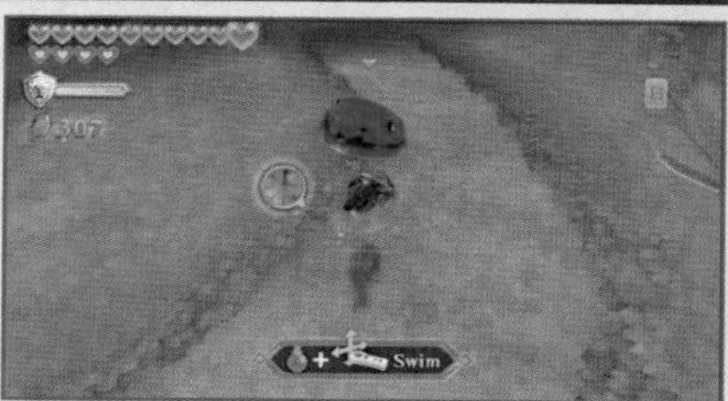

Blue Chuchus are the aquatic branch of the Chuchu family. While all Chuchus are mostly made of water or some other liquid, Blue Chuchus are so watery they can't survive except on the bottom of deep, watery areas. Where other Chuchus have to slither along the ground, Blue Chuchus can propel themselves upward through water with powerful leaps and try to grab on to adventurers who happen to be swimming by. You can defeat them with spin attacks.

After you've collected seven groups of Tadtones, three of the "scary fish" like the one you encountered earlier in Lake Floria invade the flooded woods. These fish harass you if you swim up to the upper regions of the water but won't bother you down in the depths. Defeat them by spin-attacking each fish twice. There are plenty of air bubbles, so you can stay in deep water almost indefinitely, but be wary of purple bubbles. These bubbles are poisonous.

After you've gathered twelve groups of Tadtones, go visit the Kikwi elder. Talking to him unlocks the ability to dowse for Tadtones, which can make gathering up the last five groups a bit easier. Usually it's easier to gather the large groups first, which are easy to spot, and then you may need to dowse a bit to spot the lone Tadtones even if you already know where they're supposed to be. Note that you can't dowse underwater; you need to go up to the Great Tree or a lily pad.

Once you've gathered all of the Tadtones, return to the Water Dragon and speak with her. She's as good as her word and gives you her portion of the Song of the Hero, then she drains the water out of the woods.

The Emptied Woods

Make a quick, final trip into the Deep Woods to get Goddess Cube #26. It's on the roof of Skyview Temple. Go around to either side of the temple and you can grapple to the top using your Clawshots.

Return one last time to Lake Floria, to the waterfall area just outside the entrance to the Ancient Cistern. Now that you have the Clawshots, you can snag Goddess Cube #24. Examine the cliff face opposite the Ancient Cistern's entrance for a patch of vines you can use to grapple up onto the high cliff where the cube is hidden. You can also snag an Amber Relic nearby.

Goddess's Treasure Chest Pickups: #22, #23, #24, #25, #26

Goddess's treasure chest #24 is hidden on a small island that's located right beneath Fun Fun Island. To claim it, just fly your Loftwing toward Fun Fun Island at a low elevation. The chest is sitting out in the open and contains a Gold Rupee.

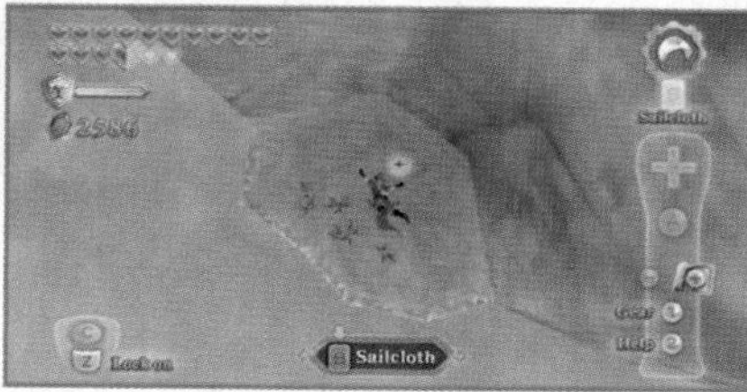

You can pick up goddess's treasure chest #25 now that you have the Mogma Mitts. It's located in the thunderhead, within an island that floats roughly between the Isle of Songs and Bug Rock. This island doesn't appear on your in-game map because it's so small that it's virtually, but not completely, impossible to stand on. If you approach the island from the right direction, though, there is one small area where Link can land if he dives off of his Loftwing.

This area contains nothing but a patch of dirt where you can dig to reveal a burrow. It's patrolled by a centipede you can just sneak past if you like. Take the exit on the right to emerge in a small fenced-in area. Climb up the patch of vines nearby to find the activated goddess's treasure chest sitting on a small platform. Open the chest to receive an invaluable Empty Bottle.

To claim goddess's treasure chest #26, you need to revisit the island where you claimed chest #11. The catch is that you don't want to visit it during the day. If you do, it's completely impossible to get into the alcove where chest #26 resides. Instead of heading directly to this island, go to Skyloft and head into Beedle's Airshop. Sleep unti nighttime on the bed inside. You wake up on the correct island. Go outside the airshop and you can climb up a ladder that leads to a platform. Dash and leap off the end of the platform to land in the alcove where chest #26 is waiting. Open the chest to claim a Rupee Medal.

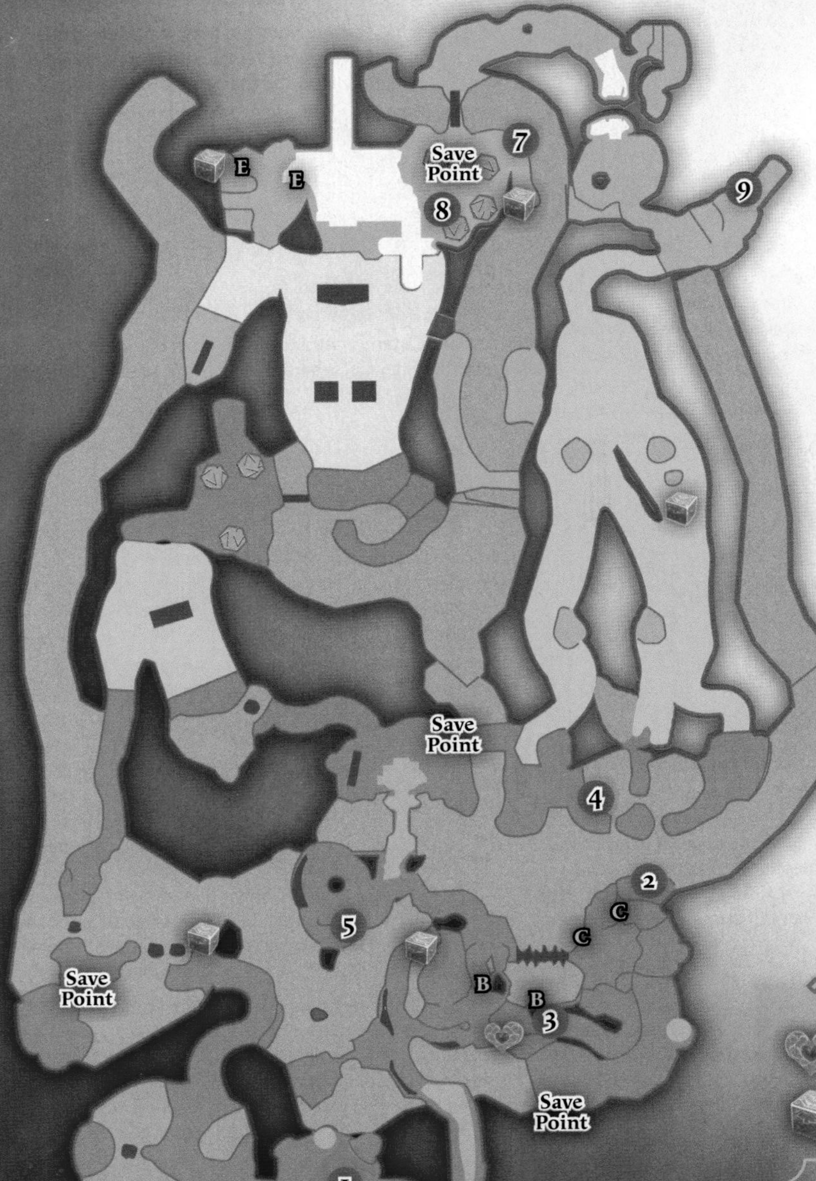

LEGEND

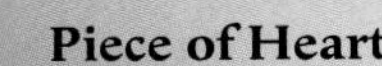
Piece of Heart

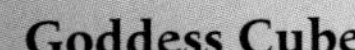
Goddess Cube

Farewell to Eldin Volcano

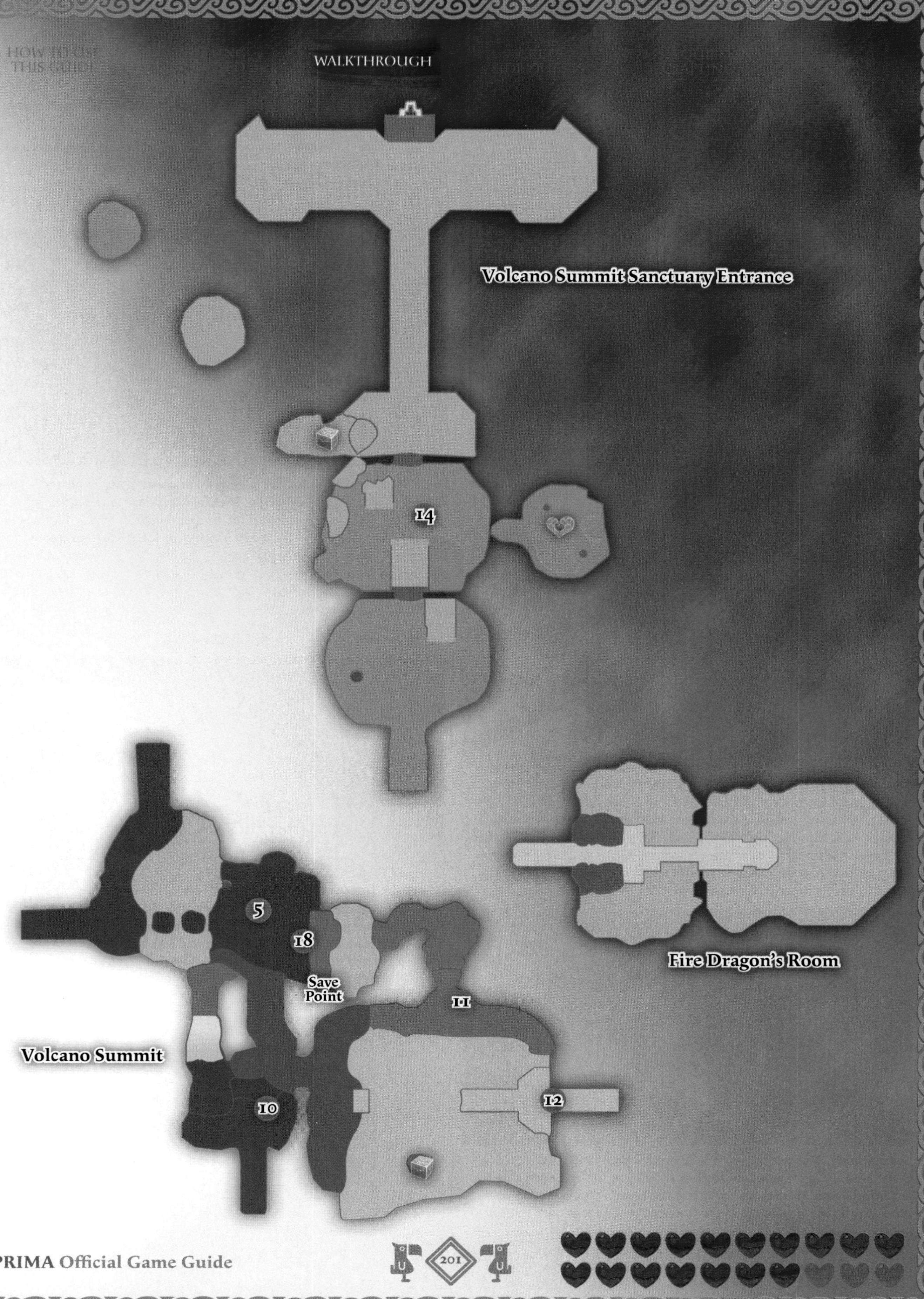
Volcano Summit Sanctuary Entrance
14
Fire Dragon's Room
5
18
Save Point
11
Volcano Summit
10
12

1. Busted

As you dive into Eldin Volcano, a cutscene kicks in instead of the usual map that lets you select a bird statue. The volcano is erupting and the updrafts knock Link wildly off course. Link comes to later in a Bokoblin prison cell, with almost all of his equipment missing. Fortunately, one of the Mogmas shows up to check on you and return your Mogma Mitts to you. Now you can burrow out of the prison cell through a temporary tunnel.

2. Underground

Now that you're out of your cell, make sure the Bokoblins don't catch you. Right now, you have absolutely no way of defending yourself. Instead, focus on sneaking around and not being spotted. The moment you're spotted, Bokoblins high up the mountain fire a boulder at you. After that, you have to attempt whatever sequence you're trying to clear all over again. Note that other enemies are still active in Eldin Volcano, and for now you simply have to run away from them.

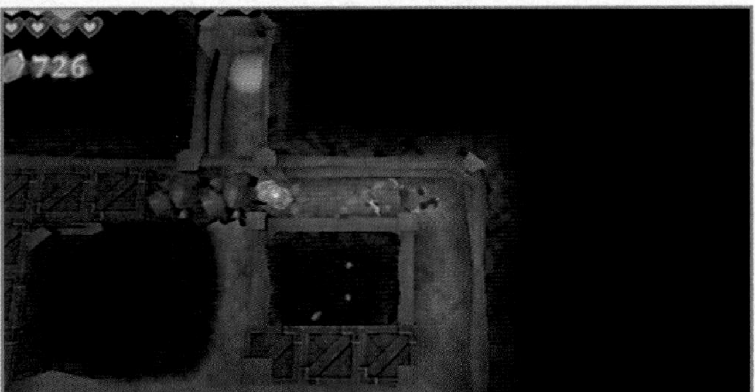

Sneak through another tiny burrow (B on the map) that's in the drop-down area, using some bombs to clear the way to the exit. You come to the other side of the Bokoblin watch station. Follow the path and you emerge just behind your old friend the skeleton bridge. A huge Bokoblin guard tower stands there now. Sneak around it by staying outside of the lighted area around the tower's base.

Dig into the burrow (C on the map) at the end of the safe, unlighted area. Climb into it and head straight to the exit. You come up just below the chest that holds your Gust Bellows.

3. Stealth

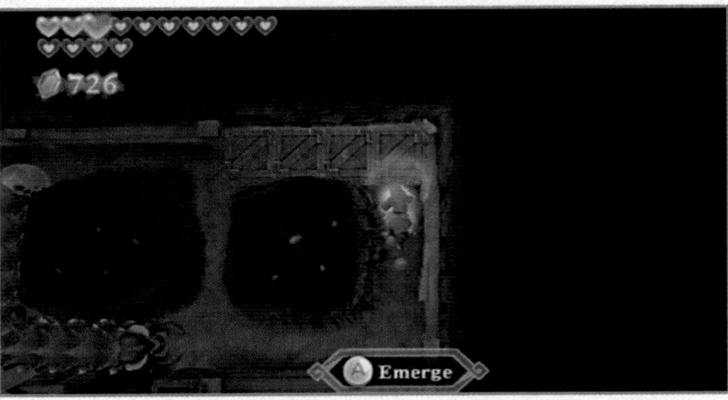

Now that you have your Gust Bellows, blow away the superheated rubble nearby. Now you can safely cross the skeleton bridge without getting caught by the Bokoblins. Now, climb up and head around the back way toward your Clawshots. Use the iron walls the Bokoblins have erected to sneak past them without being seen. At the rear of the area, crawl into the burrow (D on the map). Pass through quickly to the exit. You come out on the far side of the iron bars. Drop down to open the blue chest that contains your Clawshots.

4. Overhead

Once you have your Clawshots, grapple out of this area via a long line of flying plant targets. Grapple on to to the vines growing along the walls, then drop to a platform below. Walk around and hop onto one of the stone platforms floating by. Ride the platform until you go underneath an arch and come to a low stone area you can hop onto.

5. Bombing Raid

The blue chest containing your whip is inside the circle of light around a nearby guard tower. Sneak around it and use your Clawshots to grapple on to a vine-covered wall at the far end of the safe stone pathway. You come up on a ledge where three Bomb Flowers grow. Roll one of the bombs down the slope at the guard tower to put the light out and take out the Red Bokoblin on top of it. Snag the whip and move on.

6. More Bombing

Run up to the bars keeping you from crossing the stone bridge behind the area where you snagged your whip. Flick the whip to yank a flying plant target up out of the ground, then use your Clawshots to grapple over the bars. Save your game at the bird statue. You need to clear the passage off to your left. Pick one of the Bomb Flowers growing in this area and blast away the huge block of rubble obstructing your path.

Use another Bomb Flower to clear another large chunk of rubble behind it. Now you can ride the hot-air geyser up to the top of the mountain. Don't slide down the sandy slope; instead you want to cross the stone bridge that's near the Mogma. After that, dash across the fallen guard tower to reach the rear side of the Bokoblin village. Don't enter the area just yet. Instead, walk down the small stone walkway that stretches beneath it.

7. Bombing Hop

Here you want to get your Slingshot back. Wait for one of the platforms to float by and then ride it down to a solid area on the right-hand side of the lava flow. You must blast down the guard tower across from you, near the blue chest holding your Slingshot, so you can safely claim it. To do this, you have to grab a Bomb Flower, leap onto a stone platform drifting by, throw the bomb at the guard tower, and then leap off the platform to cross the lava flow. This sounds pretty complicated but it's perfectly possible—just accept the risk of blowing yourself up.

8. Dazed

Use the flying plant targets overhead to make your way back up to the Bokoblin village. Now you need to get your Bomb Bag back, so you can carry bombs again. To get it, you need to sneak through a well-lit area patrolled by two Bokoblins. You can only get past them by using the Slingshot to dizzy them, then running past while they can't notice you. Once you're on the other side, use the Slingshot to dizzy the Bokoblin atop the guard tower. Dash over and quickly climb down into the burrow (E on the map). Follow it to the exit to claim your Bomb Bag.

9. Final Bombing

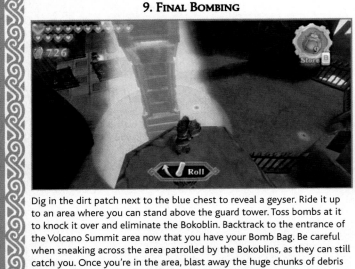

Dig in the dirt patch next to the blue chest to reveal a geyser. Ride it up to an area where you can stand above the guard tower. Toss bombs at it to knock it over and eliminate the Bokoblin. Backtrack to the entrance of the Volcano Summit area now that you have your Bomb Bag. Be careful when sneaking across the area patrolled by the Bokoblins, as they can still catch you. Once you're in the area, blast away the huge chunks of debris preventing you from entering the area.

10. Rearmed

Now that you're in the Volcano Summit, you can grab your sword. The Bokoblins helpfully left it sitting just in front of you. Save your game again at the bird statue. You can't drop into the area beyond the statue now because of iron bars. Instead, walk over the sandy slope you could also use to reach the next area. The top of the slope is blocked with rubble. Hmm.

11. Platforms

Now platforms float by on the lava. Ride one over to the stairway on the far side of the magma flow. From here, you can take another passage that leads around to the large, lower chamber by a different route. Use a thorn bud growing in the chamber to create a stone platform to hop across. Fight off the Fire Keese, then open your blue chest to get all of your stuff back.

12. Backtrack

Go around and blast the rubble blocking the sandy slope, so you have a shortcut back to the room on the right. Go back into the room on the right and pick off the Cursed Spumes with your bow. This time, head into the entrance at the top of the stairs.

13. Drawbridge

In this room, begin by cutting the rope on the pulley to the drawbridge; use your Hook Beetle to cut the ropes on the two pulley systems on either side of the drawbridge. Step inside to speak with the Fire Dragon and receive his part of the Song of the Hero. Note that after you speak with the Fire Dragon, Eldin Volcano returns to normal and many of its temporary features, like the burrows and iron walls, disappear.

14. Loot

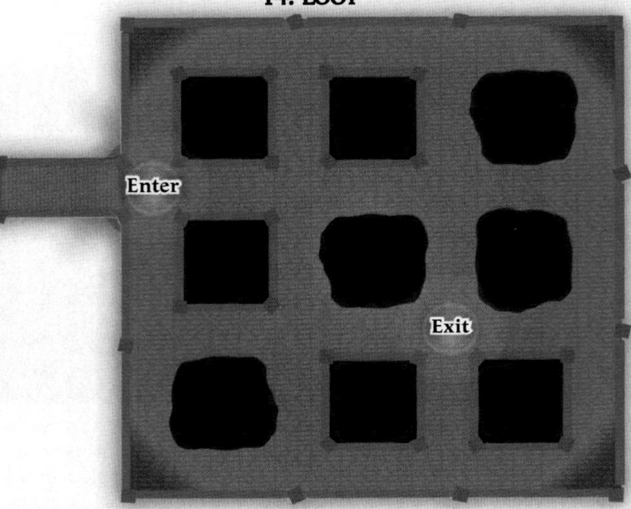

At this point, backtrack and pick up any Goddess Cubes you hadn't gotten previously in this area. Now that you're in this area with Mogma Mitts, you can also pick up a Piece of Heart. Go from the Volcano Summit to the area outside the entrance to the Fire Sanctuary. A burrow there leads into a hidden area. Inside the hidden area is a Piece of Heart and some Fairies. This should be the last bit of loot you need to get from Eldin Volcano and the last time (side quests aside) you need to visit this area.

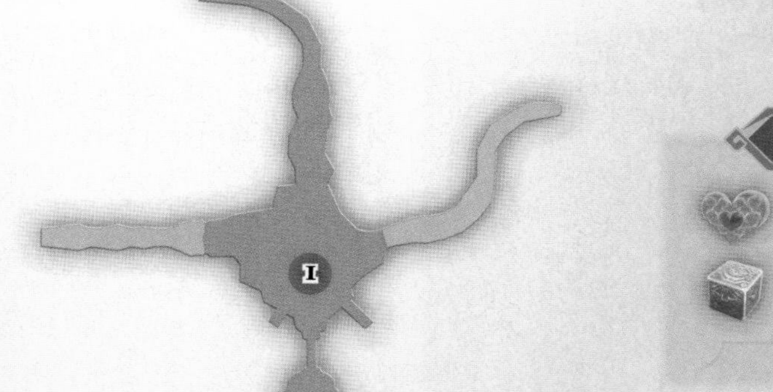

LEGEND

Piece of Heart

Goddess Cube

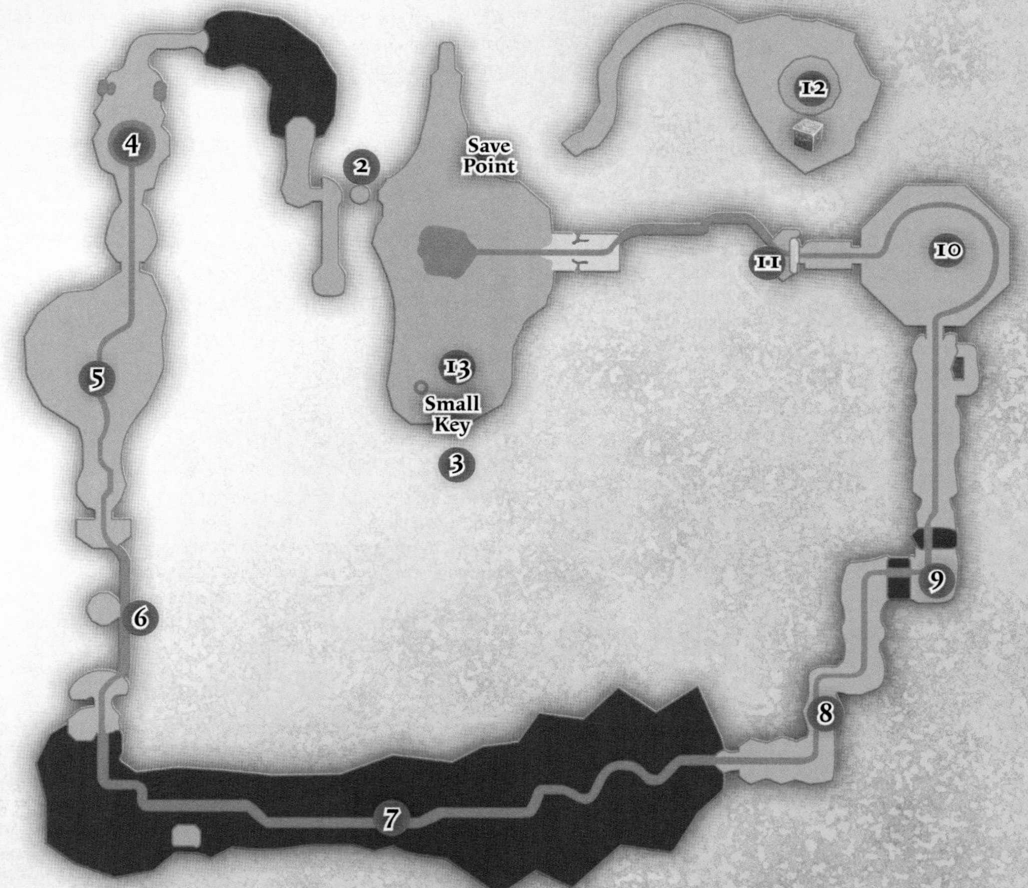

Lanayru Gorge

1. Goron's Gift

Head directly into the Lanayru Caves and speak with the Goron there. He's had time to find an opening into the Lanayru Gorge, the home of the Thunder Dragon. Roll a bomb into the tunnel to clear out some rubble, then crawl through the small tunnel to emerge into a new area. You can find a few Rupees here, but it's nothing too interesting. Move on to the Lanayru Gorge.

2. Locked Door

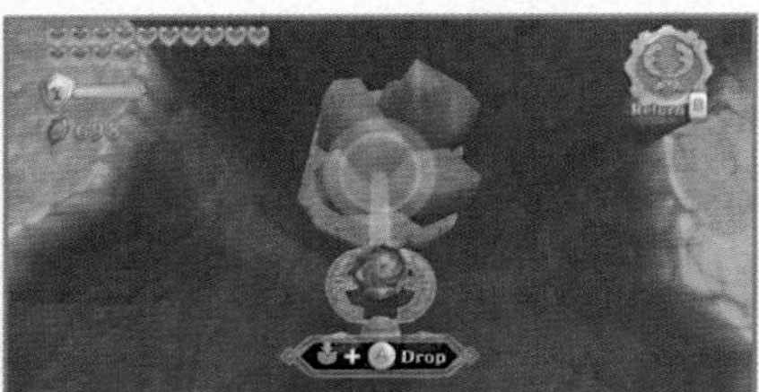

Initially, it seems that you may have gotten here far too late. The area is as run down as the rest of the present-day Lanayru Desert, and there's a dragon-shaped skeleton bleaching in the sun at the far end of the platform. Of course, the Lanayru region means Timeshift Stones. Maybe you could have a word with the Thunder Dragon if you could find one? Start exploring.

The only area you can get into right now is to your right, where a pile of rubble sits on a tall stone platform. Use the Hook Beetle to clear the rubble away with a Bomb Flower. Hop across to find a padlocked door and a stone tablet. The stone tablet mentions that passage through the door is only possible with the permission of the Thunder Dragon. So examine the area around the Thunder Dragon's skeleton to see if you can find a key.

3. Lost Key

If you look around the Thunder Dragon's skeleton on the main plateau, you won't find anything. Instead, look beneath it. Head to the far left of the padlocked door and deploy the Hook Beetle to examine the area. The Small Key is on a tiny platform far, far beneath the Thunder Dragon's plateau. Snag it with the Hook Beetle.

4. Cart Trip

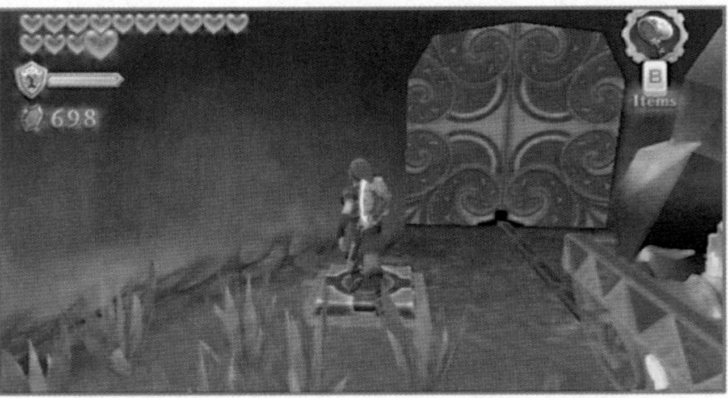

Grapple across the bottomless chasm using the flying plant targets, then climb up after you grapple on to the wall target at the end. In this area, you find an old mine cart containing a load of Timeshift Stone ore. Activate the Timeshift Stone with a thrust and get ready to follow the mine cart through the entire gorge. The mine cart sometimes comes across obstacles you have to remove. For instance, it can't pass through the door that leads out of this area unless you stand on a floor switch.

5. Running Battle

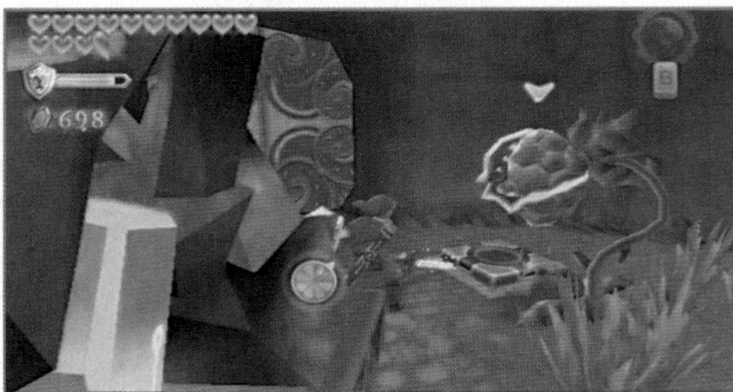

In this area, the Timeshift Stone summons many Technoblins and Deku Babas into being. Defeat the ones who advance on you, but otherwise, try to avoid fighting wherever you can. Once the mine cart travels far enough from an enemy, the foe just winks out of existence. If you get too far from the mine cart in this room, you drown in sinksand. You do need to fight the Deku Baba that spawns at the end of the room, since it's right next to the floor switch you need to hit to open the doors.

6. Quickly

In this room, the mine cart summons platforms that let you cross over a yawning chasm. Some of the stone platforms in the middle of the way, though, are patrolled by Technoblins. You must defeat them extremely quickly, which means very precise and aggressive sword slashes. You don't have enough space or time to fight them more defensively. Once the mine cart reaches the far side, grapple up to the vines and climb up to find a switch on a high platform.

7. Wall-Crawling

This area demands some fast, tricky platforming, since you have to move entirely along the walls and temporary time-shifted platforms. Follow the main set of platforms around to the end, then scramble up the vines that appear on the wall. At the top of the vines is another series of platforms. Very quickly dash across the platforms and fight a Deku Baba that appears on a stone area just beyond them. Once the Deku Baba is defeated, grapple over to a section of vines on the opposite wall. Drop to the platforms and hit the switch there.

This opens a door for the mine cart below. As the mine cart moves forward, it summons another set of vines into existence. Grapple over to them. You have to climb along this long patch of vines to keep up with the mine cart. Be sure to grab every Stamina Fruit you can and be careful leaping over the steam jets on the wall. Drop off the vines once a platform appears beneath them.

The mine cart hits another closed door, which makes this platform a safe perch. Grapple over to a wall target located on the opposite wall, then to another wall target, then drop down to the platform where the floor switch is located. Step on it to open the door. As the mine cart passes through the canyon, wall targets begin to time shift into existence. Just grapple from target to target. Be careful of the Keese that fly around this area. When you come to the last wall target, you can grapple on to a patch of vines around the door that leads out of this area.

8. Careful

Now you're in a long, narrow stone tunnel. It's nothing but sinksand in the present day, so continue to stay close to the mine cart. Green Chuchus and Deku Babas appear as the mine cart time-shifts the area around you. The area is so narrow that you have no choice but to fight them, but be very careful. If you accidentally hit the mine cart, you drown instantly in sinksand. When the cart comes to a stop before some iron bars, get out your whip so you can pull the switch on the other side.

9. Swing for Life

Stay close to the cart as it passes through the first part of the tunnel, where spiked metal devices slide rapidly back and forth across the tunnel floor. The mine cart blocks them. As the mine cart goes to pass over the first pit in this room, a Technoblin attacks you. Be very quick here. Defeat the Technoblin, then quickly get out your whip, snag the hook over the bottomless pit, and swing to the other side.

Ignore the Deku Baba on the other side. Use your whip to snag a hook that's over the next pit and swing across to solid ground. The mine cart summons a pair of Deku Babas here. You have no choice but to defeat them very quickly and carefully. Stay with the mine cart as you move carefully through another stone area full of the spiked metal sliders. When the mine cart comes to a stop at the door, dash through the sinksand up to a switch to the right. Pull the switch so you and the mine cart can move on.

10. Rushdown

Now you're in a large, solid round room. As the mine cart slowly winds around the track, you must defeat a gauntlet of strong enemies without accidentally shutting off the mine cart. You must fight Beamos, Green Chuchus, Technoblins, and a Sentrobe in rapid succession. When the mine cart reaches the door, use your whip to pull a high wall switch.

11. End of the Line

You're finally outside and heading back to the Thunder Dragon's plateau. Run across the platforms the mine cart summons and fight the Deku Baba that guards them. When the mine cart comes to a pile of rubble obstructing the track, send your Hook Beetle out to pick up one of the nearby Bomb Flowers. Bomb the rubble so the mine cart can proceed.

Fight the Deku Babas that appear in front of you, then jump across the small gap in the platforms. A Quadro Baba appears as you continue following the platforms. Defeat it quickly and move on. After this, the mine cart moves to its final destination and time-shifts the entire plateau into the past, when the Thunder Dragon was still alive.

12. The Ailing Dragon

The Thunder Dragon can't give you his part of the Song of the Hero because he's too sick to sing. Go talk to the worker robots in the area to find out what's up with his ailment. You especially want to talk to a little guy who is guarding a series of platforms. The only thing that can heal the Thunder Dragon is the Life Tree Fruit. The worker robots have planted a Life Tree Seedling for the Thunder Dragon, but it can't grow in Lanayru Desert's poor soil.

Now the worker robot by the platforms has stepped aside, so you can explore the area where they've planted the Life Tree. This area isn't time-shifted yet, since it's outside the mine cart's field of effect. Dash across the sinksand and climb up the central platform, where a stunted tree grows. Blow away the pile of sand to reveal a Timeshift Stone. Hit it to see what was going on here a thousand years ago.

The stunted tree dissolves into a tiny seedling, the seedling of the Life Tree that the worker robot mentioned before. You've seen that it's not going to thrive here, so pick it up and take it somewhere else. After you've taken the seedling, drop down and activate Goddess Cube #27 in the far corner. If you've followed this walkthrough completely, this should be the final Goddess Cube you need to activate.

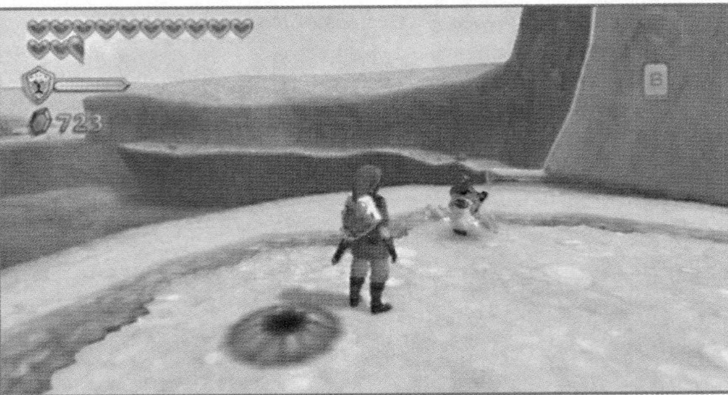

Carefully examine the hole left behind after you've picked the seedling. It looks a bit like a burrow hole, but instead of being flat, the soil is heaped at the edges. Chances are you've seen holes like this in Skyloft and the Sealed Grounds. In fact, you were shown one in a cutscene in the Sealed Grounds not too long ago, so try going back there. Since you time-shifted the area with the seedling, you need to time shift the mine cart from a distance to get out of this area. Shooting an arrow at it works, though you need a very precise shot.

13. Life Tree

Backtrack to the Sealed Grounds and examine the planting soil. If you plant it here, Fi tells you that the location for the seedling is good, but that it's going to take too long for the seedling to grow here. Good thing there's a nearby door that leads to a thousand years in the past, huh? Take the seedling back and pass through the Gate of Time. Plant the seedling in the distant past, then return to the present-day Sealed Grounds.

You find an enormous tree with a massive golden fruit dangling off of it. Dash-roll at the tree to obtain the Life Tree Fruit. Return to Lanayru Gorge and give it to the Thunder Dragon. He's happy to reward you with his part of the Song of the Hero. Now you're ready to go back to Skyloft and see Levias.

Goddess's Treasure Chest Pickups: #27

To claim goddess's treasure chest #27, return to the tiny rock island in the thunderhead where you nabbed chest #25 earlier. Dive back onto the same burrow. This time, instead of taking the right exit, take the left exit. Open this chest to nab the Small Quiver.

Farewell to Skyloft

Song of the Hero

Return to the sky and head to the thunderhead to see Levias, who automatically gives you the promised Song of the Hero. The Song of the Hero doesn't directly open the final dungeon, if you were hoping for that. It actually opens the game's final Silent Realm challenge, which is the last test Link must pass to prove that he's worthy of the Triforce. Return to Skyloft.

The Trial Gate

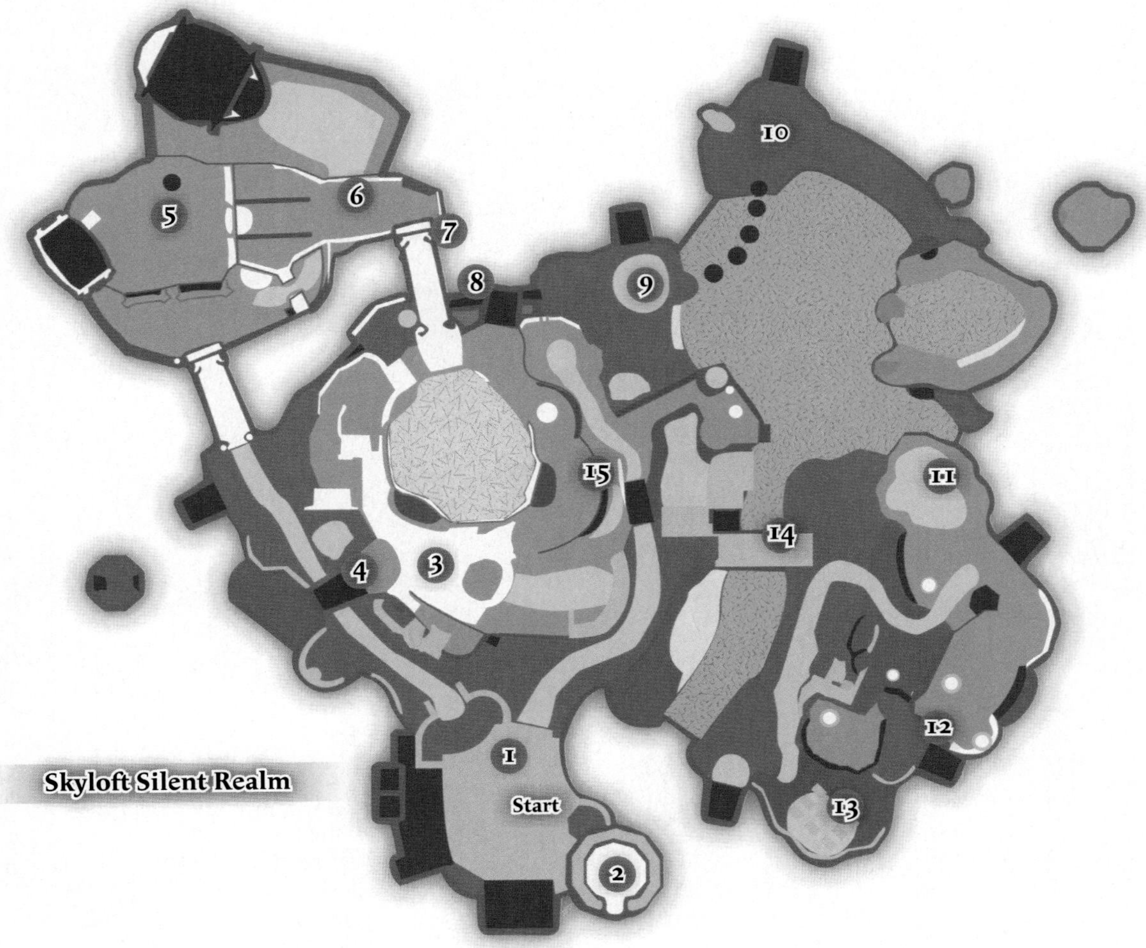

Skyloft Silent Realm

Skyloft's Trial Gate is in the plaza, in front of the Light Tower. Play the Song of the Hero there to open up the Silent Realm. This Silent Realm challenge demands all of the tricks and technqiues you've developed while clearing the others. Many of the Sacred Tears you collect here are placed in cramped areas where you either don't have a lot of room or are penned in by Watchers.

The suggested order of retrieving the tears is designed to be more safe than convenient. A real danger in the Skyloft Silent Realm is getting all of the Sacred Tears and then being unable to make it back to the start point due to the sheer density of Watchers patrolling the area. This order is meant to preserve most of the easily nabbed tears, so you can grab them if you stumble into a Watcher. One final note: It is extremely difficult to go from tear 8 to tear 9 without alerting the Watcher in that area. It's almost safest to just dash through and get to the tear as quickly as possible.

Your reward for clearing this Silent Realm is the Stone of Trials, the item that acts as the key to the final dungeon. It doesn't do anything else.

The Bird's Eye

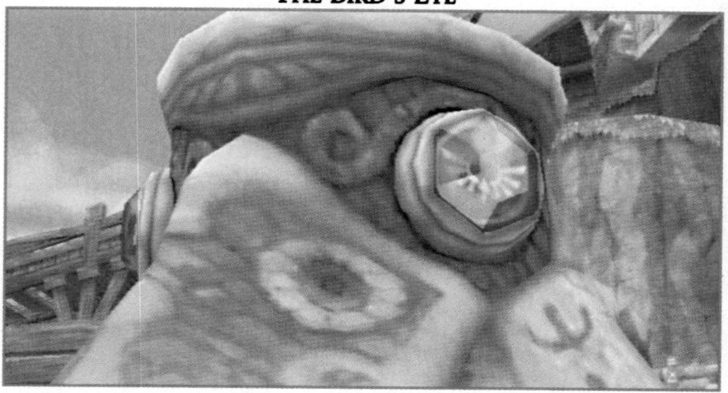

To open up the final dungeon, you need to use the Stone of Trials somewhere in Skyloft. You can try talking to Headmaster Gaepora about it, but he doesn't really know anything. The game gives you a clue about this, but it happens at the very beginning of the game.

If you explored Skyloft early on, before you found the Lumpy Pumpkin, you may have stumbled across an old man studying a statue of a bird (not to be confused with a bird statue save point) that sits on the plateau where the waterfall cave is. The bird has one red stone eye and the other somehow went missing. Hey, your Stone of Trials is just about the same size and shape as the bird's remaining eye...

Examine the statue and insert the Stone of Trials. Stand back and watch an amazing transformation take place. A hidden dungeon in the base of the Statue of the Goddess appears, along with a series of targets you can use to grapple over to its entrance. At this point, gear yourself up and buy all the potions you can carry. You're ready to finish the game.

Wait, What About...

If you're any sort of Legend of Zelda *fan, it's not hard to guess what you're thinking right now. "Wait, the final dungeon? But where's the Hylian Shield? Is it inside? Should I do something to go get it?"*

No, the Hylian Shield isn't inside the final dungeon. As for whether or not you should get it... well, it depends on what type of player you are. In Skyward Sword, *the Hylian Shield is a very different sort of item than it is in previous games. It's astonishingly powerful, because it is the only shield in the game that does not break. This means you can use it to absorb stupendous amounts of damage.*

The catch to this is that getting the Hylian Shieid is much harder than just beating the final boss without it. While the Hylian Shield was a necessary part of an adventurer's high-end kit in most Legend of Zelda *games, in* Skyward Sword *it's more something cool to show your friends. If you're skillful enough to get it, it's unlikely that you are ever going to really need it.*

So if you're a player who's mostly interested in the storyline, you should just make sure you have a Divine or Goddess Shield and get ready to finish the game. If you're a completist, go ahead and do this dungeon anyway. You have a final chance to save before the final boss. At that point, you should return to Lanayru Gorge and start working on the boss rush mode of the Thunder Dragon's Lightning Round minigame. More details on that are available in the "Secrets and Side Quests" chapter.

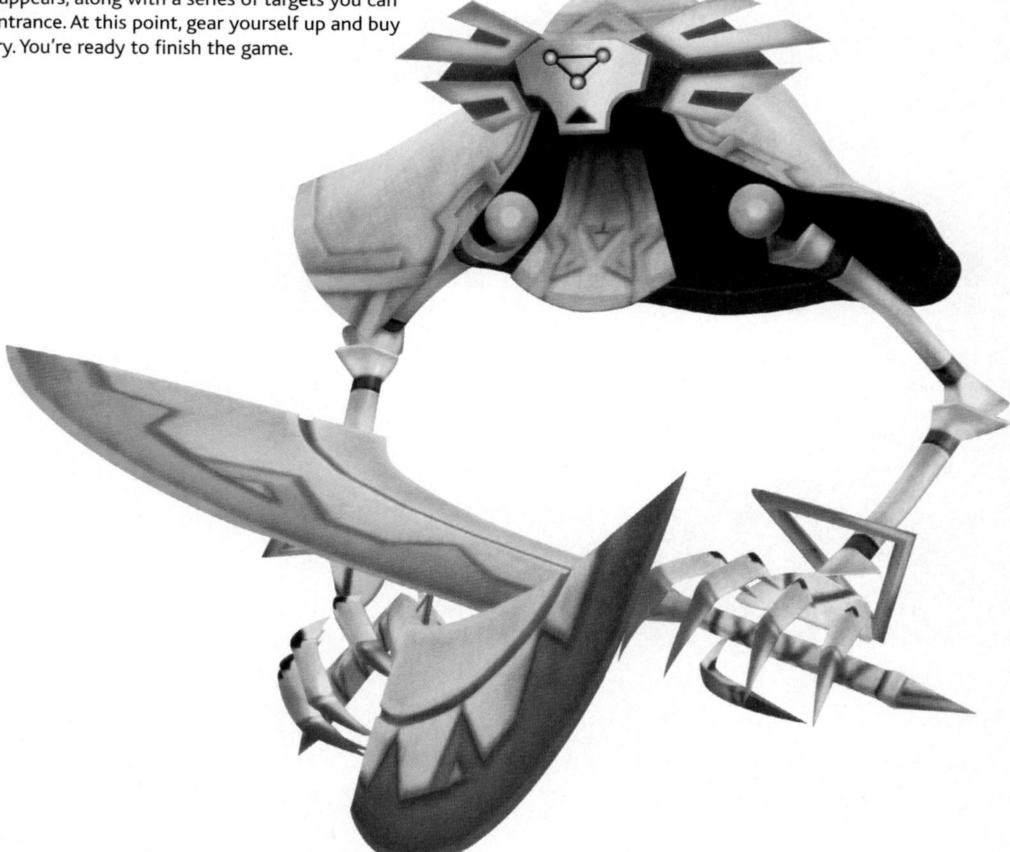

ZELDA
Skyward Sword

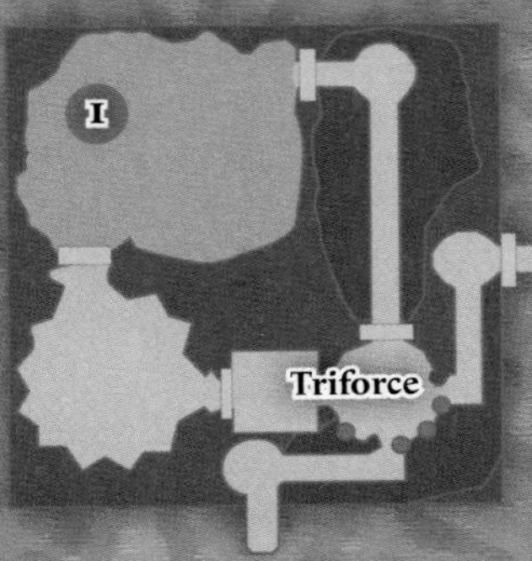
1
Triforce

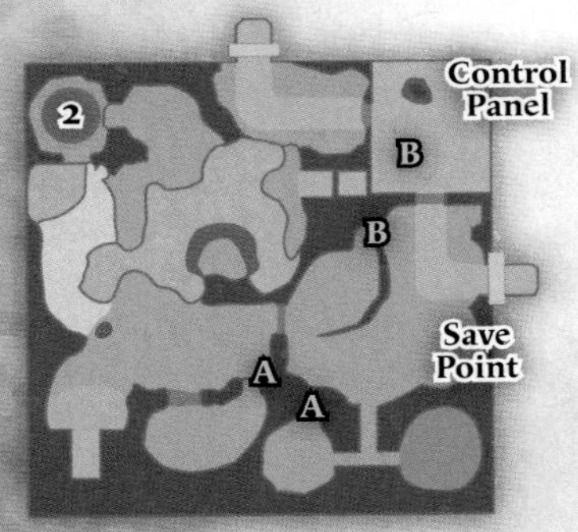
2
Control Panel
B
B
Save Point
A
A

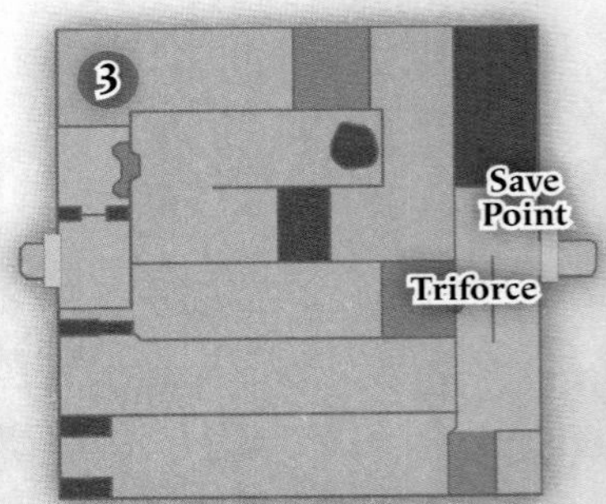
3
Save Point
Triforce

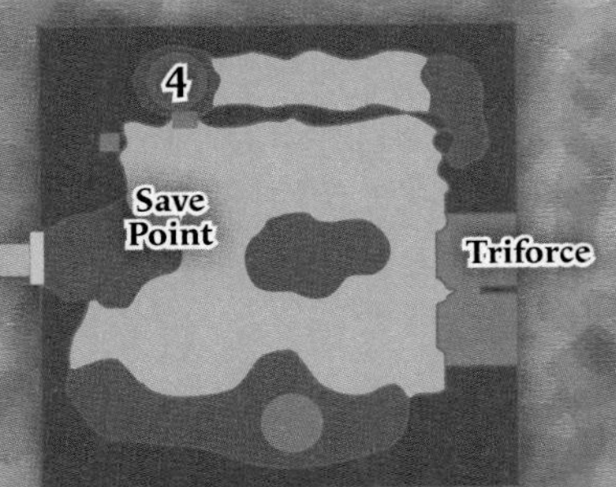
4
Save Point
Triforce

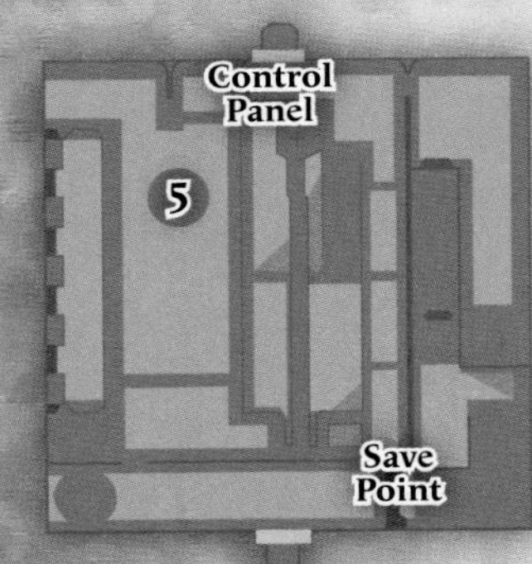
Control Panel
5
Save Point

Save Point
Goddess Wall
6

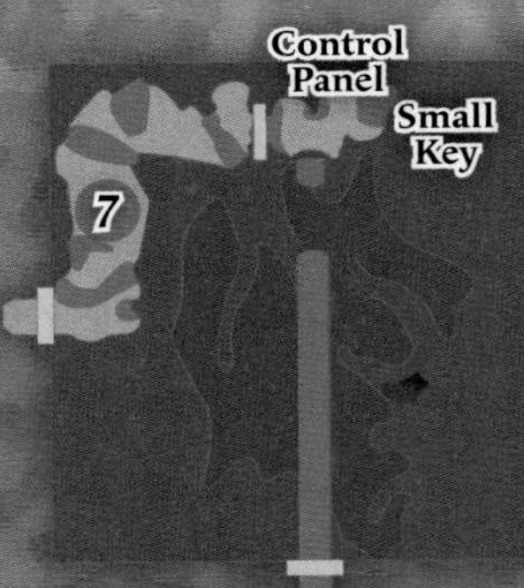
Control Panel
Small Key
7

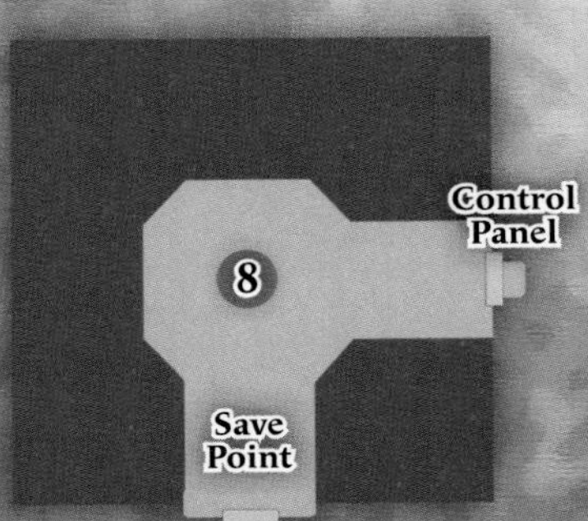
Control Panel
8
Save Point

Sky Keep

The Modular Dungeon

In most dungeons, there's a set level layout and you move through it. Sky Keep works a bit backward: you can move different parts of the dungeon around your set location. The dungeon's entire layout works like a sliding tile puzzle. The map shown indicates the default state of the rooms when you enter the dungeon. The rooms are numbered according to their default locations. Ordinarily, the numbered headers correspond to waypoints that tell you where in the dungeon to go. For Sky Keep, the numbered headers tell you in which order you must pass through the rooms. Each room is a puzzle with its own solution. Usually, all you need to figure out how to move the tiles of the rooms is a clear idea of which room you're in and which one you want to be in next.

8. The Map Room

This room is simple. Don't get used to that.

After you enter the dungeon, head into the center of the room. Open the blue chest there to receive the Dungeon Map. Next, head right to find this room's control panel. You can move the entire dungeon from any control panel, except for the room you're currently standing in.

From the starting configuration, you can only connect Room 8 to Room 6. You can opt to connect Room 6 to Room 1 or Room 5. For our purposes, connect it to Room 1. Pass through the east exit from Room 8 to Room 6.

6. The Forest Room

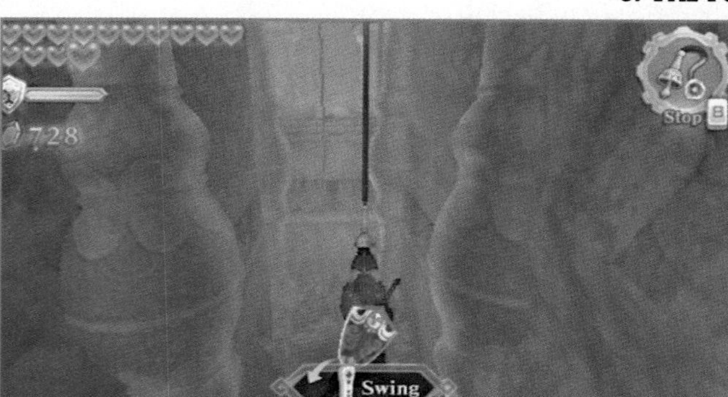

You begin in a miniature forest glen where giant mushrooms grow. Head south, through an area guarded by two Deku Babas and a Quadro Baba. When you come to the edge of the bottomless pit, launch the Hook Beetle and use it to cut through a fern on the far side. This frees a rope you can use to swing across. Begin your swing by snagging the hook in front of you with your whip. Swing from your whip to the rope and then to the other side.

A Skulltula drops down to attack you when you reach the stone platform on the other side. Defeat it, then use your bow to pick off the Furnix circling around the spinning stone pillars. Next, grapple from the nearest pillar to a second one. From the second one, grapple over to a wall target mounted in a fish's mouth on the far wall.

Three Pyrups lurk in small alcoves in the far wall. You can't pass through the area while they're alive. Have the Hook Beetle snag Bomb Flowers off the spinning pillar across from you and then go bomb the Pyrups. Once the Pyrups are eliminated, run and grab on to the rope dangling in front of you. Use it to swing onto the wooden hanging platform. Once you're on it, use the Gust Bellows to swing this wooden platform toward another one you need to jump onto.

Once you're on the second platform, face left. Use the Gust Bellows to make it swing toward the broken stone area in front of you. Leap off, then go save your game at the bird statue. Activate the goddess wall just to the left. Pull the switch on the wall opposite it to create a shortcut back into the mushroom glen. This room is solved, so now you can use it to quickly pass from one room to another. From here, pass into Room 1.

1. The Deadly Room

The door that leads to the Triforce is barred. There's another door ahead of you, but it's padlocked. The only blue chest in the dungeon is in Room 7, so you clearly need to pick up the Small Key in that room. It isn't possible right now to arrange the rooms so that you can get into Room 7 by using the control panel in Room 8. Instead, go back to Room 8 and arrange the rooms you can move so that Room 6 leads into Room 5, which contains a control panel of its own.

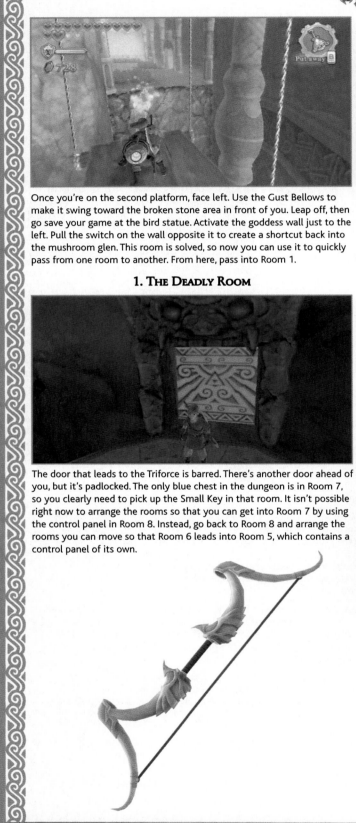

5. The Factory Room

Save your game just after you enter the room, then head all the way to the left. Pick up the Timeshift Orb and then head all the way down to the right. Swat the Technoblin that spawns in front of you. Pass through the door and down the stairs. At the bottom, in front of the ladder, you must battle a Sentrobe. After it's destroyed, set the Timeshift Orb down directly in front of the iron bars blocking in a pressure plate.

Climb up the ladder. Just inside the Timeshift Orb's area of effect should be a switch. Hit it to lift the bars. Pick up the Timeshift Orb and stand on the pressure plate. This opens a hatch in front of you. Toss the Timeshift Orb onto the conveyor belt behind the hatch. The Timeshift Orb powers the conveyor belt, which automatically carries it up to the area at the top of the ladder.

Stand on the pressure plate at the far end of the conveyor belt and your Timeshift Orb drops right out into your hands. Carry it into the next chamber and down the stairs. Fight the Technoblin that spawns in front of you. Leave your Timeshift Orb against a far wall in the lower part of the chamber. You want it to remove the barbed wire that's blocking in an arrow switch.

Go to the chamber's upper area and activate the arrow switch. This removes the iron bars to your left. Now, go back down and fetch your Timeshift Orb. Carry it up to the vane platform and set it down there. While standing on the solid area to the vane platform's left, use the Gust Bellows to move the vane platform over to the iron bars that block the track. Stand on the pressure plate that's across from the iron bars to lift them.

Now you can use the Gust Bellows to move the vane platform down the rest of the track. Pick up your Timeshift Orb and cross the vane platform to pass into the room's final chamber. Stand on the pressure plate at the left side of the room, and place the Timeshift Orb onto a conveyor belt. As the Timeshift Orb passes along the conveyor belt, it removes the barbed wire blocking in a series of five arrow switches located above it.

Run alongside the Timeshift Orb and attempt to activate each arrow switch as the orb passes by below them. It also activates a pair of Beamos that you should defeat very quickly. If you can't quite hit all five switches the first time the Timeshift Orb passes by, use your whip on the hook switch in the center of the room to reverse the conveyor belt's direction and try again.

Once all five switches are activated, the iron bars blocking in this room's control panel lift up. Configure the rooms so you can enter Room 2 from here, probably by passing through Room 1.

2. The Earth Room

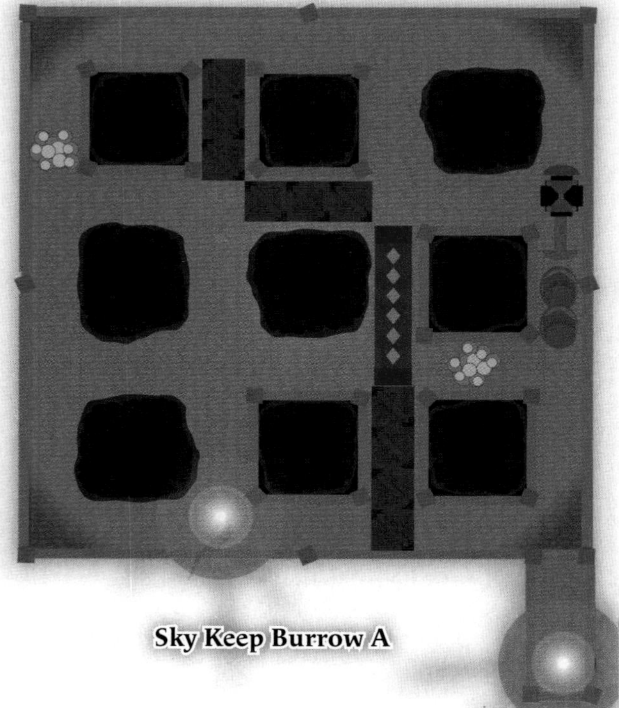

The area in front of you is barred by a red gate. To pass on, explore the chambers to the left. From the easternmost chamber, roll a bomb through a small tunnel into the westernmost chamber. Once there, fight a Red Chuchu. In the corner of the room, there's the entrance to Burrow A. Climb in and smash the boulders blocking in the red switch. Press it to open the gate. Climb out of the burrow the way you entered and circle around.

Fight the Dark Lizalfos on the far side of the gate. Once it's defeated, toss a bomb into the basket-holding statue to your left. Don't activate the switch you reveal yet. Stand on the round stone platform nearby and roll a bomb down the sandy slope. At the bottom of the slope is a basket-holding statue. Rolling the bomb into the basket reveals a second switch. Once again, don't hit it just yet.

Enter the room the switch is in, though. Climb up the vines on the right-hand side of the room. Stand at the edge of the stone platform where you emerge. Face the Bomb Flower that's at the center of a forest of saplings. Charge a Skyward Strike and then fling a horizontal sword beam at the saplings. One dead-on hit should cut them all down. Repeat the process to cut down the saplings blocking in a basket-holding statue to your left.

Use the Hook Beetle to pick up the Bomb Flower opposite you and drop it into the final basket-holding statue. This reveals a final switch. Now, you need to activate the switches in order from the lowest to the highest. So start with the one at the bottom of the sandy slope, then the first one you revealed, then the one that was blocked in by saplings. It's easiest to activate all three using the Hook Beetle while standing on the small stone platform at the top of the sandy slope.

This raises the bars blocking in a room that should be just behind you. Inside is the other entrance to Burrow A. Crawl in and use the Bomb Flower to eliminate both small piles of rubble. Now that you can pass through this burrow, you can hit the blue switch and move the red gate back into its original position. Exit through the hole you used to enter. Now that the red gate is back in its original position, there's a new passage you can enter.

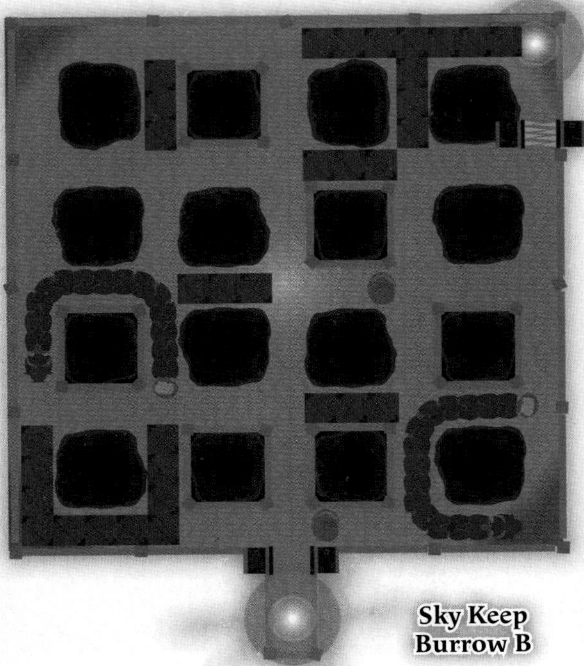

In this room is the entrance to another burrow, Burrow B. In this burrow, you cannot reach the exit until you defeat the two centipedes that patrol it. This is much simpler than it looks, since each centipede mostly sticks to its own side of the room. Once both centipedes are vanquished, you can climb out of the burrow's exit to reach the control panel. There's also a switch in the control panel's room you can hit to raise the bars blocking it in. From here, configure the rooms so you can enter Room 7.

7. Dreadfuse's Room

The moment you step into this room, you enter a battle with Dreadfuse. He's a second robot skeleton pirate from the same production line that produced Scervo, who you battled earlier on the Sandship. The only difference between this battle and the battle with Scervo is that Dreadfuse uses a shorter gangplank. This works to your advantage, making the fight a little bit shorter. The Master Sword's extra reach helps, too. Once Dreadfuse is defeated, grapple across the gap in the gangplank.

To your right is the blue chest containing the Small Key. To your left is a room containing a control panel. Now that you have the Small Key, configure the rooms so that you can pass back into Room 1. Hopefully, you didn't take too much damage fighting Dreadfuse.

1. The Deadly Room

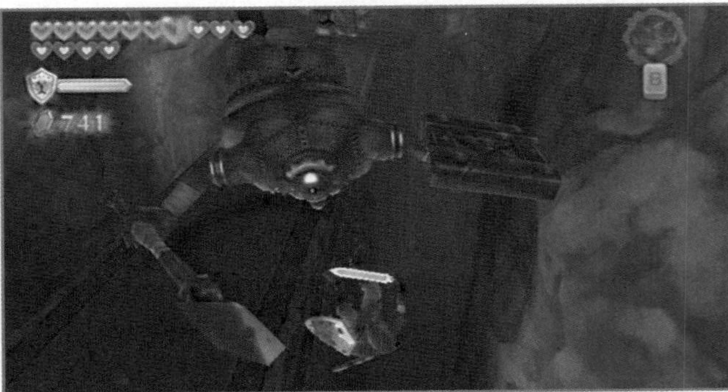

Open the padlocked door and pass through. Your first battle in the gauntlet you must run to acquire the Triforce of Courage is with a trio of Moblins with iron shields on an extremely narrow bridge. As long as you don't end up between any two of them, this should go fairly quickly provided you're using a good shield. Be sure to dodge away after you defeat a Moblin so you don't lose health to its death throes.

The next chamber contains around half a dozen Bokoblin archers and around half a dozen Blue and Green Bokoblins. When you step into the northeast corner of the room, two Stalfos rise up to join in the battle. This is probably the most dangerous of the chambers in the Deadly Room. First, carefully pick off all of the Bokoblin archers with your bow. If you miss even one, you can suddenly find your back full of arrows while you're trying to fight the other Bokoblins.

Try not to raise the Stalfos until you've defeated every other enemy in the room. If you accidentally raise the Stalfos while there are still archers in the room, you should honestly ignore the Stalfos and focus on getting rid of the archers. Now that you have the Master Sword, the Stalfos probably won't last long in a fight with you. They're only dangerous if you accidentally raise them while the room is still packed full of other enemies.

The next chamber contains a Stalmaster flanked by four Cursed Bokoblins. It's actually best to ignore the Cursed Bokoblins as you engage the Stalmaster. The room where you fight him now is much smaller than the room where you battled him the first time around. The Master Sword makes the battle go faster but doesn't make the Stalmaster any less dangerous. Use the same patient hit-and-run tactics and the Stalmaster should go down. After that, you can mop up the Cursed Bokoblins.

After you've defeated all of the sub-bosses, you can pass through into the room where you can claim the Triforce of Courage. Hit the wall switch to remove the bars blocking your path. Now you can return to Room 7 and plot out a course to the other two Triforce pieces. Once you've claimed the first Triforce, you can gather the other two in whatever order you like.

3. The Lava Room

This room is a tricky platform maze you must navigate to the Triforce. The center path is barred, so head left to a metal grate. Hit the thorn bud above to create a stone platform and ride it toward the far side of the room. Battle the Fire Keese that attack you along the way. While you're riding this stone platform, send the Hook Beetle over to hit a switch just ahead of you. At the end of the lava flow your platform is riding on, there's a low fence to your right.

You can jump over it, provided you've hit a thorn bud to create a platform on the other side. By hitting the switch, you've created a current that the new platform can ride on. It may take a few tries to get this right. Just be patient. While you're riding the second platform, fire the Hook Beetle at a switch on the far wall ahead of you. Now you can pass underneath the wall and into a low tunnel.

Hop off the stone platform and onto another iron grate. Hit the switch on the wall behind to open up a shortcut to the room's entrance, then save your game so you don't have to repeat the area you just passed through. When you're ready, hit the thorn bud above you to create a stone platform. Fight a swarm of Dark Keese that attacks as you ride to the far end of the room.

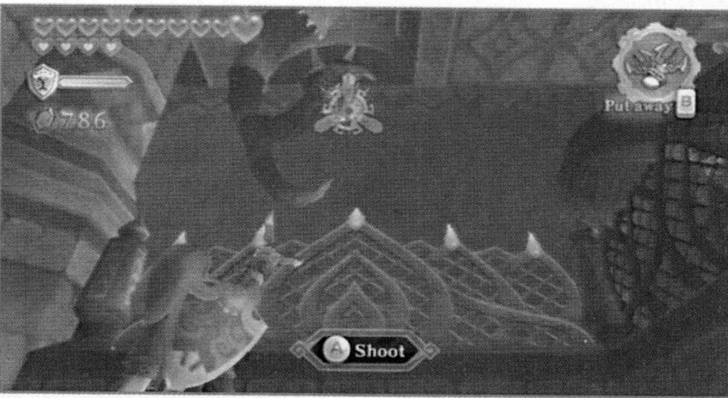

Before you get there, send the Hook Beetle ahead and to the right to flip a crystal switch on the wall. Get ready to create a new stone platform and jump across a low fence onto it. Ride this second platform around a curve in the lava flow until you come to a third platform that's rising up and down on a fountain of lava. Leap across from your platform to the new one while the fountain isn't gushing.

TIP

An alcove nearby hides a Silver Rupee. You can grab it with the Hook Beetle.

While standing on the fountain platform, you can hit a thorn bud to create a new stone platform on the other side of an iron fence. Before you do this, use the Hook Beetle to hit the switch a second time. This creates a current in the lava, so the new stone platform you're about to create can flow downstream. You can jump the fence onto the new platform if you do so while the fountain platform is high. You must time the creation of the new platform so that it's completely solid when you jump onto it. While the fountain platform is high, leap across the iron fence to your side and land on a new stone platform.

This final stone platform flows down a final river of lava. Hop off it when it passes under the iron grate, then hop back on. Use your bow to pick off the Cursed Spumes. At the end of this lava passage is a wall platform you can grapple on to. Climb to the platform above it to find the chamber where you can claim the Triforce of Power. Hit the wall switch behind you to pass back into this room's entrance area. Save at the bird statue, then backtrack into a room with a control panel. Carefully configure the remaining rooms so you can get into Room 4.

4. The Desert Room

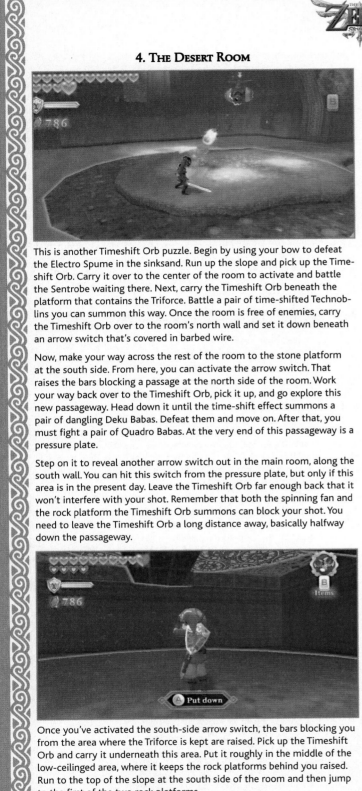

This is another Timeshift Orb puzzle. Begin by using your bow to defeat the Electro Spume in the sinksand. Run up the slope and pick up the Timeshift Orb. Carry it over to the center of the room to activate and battle the Sentrobe waiting there. Next, carry the Timeshift Orb beneath the platform that contains the Triforce. Battle a pair of time-shifted Technoblins you can summon this way. Once the room is free of enemies, carry the Timeshift Orb over to the room's north wall and set it down beneath an arrow switch that's covered in barbed wire.

Now, make your way across the rest of the room to the stone platform at the south side. From here, you can activate the arrow switch. That raises the bars blocking a passage at the north side of the room. Work your way back over to the Timeshift Orb, pick it up, and go explore this new passageway. Head down it until the time-shift effect summons a pair of dangling Deku Babas. Defeat them and move on. After that, you must fight a pair of Quadro Babas. At the very end of this passageway is a pressure plate.

Step on it to reveal another arrow switch out in the main room, along the south wall. You can hit this switch from the pressure plate, but only if this area is in the present day. Leave the Timeshift Orb far enough back that it won't interfere with your shot. Remember that both the spinning fan and the rock platform the Timeshift Orb summons can block your shot. You need to leave the Timeshift Orb a long distance away, basically halfway down the passageway.

Once you've activated the south-side arrow switch, the bars blocking you from the area where the Triforce is kept are raised. Pick up the Timeshift Orb and carry it underneath this area. Put it roughly in the middle of the low-ceilinged area, where it keeps the rock platforms behind you raised. Run to the top of the slope at the south side of the room and then jump to the first of the two rock platforms.

You should be able to grapple into the area and pass into the adjoining room, where the Triforce of Wisdom waits. Once you have a completed Triforce, this dungeon automatically ends. Settle back to enjoy the cutscenes, but don't put your controller down for long.

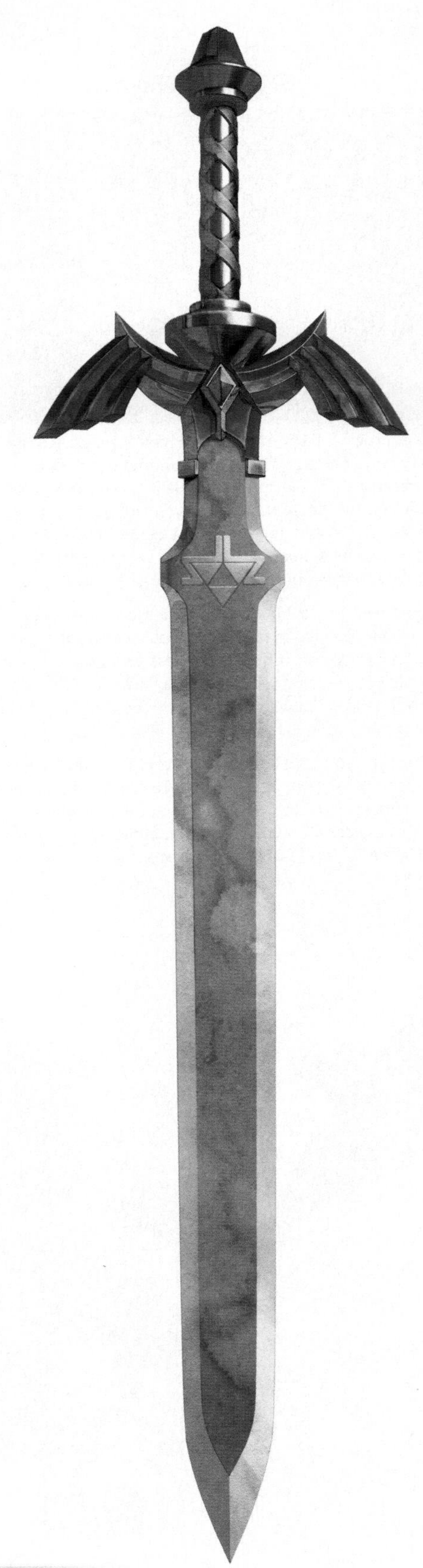

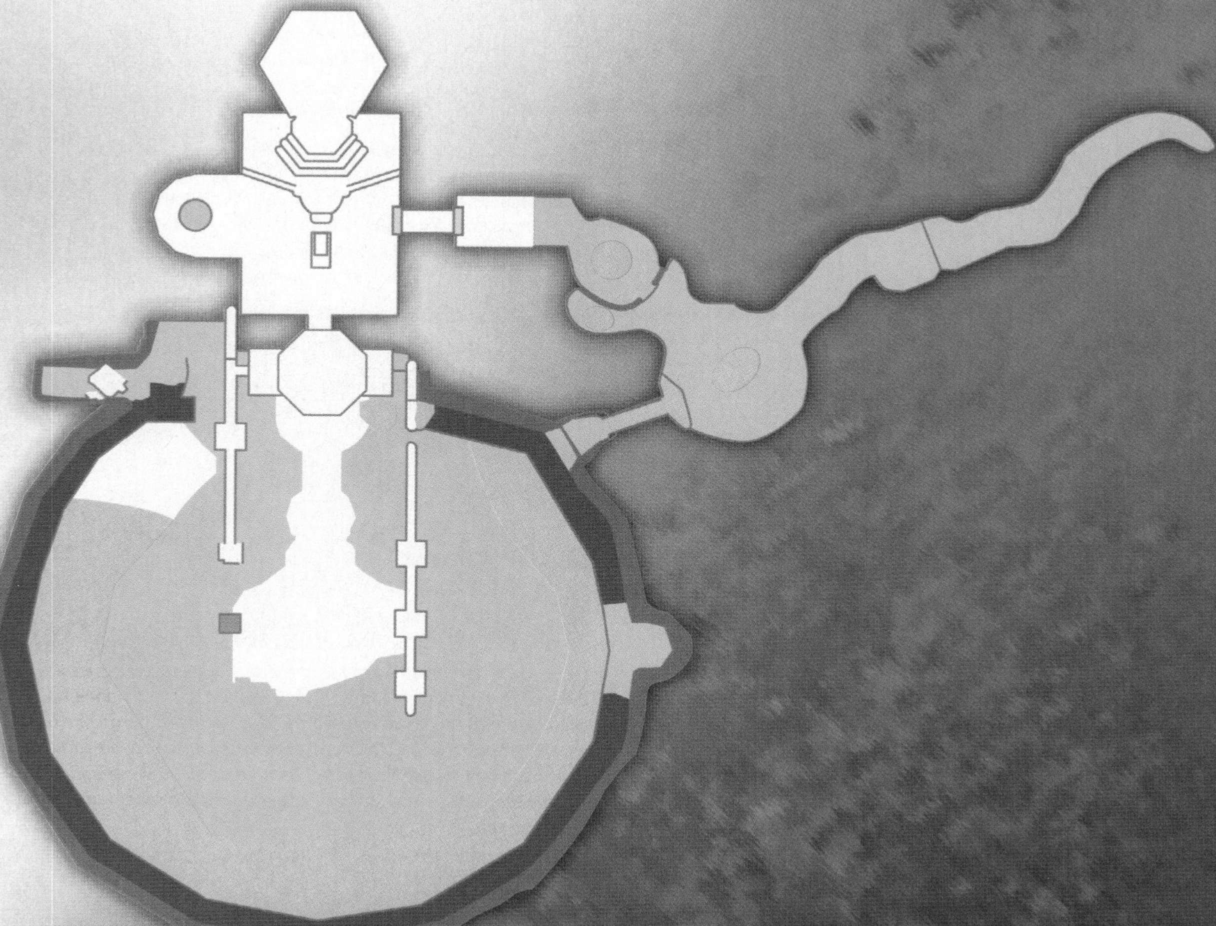

THE NEW SEALED GROUNDS

Your actions at Sky Keep have had far-reaching effects, changing the map of the Sealed Grounds forever. Before you can enjoy your victory, though, you have one last challenge waiting for you in the past. Pass through the Gate of Time at the new Sealed Grounds to meet the game's two final challenges.

BOSS: GHIRAHIM

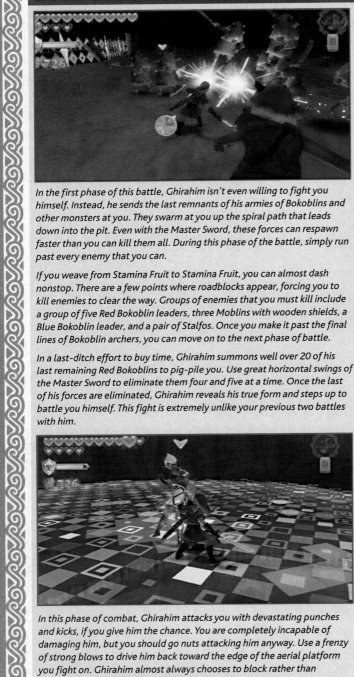

In the first phase of this battle, Ghirahim isn't even willing to fight you himself. Instead, he sends the last remnants of his armies of Bokoblins and other monsters at you. They swarm at you up the spiral path that leads down into the pit. Even with the Master Sword, these forces can respawn faster than you can kill them all. During this phase of the battle, simply run past every enemy that you can.

If you weave from Stamina Fruit to Stamina Fruit, you can almost dash nonstop. There are a few points where roadblocks appear, forcing you to kill enemies to clear the way. Groups of enemies that you must kill include a group of five Red Bokoblin leaders, three Moblins with wooden shields, a Blue Bokoblin leader, and a pair of Stalfos. Once you make it past the final lines of Bokoblin archers, you can move on to the next phase of battle.

In a last-ditch effort to buy time, Ghirahim summons well over 20 of his last remaining Red Bokoblins to pig-pile you. Use great horizontal swings of the Master Sword to eliminate them four and five at a time. Once the last of his forces are eliminated, Ghirahim reveals his true form and steps up to battle you himself. This fight is extremely unlike your previous two battles with him.

In this phase of combat, Ghirahim attacks you with devastating punches and kicks, if you give him the chance. You are completely incapable of damaging him, but you should go nuts attacking him anyway. Use a frenzy of strong blows to drive him back toward the edge of the aerial platform you fight on. Ghirahim almost always chooses to block rather than counterattack. You can drive Ghirahim off the edge of the platform and down to the next level.

When you do, leap down after him and execute a Fatal Blow. This lets you damage the diamond-shaped weak point on Ghirahim's chest. After you've done this, combat goes to its next phase. Ghirahim begins guarding himself more intelligently, hands glowing with power. To drive him back now, you must use strikes that exploit the gap he inevitably leaves in his guard. If he holds his hands above each other, for instance, use a horizontal strike.

If you use the incorrect type of attack when he's guarding, then Ghirahim swiftly dodges to slide around you. This effectively makes the two of you change places, which is extremely dangerous if you've already driven Ghirahim to the very edge of the battlefield. You have to slow down a little bit in this phase of combat to be careful, but don't let up for long. There's no reason to give Ghirahim extra time to take potshots at you.

Once you drive him off the edge of the second platform, use another Fatal Blow on him. On the third platform, Ghirahim doesn't change his attack pattern. Simply try to drive him off and use a Fatal Blow on him one more time. The last aerial platform descends to the ground, where the two of you are going to finish this battle. The third Fatal Blow has aggravated Ghirahim's weak point, making it larger. He pulls a saber out and begins to duel with you.

This phase of battle is a little more like your old duels with Ghirahim. You can shield-bash his sword attacks to momentarily stagger him. The main difference, though, is that you can't damage Ghirahim with any attack besides a thrust at his weak point. When he hurls his projectiles at you, shield bashing them won't deal even a little damage to him. In addition to his old moves, Ghirahim can now hurl sinister red sword beams at you with his sword. You can dodge these or use your shield to block, but you can't shield-bash them.

Once enough of your thrusts strike true, Ghirahim begins the final phase of combat. He summons a tremendous zweihander. So long as he has this sword intact in his hands, you cannot damage him. He uses the blade to protect his weak point. The only way to hurt him now is to successfully shield-bash one of Ghirahim's attacks. This sends Ghirahim into a guarding stance. Begin savagely attacking his sword.

Your own Master Sword is more powerful, and if you hit the zweihander enough times with crosswise slashes, you can actually cut it in half. Once you do this, you must quickly thrust at Ghirahim's weak point. If your strike is not true, Ghirahim reforms his sword and attacks you again. Once you have hit Ghirahim's weak point twice in this phase, the battle will end.

At this point, you have your last chance to save your game. This is the game's "point of no return." Going forward initiates the very last boss battle. If there's anything left in the game that you want to accomplish before it's all over, then go and do it now. In particular, players interested in getting the Hylian Shield and clearing the Thunder Dragon's Lightning Round should take this opportunity to go to Lanayru Gorge. If you're ready to end your game, then continue.

FINAL BOSS: DEMISE

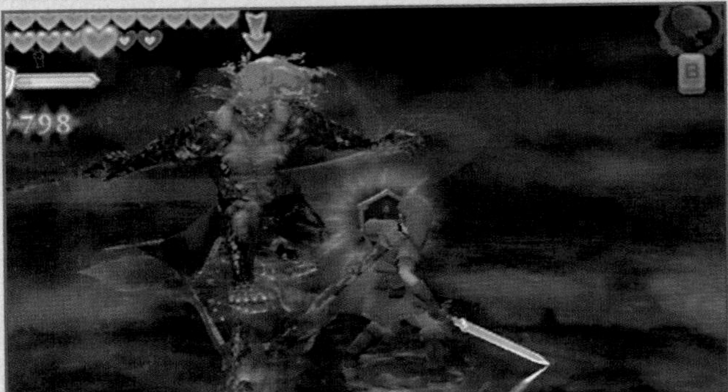

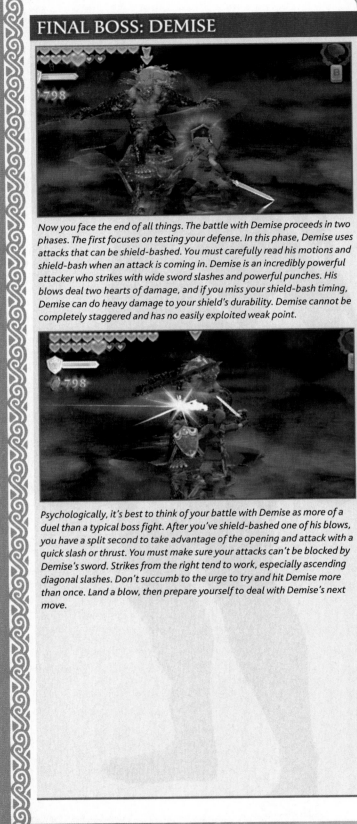

Now you face the end of all things. The battle with Demise proceeds in two phases. The first focuses on testing your defense. In this phase, Demise uses attacks that can be shield-bashed. You must carefully read his motions and shield-bash when an attack is coming in. Demise is an incredibly powerful attacker who strikes with wide sword slashes and powerful punches. His blows deal two hearts of damage, and if you miss your shield-bash timing, Demise can do heavy damage to your shield's durability. Demise cannot be completely staggered and has no easily exploited weak point.

Psychologically, it's best to think of your battle with Demise as more of a duel than a typical boss fight. After you've shield-bashed one of his blows, you have a split second to take advantage of the opening and attack with a quick slash or thrust. You must make sure your attacks can't be blocked by Demise's sword. Strikes from the right tend to work, especially ascending diagonal slashes. Don't succumb to the urge to try and hit Demise more than once. Land a blow, then prepare yourself to deal with Demise's next move.

Once you knock Demise over, he rises again, more furious and powerful than ever. This phase focuses on testing your offense. You can shield-bash some of Demise's attacks here, but it can't be the centerpiece of your strategy. Shield bashes won't stagger Demise once this phase of combat begins. Demise electrifies his sword and sometimes even absorbs the power of striking lightning bolts. He attacks with sword beams and great sweeps of his electric sword. You cannot hit Demise with ordinary sword blows when he's electrified, nor can you afford to let your blade cross his. Regular attacks cannot knock Demise out of an attacking animation or inflict hit-stun.

There are two things you can do to damage Demise here. You can focus on hitting him with quick thrusts if you get an opening where he's not electrified. When he's electrified, you can successfully hit him with vertical spin slashes. This does not electrocute you and can even inflict momentary hit-stun. Take advantage of these rare chances to strike again. Note that if you spend a lot of time shield-bashing Demise's attacks, he may attack you with a devastating three-hit sword combo. You can shield bash every move in the combo, but the timing for this is very tight and your shield can take tremendous damage if you foul up. Focus on dodging instead, trying to get into position for a quick attack.

When you've damaged Demise enough during the battle's second phase, he falls over. You must quickly execute a Fatal Blow on him in order to finish the battle. If your timing is off, the Fatal Blow misses, Demise stands up, and you have to go through a shortened version of the second phase of battle all over again. Once you successfully execute a Fatal Blow on Demise, you've beaten the game. Sit back and enjoy the ending. You've earned it.

HERO MODE

You've defeated Demise, you've enjoyed the game's ending cutscenes...but *Skyward Sword* isn't over just yet. After you finish the game, you receive a prompt to create a Hero Mode save file. Hero Mode is a high-difficulty version of *Skyward Sword* designed for advanced players. If you can breeze through the Thunder Dragon's Lightning Round, this version of the game is for you. Here's a list of what changes in Hero Mode:

- **Every enemy in the game does double damage. Yes, that means enemies who could attack and do two full hearts of damage to you in the regular game can do four hearts of damage in Hero Mode. They call it Hero Mode for a reason.**
- **You cannot ordinarily gather hearts anywhere. Not from enemies, not from pots, not growing wild. The only way to make hearts spawn as they do in the regular game is to carry the Heart Medal.**
- **When you acquire the True Master Sword, you no longer have charge time before launching a Skyward Strike. That is, simply tilting your Wii Remote briefly into a vertical position makes you instantly able to fire a sword beam.**
- **Certain lines of dialogue change. You must discover which ones for yourself. Some of the secrets of Hero Mode must be earned.**
- **You can skip all cutscenes, even when watching them for the first time.**
- **If you can make it to the Thunder Dragon's Lightning Round, you can play through a twelve-stage boss rush that includes a fight with Demise.**

Just to confirm what is and isn't in Hero Mode, here's a list of the things that do not change:

- **The story and ending are basically the same. If you play Hero Mode, do it for the challenge.**
- **The dungeon layouts, game flow, and puzzles remain basically the same. This isn't a Master Quest.**
- **Enemy placement is largely the same. When everything does double damage, the default locations are dangerous enough.**
- **The items are the same, though you may find you suddenly care a lot more about having and using Guardian Potions.**

The ultimate bragging-rights challenge for *The Legend of Zelda: Skyward Sword* is to defeat all 12 phases of the Thunder Dragon's Lightning Round in Hero Mode. If you can do this, you may actually be a hero of legend yourself.

Secrets & Side Quests

Gratitude Crystals Collection Guide

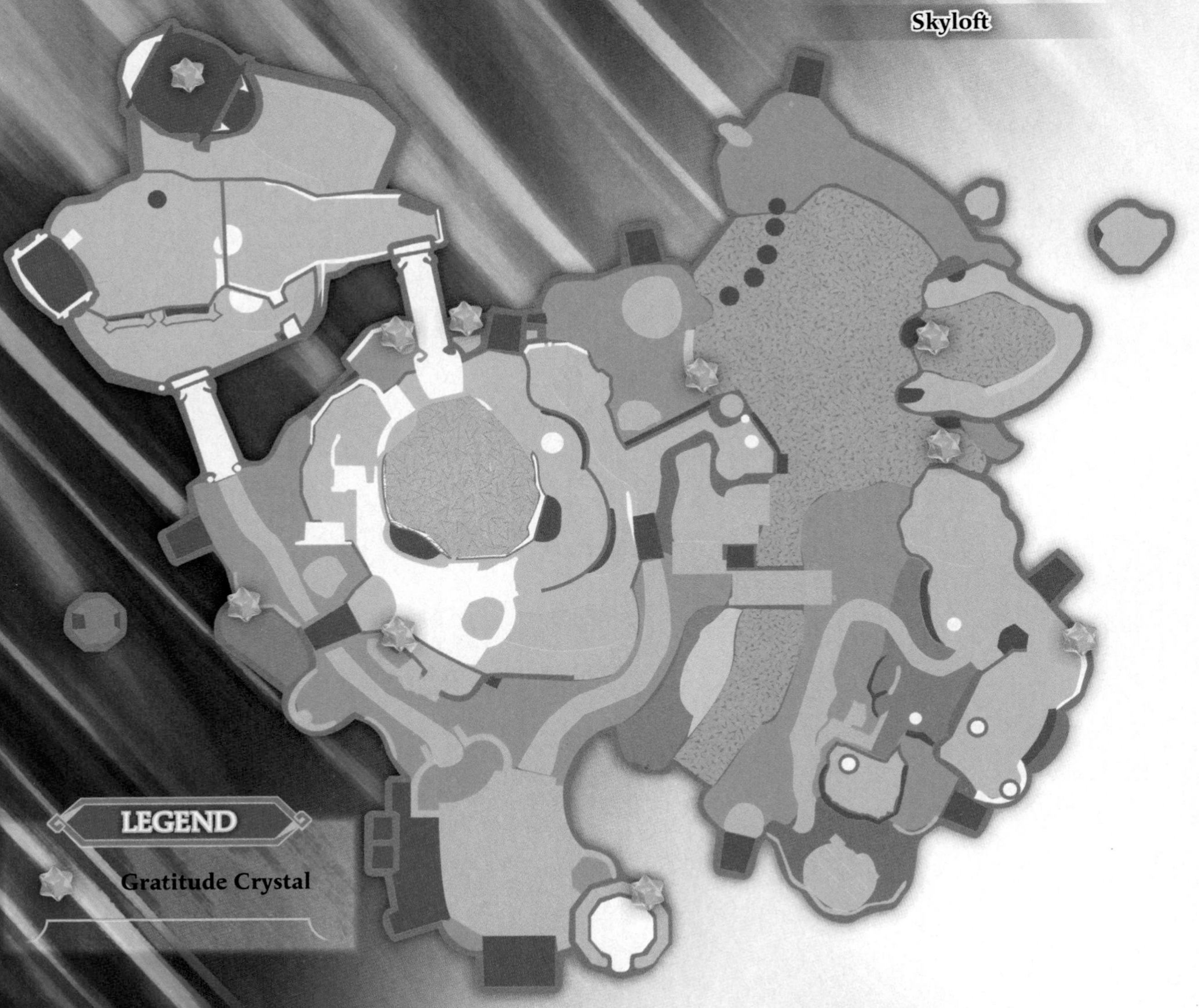

Skyloft

LEGEND

Gratitude Crystal

This guide covers how to acquire all of the game's Gratitude Crystals. By gathering them and giving them to Batreaux, you can earn handsome rewards that include Pieces of Heart, Rupees, and larger wallets to let you carry more Rupees. You can begin gathering Gratitude Crystals after you clear the Skyview Temple dungeon, which unlocks the game's first request.

There are two ways to gather Gratitude Crystals. One is to go out at night and find the 15 loose Gratitude Crystals scattered throughout the sky. Many of these crystals lie in plain sight, and once you obtain the Master Sword you can dowse for the rest of them. Twelve of the Gratitude Crystals you need are scattered around Skyloft, some indoors and some outdoors. Gratitude Crystals occur indoors only in the Knight Academy and a handful of other locations. Remember that all Gratitude Crystals can be snagged by the Hook Beetle.

There's one inside the Sparring Hall, up in the rafters.

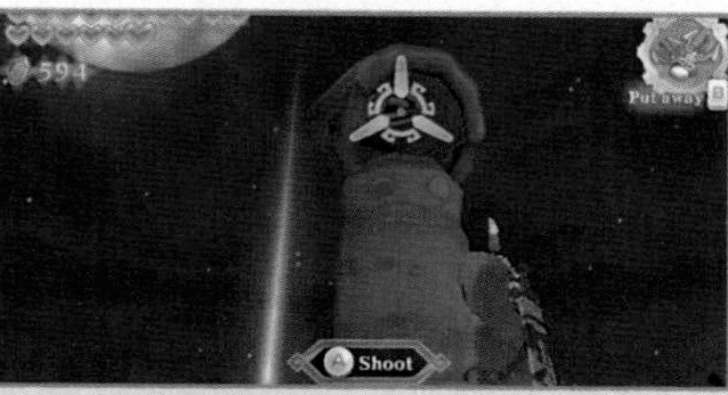

Grapple up into this chimney to sneak into Zelda's room and grab the Gratitude Crystal (and Piece of Heart) there.

There's one inside Orielle and Parrow's house, in a corner.

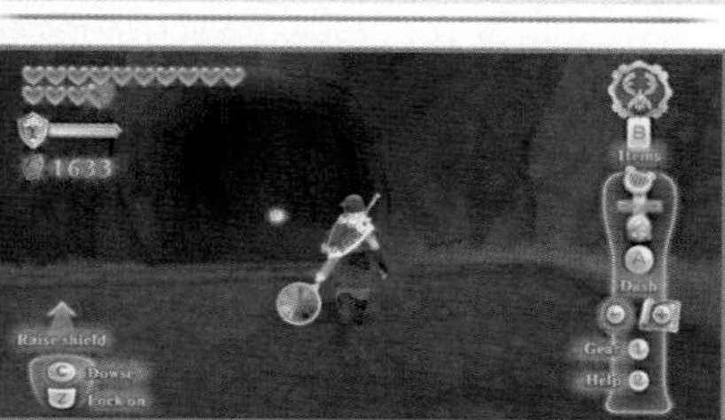
Pass through the waterfall cave to grab this Gratitude Crystal, hidden in the cave where your Loftwing was penned up earlier in the game.

TIP

Three of the loose Gratitude Crystals are available only at night on other islands in the sky, but you can pick those up while accepting other gratitude requests there.

The other way to gather them is to take requests from townsfolk. You can earn 65 of the 80 Gratitude Crystals required to finish Batreaux's quest this way. Some characters may ask you to run errands or perform basic tasks for them, while others may send you to find lost objects or fetch items from the bazaar. After you finish one of these requests, you're given a stack of five Gratitude Crystals. Each townsperson is part of only one Gratitude Crystal quest. It is possible to accept a quest before you meet the requirements necessary for finishing it.

LEGEND

Gratitude Crystal

Knight Academy

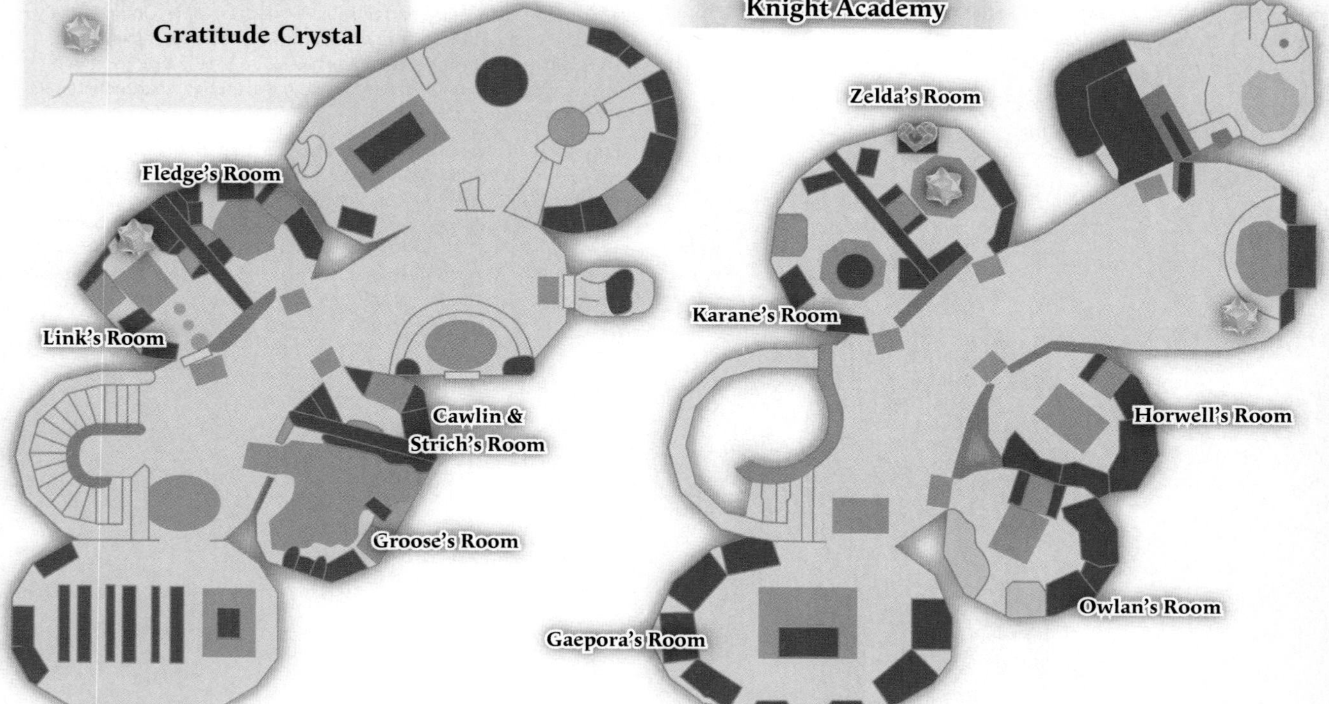

Fledge's Room
Link's Room
Cawlin & Strich's Room
Groose's Room
Zelda's Room
Karane's Room
Horwell's Room
Owlan's Room
Gaepora's Room

Night and Day

You can change the time of day in Skyloft by going to sleep in any bed. You need to do certain things at night to complete several Gratitude Crystal requests, especially the first one, and to gather the "loose" Gratitude Crystals lying around the sky. Gathering Gratitude Crystals is, in fact, one of only two reasons to ever be active at night (the other is the secret shops, which are covered in the next section).

There are a few things to remember about being active in Skyloft at night. One is that you can't fly your Loftwing at night. If you jump off the edge of Skyloft and attempt to summon your bird, absolutely nothing happens. Skyloft plays host to a species of insect, the Starry Firefly, that can only be caught at night or in the waterfall cave. Certain doors that are open during the day become locked at night. The shopkeepers from the bazaar all go back to their homes, where you can interact with them.

Finally, monsters roam Skyloft at night. You primarily encounter Keese and Green Chuchus that should be easily defeated, but they respawn persistently. Pets become feral at night. While you can drive them away with your sword, you absolutely cannot defeat them permanently.

Batreaux's Rewards

Here is a list of the rewards you get by visiting Batreaux after obtaining certain numbers of Gratitude Crystals. To get all of the rewards, it is absolutely necessary to find and complete every single gratitude request you can get from townspeople. You also need to gather up all of the loose Gratitude Crystals in the sky.

GRATITUDE CRYSTAL REWARDS

NUMBER	REWARD
5	Medium Wallet
10	Piece of Heart
30	Big Wallet, Cursed Medal
40	Gold Rupee
50	Giant Wallet
70	Gold Rupee x 2
80	Tycoon Wallet

Wryna's Request: Find Kukiel

Characters: Wryna, Kukiel

I assure you, nothing would fill my
heart with joy more than to be friends
with the fine people of this town.

You get this request automatically after placing the Ruby Tablet fragment into the Ancient Tablet's aperture in the Statue of the Goddess. Wryna's daughter, Kukiel, has gone missing and she fears a monster is somehow involved. Talk to Parrow in the plaza and his sister Orielle to receive the most useful clues: that there is a monster rumored to live in the graveyard and an old man who spends most of his time hanging out at the Lumpy Pumpkin claims to have seen it. Fly out there and speak to him.

The old man tells you that if you go out to the graveyard at night and hit the headstone closest to the tree, the door to the storehouse will mysteriously open. You also need to push the headstone after you hit it with your sword. This opens the door to the storehouse. When the storehouse in the graveyard opens, walk to the ladder and climb down. This takes you to an isolated house that sits on a series of isolated platforms beneath Skyloft.

You'll find Kukiel inside the house with her "friend," who turns out to be a horrible-looking monster named Batreaux. Despite Batreaux's terrifying visage, he's actually a kind-hearted soul who loves people. Unfortunately, he scares the snot out of most townspeople and so he can't live above in Skyloft with everyone else. Batreaux has heard that if a monster can obtain enough Gratitude Crystals from humans, though, that monster will transform into a human.

Naturally, Batreaux wants Link to go out and gather all the Gratitude Crystals for him. While this may sound a bit like helping Batreaux game the system, it's ultimately for the best that you go out and do this for the poor guy. Begin after you meet Batreaux by sleeping until morning, then going to Jakamar's House and speaking to Wryna inside. Kukiel has returned home, as she promised you last night. Her mother gives you your first stack of five Gratitude Crystals.

Parrow's Request: Find Orielle

Characters: Parrow, Orielle

You'll find Parrow pacing in the plaza when you can accept this request. He's worried because his sister went out for a flight and never came back. He says she went to the western sky. Go soaring around there and you'll find her on an island in the area between Fun Fun Island and the Lanayru Desert entrance. The island is relatively low, so if you're flying too high you may not be able to see her.

Speak with her and she says that her Loftwing has been injured. She sends you back to get some medicine from her brother. He gives you a bottle full of Mushroom Spores to carry back to her and tells you to keep the Empty Bottle after you're done. Fly back to the island and give the medicine to Orielle to finish off the quest and get five Gratitude Crystals. Go back to Skyloft and talk to Parrow to get five more.

Dodoh's Request: Find My Party Wheel

Characters: Dodoh

Requires: Scrapper

Drop by Fun Fun Island after you've activated Scrapper. The odd fellow who runs the place, Dodoh, is down in the dumps because his party wheel fell beneath the clouds. Agree to go find it for him and Fi adds it as a dowsing target. The party wheel is located in the Lanayru Desert, so head there on your Loftwing.

Use the bird statue marked "Desert Entrance" to arrive close to your objective. Hit the Timeshift Stone next to the mine cart. This causes plants to bloom in the nearby area, which causes a patch of vines to spring into existence on a nearby cliff. Cross the vine patch and shimmy across another nearby wall to reach another cliff. You need to climb across while dangling from a narrow ledge. It's a long way to go while hanging by your fingers, but there's a Stamina Fruit that helps you make it.

Keep going until you reach a cliff on the opposide side. Be careful of the sides of this area as you make your way to the party wheel, as you can fall down the slope and get dumped into a chasm to your right or back into the desert on your left. There's a blue chest containing a random treasure in this area you can snag while you're here, too. Once you claim the wheel, Scrapper can deliver it to Dodoh. This opens up the Fun Fun Island minigame, Dodoh's High Dive.

Cawlin's Request: Deliver a Letter

Characters: Cawlin, Karane, Phoeni

This request chain begins when you overhear at the bazaar that people in the Knight Academy are hearing strange sounds from the bathroom at night. Sleep until nighttime and approach the bathroom. You hear a voice begging for help. Try to enter the bathroom and you hear the mysterious voice begging you for paper.

The next morning, you can find Cawlin standing next to the Knight Academy's entrance with a speech balloon over his head. It seems Cawlin is having girl troubles. He hands you a very important piece of paper and tells you that it absolutely must be delivered to someone. No, it's not for Phoeni, it's a (probably doomed) love letter for your classmate Karane.

Once you have the paper, you can choose what to do with it. You can ignore Cawlin and give it to Phoeni anyway, or you can actually give it to Karane. If you give it to Karane, Cawlin is extremely grateful and you get five Gratitude Crystals, though you find out Cawlin doesn't really stand a chance.

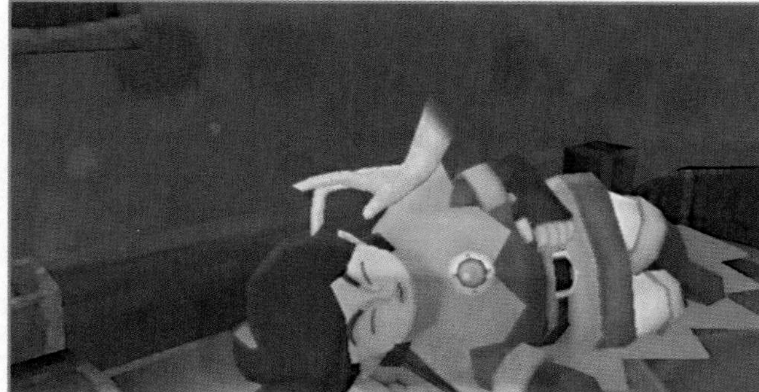

If you give it to Phoeni, then at first it seems you've accomplished nothing besides ruining Cawlin's life. Visit Cawlin's room at night, though, and you find Phoeni's spectral hand caressing him in his sleep. In this case, you get five Gratitude Crystals from the lovestruck ghost.

Fledge's Request: I Want to Be Strong

Characters: Fledge

Requires: An Empty Bottle

Talk to Fledge as he walks around the area by the plaza. He shyly admits that he's training at night to get stronger. Sleep until nighttime and go visit Fledge in his room at the Knight Academy. He's trying hard, but he just doesn't have the stamina to stick with his training. The next day, go to the bazaar and buy him a Stamina Potion. Give it to him in his room at night.

Speak to Fledge again the next day. His training is going better now, but he's afraid he's hitting a plateau. Visit him in his room at night and he requests another Stamina Potion. Pick it up at the bazaar and give it to him the next night.

Talk to Fledge the next day. His training is going better and he invites you to visit him again in his room at night. Visit him a third time and Fledge thanks you for all the help you've given him with training. He's so thankful, in fact, that you get five Gratitude Crystals.

After you finish Fledge's gratitude request, he begins hanging around the Sparring Hall during the day. Speak with him to play the Pumpkin Pull minigame.

Mallara's Request: Clean My House

Characters: Mallara, Pipit

Requires: Gust Bellows

Enter Pipit's House in Skyloft after you acquire the Gust Bellows in Lanayru Mining Facility. You find the interior absolutely covered in dust. Mallara asks if you'd be so kind as to clean it up for her. To do this, you must use the Gust Bellows to blow every single speck of dust off of the interior. If you miss even a tiny patch, you aren't actually finished. She automatically lets you know when the house is completely clean. Your reward is a Red Rupee and five more Gratitude Crystals.

Stop by Pipit's House at night after completing this request. You can learn something interesting about Pipit.

Bertie's Request: Find the Baby's Rattle

Characters: Bertie, Luv, Bertie's Baby

Requires: Gust Bellows, Clawshots

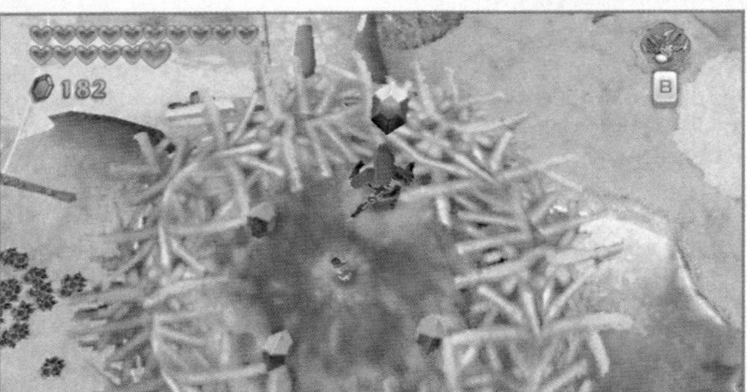

Visit Bertie's House at night after you've obtained the Clawshots to find out that he has a problem. Luv is a heavy sleeper, which leaves him up all night dealing with the fussy baby. The baby used to sleep through the night, but that was before its rattle disappeared. All Bertie knows about where the rattle got off to is that a bird took it.

Use your Clawshots to grapple up to the top of the great waterfall that overlooks Skyloft. Stand on the small stone area just to the left of the falls and leap off. There's a big bird's nest atop a windmill you can dive into if you leap from the top of the waterfall.

When you land in the bird's nest, use the Gust Bellows to blow away sand that's collected around a brightly colored object. It's the rattle. Pick it up, wait until nighttime, and then take it back to Bertie to receive five Gratitude Crystals from him.

Sparrot's Request: Find My Crystal Ball

Characters: Sparrot

Requires: Scrapper, Clawshots

Once the fortune-teller disappears from the bazaar, visit him at his home at night. It seems Sparrot is dejected because he's lost his crystal ball and can't imagine where he'll find a replacement. Offer to help him and you gain the ability to dowse for crystal balls. You get a hint that you should look at Eldin Volcano. Even better: Dive into the bird statue next to the Earth Temple.

Dowsing quickly reveals that there's a crystal ball above and to the left of the Earth Temple's entrance. To get it, use the nearby wall target to grapple up. Examine it and you can summon Scrapper to carry it back up to Skyloft. Head back to Sparrot's House to deliver his new crystal ball. You receive five Gratitude Crystals in return.

Instructor Owlan's Request: I Want a Rare Plant

Characters: Owlan, Oolo

Requires: Scrapper, Faron's Part of the Song of the Hero

Speak with Instructor Owlan in his room after you've activated Scrapper. Owlan is a collector of rare plants who's desperate to find something really new and exciting. He asks if you'll look for something for him on the surface world. Agree and you get the ability to dowse for rare plants. Head to Faron Woods.

Dowsing leads you to Oolo living nearby. Oolo complains about having to hide all the time and wonders if it could live somewhere less dangerous. Offer to take Oolo back to Skyloft and it readily accepts. Present Oolo to Instructor Owlan to receive five Gratitude Crystals.

Kina's Request: The Pumpkin Patch

Characters: Pumm, Kina, Guld

Requires: Song of the Hero

You can do phases of this gratitude request earlier in the game, but it all makes a bit more sense if you knock it out all at once. To start with, go to the Lumpy Pumpkin after you've assembled all the pieces of the Song of the Hero. The Lumpy Pumpkin's owner thinks of something else for you to do: help his daughter pick this year's pumpkin harvest. Go talk to her at the pumpkin patch behind the Lumpy Pumpkin. The pumpkin-picking task is accomplished by playing a minigame where you must carry a big stack of pumpkins over to the shed without dropping any. The secret is to move slowly and keep the pumpkin stack upright by moving in the opposite direction when it tilts.

Succeeding at the pumpkin-carrying minigame opens up a harp-playing minigame. Sleep in one of the Lumpy Pumpkin's beds so you can enter the area at night. Just play the harp once to progress the quest chain. As long as you don't completely fail the minigame, you should do well enough to progress this quest chain. After you play, the Lumpy Pumpkin's owner decides that you've paid off the chandelier. He rewards you for all your hard work with a Piece of Heart. Stay overnight at the Lumpy Pumpkin again and you can admire its sturdy (and gaudy) new chandelier in the morning.

Go outside and talk to Kina. She should now have the speech bubble above her head that initiates this request. She wishes that there was someone who could help her plow the pumpkin fields for next year. Agree to help Kina and Fi gives you the ability to dowse for someone good at plowing pumpkin patches. Go to Eldin Volcano to start your search. Dowsing should eventually bring you to the cave that leads to the interior area where you flushed out a group of Bokoblins much earlier in the game.

Now that you've taken care of the Bokoblins and all of Eldin Volcano's troubles are over, the Mogmas have moved back into their ancestral home. You can talk to every Mogma NPC who's helped you in the game by traveling to the different rooms. One of them mentions that the elder, Guld, has been down in the dumps lately. To talk to him, you need to dive onto a platform near the entrance where he's resting. Speak to Guld and the old Mogma mentions he hasn't been feeling well lately—the heat's getting to him in his old age. He wonders if there's a place he could work that would be much cooler.

Tell him you know of a place and he agrees to go with you. Scrapper can carry him back to the Lumpy Pumpkin. Head back to Skyloft and fly there to escort Guld to his new home. Plowing the pumpkin patch is no trouble for Guld, and Kina's happiness seems to be all the reward he needs. Kina gives you five Gratitude Crystals. You can also pick up a spare Gratitude Crystal in the Lumpy Pumpkin's upstairs area and another outside in the pumpkin shed.

Beedle's Request: Find My Beetle

Characters: Beedle, Strich

Requires: Bug Heaven

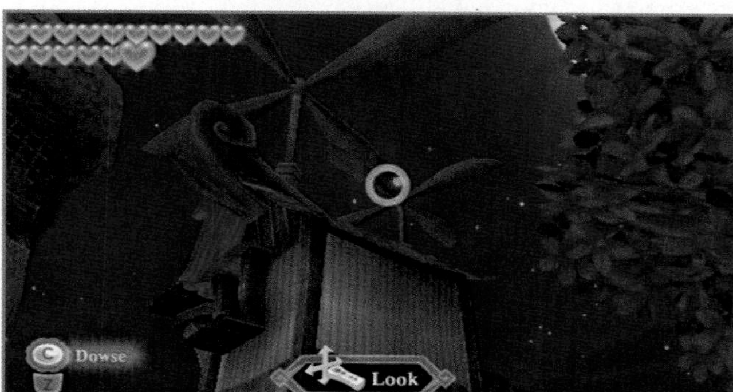

To get Beedle's request, you must sleep in the bed in his airshop and choose to wake up in the middle of the night. This takes you to a tiny island in the far northeast corner of the sky where Beedle parks the airshop at night. Beedle's beloved and extremely rare Horned Colossus Beetle has gone missing. While you're here, nab the spare Gratitude Crystal located atop the airshop's rotor with the Hook Beetle.

Go talk to Strich at his bug island in the thunderhead. He's in a fantastic mood because he found a super-rare insect. Once you explain that it's probably Beedle's Horned Colossus Beetle, Strich is a bit crestfallen. He finally says that he'll hand Beedle's Insect Cage over if you can catch 10 predetermined insects on the Bug Heaven course in less than three minutes.

Once you have the Beedle's Insect Cage, go board the airshop and spend the night there. Give it to Beedle then to get your reward of five Gratitude Crystals. As an additional reward, Beedle lets you buy anything from his shop for half off. This is an excellent time to pick up the Piece of Heart, or the final slot for your Adventure Pouch.

Peatrice's Request: Do You Love Me?

Characters: Peatrice, Peater

Requires: Visiting the Item Check Frequently

And that's why I won't ask any more of you. I'll just watch over you, protecting you from afar, keeping a vigilant eye on your items.

Chances are the final request you get is going to be from Peatrice, the Item Check girl. At the beginning of the game she's bored by you, but the more you visit Item Check the more she warms up to you. Actually, she warms up to you a bit too much. Eventually, her father, Peater, grows concerned about her, believing "some rascal" has stolen her heart.

Eventually, you should see a speech bubble over Peatrice's head after Peater tells you about his troubles. Peatrice invites you to visit her house at night. Speak to her there to complete the quest. If Peatrice believes that you share her feelings, you get the Gratitude Crystals from her. If you convince her that her feelings aren't reciprocated, you can the Gratitude Crystals from her father.

NOTE

Transforming Batreaux into a human changes Skyloft significantly. Once Batreaux becomes a human, monsters stop spawning in Skyloft at night. This is good if you want to catch Starry Fireflies without being bothered and bad if you like to grind for Monster Claws and Jelly Blobs in the waterfall cave.

Secret Shops of Skyloft

There are three secret shops in Skyloft that you can only visit at night. Two are useful for making money and one is invaluable if you need treasures and have some Rupees burning a hole in your wallet. Here's a guide to taking advantage of the secret shops of Skyloft.

Rupin's Night Shop

Rupin runs the Gear Shop in Skyloft by day. By night, you can visit his home to sell spare treasures you've acquired. Rupin buys only four treasureseach night. Which four treasures he selects is entirely random. You can change Rupin's selection by repeatedly sleeping in a bed until nighttime. There's even a bed in Rupin's house you can use for this purpose. You can make a lot of money by sleeping until Rupin decides that he wants Jelly Blobs or Amber Relics.

RUPIN'S NIGHT SHOP

TREASURE	BUY PRICE
Hornet Larvae	20
Bird Feather	20
Tumbleweed	20
Lizard Tail	20
Eldin Ore	30
Ancient Flower	30
Amber Relic	30
Dusk Relic	30
Jelly Blob	30
Monster Claw	30
Monster Horn	30
Ornamental Skull	30
Evil Crystal	30
Blue Bird Feather	100
Golden Skull	100
Goddess Plume	100

Strich's Night Shop

Your classmate Strich runs a bug-buying business out of his dorm room at night. He buys three randomly selected species of bugs every night. As with Rupin's random selections, you can force Strich's list to change by repeatedly sleeping until nighttime. It's worth checking in with Strich regularly, since you can make a lot of money if you happen to have a lot of Sand Cicadas or Faron Grasshoppers on hand when he wants to buy them.

STRICH'S NIGHT SHOP

BUGS	BUY PRICE
Deku Hornet	1
Blessed Butterfly	5
Gerudo Dragonfly	30
Starry Firefly	30
Woodland Rhino Beetle	20
Volcanic Ladybug	20
Sand Cicada	50
Sky Stag Beetle	20
Faron Grasshopper	40
Skyloft Mantis	10
Lanayru Ant	20
Eldin Roller	40

The Moonlight Merchant

Enter the waterfall cave in Skyloft at night. Look for three Blessed Butterflies flying about, as they would over a Gossip Stone. Play your harp. Instead of a Gossip Stone, you summon the Moonlight Merchant, a devious stone that sells rare treasures acquired on the black market. His prices are high, but much of what he offers is much easier to buy than find yourself.

THE MOONLIGHT MERCHANT

TREASURE	PRICE
Monster Horn	100
Dusk Relic	100
Evil Crystal	100
Blue Bird Feather	200
Golden Skull	200
Goddess Plume	200

Minigames (And How to Beat Them)

You discover a lot of minigames to play in *The Legend of Zelda: Skyward Sword*. Some are just for fun or ways to earn money, while others give you chances to earn valuable Pieces of Heart. Here's a guide to who's who and what's what when it comes to minigames.

Bug Heaven

Strich awaits on an island in the thunderhead. This island is a specially constructed "bug paradise," where Strich is raising at least one of every type of bug in the world. In Strich's minigames, you pay a fee to see how quickly you can catch the bugs from a pre-set list. Strich charges 20 Rupees for the Beginner course and 50 Rupees for the Wrangler course.

The Beginner list of bugs you must catch is: Skyloft Mantis, Volcanic Ladybug, Lanayru Ant, Sky Stag Beetle, Starry Firefly.

The Wrangler list of bugs you must catch is: two Faron Grasshoppers, one Woodland Rhino Beetle, one Skyloft Mantis, one Blessed Butterfly, one Lanayru Ant, one Sand Cicada, one Gerudo Dragonfly, and two Eldin Rollers.

Aside from knowing how to catch each bug in the wild, doing well in Bug Heaven just involves memorizing where all the bugs in the island are and figuring out the shortest path from one type to another. You can easily figure this out through simple trial and error.

Strich gives his best rewards if you can clear either of his courses in less than two minutes. You can also get special rewards for clearing the Wrangler course in less than three minutes. The best rewards are always a stack of five bugs of a given type, with rarer bugs awarded for completing more difficult goals.

BUG BEGINNER COURSE REWARDS
Deku Hornet x5
Blessed Butterfly x5
Skyloft Mantis x5
Sky Stag Beetle x5

BUG WRANGLER COURSE REWARDS (LESS THAN THREE MINUTES)
Woodland Rhino Beetle x5
Gerudo Dragonfly x5
Lanayru Ant x5
Volcanic Ladybug x5

BUG WRANGLER COURSE REWARDS (LESS THAN TWO MINUTES)
Eldin Roller x5
Sand Cicada x5
Faron Grasshopper x5
Starry Firefly x5
Volcanic Ladybug x5

Clean Cut

Peater charges 10 Rupees to see if you can chop a falling piece of bamboo more than 27 times while it's in midair. If you succeed, he rewards you with a random rare treasure.

Dodoh's High Dive

Dodoh's High Dive is a complicated diving minigame where Link pays 20 Rupees to be shot out of a cannon. While diving back down to earth, you can guide Link through rings to build up a score multiplier that goes as high as x10. Hitting any of the Dodoh Ball hazards on your fall reduces your score multiplier. Beneath you is a spinning wheel whose slots are marked by Green, Blue, and Red Rupees. If you land on the Red Rupee space with a modifier of x5, your reward is 100 Rupees.

There's also a Rupoor space you can land on that immediately penalizes you 10 Rupees, a brown slot that gives you nothing, and a special 50-Rupee space. If you land on the 50-Rupee space with a x10 modifier, you win 500 Rupees and a Piece of Heart.

Harp Performance

Go to the Lumpy Pumpkin at night and you can perform on your harp as part of a duet with Kina. Your performance is scored based on how well you keep time with the audience. A good performance is worth 50 Rupees.

Rickety Coaster

A trip on the Rickety Coaster courses at the Shipyard in the Lanayru Sand Sea costs 20 Rupees for the Beginner course and 50 Rupees for the Expert course. If you can finish the Beginner course in less than 60 seconds, you're rewarded with a rare treasure. If you can finish the Expert course in less than 65 seconds, you can win a Piece of Heart.

Pumpkin Pull

After you finish Fledge's gratitude request, he offers you a new minigame just outside the Sparring Hall. Pay Fledge 20 Rupees and he offers to toss pumpkins into the air for you to shoot down with your bow. You get points for each pumpkin you shoot down. It begins at 10 points and goes up to 50 with each consecutive shot, with double points offered for hitting special sparkling pumpkins. If you can get more than 600 points in this challenge, Fledge gives you a Piece of Heart.

The Thunder Dragon's Lightning Round

This is it, the biggest minigame Skyward Sword has to offer. You can play the Thunder Dragon's Lightning Round any time after receiving the Thunder Dragon's portion of the Song of the Hero. There are two aspects to the Lightning Round: the Silent Realm trials (a time trial mode) and the combat trial (basically a boss rush mode).

For the Silent Realm trials, you can opt to enter any Silent Realm map you've cleared already in the game. If you can finish it, the Thunder Dragon gives you a reward based on how quickly you manage to finish. This reward can be anything from 5 Rupees to 100 Rupees, depending on how your completion time compares to the Thunder Dragon's goal time.

The Thunder Dragon always gives you 50 Rupees the first time you play through a given Silent Realm trial. If you beat your best time for a given Silent Realm, you always get 50 Rupees. If you can finish the trials while beating the Thunder Dragon's goal time, you get a random rare treasure. You only get the rare treasure if you qualify for that reward, unless you also beat your personal best time or were playing the Silent Realm trial for the first time.

SILENT REALM	TIME TO BEAT
Faron Woods	3:00
Lanayru Desert	4:15
Eldin Volcano	6:00
Skyloft	4:00

The Thunder Dragon's battle trial lets you relive any boss battles you've already fought, with the exception of the battle against Bilocyte. To win a prize from the Thunder Dragon, you must clear a certain number of battles in succession without using any Adventure Pouch items besides your shield. You only have access to tools and items that you would've had during the initial fight. You can select from any of 11 boss fights on a first pass through the game, provided you come here after saving at the point of no return. The Thunder Dragon offers you a reward after each battle you clear, or the chance to continue on and try for an even bigger reward by beating another battle. If you visit this minigame while playing in Hero Mode, an additional twelfth battle with Demise is available.

THUNDER DRAGON REWARDS

BATTLES WON	REWARD
1	20 Rupees
2	Small Treasure
3	100 Rupees
4	Piece of Heart (200 Rupees after first victory)
5	300 Rupees
6	Rare Treasure
7	500 Rupees
8	Hylian Shield (if you have already obtained the Hylian Shield or if both your Adventure Pouch and Item Check are full, you receive 1,000 Rupees)
9	2,000 Rupees
10	3 Rare Treasures
11	3,000 Rupees
12	9,900 Rupees

The way the battle trial works is that you pick the first battle you want to repeat yourself, then the Thunder Dragon picks subsequent battles randomly. While the Thunder Dragon's battle trial is primarily a test of player skill and memorization, there are some strategies you can use to help yourself get farther and hopefully acquire at least the Hylian Shield. Try to pick a battle that you find genuinely difficult for the first round, so it doesn't hit you as an unpleasant surprise in the Thunder Dragon's random selections.

You can also begin by picking a battle that's easy to lose under "time out" conditions, like the second or third battle with The Imprisoned. When you're fighting the bosses for the big rewards, focus most on not taking any damage. The Thunder Dragon does time your fights and offers you 50 Rupees whenever you beat your best time on a given boss. Still, it's not worth rushing to grab this reward if you're trying to survive eight rounds so you can claim the Hylian Shield. When you fight in a boss room that lets you refill your health from jars or heart flowers, always do so. If you simply repeat battles you find difficult until you begin to find them easy, you can get farther and farther in the Thunder Dragon's Lightning Round.

Items, Equipment, and Crafting

Treasure-Hunting Guide

There are 16 types of treasure in *The Legend of Zelda: Skyward Sword*. You find them in a variety of ways and in a variety of places, but you use all of them for one purpose: to improve Link's equipment. This section of the guide is a reference for players who either want to know the requirements for upgrading something or want to know how to find treasures that they're missing.

Note that the game divides treasures into two categories, small and rare. The first three rows of treasures on your item screen count as small, while the bottom row counts as rare. While these categories roughly describe the rarity of the treasures involved, there are some small treasures that can actually be pretty difficult to obtain.

How Much Treasure Do I Need?

There's only so much equipment to upgrade in *Skyward Sword*, so it stands to reason that you only need to acquire so much treasure. Here's a list of the bare minimum number of all treasures you need to obtain to upgrade all of Link's equipment. Anything you acquire over this amount you can just sell off to Rupin to make some extra Rupees. Some treasures you can easily acquire more than enough of just by exploring the game, while others you need to go out of your way to get.

TOTAL AMOUNT OF TREASURE

Treasure	Total Number	Treasure	Total Number
Hornet Larvae	4	Jelly Blobs	8
Bird Feathers	5	Monster Claws	17
Tumbleweeds	16	Monster Horns	8
Lizard Tails	7	Ornamental Skulls	12
Eldin Ores	7	Evil Crystals	4
Ancient Flowers	7	Blue Bird Feathers	5
Amber Relics	25	Golden Skulls	4
Dusk Relics	13	Goddess Plumes	3

How Do I Get Treasures I'm Missing?

If you're trying to make a particular item and need to quickly amass some amount of a treasure, you probably want to go grind for it real quick. It's smartest to wait until toward the end of the game to grind, since otherwise you might get what you want out of a random treasure chest or by summoning a Gossip Stone. Bear in mind that at some points in the game, you simply can't obtain certain treasures. You can't get Tumbleweeds before you can go to Lanayru Desert, for instance. Here's a quick list of the best ways to grind for certain treasures, if you want to get some fast.

Hornet Larvae

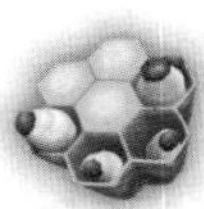

The only place in the game you can acquire Hornet Larvae is in the Deep Woods area of Faron Woods. If you're grinding for them, the best place for it is the tree just outside Skyview Temple. Shoot at the Deku Hornet hive up in the tree, use your Bug Net to catch or drive away the Deku Hornets, then go over where the hornet nest fell to claim the Hornet Larvae. You can reset the Deku Hornet nest by rapidly walking in and then back out of Skyview Temple, which lets you quickly get all the Hornet Larvae you need.

Bird Feathers

You get Bird Feathers by catching small pink birds and small yellow birds in your Bug Net. The birds gather in many different areas in Faron Woods. If you're not at the very end of the game, the Sealed Grounds is one of the best places to catch birds. You can walk in and out of the Sealed Temple to reset the birds that roost just in front of the entrance. If you are at the end of the game, a good place to hunt birds is around the "In the Woods" bird statue in Faron Woods.

Tumbleweeds

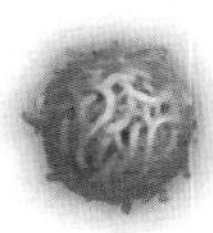

You get Tumbleweeds by catching the ones that blow around Lanayru Desert regions in your Bug Net. These Tumbleweeds have a chance of spawning and blowing across the screen every time you stop after moving for a short distance. If you simply run without stopping, no Tumbleweeds spawn. The entrance area of Lanayru Desert itself is a good place to hunt for Tumbleweeds, since you've got lots of room to run around.

Lizard Tails

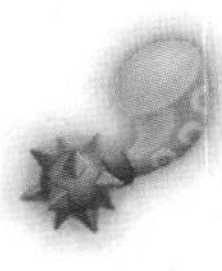

You can only get Lizard Tails by defeating Lizalfos. It is possible to grind for Lizard Tails, though usually you get all that you need in the course of exploring the game. If you do end up having to grind for Lizard Tails, an excellent place to hunt Lizalfos is the Shipyard at the Lanayru Sand Sea. You can fight the pair of Lizalfos who appear on the platform near the entrance, leave, then come right back and fight them again.

Eldin Ores

Eldin Ore only appears in Eldin Volcano areas. If you dig around in that area's dirt patches with any frequency, you should end up with far more than you need. If you need to get some Eldin Ore fast, it can be good to explore the area just in front of the entrance to the Fire Sanctuary. You usually get a couple of Eldin Ores from one of the dirt patches just across from the Gossip Stone.

Ancient Flowers

You can only find Ancient Flowers growing in time-shifted areas of Lanayru Desert. You should get plenty throughout the course of the game, but if you need to get some fast, try a quick pass through the Lanayru Mine or the area just outside the Temple of Time. Basically, any area of Lanayru Desert that's loaded with Timeshift Stones can produce lots of Ancient Flowers if you just run around activating them.

Amber Relics

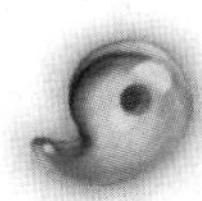

Even with as many Amber Relics as you need to upgrade equipment in this game, you should never ever lack for them. If you pick up even half of the ones you stumble across while exploring the game's dungeons, you should have more than enough to make whatever you want. If for some reason you do need Amber Relics fast, the first few rooms of Skyview Temple and the Faron Woods contain plenty of them.

Dusk Relics

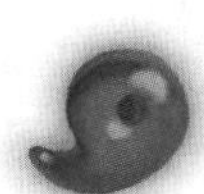

Dusk Relics can be a bit tricky, because you can only get them from random treasure drops and in the Silent Realm. You can't typically get into a Silent Realm whenever you want, unless you wait until the Thunder Dragon's Lightning Round is open. Then you can take the Thunder Dragon's Silent Realm challenges, which let you enter any Silent Realm maps. Even if you fail these challenges, you get to keep any treasures you pick up in them.

Jelly Blobs

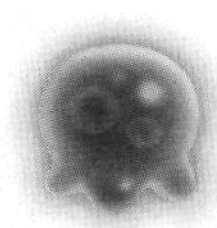

Jelly Blobs drop when you defeat monsters that the game considers "squishy." In practice, this means Chuchus, Deku Babas, and Arachas. You may need to hunt for these early in the game, though eventually you end up carrying around tons of them you don't need anymore. When you need to hunt for Jelly Blobs, it's usually quickest to just run into the waterfall cave in Skyloft and hunt the Green Chuchus that live inside.

Monster Claws

All types of Keese drop Monster Claws, though you still have a tendency to run short of them. When you need to get a few extra, the waterfall cave in Skyloft is a good place to fight lots of Keese and not much else. Once monsters stop appearing in Skyloft, you can go on Keese hunts in Eldin Volcano. The Fire Keese tend to spawn in packs and aren't especially dangerous to you later on in the game.

Monster Horns

You can only obtain Monster Horns from Bokoblin leaders. Sometimes they drop Monster Horns when you defeat them. A more reliable way to obtain Monster Horns from them, though, is to steal them by using the whip. A good place to hunt is the Bokoblin village just to the left of the Earth Temple's entrance in Eldin Volcano. There's a Blue Bokoblin leader there you can steal from or just repeatedly defeat. To steal a Monster Horn, just flick the whip at the Bokoblin leader and then yank quickly back. This pulls the Monster Horn from the leader's belt or hand and into your possession.

Ornamental Skulls

All types of Bokoblins can drop Ornamental Skulls. You typically only have to go hunt for them early in the game, since later on you've defeated so many Bokoblins it's inevitable that you end up with a stack of the skulls. When you need to hunt Bokoblins, Eldin Volcano's sandy slopes and villages are excellent places to search for them. You can also try hunting in Faron Woods, though there the Bokoblins tend to spawn in smaller groups.

Evil Crystals

In a certain sense, it's not really possible to grind for Evil Crystals. In theory, any enemy that's Cursed or can inflict curses can drop an Evil Crystal. In practice, you tend to get them only from Dark Lizalfos and Cursed Bokoblins. These aren't enemies you can casually go out and hunt. If you didn't get all the Evil Crystals you need while passing through the Ancient Cistern, you're probably best off buying the rest from the Moonlight Merchant.

Blue Bird Feathers

You have lots of chances to get Blue Bird Feathers in the game, but it's surprisingly difficult to just go out and grind for them. To get a Blue Bird Feather, you have to catch one of the rare small blue birds that sometimes spawn with small bird groups. You usually have better luck traveling from one spawn point to another than trying to reset one spawn point repeatedly. The Sealed Grounds is an especially good place to hunt, as are Skyview Spring and the "In the Woods" bird statue in Faron Woods.

Golden Skulls

Golden Skulls aren't actually very rare. You get them by fighting Bokoblins later in the game, with rarer types of Bokoblins like Technoblins dropping them a bit more frequently. Due to the sheer volume of Bokoblins you fight in this game, chances are you can easily amass a good-sized pile of Golden Skulls just from battling your way through dungeons. If you need to hunt for Golden Skulls, just wait until late in the game and hit up Eldin Volcano.

Goddess Plumes

There are a few ways you can try to grind for Goddess Plumes. They appear sometimes in the Silent Realm, so you can wait until late in the game and grind for them at the Thunder Dragon's Lightning Round. You can also try farming the one that appears in Lanayru Mining Facility in the room where you get the Gust Bellows. Running in and out of the dungeon, that Goddess Plume is going to have a good chance of being in that particular pile of sand when you blow it away.

Upgrade Recipe List

RECIPE LIST

ITEM	UPGRADE PRICE	TREASURE	TREASURE	TREASURE	TREASURE	RESULT
Slingshot	50	2 Dusk Relics	2 Amber Relics	3 Jelly Blobs	—	Scattershot
Hook Beetle	50	2 Ancient Flowers	2 Hornet Larvae	1 Golden Skull	—	Quick Beetle
Quick Beetle	50	3 Ancient Flowers	4 Amber Relics	1 Blue Bird Feather	1 Goddess Plume	Tough Beetle
Wooden Bow	50	3 Tumbleweeds	3 Monster Claws	2 Eldin Ores	1 Evil Crystal	Iron Bow
Iron Bow	100	5 Tumbleweeds	3 Lizard Tails	2 Evil Crystals	1 Goddess Plume	Sacred Bow

RECIPE LIST

ITEM	UPGRADE PRICE	TREASURE	TREASURE	TREASURE	TREASURE	RESULT
Bug Net	100	3 Tumbleweeds	2 Ancient Flowers	1 Evil Crystal	—	Big Bug Net
Wooden Shield	30	2 Amber Relics	1 Monster Claw	1 Jelly Blob	—	Banded Shield
Banded Shield	50	2 Monster Claws	3 Amber Relics	2 Tumbleweeds	1 Ornamental Skull	Braced Shield
Iron Shield	50	2 Eldin Ores	2 Ornamental Skulls	2 Monster Claws	—	Reinforced Shield
Reinforced Shield	100	3 Eldin Ores	3 Monster Claws	3 Tumbleweeds	1 Blue Bird Feather	Fortified Shield
Sacred Shield	100	3 Ornamental Skulls	1 Dusk Relics	2 Bird Feathers	—	Divine Shield
Divine Shield	150	3 Monster Horns	4 Dusk Relics	3 Bird Feathers	1 Blue Bird Feather	Goddess Shield

RECIPE LIST

ITEM	UPGRADE PRICE	TREASURE	TREASURE	TREASURE	TREASURE	RESULT
Small Seed Satchel	50	4 Amber Relics	3 Monster Claws	3 Ornamental Skulls	—	Medium Seed Satchel
Medium Seed Satchel	100	5 Amber Relics	3 Monster Claws	1 Golden Skull	1 Blue Bird Feather	Large Seed Satchel
Small Quiver	50	3 Monster Horns	3 Dusk Relics	5 Amber Relics	—	Medium Quiver
Medium Quiver	100	2 Monster Horns	3 Dusk Relics	1 Golden Skull	1 Goddess Plume	Large Quiver
Small Bomb Bag	50	1 Lizard Tail	3 Ornamental Skulls	1 Blue Bird Feather	—	Medium Bomb Bag
Medium Bomb Bag	100	3 Lizard Tails	4 Jelly Blobs	2 Hornet Larvae	1 Golden Skull	Large Bomb Bag

Bug-Catching Guide

There are 12 types of bugs in *The Legend of Zelda: Skyward Sword*. Each bug has a favored type of environment and usually occurs in a certain type of place in a certain region. You primarily use bugs as ingredients when brewing potions. So unless you're interested in making high-end potions, you don't need to mess with this part of the game. This section of the guide is a reference for players who want to make specific high-end potions. While they aren't entirely necessary in the main game, they can be fun to play around with and invaluable when you're playing the game in Hero Mode.

While you can stop hunting treasures when you've obtained certain numbers, potions are consumables. That means what types of bugs you need and how many of them you need depend on how many potions you use and what types you're interested in using. You definitely won't stumble upon the bugs you need to brew a particular potion by accident. To be serious about potion brewing, you need to be willing to go out and hunt down the bugs you want. You also want to upgrade your Bug Net into a Big Bug Net before going on serious bug hunts, since the Big Bug Net makes it much easier to catch bugs successfully.

Where Do I Hunt for Bugs?

Deku Hornet

You only encounter Deku Hornets in the Deep Woods, where they build nests in trees. You can catch tons of them at once and usually have a lot more on hand than you really need. To catch Deku Hornets, just shoot down one of their nests. This disturbs an entire swarm of them, which lets you catch them nine at a time.

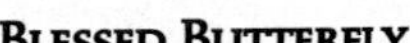

Blessed Butterfly

Blessed Butterflies can literally be found in every region of the game, but if you want to catch a lot of them quickly, it's best to stick to Skyloft. There's a road that runs from the Knight Academy to the plaza where you can usually find four to five Blessed Butterflies spawning regularly.

Gerudo Dragonfly

Gerudo Dragonflies spawn in Lanayru Desert, usually in groups of two. They're relatively common spawns, so there's no especially good part of the desert to go for hunting them. Simply running around the desert for a bit should give you ample opportunities for catching five or six.

Starry Firefly

Starry Fireflies can only be found in the sky at night. You can catch them in Skyloft or on the handful of islands in the sky where you spend the night. If you want to catch a lot of Starry Fireflies at once, spend the night in Beedle's Airshop. The island where Beedle passes the night always spawns a pair of Starry Fireflies right next to each other.

Woodland Rhino Beetle

You can catch Woodland Rhino Beetles in a handful of locations in Faron Woods. The best by far is a vine-covered wall behind the Sealed Grounds. Two of the Rhino Beetles spawn in this location pretty consistently. You don't use the Bug Net to catch these insects. Instead, dash-roll at the walls they climb on and knock them over.

Volcanic Ladybug

You can find Volcanic Ladybugs, usually in groups of two, throughout Eldin Volcano. There is no area where they spawn that is particularly more convenient than any other. Just investigate walls as you run through Eldin Volcano and try to pick up as many as you can at once.

Sand Cicada

Sand Cicadas make a very distinct sound. You always know when you're near one by the sound of its high-pitched trilling chirps. You usually find them one at a time, clinging to the side of a wall. There's one near the entrance of Lanayru Desert that's particularly convenient and easy to catch.

Sky Stag Beetle

Sky Stag Beetles only occur in Skyloft, climbing along the trunks of trees. You can find one pretty consistently if you check the tree next to the pumpkin patch near Gondo's place. It's hard to catch lots of Sky Stag Beetles at once, since bugs in Skyloft don't respawn unless you go to sleep until morning to refresh the map.

Faron Grasshopper

Faron Grasshoppers most frequently occur in the tall grass in Faron Woods. Just run around for a bit in the parts of Faron Woods nearest the exit from the Sealed Grounds and you should be able to catch four or five. While Faron Grasshoppers spawn one at a time, there are a lot of spawn points for them in Faron Woods.

Skyloft Mantis

Skyloft Mantises may be the rarest and most frustrating bugs to catch in the game. There are a few areas in Skyloft where they spawn. After you've finished Bateaux's gratitude quests, they tend to appear more often. You can usually find a Skyloft Mantis in the pumpkin patch over by Gondo's house.

Lanayru Ant

Lanayru Ants only occur in regions of Lanayru Desert, usually two or three at a time. If you explore the port area of the Lanayru Sand Sea, you can find a group that often boasts six or seven Lanayru Ants at once. A couple of quick trips here usually nets you Lanayru Ants to spare.

Eldin Roller

Extreme care is called for when catching Eldin Rollers, since they often run around your feet and end up getting themselves stepped on. There are a few good areas for finding Eldin Rollers in Eldin Volcano, but one of the best is the area outside the entrance to the Fire Sanctuary. There's a patch of dirt you can dig in there that fairly consistently yields two Eldin Rollers.

Potion Recipe List

POTION RECIPES

POTION	UPGRADE PRICE	BUGS	BUGS	BUGS	BUGS	RESULT
Heart Potion	20	1 Woodland Rhino Beetle	3 Blessed Butterflies	1 Volcanic Ladybug	—	Heart Potion+
Heart Potion+	30	3 Deku Hornets	3 Blessed Butterflies	1 Sand Cicada	1 Eldin Roller	Heart Potion++
Revitalizing Potion	20	3 Deku Hornets	2 Skyloft Mantises	2 Woodland Rhino Beetles	—	Revitalizing Potion+
Revitalizing Potion+	30	3 Lanayru Ants	2 Woodland Rhino Beetles	1 Gerudo Dragonfly	1 Sand Cicada	Revitalizing Potion++
Stamina Potion	20	3 Volcanic Ladybugs	2 Sky Stag Beetles	2 Gerudo Dragonflies	1 Faron Grasshopper	Stamina Potion+
Air Potion	20	2 Sky Stag Beetles	2 Skyloft Mantises	2 Lanayru Ants	—	Air Potion+
Guardian Potion	40	1 Faron Grasshopper	2 Eldin Rollers	3 Blessed Butterflies	3 Starry Fireflies	Guardian Potion+

MAPS

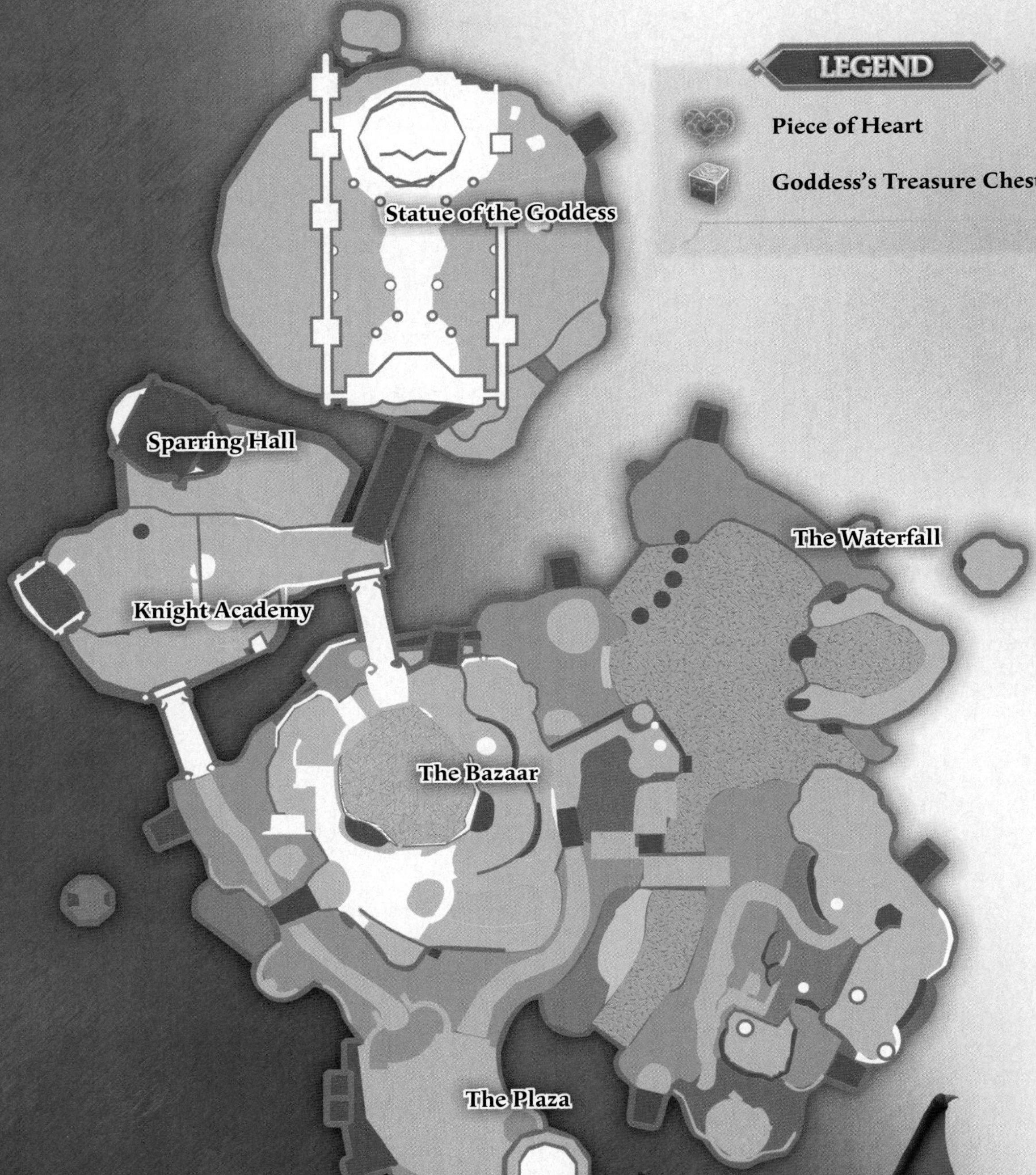

LEGEND

Piece of Heart

Goddess's Treasure Chest

Statue of the Goddess

Sparring Hall

Knight Academy

The Waterfall

The Bazaar

The Plaza

SKYLOFT

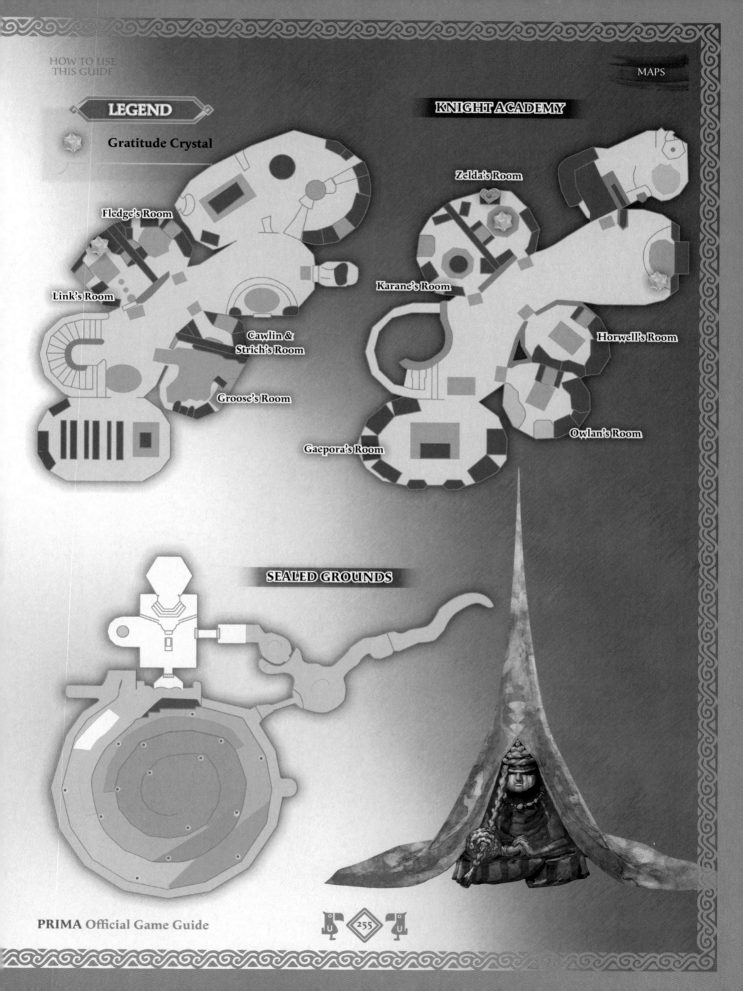

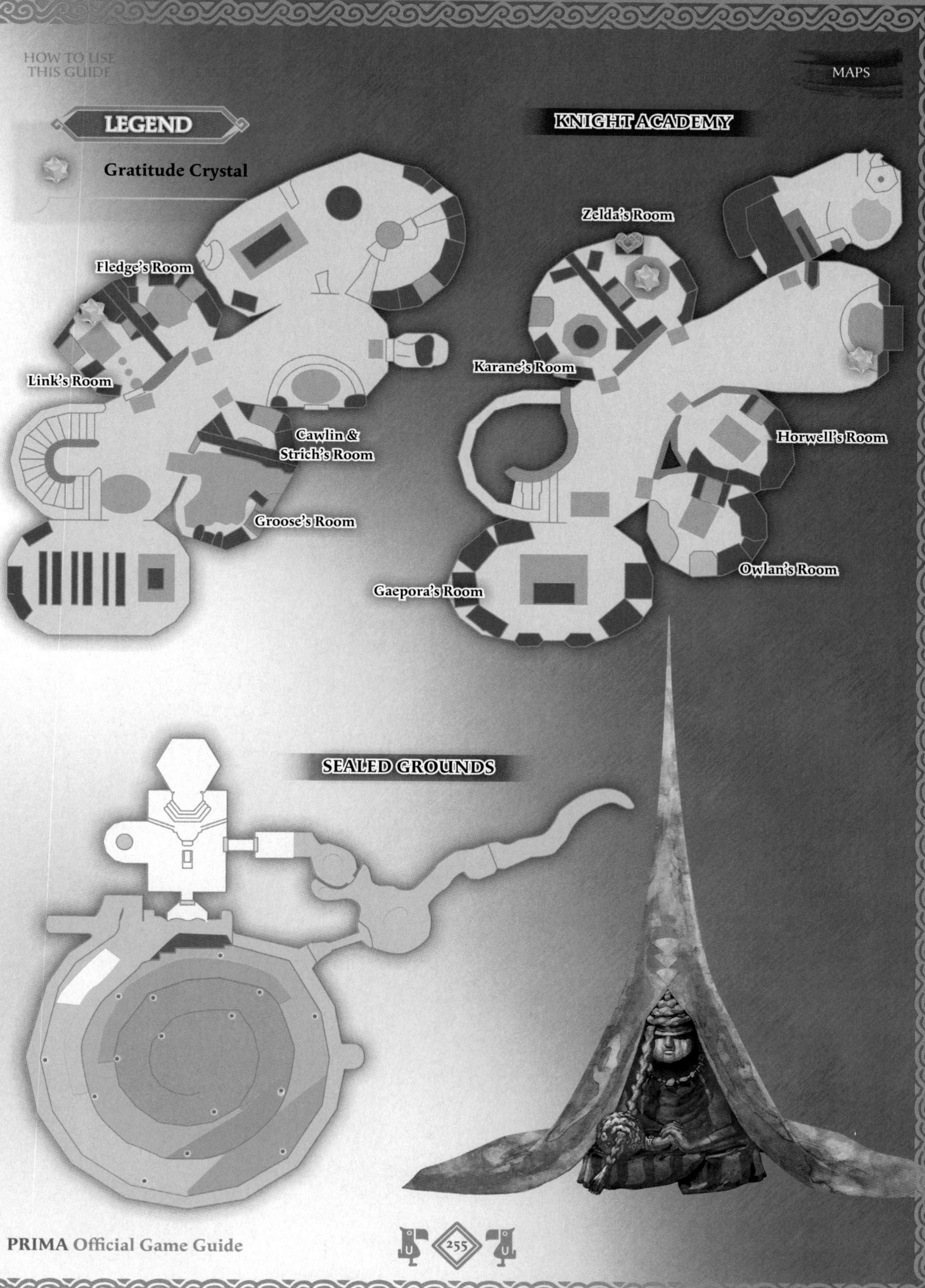
LEGEND
Gratitude Crystal
KNIGHT ACADEMY
Fledge's Room
Link's Room
Cawlin & Strich's Room
Groose's Room
Zelda's Room
Karane's Room
Horwell's Room
Owlan's Room
Gaepora's Room
SEALED GROUNDS

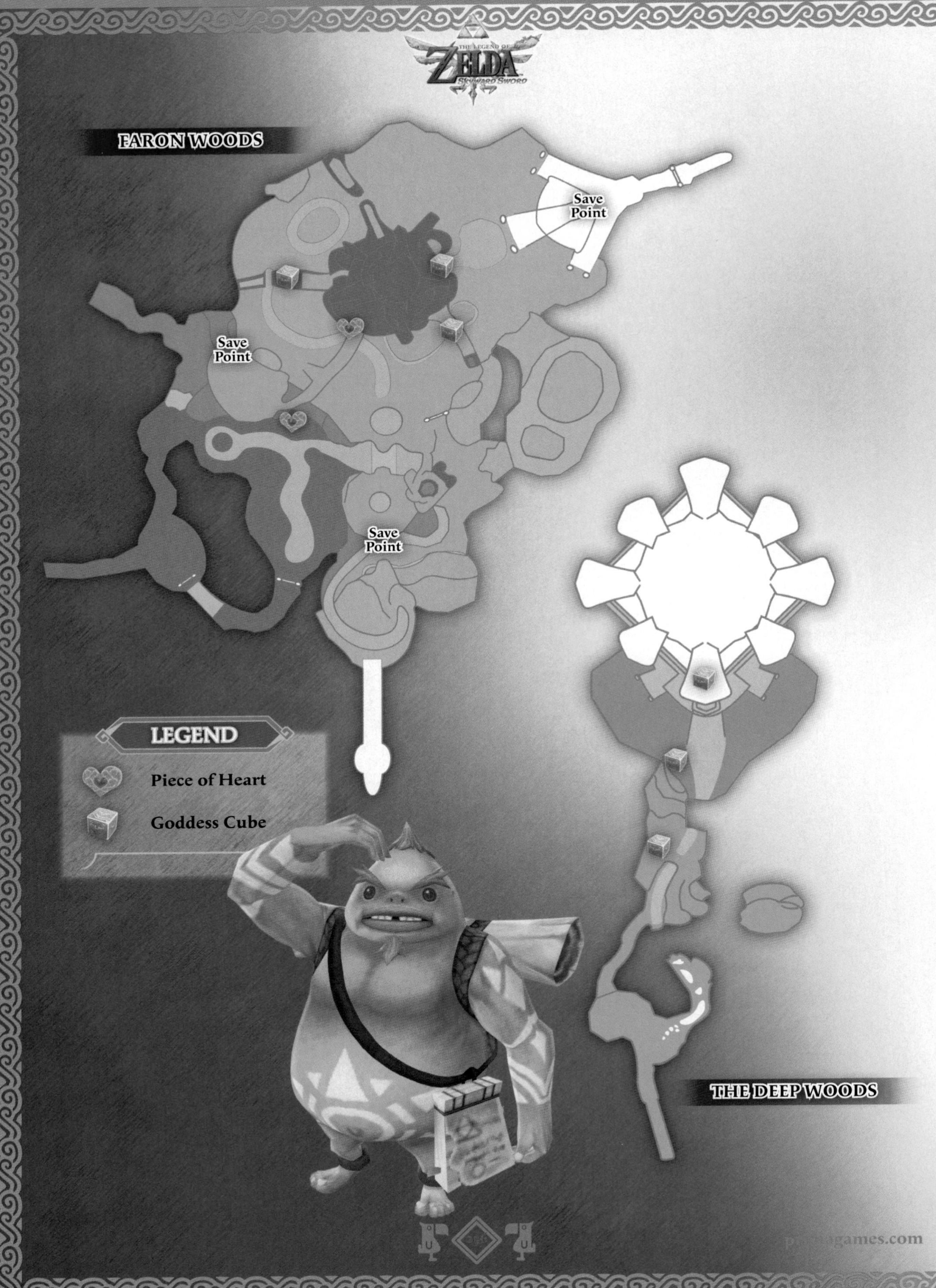
THE LEGEND OF
ZELDA
SKYWARD SWORD
FARON WOODS
Save Point
Save Point
Save Point
LEGEND
Piece of Heart
Goddess Cube
THE DEEP WOODS

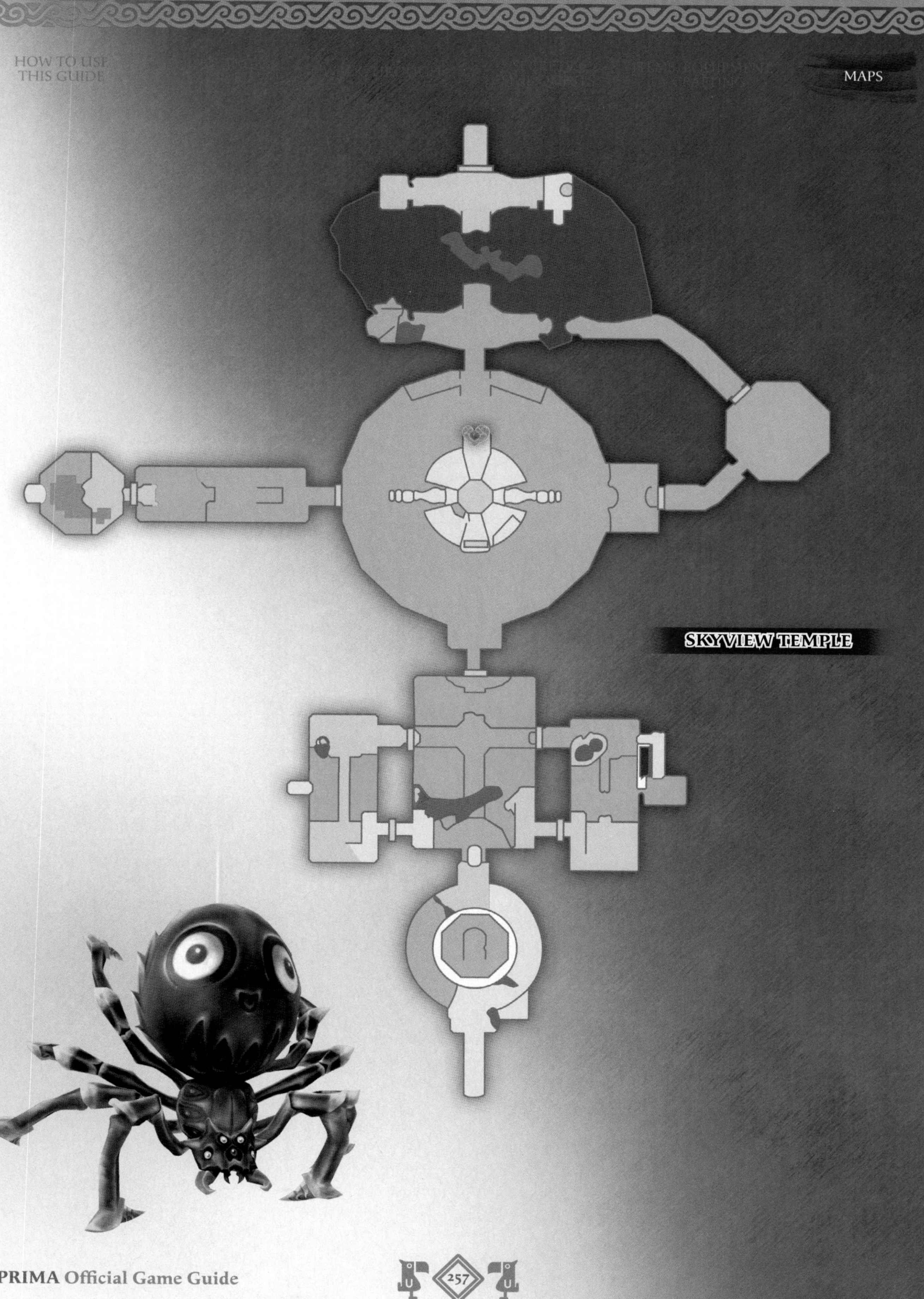
SKYVIEW TEMPLE

LEGEND

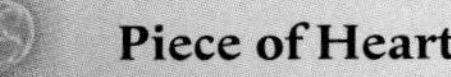
Piece of Heart

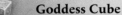

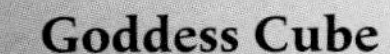
Goddess Cube

ELDIN VOLCANO

ELDIN VOLCANO INTERIOR

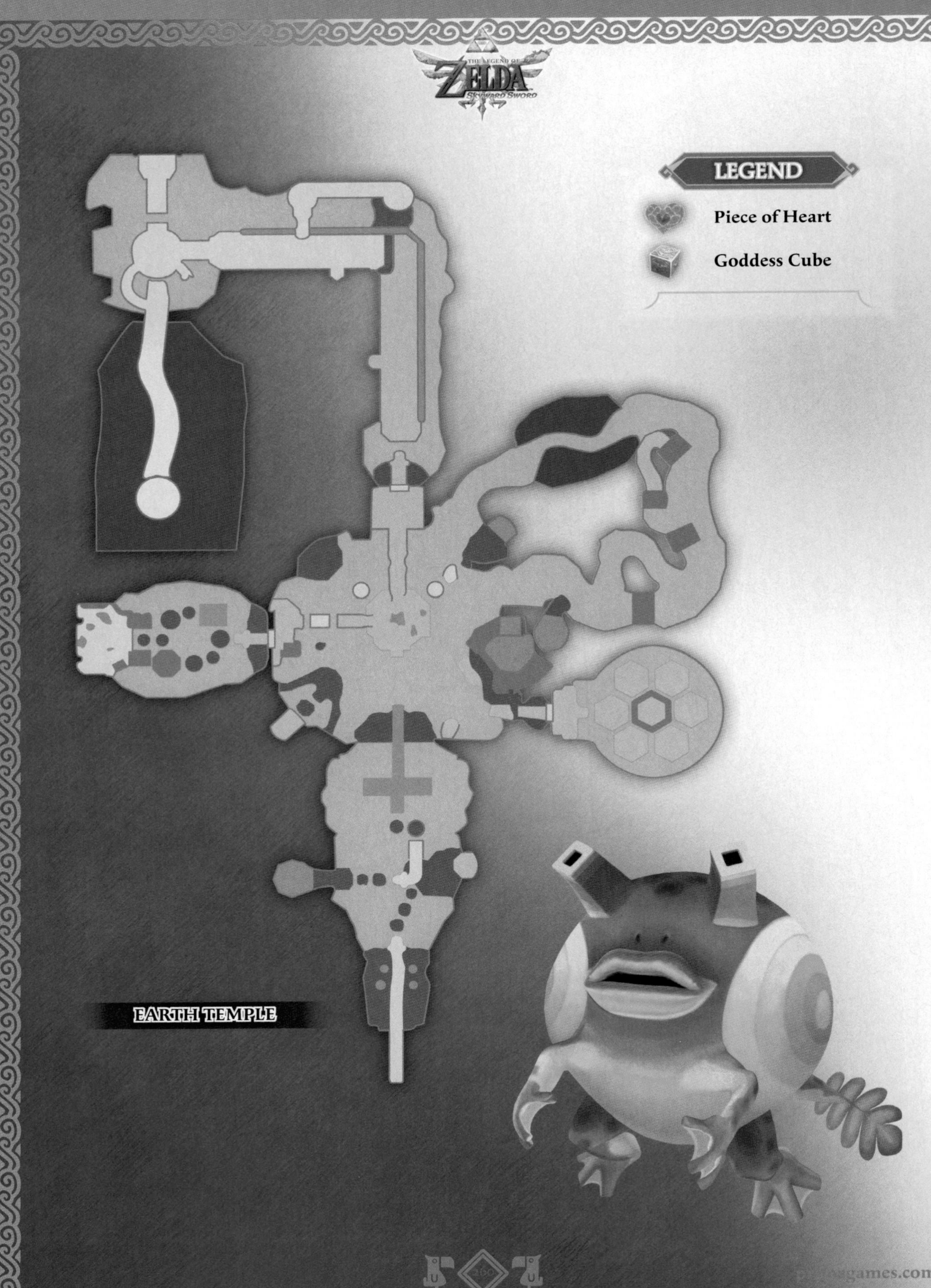
THE LEGEND OF
ZELDA
SKYWARD SWORD
LEGEND
Piece of Heart
Goddess Cube
EARTH TEMPLE

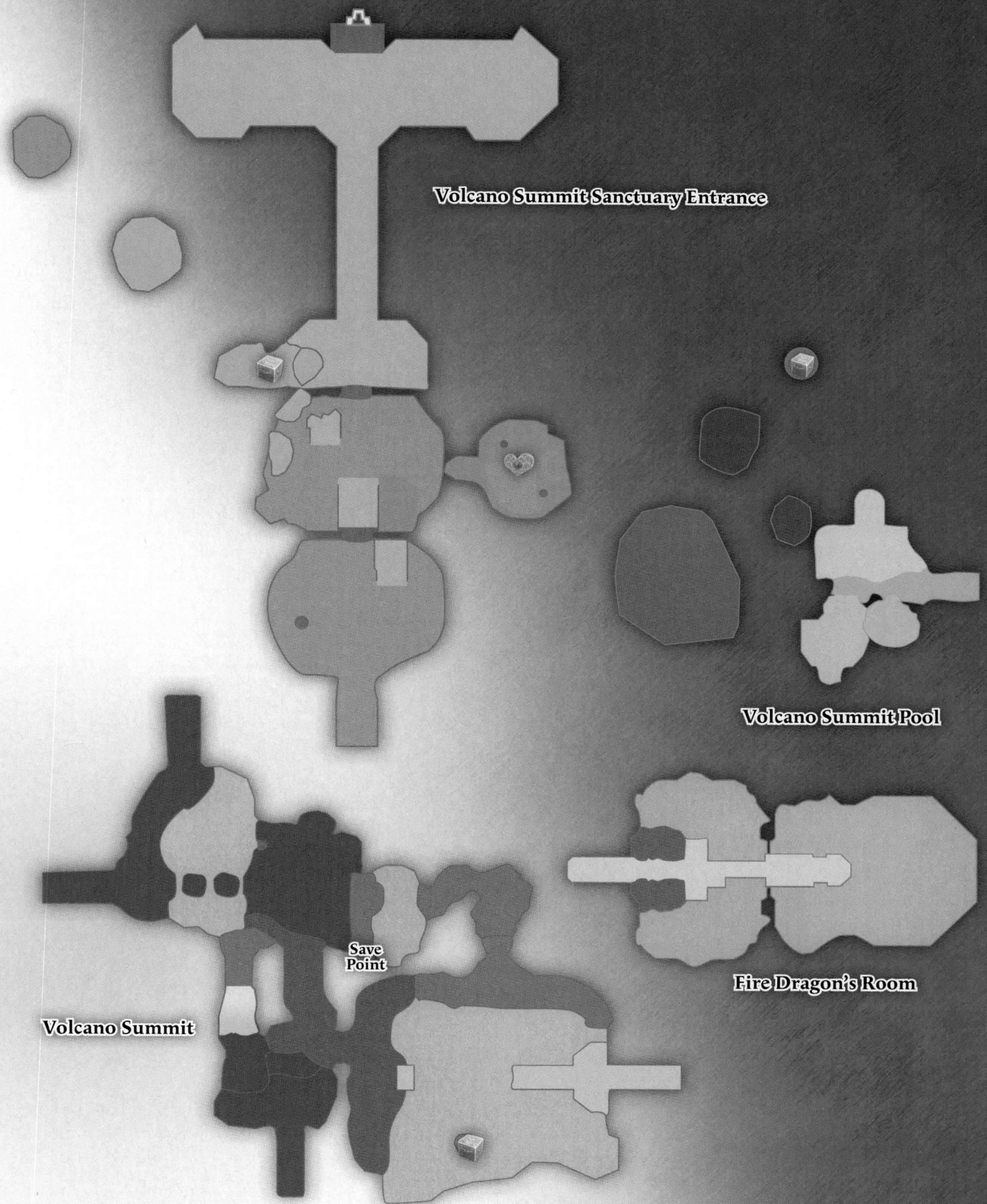

Volcano Summit Sanctuary Entrance

Volcano Summit Pool

Fire Dragon's Room

Save Point

Volcano Summit

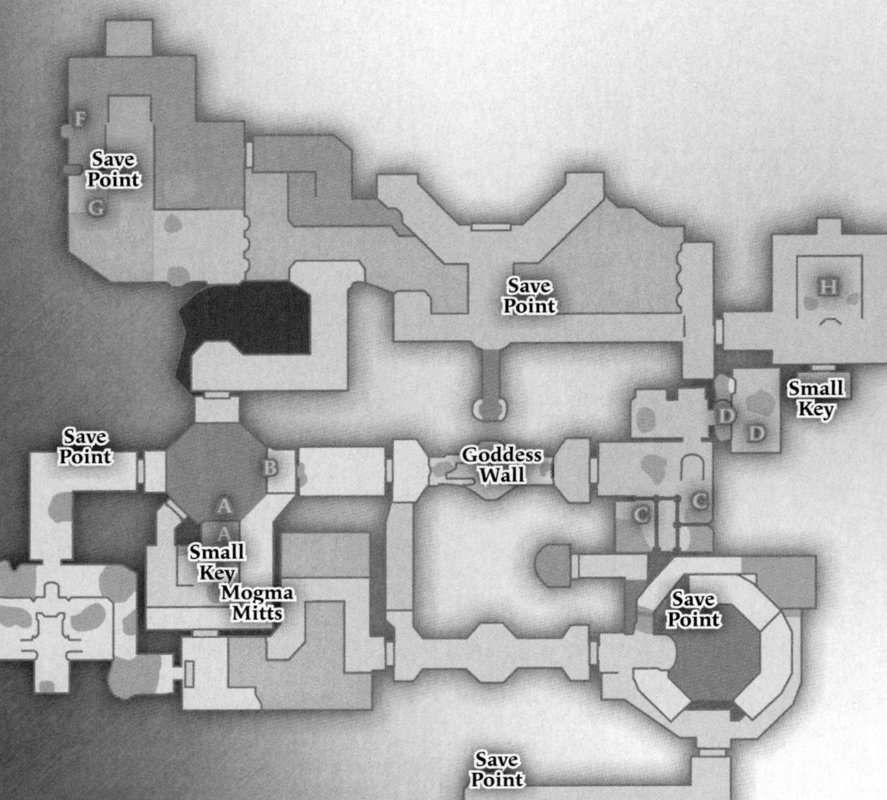

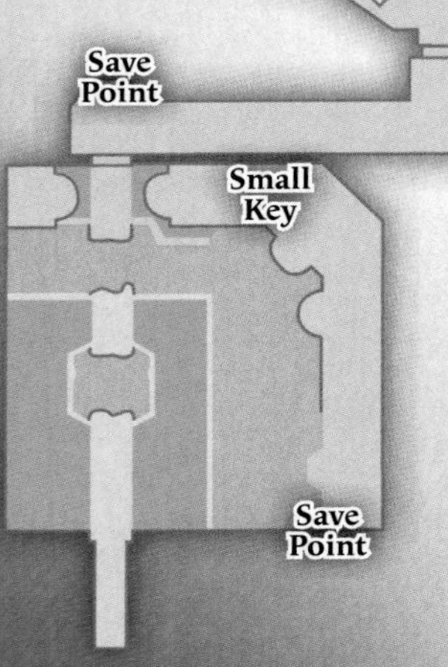

FIRE SANCTUARY

LEGEND

Piece of Heart

Goddess Cube

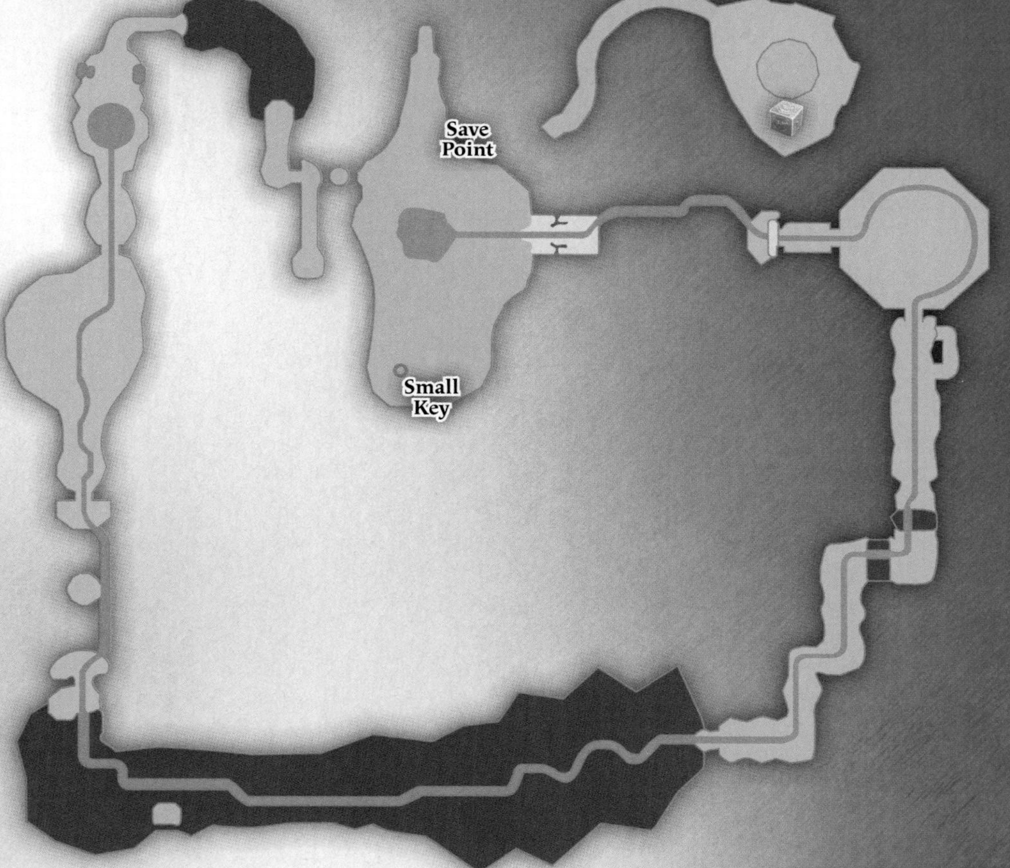

LANAYRU GORGE

LANAYRU MINE

LANAYRU MINING FACILITY

Ancient Circuit

Save Point

Save Point

Gust Bellows

Save Point

Small Key

Save Point

LEGEND

 Piece of Heart

 Goddess Cube

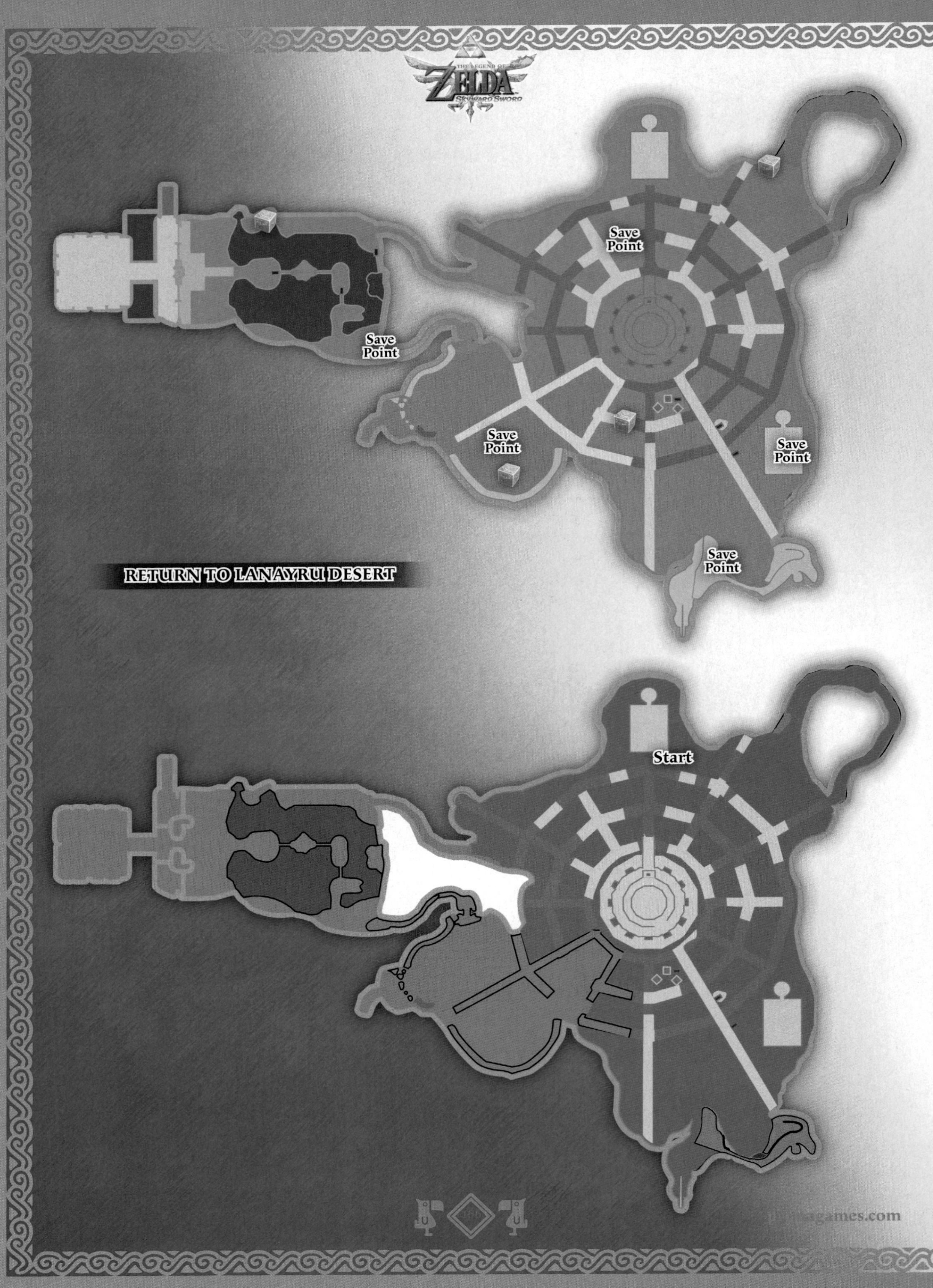
THE LEGEND OF
ZELDA
SKYWARD SWORD
Save Point
Save Point
Save Point
Save Point
Save Point
RETURN TO LANAYRU DESERT
Start

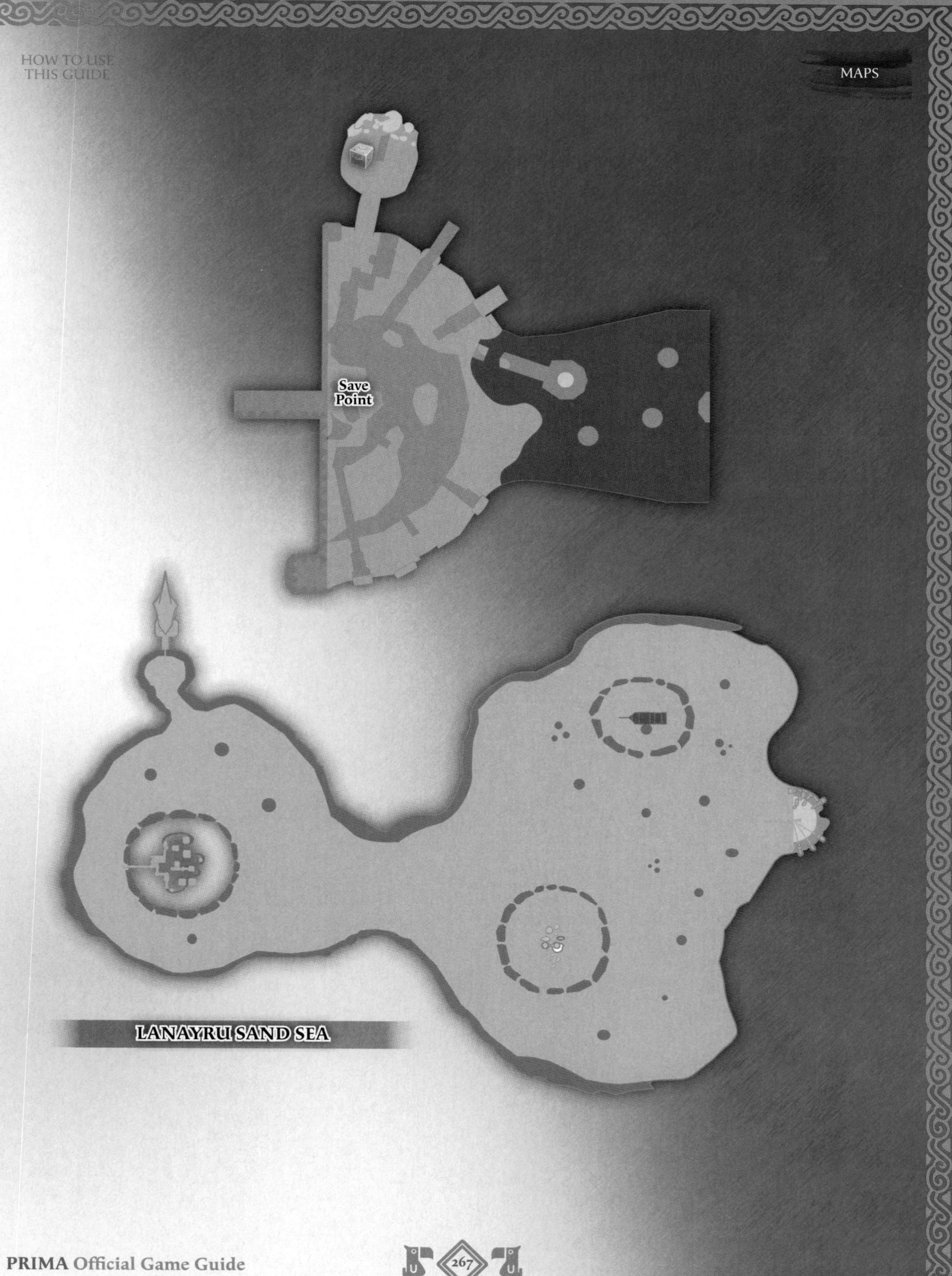
Save
Point
LANAYRU SAND SEA

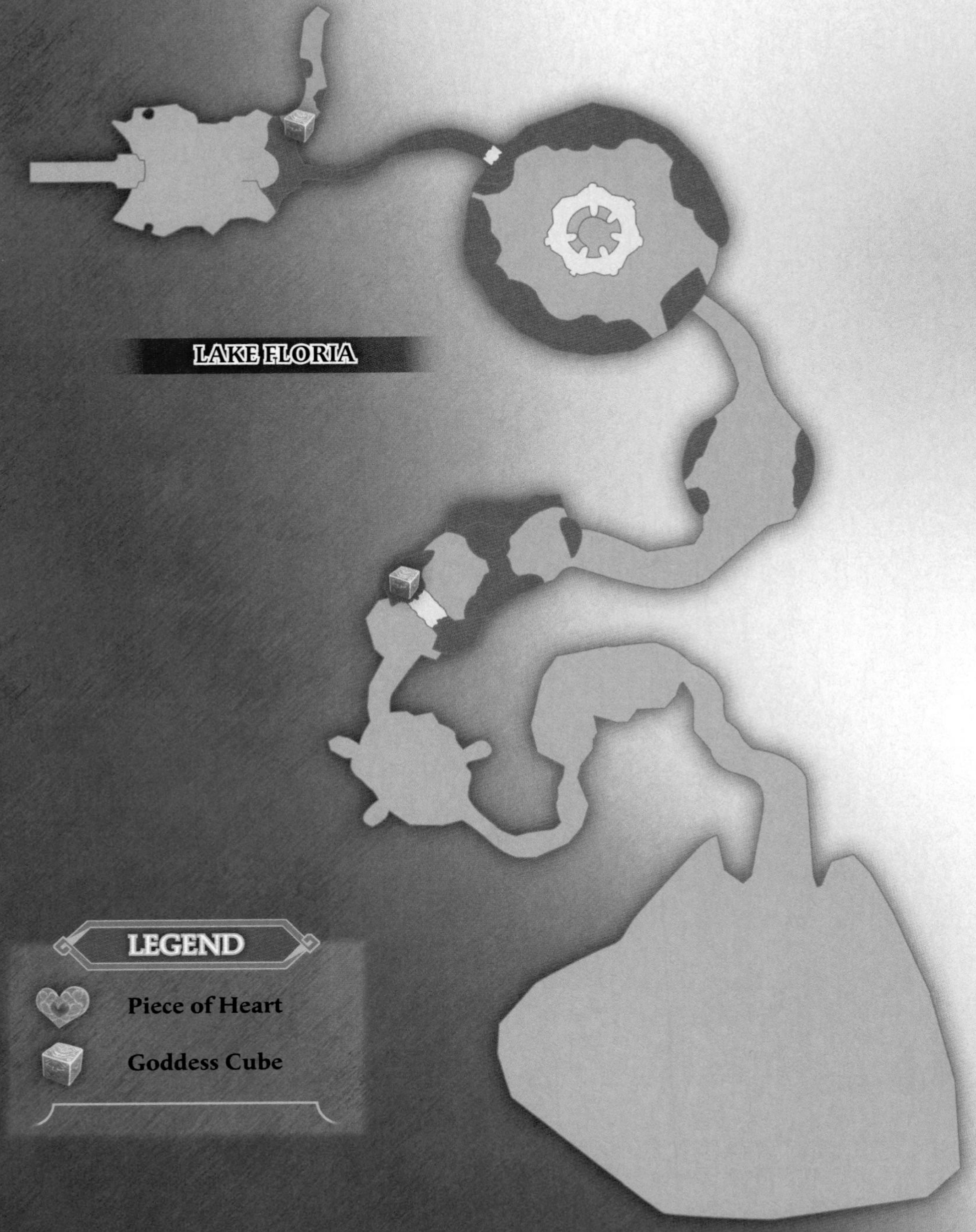

LAKE FLORIA

LEGEND

 Piece of Heart

 Goddess Cube

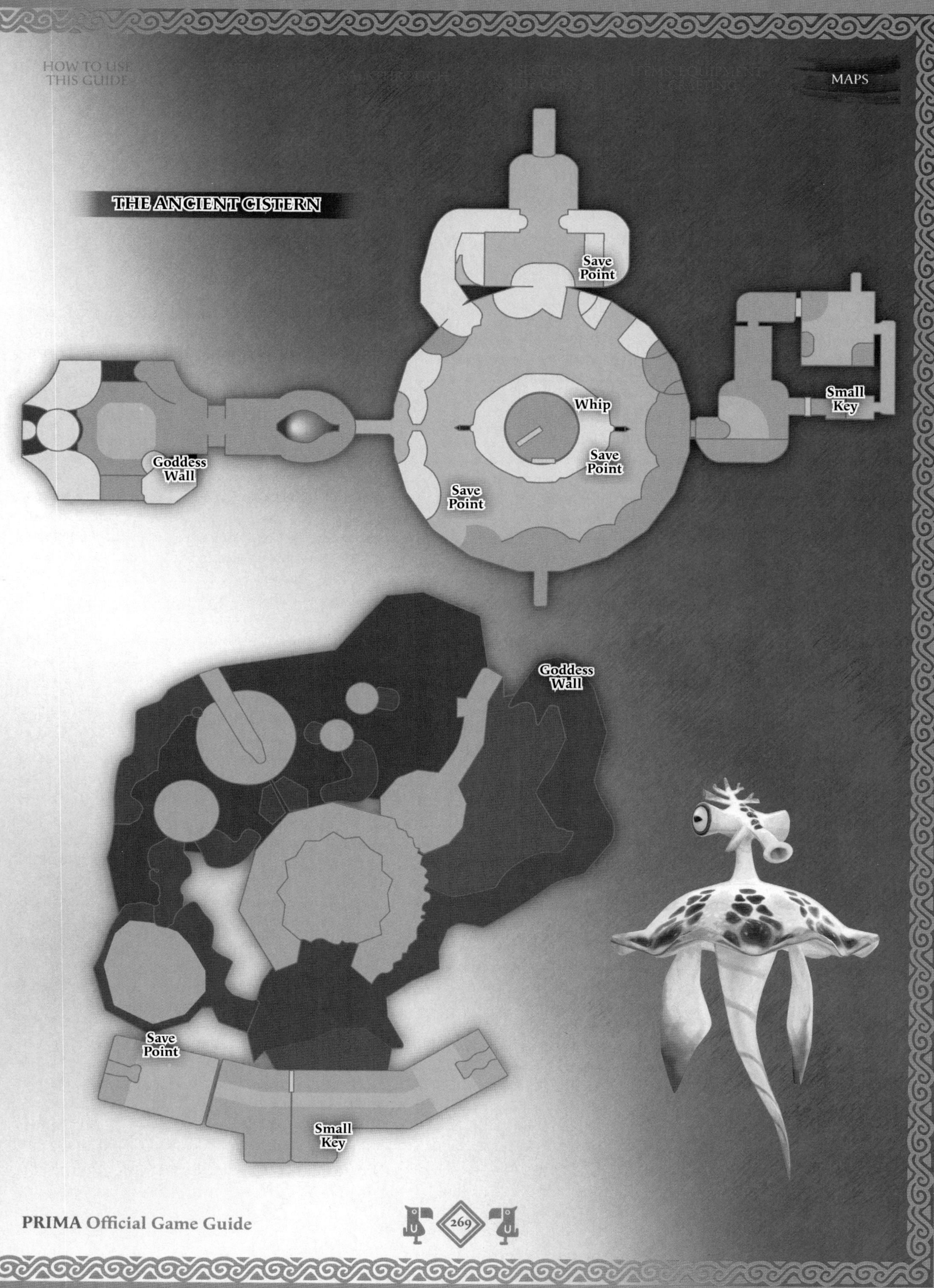
THE ANCIENT CISTERN
Save Point
Small Key
Whip
Save Point
Goddess Wall
Save Point
Goddess Wall
Save Point
Small Key

Index

PRIMA OFFICIAL GAME GUIDE

WRITTEN BY ALICIA ASHBY

Product Manager: Jesse Anderson
Copyeditor: Deana Shields
Design & Layout: Marc W. Riegel
Manufacturing: Stephanie Sanchez
Maps: Philip Roes
Technical Editor: Alexander Musa

Prima Games would like to thank: Yugo Sato, Kaori Yagi, Emiko Ohmori, Zac Evans, Allen Perez, Sean Craig, Jeffery Fox, Adam Henderson, Amber Kenyon, Yvette Lessard, Eric Styner, Sean Taylor, Blake Caplan, Noriyoshi Iwata, Michael Keough, Nate Bihldorff, Erik Peterson, Shannon Jaye Roberts, Austin A. King, Scott Willson, Stacy Kolden, Marissa Sipos, Shaida Boroumand.

ISBN 978-0-307-89204-1
Printed in the United States of America

11 12 13 14 LL 10 9 8 7 6 5 4 3 2 1

Prima Games
An Imprint of Random House, Inc.
3000 Lava Ridge Court, Suite 100
Roseville, CA 95661
www.primagames.com

ALICIA ASHBY

Alicia Ashby got her start at DoubleJump Books, working on guides including Castlevania: Dawn of Sorrow, Persona 4, and Rogue Galaxy (produced in partnership with Prima). She has written as a games journalist since 2004 for outlets including GamePro, Retro Gamer, and Engage Digital. She lives in southwestern Virginia with her husband, two cats, and too many comic books.